PRACTICAL WINDOWS ADMINISTRATION SCRIPTING

LIMITED WARRANTY AND DISCLAIMER OF LIABILITY

THE CD-ROM THAT ACCOMPANIES THE BOOK MAY BE USED ON A SINGLE PC ONLY. THE LICENSE DOES NOT PERMIT THE USE ON A NETWORK (OF ANY KIND). YOU FURTHER AGREE THAT THIS LICENSE GRANTS PERMISSION TO USE THE PRODUCTS CONTAINED HEREIN, BUT DOES NOT GIVE YOU RIGHT OF OWNERSHIP TO ANY OF THE CONTENT OR PRODUCT CONTAINED ON THIS CD-ROM. USE OF THIRD-PARTY SOFTWARE CONTAINED ON THIS CD-ROM IS LIMITED TO AND SUBJECT TO LICENSING TERMS FOR THE RESPECTIVE PRODUCTS.

CHARLES RIVER MEDIA, INC. ("CRM") AND/OR ANYONE WHO HAS BEEN INVOLVED IN THE WRITING, CREATION, OR PRODUCTION OF THE ACCOMPANYING CODE ("THE SOFTWARE") OR THE THIRD-PARTY PRODUCTS CONTAINED ON THE CD-ROM OR TEXTUAL MATERIAL IN THE BOOK, CANNOT AND DO NOT WARRANT THE PERFORMANCE OR RESULTS THAT MAY BE OBTAINED BY USING THE SOFTWARE OR CONTENTS OF THE BOOK. THE AUTHOR AND PUBLISHER HAVE USED THEIR BEST EFFORTS TO ENSURE THE ACCURACY AND FUNCTIONALITY OF THE TEXTUAL MATERIAL AND PROGRAMS CONTAINED HEREIN. WE HOWEVER, MAKE NO WARRANTY OF ANY KIND, EXPRESS OR IMPLIED, REGARDING THE PERFORMANCE OF THESE PROGRAMS OR CONTENTS. THE SOFTWARE IS SOLD "AS IS" WITHOUT WARRANTY (EXCEPT FOR DEFECTIVE MATERIALS USED IN MANUFACTURING THE DISK OR DUE TO FAULTY WORKMANSHIP).

THE AUTHOR, THE PUBLISHER, DEVELOPERS OF THIRD-PARTY SOFTWARE, AND ANYONE INVOLVED IN THE PRODUCTION AND MANUFACTURING OF THIS WORK SHALL NOT BE LIABLE FOR DAMAGES OF ANY KIND ARISING OUT OF THE USE OF (OR THE INABILITY TO USE) THE PROGRAMS, SOURCE CODE, OR TEXTUAL MATERIAL CONTAINED IN THIS PUBLICATION. THIS INCLUDES, BUT IS NOT LIMITED TO, LOSS OF REVENUE OR PROFIT, OR OTHER INCIDENTAL OR CONSEQUENTIAL DAMAGES ARISING OUT OF THE USE OF THE PRODUCT.

THE SOLE REMEDY IN THE EVENT OF A CLAIM OF ANY KIND IS EXPRESSLY LIMITED TO REPLACEMENT OF THE BOOK AND/OR CD-ROM, AND ONLY AT THE DISCRETION OF CRM.

THE USE OF "IMPLIED WARRANTY" AND CERTAIN "EXCLUSIONS" VARIES FROM STATE TO STATE, AND MAY NOT APPLY TO THE PURCHASER OF THIS PRODUCT.

PRACTICAL WINDOWS ADMINISTRATION SCRIPTING

BOBBY MALIK

CHARLES RIVER MEDIA
Boston, Massachusetts

Cover Design: Tyler Creative

CHARLES RIVER MEDIA
25 Thomson Place
Boston, Massachusetts 02210
617-757-7900
617-757-7969 (FAX)
crm.info@thomson.com
www.charlesriver.com

This book is printed on acid-free paper.

Bobby Malik. *Practical Windows Administration Scripting.*
ISBN: 1-58450-461-7

Library of Congress Cataloging-in-Publication Data
Malik, Bobby.
Practical Windows administration scripting / Bobby Malik.
p. cm.
Includes index.
ISBN 1-58450-461-7 (alk. paper)
1. Microsoft Windows (Computer file) 2. Operating systems (Computers) 3. Programming languages (Electronic computers) I. Title.
QA76.76.O63M345 2006
005.4'46—dc22

2006007734

06 7 6 5 4 3 2 First Edition

CHARLES RIVER MEDIA titles are available for site license or bulk purchase by institutions, user groups, corporations, etc. For additional information, please contact the Special Sales Department at 800-347-7707.

Requests for replacement of a defective CD-ROM must be accompanied by the original disc, your mailing address, telephone number, date of purchase and purchase price. Please state the nature of the problem, and send the information to CHARLES RIVER MEDIA, 25 Thomson Place, Boston, Massachusetts 02210. CRM's sole obligation to the purchaser is to replace the disc, based on defective materials or faulty workmanship, but not on the operation or functionality of the product.

This book is dedicated to my late father Professor Virendra Malik and to my wife Vibha, and my two sons Ankit and Devsh.

Contents

Preface

ABOUT THIS BOOK

This book is a practical guide to Windows scripting. This book is for experienced Windows systems administrators and engineers automating and administering Windows tasks. Through its practical scripting approach, this book will arm you with a thorough understanding of available Microsoft Windows scripting technologies and their practical applications in Windows systems administration and engineering arena.

This book concentrates solely on scripting for windows administration and engineering tasks using Microsoft Scripting technologies. This book is full of practical techniques and scripts that you can use as is or modify them to create your own custom administration tools.

Why This Book?

It is easy to automate and administer Windows tasks with scripts. However, there is a great deal of scripting fear amongst administrators and engineers based on the steep learning curve, the lack of understanding of various available scripting technologies and how to effectively use these technologies for systems administration and automation. This book dispels this fear by putting these technologies into perspective and creating practical systems administration and automation examples, to the extent that scripting becomes a systems administrator's aid, rather than hindrance.

Why Did I Write This Book?

I enjoy writing scripts and have been writing scripts to automate administrative tasks for almost my entire career both as an administrator and as a Windows engineer.

At first, I mostly wrote batch scripts that used command line utilities to automate simple administrative tasks. When batch scripts started to limit me (that is, I was unable to work with text files), I moved to writing Perl scripts. Perl scripts provided more flexibility (I was able to read, write, and search text files), but required more work and had one problem: you were required to install Perl interpreter on every windows system to run the Perl scripts. Not every organization was prepared to install PERL on every system. This limited my capability as administrator to manage multiple systems for my clients. Therefore when Microsoft included Windows Scripting Host and VBScript in Windows 2000, I was very happy and finally graduated to a language that was both flexible and available. Today, I mostly write scripts in VBScript as it is an easy language that is used by most Windows administrators and engineers.

Over the years I have written thousands of scripts to automate and manage Microsoft Windows operating systems, databases, applications, hardware and more. As a result I have gathered a wealth of information and a script for almost every task that an administrator does on a system. I wanted to share this wealth of information with all Windows administrators and engineers willing to quickly learn and use the Windows scripting technologies. And what can be better than writing a book to share such information. This is that book.

When I thought of writing a book, I imagined writing a practical book with a practical approach that provided complete scripts that could be run with little or no modification. Practically speaking, there is no one technology that suffices all scripting administration needs, therefore, in this book I have leveraged all of the Windows scripting technologies to create tools that you can use as is, or with few changes, to administer and engineer your Windows environment.

Is This Book for You?

This book was created particularly for experienced Windows Systems administrators, engineers, and help-desk technicians interested in using Windows Scripting technologies to automate and manage their Windows environment. If you are a Windows systems administrator or an engineer who is well versed with Windows administration tasks (such as managing services, disks, registry, etc.) and have basic Windows scripting or programming knowledge, this book is for you.

This book is not for a new (beginner) systems administrator or Windows engineer with no prior knowledge of scripting or programming. However, this book can help others interested in learning how to script. Although, this book is organized and focused toward systems administration using VBScript, it is likely to help others who simply want to learn how to use specific technologies such as Script Runtime —`FileSystemObject` and `Dictionary`—objects may benefit from this book.

This book, however, does not cover scripting for Systems Management Server, Microsoft SQL server, and the Exchange Server. However, these products can be managed using the Microsoft scripting technologies outlined in this book. For this reason, this book may appeal to you, if you are responsible for managing and automating these products.

Foreword

As enterprises continue to leverage the Microsoft Windows platform for more and more purposes, the requirement to automate basic system administration, system updates, and repetitive tasks becomes essential.

Scripting and automation is an integral part of managing large computer platforms. The need for advanced scripting and automation is amplified with the current industry focus on maintaining security where significant changes to systems need to be engineered, tested, and implemented very quickly to avoid security exploits from causing catastrophic downtime.

The requirement to stay within currently supported operating system and infrastructure software versions for vendor support agreements is also driving the requirement to script system administration tasks. Eliminating human error and ensuring consistency by implementing changes programmatically is critical to large enterprise environments as well.

Organizations that rely on computers and the resultant information technology staff are constantly under pressure to reduce costs and provide more functionality with fewer resources. The investment in implementing scripts to maintain and enhance the computing platform allows administrators to focus more of their time on activities that are considered value-added by the organizations that they support. The current focus on the total cost of ownership by chief operating officers necessitates the utilization of scripting and automation.

Bobby Malik is an expert script author and has developed many scripts to solve diverse problems faced by large, complex computing environments. Through the use of many different scripting technologies, including VBScript, Bobby has developed solutions that have saved countless hours of manual work. He has developed frameworks and libraries allowing beginner and intermediate script authors the ability to leverage his past experiences to develop sophisticated scripts on their own. Bobby's passion for scripting and sharing his knowledge has driven him to write this practical book.

Tal Sadan
Director, Global Technologies Infrastructure
Merrill Lynch

Part I Scripting Basics

In This Part

- How to use this book
- Microsoft Windows scripting technologies
- Scripting standards

This part covers various Microsoft scripting technologies that you can use to create scripts for automation and Windows administration. This part also lists guidelines that you can use to create scripting standards best suited for your and your organization's needs.

1 How to Use This Book

In This Chapter

- Introduction to Scripting
- Conventions
- What you need to use this book
- How this book is organized
- Where you can get the code for this book
- How to install and run scripts included with this book
- Where you can send your feedback

INTRODUCTION TO SCRIPTING

Scripts have been an integral part of the UNIX operating system. For years, UNIX administrators and engineers have enjoyed the privilege to automate and administer local and remote UNIX systems by writing simple readable scripts.

Microsoft operating systems also provided scripting support in the form of batch files. Although batch files are a good start, large batch files can be difficult to write and debug. Moreover, batch scripts cannot make use of technologies such as the Microsoft's ActiveX components (ActiveX components are covered later in this book). Therefore, an administrator had to use utilities such as the isMember.exe resource kit utility or the Reg.exe utility or write custom programs (to take advantage of the ActiveX objects [commonly known as COM objects] and the Windows API you had to write program in Microsoft Visual Basic®, C, C++ or other languages and then write a batch script to automate the process), to accomplish the administrative tasks. Since most administrators are not programmers, they were limited by the available utilities.

With the Windows 98 (and above) operating system, Microsoft bundled Windows Script Host (WSH). WSH supported running scripts written in VBScript and Jscript. As a part of Windows 2000, Microsoft also introduced other technologies, such as Active Directory Services Interface (ADSI), Windows Management Instrumentation (WMI) and Microsoft HTML Applications (HTA) making automation and administration easier than before.

This book focuses on these technologies and how they can be used to manage Windows administration tasks. In this book you will learn how to automate and administer several windows administration tasks that you, as an engineer or an administrator, do on a daily basis. This book begins with an introduction to Microsoft Windows scripting technologies. You will then learn how you can use different technologies to accomplish a task and how you can integrate together these technologies to create tools that you can use to automate and administer your Windows environment.

CONVENTIONS

In this book, you will find the following standard conventions. For example, a Note is shown as an icon.

A Note offers additional explanation of how something works or points out a particular caveat to an approach or technique.

Similar to a Note, a Tip also provides an optional approach that you may want to consider. However unlike a note, a Tip is a definite approach to a solution.

Additional Resource: Additional resources are references (or additional reading) to external (not provided in the book) sources that you may consider reading.

Reference (to a chapter / page / appendix): These are internal references to the text or a topic in the book. At times you may see references to a page in the book or to an appendix included at the back of the book. For example, for additional information on Script Store Tool, read the Appendix located at the back of this book.

WHAT YOU NEED TO USE THIS BOOK

This book is on scripting Windows administration tasks. Therefore, you would at minimum require a computer running Windows 2000 operating system that you can use to create and run the scripts included with this book or the scripts that you create.

Most scripts in this book will run on Windows 2000 and above systems. However, some scripts will only run on Windows XP® or a Windows 2003 operating system because they are created specifically for these operating systems, such as the scripts created in Chapter 5 and Chapter 6. Besides a computer system running Windows 2000 or above operating system, you will also require the following:

Windows Script Host

You need Windows Script Host (WSH) Version 5.6 installed on your system. It is a free download available from Microsoft at *http://www.microsoft.com/downloads/details.aspx?FamilyId=C717D943-7E4B-4622-86EB-95A22B832CAA&displaylang=en*. If you are running Windows XP or Windows 2003, however, you already have Windows Script Host v5.6.

Text Editor

You will need a text editor to write a script. You can either use a basic editor, such as Notepad.exe that is built into Windows, or use an editor that you are most familiar with.

If Microsoft Office XP or Office 2003 is installed on your system, you can also use the Microsoft Script Editor® (MSE) (Figure 1.1 shows the Microsoft Script Editor when launched). You can either launch MSE from the Macros menu under the Tools menu from inside of the Microsoft Office components, such as MS Word, or launch it directly by running MSE7.EXE from your MS Office folder. Alternatively, you can also use Visual Studio or even MS Word. However, these tools save files in their own format that the scripting host cannot decipher, and you will need to be sure to save the files in a text format.

The Toolbox window does not provide you any tools for scripts. You can expand the Text window view by closing the Toolbox window. You can expand the Text window by closing or setting the Project window to auto hide.

Microsoft Script Editor remembers the script that was last selected when the editor was closed. When reopened, it sets the focus to the same script. Therefore, you would need to change focus to the script that you wish to edit after the tool is loaded successfully.

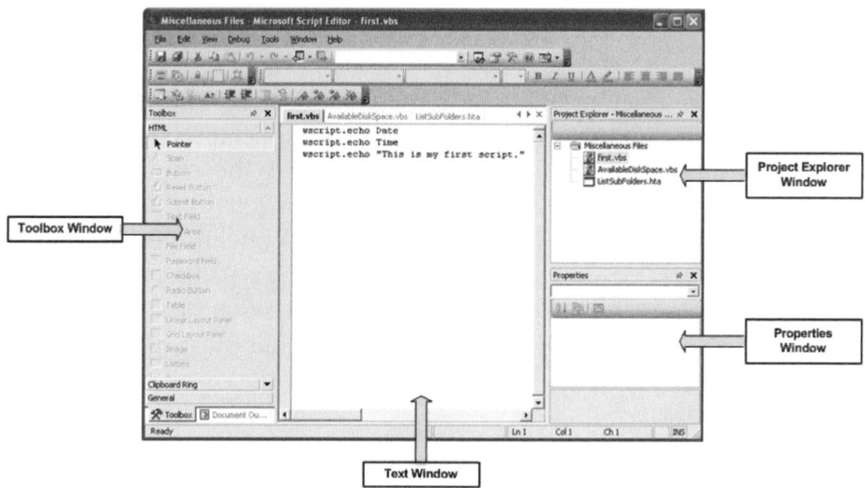

FIGURE 1.1 Microsoft Script Editor.

The right-click menu of a script lists Notepad (and/or other editors you have installed on your system) that you can use to edit a script. You can also add MS Script Editor as an option to this menu by adding the following registry key and values:

```
[HKEY_CLASSES_ROOT\VBSFile\Shell\MS Editor]
@="&MS Script Editor"

[HKEY_CLASSES_ROOT\VBSFile\Shell\MS Editor\Command]
@="C:\\Program Files\\Microsoft Office\\OFFICE11\\MSE7.EXE %1"
```

ON THE CD

Alternatively, you can use the `SetScriptEditor.hta` script included on the CD-ROM at scripts\chapter01 to add Microsoft Script Editor to the right-click menu of a script. Figure 1.2 shows a Microsoft Internet Explorer–type window that is displayed when you launch the `SetScriptEditor.hta` script. You can either accept the default values or modify them as needed.

HTML Editor

You can use Notepad.exe to write HTML code for your scripts. However, if you are not comfortable with writing HTML code in a plain text editor, you can use other HTML editors, such as Microsoft FrontPage, Macromedia Dreamweaver, Macromedia Homesite, or any HTML editor that is available to you for writing HTML Application (HTA) scripts.

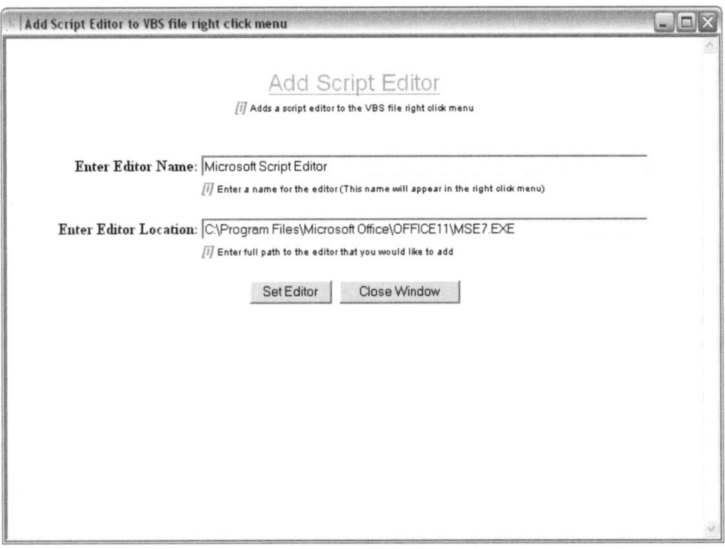

FIGURE 1.2 Script Editor Application window.

You can also use Microsoft Script Editor to create new HTML files that you can later save as HTA scripts. Opening or creating an HTML file will enable you to take advantage of the tools listed in the Toolbox window.

Microsoft XML Notepad

Many scripts in this book use XML as an output or an input file that you may need to edit. Although you can use Notepad to edit the XML documents, XML Notepad is an excellent choice for editing or creating new XML files. Unfortunately, you cannot download the tool from Microsoft.com, and you will have to search the Internet for it (*google.com*), to download it from a non-Microsoft site. Microsoft, however, does provide articles on how to use the utility to create an XML document that you can read at *http://support.microsoft.com/default.aspx?scid=kb;en-us;296560.*

Windows Script Component Wizard

For creating Windows Script Components (covered in Chapter 2), you will need to download and install the free Windows Script Component Wizard available from Microsoft at *http://www.microsoft.com/downloads/details.aspx?FamilyId=408024ED-FAAD -4835-8E68-773CCC951A6B&displaylang=en.*

Windows Script Encoder

Chapter 1 covers the script encoding for which you need the script encoder command line tool, also available free of cost from Microsoft at *http://www.microsoft.com/downloads/details.aspx?FamilyId=E7877F67-C447-4873-B1B0-21F0626A6329&displaylang=en.* You must download and install this tool to encode your scripts.

Active Directory / Domain

Although this book does not cover Active Directory (AD) management (such as creating users and groups and managing organizational units) using scripts, it is best to have an AD domain. Because the book does contain scripts that require domain authentication, you need an Active Directory environment, that is, you must be running a domain environment with at least one domain controller running Active Directory. It is also important that you join your test machine (where you will run your scripts) to the domain as a member system (server or workstation).

TIP

If you have access to only one test machine, consider installing Windows 2003 server as a domain controller on that machine. Most scripts in the book will run on Windows 2003 server.

Windows 2003 Terminal Server

Chapter 5 covers scripting for Terminal Server, therefore you must have a computer system running Windows 2003 with Terminal Services enabled.

Windows 2003 with SP1 and Windows XP with SP2

The last chapter of the book (Chapter 6) covers scripting for Windows Firewall. Windows Firewall is installed by default when you install Service Pack 1 (SP1) on Windows 2003 and Service Pack 2 (SP2) on Windows XP. To run scripts included in that chapter, you must have a computer system installed with SP1 on Windows 2003 and SP2 on Windows XP operating systems.

Access to a Remote System

Most scripts can be run locally, that is, they can be run to configure and query the same system the scripts are running on. To manage a remote computer, however, you must have an administrative access on the remote computer system. The remote system should also be running Windows 2000, Window XP, or Windows 2003, depending on the task you need to accomplish.

Script Store Tool

"Once bitten, twice shy." If you are not using the script, it is best practice to rename the script file extension to .txt. By changing the extension, you avoid accidentally running a script that may cause damage to the environment (text files when double-clicked, will by default, open up with Notepad.exe for editing).

You can, optionally, use the Script Store (ScriptStore.exe) tool (included with this book) to securely save and retrieve your scripts (the scripts are encrypted before they are stored as text files). Script Store also allows you to edit and run your scripts with Wscript.exe, Cscript.exe, or MSHTA shells. Figure 1.3 shows the Script Store tool window.

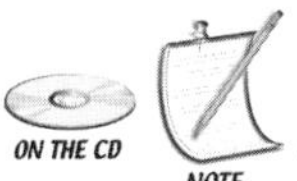

This is not an editing tool. The tool does not save changes made to your script. It simply allows you to change the text in the script before running the script. The program is located on the CD-ROM in the Programs folder.

Reference: How to install and use the Script Store tool is covered in the Appendix located at the back of this book.

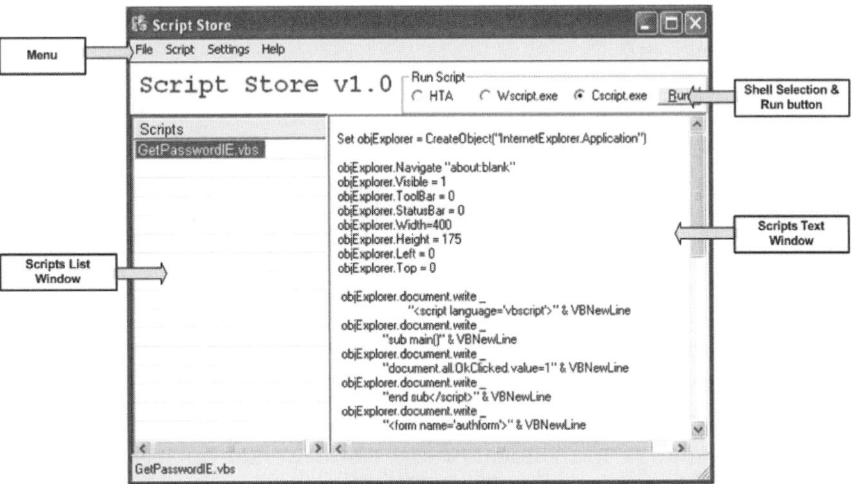

FIGURE 1.3 Script Store tool.

RunAs

Typically, you may run your scripts with administrative privileges in the test environment. In the production environment, however, you may want to run the scripts under a less privileged account. Although some tasks can be done only if you run your scripts with administrative privileges, such as creating an account in the domain, it is good practice to run your script with minimum privileges to minimize risk of damaging your environment. For example, you require only read privilege to the Active Directory to retrieve user account information. Therefore, you should run your enumeration script as a user that has only read permissions to the Active Directory or the Organizational unit.

TIP

You can use `RunAs` *command (included in Windows 2000 and above) to run the scripts under a specific user context.* (`RunAs` *is also discussed in Chapter 3.)*

HOW THIS BOOK IS ORGANIZED

This is not just another scripting book on the market. It has several distinct features that make learning to script easier and enjoyable.

Two-Part Book

This book is designed for both a systems administrator with little or no scripting knowledge and an administrator experienced in scripting. Therefore, for ease this book is divided in two part:

Part I: "Scripting Basics" introduces you to the available Windows scripting technologies.

Part II: "Advanced Windows Administration Scripting" delves deeper into scripting and teaches you how to manage and configure the ten most important Windows administration tasks.

Part I

This part of the book contains the basics of scripting and introduces you to the key Microsoft Windows scripting technologies. This part of the book also introduces you to scripting standards and guidelines that can help you build scripting standards best suited for you and your organization.

Chapter 2, *Microsoft Windows Scripting Technologies,* begins with an introduction to the VBScript scripting language you use in the rest of the book to write scripts. This chapter teaches you how to run a script and what script shells you can run the scripts in. It also introduces you to the various Windows scripting technologies, such as WMI, ADSI, MSXML Dom, and Windows script components that the scripts in Part II of the book are based on. Chapter 3, *Scripting Standards,* covers good practices that will help you create your own scripting standards. It lists guidelines for naming scripts, writing code, standardizing input and output formats, including comments and documenting your scripts.

If you have limited scripting knowledge, then you should read this part of the book first to acquire required scripting knowledge before moving on to the advanced part of the book.

Short of Chapter 2, *Microsoft Windows Scripting Technologies*, there is no sacred order to this book. Read whichever chapter interests you. The book's purpose is to help you learn the available scripting technologies and how to use these technologies practically to administer Windows administration tasks. Just remember that the scripts in every chapter use the technologies explained in the Chapter 2. While you can skip around in Part II of the book, it is essential to read Part I, especially if you are not well versed in scripting technologies.

Part II

This part covers three different Windows administration tasks that you as an administrator and/or an engineer administer.

Chapter 4 covers IIS 6.0 management scripts. In this chapter you learn how to use WMI IIS6 provider to manage IIS 6.0. Scripts in this chapter are created to take advantage of the Microsoft XML Document Object Model that allows you to read and write to XML files. Scripts in this chapter are WSF (Windows Script File) scripts that can take advantage of better argument handling. Chapter 4 also includes the Input, Process and Output model for each script. This chapter also demonstrates the Input, Process and Output relationships (explained later in this chapter) for each script in the chapter.

Chapter 5 covers Windows Terminal Services in Windows 2003 management using Terminal Service classes in WMI. The scripts in this chapter extensively use XML files as input configuration files. The scripts in this chapter can be used to retrieve Terminal Service information; change Terminal Service settings, add or delete an account on a terminal server, set Terminal Services Environment settings, and more.

Chapter 6 introduces Windows XP SP2 and Windows 2003 SP1 specific management through scripts. Scripts in this chapter allow you to manage the Windows Firewall settings. Using these scripts, you can do several tasks from enabling or disabling the firewall to configuring individual ICMP settings. This chapter covers three types of scripts: WSF, VBS and HTA scripts.

How a Chapter or a Topic Is Organized

The best method of learning to script is to start writing scripts, and that is how each chapter in this part is generally organized. A chapter or a topic may begin with a base script followed by the steps or description of the script.

All chapters in this part are generally organized in the following order:

- Introduction to the chapter
- What is covered

- Minimum requirements
- Before reading this chapter
- Topics
- Summary

Multiple Scripts for a Task

Most books illustrate a single method that uses a single technology to accomplish a task. In this book, however, you may see multiple approaches that use multiple technologies to accomplish the tasks. For example, you may see a script that displays a message on the user's screen using `MSGBOX` method in VBScript, and at the same time there may be another script that uses `Echo` method in Windows Script Host (commonly known as WSH) to display a message. Similarly, there may also be an HTA script that displays the message in an Internet Explorer window. There may also be an example that writes to an external file.

The output and the input may depend on the type of shell the script is run under. Following is how it is organized in the book.

- Run with Wscript.exe
  Input: Internet Explorer or `Inputbox` or external files

  Output: Internet Explorer or `Wscript.Echo` or `Msgbox` or `Popup` or external files
- Run with Cscript.exe
  Input: Internet Explorer or `Inputbox` or `Wscript.stdin` or external files

  Output: Internet Explorer or `Wscript.Echo` or `Wscript.Stdout` or external files
- Run with MSHTA (if created as an HTA script)
  Input: Internet Explorer or external files

  Output: Internet Explorer or external files

Single Component for Common Functions

Scripts may contain functions and subroutines. Some may be common, and others may be unique to the script that they were written for. In this book, all the common functions and subroutines, such as `GetComputerName` function, the `WriteLog` method, and the `CheckError` function are compiled into a single-script component for reusability of code, as you see in the real-world implementations. The common component (`SWAT_1.WSC`) is available on the CD-ROM at Scripts/AdditionalScripts. A sample script (`SWAT_1.HTA`) is also included in the same folder that illustrates the methods of the common component.

ON THE CD

Three Parts of a Script

For the most part, a script does three things: it takes an input, processes it, and outputs the result. Therefore, every script in this book can be broken down into these three parts:

Input: All inputs to the script, such as the command line arguments passed to the script at runtime or the input constants or variables specified in the script.

Process: All types of processing, such as using code to query operating system information and formatting the output.

Output: Writing output to the screen, output files, such as a text file or an XML file.

There is no processing without an input, and there is no output without processing. Figure 1.5 displays this relationship.

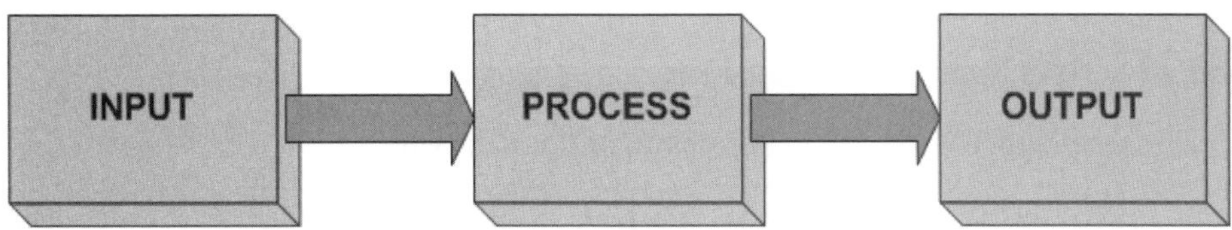

FIGURE 1.5 Input, process, and output relationship.

The input, process, and output relationship is demonstrated in Chapter 4.

Where You Can Get the Code for This Book

The CD-ROM included on the book contains all its code. The CD-ROM also includes the images from the book, arranged by chapter. For more details, see, Appendix located at the back of the book.

HOW TO RUN THE SCRIPTS INCLUDED WITH THIS BOOK

The scripts included on the CD-ROM accompanying this book were created for running in a test environments only. Therefore, you must not run the scripts in any environments other than your test environment because these scripts are available on AS-IS basis with all faults and without any warranty whatsoever, written or implied. (It is good practice to thoroughly test your scripts in a test environment before running on or against a production system.)

Installing Scripts

ON THE CD

To use the scripts included on the CD-ROM, you need to install the Scripts.msi package. The Scripts.msi file in the CD-ROM (in the scripts folder) contains script files for all the chapters in the book. You will require Microsoft Installer version 2.0 at the minimum to install the MSI package. You can choose the installation location for the scripts. You must agree to the terms and conditions in order to install the package.

NOTE

By silently installing the package, you automatically agree to the terms and conditions of the agreement. You can silently install the package by issuing the following command in the command prompt window: `%systemroot%\system32\msiexec.exe /i scripts.msi /qb! /lve c:\scripts.log`

Silently installing the package will install the scripts in your Program files folder on the system drive (generally C:\Program files).

Type of Scripts and How to Run Them

The scripts included with the book are of the following type:

.VBS: *VBScript files*: Can be run with Wscript.exe and Cscript.exe. It is preferred that you run the scripts with Cscript.exe.

.WSF: *Windows Script files*: Can be run with WScript.exe or Cscript.exe. It is preferred that you run the scripts with Cscript.exe.

.WSC: *Windows Script Components*: Helper DLL that should be registered for use in your scripts. You can right-click and select Register to register the script components in the operating system. The script components must be available when used in the scripts.

.HTA: *HTML Application*: Runs with MSHTA.EXE. You can simply double-click an HTA file to run it.

WHERE YOU CAN SEND YOUR FEEDBACK

Everyone associated with this book has worked hard so you can get the most out of this book. We have tried to understand your needs and expectations and tried to meet those expectations. Please let us know your thoughts about this book: good or bad; what you liked or disliked about the book. Also let us know if you find errors in the book or the code accompanying the book. This will greatly help us in improving future books. You can send us your feedback at *crm.info@thomson.com.*

You can also find more information about Charles River Media on the Web at *http://www.charlesriver.com.*

SUMMARY

In this chapter, you learned how this book is organized, how a chapter and a topic within the chapters is organized, and how to best read the book. This chapter also introduced you to the tools that you will need for this book. Moreover, it covered who should read the book, whether this book is for you, and where you can send the feedback. In Chapter 2, *Microsoft Windows Scripting Technologies,* you will learn about several Windows scripting technologies that will be used throughout the rest of this book. In essence Chapter 2 covers the basics of scripting that you must read before beginning Part II of the book.

2 Microsoft Windows Scripting Technologies

In This Chapter

- VBScript (VBS)
- Windows Script Host (WSH) and HTML Applications (HTAs)
- VBScript Runtime objects
- Windows Script Components
- Microsoft XML (MSXML) Document Object Model (DOM)
- Windows Management Instrumentation (WMI)

This chapter introduces you to available Microsoft scripting technologies, such as VBScript, Windows Script Host, MSHTA, Windows Script, MSXML, Windows Management Instrumentation, and the Windows Script Component.

VBSCRIPT

VBScript® (Microsoft Visual Basic Scripting Edition) is a scripting language that originated from Microsoft Visual Basic (VB). As a result VBScript is very similar in syntax with Visual Basic. However, VBScript is only a subset of VB, therefore it does not have a VB-like integrated development environment (IDE) that you can use to develop your scripts. Also, do not expect to be able to write a GUI-type program that you can write in VB with VBS. Nonetheless similar to VB, VBScript is also an easy language to learn.

Originally intended as a client-side Web page development language for Internet Explorer® (IE) Version 3.0, VBScript was introduced by Microsoft in 1996. However, VBScript gained popularity only after Microsoft released VBScript Version 2.0, which included support for server-side scripting in IIS 3.0 (Internet Information Server 3.0). By embedding VBScript inside Active Server Pages (commonly known as ASP pages), programmers were able to use VBScript as a means of accessing server-side information and provide dynamic content.

VBScript gained further popularity when Microsoft released WSH with VBScript Version 3.0. Those who worked with Visual Basic found that they now had a tool to quickly automate tasks.

In VBScript 4.0, Microsoft included the ability to access Windows file system. VBScript v5.0 was released along with and included in Windows 2000 operating system. VBScript was updated to 5.6 when Microsoft released Windows XP® and Internet Explorer® 6.0 (IE) in 2001, which is the current version. Since then, Microsoft has released only security updates for v5.6 that you can install by visiting the Microsoft Windows Update site.

Introduction to VBScript

VBScript is a scripting language as opposed to VB, which is a programming language. It differs in that VB code is compiled into a binary executable program (as .EXE or .DLL extension) before it can be run and used, whereas a VBScript is interpreted at runtime. This means that a VBScript script is written and stored in clear text (using text editing tools such as Notepad included with Windows), and in order to run, it requires an execution environment, such as WSH or MSHTA (covered later in this chapter). For example, do the following to create a script and run it:

1. Open Notepad (or a text editor of your choice)
2. Type the following in the editor window: `wscript.echo Wscript.Name & " " & wscript.version`
3. Save the text file as `DisplayWSHVersion.vbs`
4. Open a command prompt window, change directory to the folder where you saved the `DisplayWshVersion.vbs`, type the following command and press the Enter key: `Cscript //NOLOGO DisplayWshVersion.vbs`
5. Running the `DisplayWshVersion.vbs` will display the following output: `Windows Script Host 5.6`

Since VBScript requires an environment to run in, it is limited by the constraints imposed by the environment. For example, the `curDateTime.hta` script in Listing 2.1 can be run only with MSHTA shell, as compared to the script in Listing 2.2 that can be run in the WSH environment. The code in Listing 2.1 includes HTML code that WSH cannot interpret and therefore throws an error, as shown in Figure 2.1; whereas running the code in Listing 2.2 with MSHTA only displays the content in an IE-type window, as shown in Figure 2.2.

LISTING 2.1 `curDateTime.hta` Run with MSHTA Shell

```
<Script Language="VBScript">
document.write now
  </Script>
```

LISTING 2.2 `curDateTime.vbs` Run with the Wscript.exe Shell in WSH

```
wscript.echo Now
```

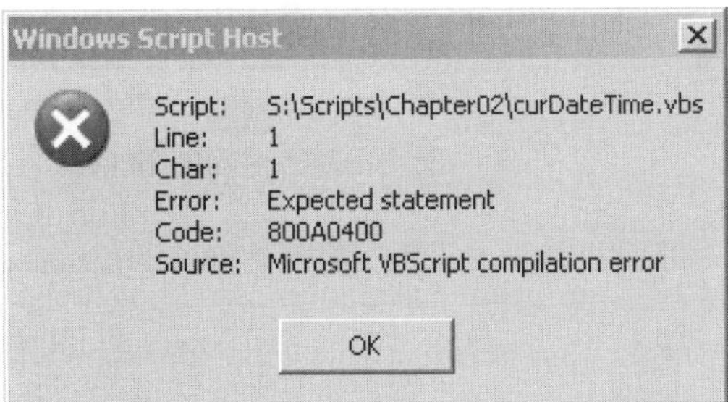

FIGURE 2.1 Error displayed by running the code in Listing 2.1 with WSH.

FIGURE 2.2 Code in Listing 2.2 shown as text in Internet Explorer-type window when run with MSHTA shell.

NOTE

Running `curDateTime.hta` *with WSH will not generate the error shown in Figure 2.1. To recreate the error, do the following:*

1. *Change the* `curDateTime.vbs` *script extension to* `curDateTime.vbs_`
2. *Change the* `curDateTime.hta` *to* `curDateTime.vbs`
3. *Run the* `curDateTime.vbs` *script. You should see the error shown in Figure 2.1.*

Do not forget to rename the script files back to their original names.

Over and above the code limitations, you also cannot run a script with an .HTA (dot HTA) extension with the WSH script. For example, if you try to run the `curDateTime.hta` with WSH, it is similar to executing `DisplayWshVersion.vbs`, as the following command shows:

```
Cscript //NOLOGO curDateTime.hta
```

you would receive the following error:

```
Input Error: There is no script engine for file extension ".hat".
```

A typical VBScript may include the following: comments, conditional statements, built-in functions, objects—its properties and methods, constants and variables, collections and arrays, iteration and looping as shown in the Figure 2.3.

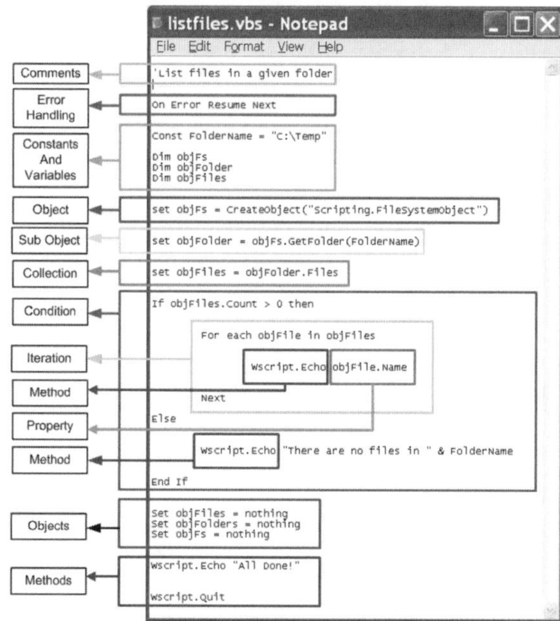

FIGURE 2.3 A typical VBScript.

Constants and Variables

Similar to other languages, VBScript also needs to be able to store and retrieve data from memory as it executes. For this, VBScript provides three statements that can be used to define constants and variables. Using these statements you can declare constants and variables that the script uses to store and retrieve data from the memory. Table 2.1 summarizes these statements.

TABLE 2.1 VBScript Statements That Define Temporary Data Storage

Statement	Description
`Const`	Declares constant
`Dim`	Declares variable or an array
`ReDim`	Allocates or reallocates memory space for a dynamic array

Constants

Constants are values that do not change during the execution of the script. For example, if a script has a value that will never change during script execution, it can be stored as a constant. Constants are generally used to represent literals (literals are hard-coded values that do not stand for anything else but literally the value that they represent). In Listing 2.3 for instance, the `FOR_READING` constant that holds value `1` literally represents `1` and nothing else.

LISTING 2.3 Constant Declared with a Static Value

```
Const FOR_READING = 1Dim objFs, objFile, sLine
 Set objFs = CreateObject("Scripting.FileSystemObject")
     Set objFile = objFs.OpenTextFile(sFileName,FOR_READING)
         sLine = objFile.ReadAll
        wscript.echo sLine
      objFile.Close
   Set objFile = nothing
   Set objFs = nothing
```

Constants can be declared using the `Const` statement as seen in Listing 2.3. The `Const` statement has the following syntax

```
[Public | Private] Const CONSTANT_NAME = expression
```

Constants can be declared as either `Public` or `Private`. If the constant is declared as `Public` it is exposed to the entire script. Declaring it as private limits the constant to the procedures (procedures are covered later in this chapter) where it is defined. Both `Public` and `Private` are optional keywords; that is, the keywords need not be included as a part of the syntax. However, if the `Private` or `Public` keyword is missing, a constant is declared as public. Within procedures, by default, constants are always declared as private.

`CONSTANT_NAME` is the name assigned to the constant and `expression` is the assigned value. Constants can be assigned numeric, string, or date values. Listing 2.3 (earlier in this chapter) is an example of a constant that is assigned a numeric value. Listing 2.4 on the other hand, is an example of a string value assigned to the constant; the string value must be placed within quotes. Listing 2.5 illustrates how to assign a date value to a constant. The date value must be placed within pound signs, as seen in Listing 2.5.

LISTING 2.4 Assign String Value to a Constant

```
Const MSG_COPYRIGHT = "COPYRIGHT 2005 CRM"
    Wscript.echo MSG_COPYRIGHT
```

LISTING 2.5 Assign Date Value to a Constant

```
Const START_DATE = #07-01-2005#
    Wscript.Echo START_DATE
```

VBScript Runtime Constants

Besides the constants that you declare, VBScript also provides a large collection of intrinsic constants that you can use in your scripts. These constants are predefined and can be used as is without declaration.

Using VBScript runtime constants you can simplify your code and make it easier to read and understand. For example, the following code line uses `vbYesNo` message box (`MsgBox`) function (covered later in this chapter) constant to pop up a dialog box that displays the `Yes` and `No` buttons.

```
Msgbox "Are you sure you want to close this script", vbYesNo
```

Similarly, VBScript script also provides date format constants, listed in Table 2.2.

TABLE 2.2 Date Format Constants

Constant	Value	Description
vbGeneralDate	0	Displays a date and/or time. Date and time display is determined by your system settings.
vbLongDate	1	Displays date in long date format
vbShortDate	2	Displays date in short date format
vbLongTime	3	Displays time in long time format
vbShortTime	4	Displays time in short time format

The following is an example of the date format constant used to display a short date:

```
wscript.echo FormatDateTime(Date(),vbShortDate)
```

and the following example demonstrates the use of `vbLongDate` date format constant used to display a date in long date format:

```
wscript.echo FormatDateTime(Date(),vbLongDate)
```

Another important set of intrinsic constants that VBScript provides is the string constants. Table 2.3 lists these constants.

TABLE 2.3 String Constants

Constant	Value	Description
`vbCr`	`Chr(13)`	Carriage return
`vbCrLf`	`Chr(13) & Chr(10)`	Combination of carriage return and line feed
`vbLf`	`Chr(10)`	Line feed
`vbNewLine`	`Chr(13) & Chr(10)` or `Chr(10)`	Windows-platform specific new line character; e.g. in Window 2000 the new line character is `Chr(13) & Chr(10)` and in Windows 98 it is `Chr(10)`
`vbNullChar`	`Chr(0)`	Character with 0 value
`vbNullString`	String with 0 value	Not the same as a zero-length (""); used for calling external procedures
`vbTab`	`Chr(9)`	Horizontal tab

Most scripts provide an output that you generally need to format for readability. For instance, consider the code shown in Listing 2.6 that echoes the last modified date and the size of a given file.

LISTING 2.6 Display Unformatted Output

```
Wscript.echo objFile.DateLastModified & objFile.Size
```

When the script in Listing 2.6 is run, the script pops up a dialog box that displays the last modified date and the size of the file, as seen in Figure 2.4. However, since there is no space or a tab between the properties displayed in the pop-up message box, it is less readable and understandable. By simply adding a tab and using `vbTab` string constant, as shown in Listing 2.7, the text seems more legible. Figure 2.5 shows the formatted output.

LISTING 2.7 Display a Tab-Formatted Output

```
Wscript.echo objFile.DateLastModified & vbTab & objFile.Size
```

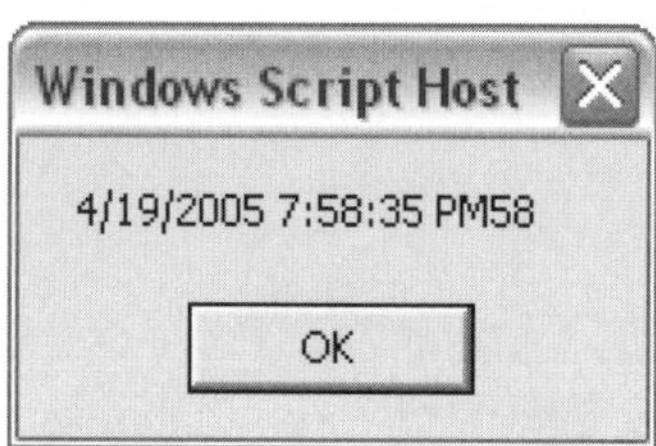

FIGURE 2.4 Non-formatted output.

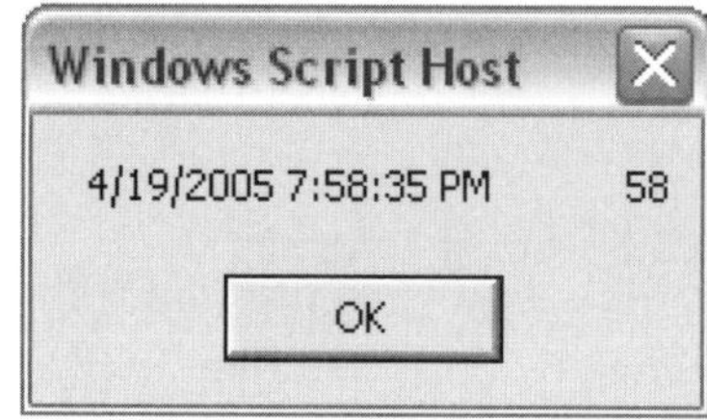

FIGURE 2.5 Tab-Formatted Output.

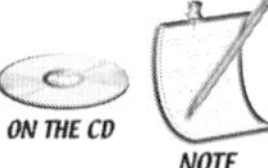

Complete scripts for listings 2.6 and 2.7 are available on the CD-ROM at Scripts\Chapter02 as `DisplayFileProperties_bad.wsf` *and* `DisplayFileProperties_good.wsf`*. The scripts take* `filename` *as a parameter. To run the script use the following syntax:*

```
DisplayFileProperties_bad.wsf /f:filename
DisplayFileProperties_good.wsf /f:filename
```

Running the script without providing the `filename` *parameter will display the syntax for the script.*

The same code can also be written using the `CHR(9)` (by passing the number `9` to the `CHR` function in VBScript) as shown in Listing 2.8. However, it is easier to remember constants than to remember different ASCII character numbers, such as `CHR(9)` for tab, `CHR(13) & CHR(10)` for new line, `CHR(13)` for carriage return. Moreover, using constants also makes your code more readable and understandable.

LISTING 2.8 Display Tab-Formatted Output Using `CHR(9)` Instead of `vbTab` Constant

```
Wscript.echo objFile.DateLastModified & CHR(9) & objFile.Size
```

Variables

Variables are memory locations identified by a name. Scripts use these named memory locations to store and retrieve data that they work with during execution. Variables are declared in the script using the `DIM` statement. Listing 2.9 shows the syntax for `DIM` statement.

LISTING 2.9 `DIM` Statement Syntax

```
Dim VariableName
```

The VariableSyntax.tif included on the CD-ROM at images/chapter02 describes the complete syntax of the `DIM` *statement as included in VBScript documentation provided by Microsoft.*

In Listing 2.9, the `VariableName` is the name of the variable being defined. For example, the following statement declares the variable named `sLogFileName`

```
Dim sLogFileName
```

The `DIM` statement also allows you to declare multiple variables with a single `DIM` statement. By separating the variable names with a comma, more than one variable can be declared in a single line. For example, the following declares `dtDateLastModified`, `iFileSize`, and `sLogFileName` using a single `DIM` keyword:

```
Dim dtDateLastModified, iFileSize, sLogFileName:
```

Although it is not essential to leave a space after a comma, it is good practice to do so; it will make your code more readable.

After the variable is defined, you can assign it a value, as shown in Figure 2.6:

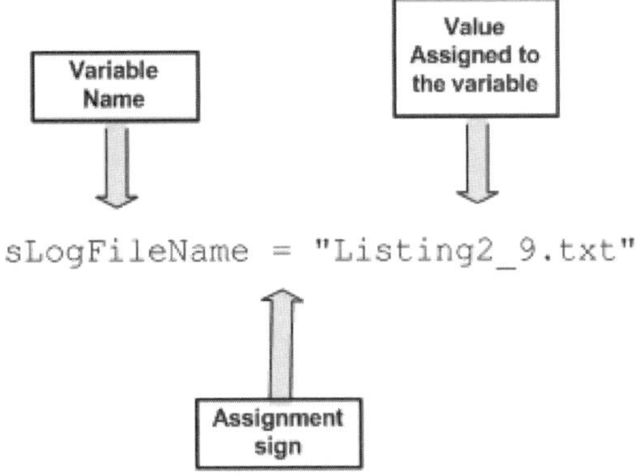

FIGURE 2.6 Assigning value to a variable.

You assign a value to a variable using the `=` (equal to) sign. For example, the `sLogFileName` variable is assigned the `Listing2_9.txt` value in Figure 2.6.

Variables can also be used in VBScript without explicitly declaring them. That is, you can directly assign a value to a variable without explicitly declaring the variable using the `DIM` statement, as the `sLogFileName` variable in Listing 2.10 is assigned the `Listing2_9.txt` value.

LISTING 2.10 `sLogFileName` Variable Used in the Script without Implicit Declaration

```
sLogFileName = "Listing2_9.txt"
        Set objFs = CreateObject("scripting.FileSystemObject")
          Set objFile = objFs.CreateTextFile(sLogFileName)
```

```
            objFile.writeline _
                "This is a sample text file created by Listing2_9.vbs"
               objFile.close
            Set objFile = nothing
         Set objFs = nothing
```

Even though the `sLogFileName` variable in Listing 2.9 is not explicitly declared, running the script does not generate any errors. This is because VBScript knows how to handle variables not explicitly declared.

To force-declare the variables though, you can use the `Option Explicit` statement. The `Option Explicit` statement must be included as the first statement in the script. For example, to force declare the variables for the script in Listing 2.10, add the `Option Explicit` statement at the beginning of the script as shown in Listing 2.11.

LISTING 2.11 The `Option Explicit` Statement Added to the Script in Listing 2.10 to Force Variable Declaration

```
Option Explicit
sLogFileName = "Listing2_9.txt"
  Set objFs = CreateObject("scripting.FileSystemObject")
    Set objFile = objFs.CreateTextFile(sLogFileName)
      objFile.writeline _
          "This is a sample text file created by Listing2_9.vbs"
         objFile.close
      Set objFile = nothing
    Set objFs = nothing
```

After adding the `Option Explicit` statement, as shown in Listing 2.11, when you run the script without explicitly declaring the `sLogFileName` variable, the script will throw the following error:

```
listing2_10.vbs(3, 5) Microsoft VBScript runtime error: Variable is
undefined: 'sLogFileName'
```

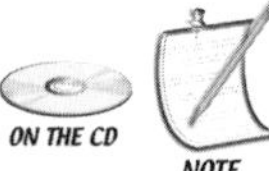
ON THE CD NOTE

`Listing2_10.vbs` included on the CD-ROM is a complete script that includes the `Option Explicit` and the `DIM` statement, and it declares the `objFs`, `objFile` and the `sLogFileName` variables.

Arrays

Arrays are like documents that contain multiple pages. For example, if you create a Word document, the new document is created with one page added to the document. As you type more data into the document, Word keeps adding more pages and keeps marking them with page numbers.

As a Word document is divided into multiple pages identified by the page number, similarly, an array is a variable divided into elements that are identified by index numbers. Index numbers always begin with `0`. For example, an array of 5 elements will be created in the memory, as shown in Figure 2.7.

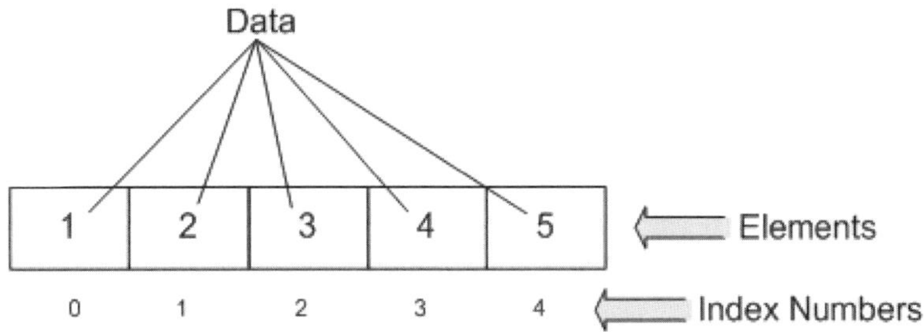

FIGURE 2.7 Array of five elements represented in memory.

You declare an array variable as you declare variables using the `DIM` statement. However, when declaring an array variable, you also include the information describing the size and the dimension of the array. For example, the following creates an array of 5 elements:

```
Dim arrNumbers(4)
```

Since index numbers of an array always begin with `0`*, to declare an array that would contain* `5` *elements, you pass the highest element number minus 1, which is* `4 (5 - 1 = 4)` *in this example.*

A single dimension array has only one index. For example, `MyArray(10)` *will have ten (0-9) elements in the single index. Whereas* `MyArray(10,20)` *will have ten (0-9) elements in the first index and twenty (0-19) elements in the second index. To retrieve a value from the single dimension array, you must use* `arrayname(elementnumber)` *such as* `MyArray(5)`*. To retrieve a value in two-dimensional array such as* `MyArray(10,20)`*, you must use* `arrayname(index1-elementnumber,√ index2-elementnumber)` *such as* `MyArray(5,15)`*. VBScript supports up to 60 dimension arrays.*

You reference a page in a document with its page number. Similarly, you reference an element of an array with its index number. For example, to echo the data stored in the third element of the `arrNumbers` array, do the following:

```
Wscript.echo arrNumbers(2)
```

To retrieve the value stored in the element of an array, you simply reference it like this:

```
ArrayName(IndexNumber)
```

To set the value of an element in the array, you use the = (equal to) assignment operator. For example, the following assigns a string value to the first element (with the index number of 0) of the `arrStrings`:

```
arrStrings(0) = First element in the array.
```

You can assign a value only to an element of an array. For example: `ArrayName(IndexNumber) = assignedValue`. *Assigning a value as* `ArrayName = assignedValue` *will generate a* `type mismatch` *error.*

Datatypes

While a variable is a container for a value that might be modified during a script's execution, a *datatype* is the kind of value (a character string, an integer number, an object, and so on) stored in a variable.

For those who are familiar with VB, you may remember that in VB you can declare a variable and restrict it to a particular data type. For example, the following restricts the `sLogFileName` variable to be able to hold only *string*-type values:

```
Dim sLogFileName as String
```

Variables in VBScript, on the other hand, cannot be restricted to hold a particular type of value. Variables in VBScript are only *variant* type that can store any kind of data. When you need to use a variable that represents a number, you simply assign a number to the variable, without quotation marks, as shown in the following example:

```
Dim Number
Number = 1
```

And to assign string data to a variable, you simply wrap the data within quotation marks, as shown in the following example:

```
Dim Number
Number = "1"
```

This makes it easier to work with variables in scripts; you do not have to declare in advance the type of data that will be stored in the variable. However, since the variable type is not declared in advance, it is up to VBScript to interpret the datatype of the variable. For example, if no other information is available, the datatype of a variable is considered to be string type which could produce unexpected results, as in that case of the following script:

```
FirstValue = inputbox("Enter first value")
SecondValue = inputbox("Enter second value")
wscript.echo FirstValue + SecondValue
```

If you type `1` in the first `inputbox` and `1` in the second `inputbox`, you would expect the script to display `2` and not `11` as displayed by the script. This happens because VBScript interprets the variables as string datatype and concatenates the values stored in `FirstValue` and the `SecondValue` variables instead of performing the mathematical addition.

You can, however, force addition (instead of concatenation) by converting the two input values using the built-in `CInt` function in VBScript; the `CInt` function converts the string-type data into integer-type data (built-in functions are described later in this chapter). If both the variables are of the integer type, VBScript will perform addition instead of concatenation. The following code displays the correct result of `2`, when `1` and `1` are typed in the two input boxes at runtime:

```
FirstValue = inputbox("Enter first value")
SecondValue = inputbox("Enter second value")
wscript.echo CInt(FirstValue) + CInt(SecondValue)
```

Objects, Methods, and Properties

VBScript provides conditional expression evaluation (`If…Then…Else` statement), loops (`Do…Loop` statement), iteration (`For each…Next` statement), and the ability to create subroutines (`Sub` and `Function` statement). However, VBScript does not provide any access to Windows operations (such as access to drives, files, and folders).

For example, VBScript does not have any built-in method to manage services or processes running on the Windows system. This is because VBScript was primarily designed for Web development that does not require such functionality. However, these functionalities are supported in VBScript through automation objects. Automation objects extend intrinsic capabilities in VBScript that can be used to manipulate and communicate information by invoking the `Methods` and `Properties` exposed by the object.

Automation objects are based on automation technology, a feature of COM (Component Object Model), which allows features of an application to be shared with other applications. For example, the IE application shares the `navigate` method that you can use in a script to open a new window and navigate to a site, such as Microsoft.com, as the script in Listing 2.12 can do.

LISTING 2.12 The `Navigate` Method in IE, Used in a Script to Open a New IE Window, and Navigate to `www.Microsoft.com` Web Site

```
Set objExplorer = CreateObject("InternetExplorer.Application")
  objExplorer.visible = true
  objExplorer.Navigate "http://www.Microsoft.com"
set objExplorer = nothing
```

For manipulation, every object typically exposes properties and methods. For example, in Listing 2.12, the `InternetExplorer.Application` object exposes the `Navigate` method that when invoked opens a new IE window and takes you to the Microsoft.com site. The object also provides the `Visible` property that the script that when set to `True` makes visible the IE window created by the `Navigate` method. There are several other properties and methods that the `InternetExplorer.Application` object also exposes that you can use in your scripts to manipulate the Internet Explorer window. For instance, the `GoHome` method that takes you to the home page of the browser, the `MenuBar` property that can be set to hide or show the menu bar, the `Resizable` property that enables and disables window resizing, and the `Quit` method that closes the window.

Similar to the `InternetExplorer.Application` object, the `Winmgmts:object` in WMI (WMI is covered in detail later in this chapter) also exposes several features that can be used in a script to manipulate various tasks in Windows, such as stopping a service as shown Listing 2.13:

LISTING 2.13 Stop a Service Using `StopService` Method Provided by `WIN32_SERVICE` Class of the `Winmgmts:` Object.

```
Dim objService
  Set objService = getobject("winmgmts:win32_service.name='Alerter'")
  ObjService.StopService
Set objService = nothing
```

Connecting to the Object

Before you can use the methods and properties exposed by an object in your scripts, you must establish a connection to the object; just like when you connect to the database before querying the data. To connect to an automation object, VBScript provides two methods: `CreateObject` and `GetObject`.

The `CreateObject` method is used to create an interface to a new instance of an application.

Following is the syntax for the `CreateObject` method:

```
CreateObject(Object [,location])
```

A new instance of an object is like a new copy of the object in memory. For example, you can create a new instance of the `FileSystemObject` object and store it in `objFs` variable in the memory as shown in the following example:

```
Set objFs = CreateObject("Scripting.FileSystemObject")
```

Similarly, you can also create another new instance of the same `FileSystemObject` and store it in the `oFileSystem` variable in the same script, as shown in the following example:

```
Set oFileSystem = CreateObject("Scripting.FileSystemObject")
```

Generally, there is no need to create multiple instances of the same object within a script unless you need to isolate the instances for a specific reason, such as declare within individual procedures.

`CreateObject` is generally used when it's uncertain that the application to interface is not running. For example:

```
Set objExplorer = CreateObject("InternetExplorer.Application")
```

The statement in Listing 2.12 (earlier in this chapter) creates a new instance of the `InternetExplorer.Application` object. The object returned in `objExplorer` is a reference to the `InternetExplorer.Application` object created in the statement. The reference to the `InternetExplorer.Application` object is created by using the special `Set` keyword in VBScript.

Whenever you create an object using the `Set` keyword, the system allocates memory for the variable and stores the object in the variable. Since memory is limited in a system, it is best practice to release the object in the memory if you have no further use of the object, by setting the variable to nothing. This can be done by issuing the following statement: `set variableName = nothing`.

On the other hand, `GetObject` is used with an application that's already running. For example, the `Set objService = getobject("winmgmts:win32_service.name= 'Alerter'")` statement in Listing 2.13 (earlier in this chapter) gets an instance of the `Winmgmts:` object using the `GetObject` method. Similar to the `CreateObject` method, the object returned in `objService` is a reference to the `Winmgmts:` object.

Generally applications that run as a service, for example the WMI service, support the use of the `GetObject` method. However, you should refer to the documentation for the application to learn if the application supports the `GetObject`, `CreateObject`, or both the methods.

Calling Object Methods

After connecting to the object, you can call a method in the following manner:

```
ObjectReference.Method
```

The example in Figure 2.8 demonstrates how the `InternetExplorer.Application` object's `Navigate` method is called.

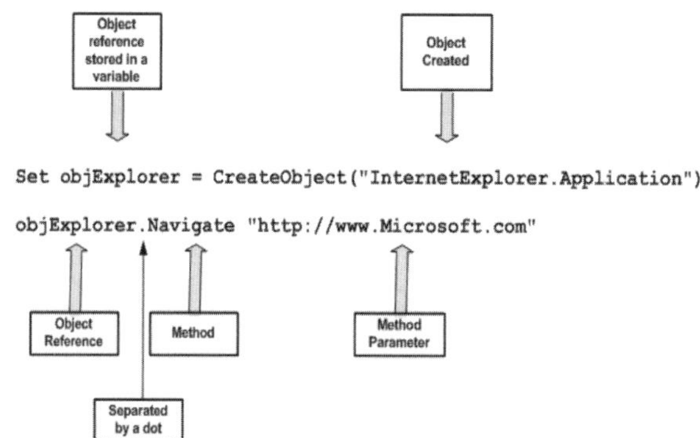

FIGURE 2.8 Demonstrates how to invoke a method.

Retrieving and Setting Object Properties

After successfully connecting to the object, you can also retrieve or set the object's properties. Properties are retrieved in a similar manner as the methods called. Therefore, to retrieve properties you can use similar syntax used to invoke a method, that is `ObjectRefrence` and `ObjectProperty` separated by a dot (period) as the following demonstrates:

```
ObjectReference.ObjectProperty
```

For example the following retrieves the `InternetExplorer.Application` object's visible property:

```
objExplorer.Visible
```

To set a property however, you must use the = (equal to) assignment operator; similar to assigning a value to a variable. The following example sets the `InternetExplorer.Application` object's `Visible` property to `TRUE`:

```
objExplorer.Visible = TRUE
```

Conditional Statements

At times you need to make decisions in your scripts. For example, the code in Listing 2.14 displays if the `Yes` or `No` was answered for the `Are you a scripting guy?` question.

LISTING 2.14 Example of Decision Making with VBScript

```
Question = "Are you the scripting guy?"
Windowtitle = "Confirm"

Answer = MsgBox (Question,VBYesNo+VBQuestion,WindowTitle)
Select case Answer
  case vbYes
    Message = "Yes"
  case vbNo
    Message = "No"
End Select
Wscript.echo Message
```

For making decisions, VBScript provides the `If…then…else` and the `Select…Case` statements. The script in Listing 2.14 uses the `Select…Case` statement to decide if the question was answered in `Yes` or `No`; based on the result returned, in the `Answer` variable by the `Msgbox` function, the `Select…Case` statement sets the `Yes` or the `No` value to the `Message` variable that the script echoes on the screen.

Select...Case Statement

The `Select…Case` statement can be used to make a decision based on the value of the expression passed to the statement. The `Select…Case` statement has the following syntax:

```
Select Case expression
   [Case expressionlist-n
      [statements-n]] . . .
   [Case Else
      [elsestatements-n]]
End Select
```

The example in Listing 2.15 demonstrates the use of the `Select…Case` statement; the script when executed displays the computer role (Standalone Workstation, Member Server, Backup Domain Controller, and so on) based on the value of the `r` variable passed to the `Select…Case` statement.

LISTING 2.15 This Script Demonstrates the Use of `Select Case` Statement

```
Dim objWMI
Dim colComputerSystem
Dim objItem
Dim r, Role
Set objWMI = getobject("winmgmts:")
Set colComputerSystem = objWMI.instancesof("Win32_computersystem")
for each objItem in colComputerSystem
  r = obvjItem.DomainRole
  select case r
   case 0 : Role = "Standalone Workstation"
   case 1 : Role  = "Member Workstation"
   case 2 : Role  = "Standalone Server"
```

```
      case 3 : Role = "Member Server"
      case 4 : Role  = "Backup Domain Controller"
      case 5 : Role  = "Primary Domain Controller"
      case else : Role = "Unknown"
    end select
    Wscript.echo Role
  next
  Set colComputerSystem = nothing
  Set objWMI = nothing
```

If...then...else Statement

The script in Listing 2.14 (earlier in this chapter) can also be written as

```
Question = "Are you the scripting guy?"
Windowtitle = "Confirm"
 Answer = MsgBox (Question,VBYesNo+VBQuestion,WindowTitle)
 If Answer = vbYes then
      Message = "Yes"
 Else
      Message = "No"
 End if
Wscript.echo Message
```

Although, in the previous code the `Select…Case` statement is replaced by the `If…then…else` statement, it also produces the same result as the script in Listing 2.14 (earlier in this chapter).

In VBScript `If…then…else` is another way of making decisions that can be used in place of the `Select…Case` statement. The syntax for the `If…then…else` statement is as follows:

```
If condition Then
    [statements]
[
[Elseif condition then
    [elseif statements]
Else
    [else statements]
]
End if
```

The `If…then…else` statement can also be written in a single line as: `If condition Then statements [Else elsestatements]`

For example, the code in Listing 2.14 (earlier in this chapter) can also be modified as follows:

```
Question = "Are you the scripting guy?"
Windowtitle = "Confirm"
    Answer = MsgBox (Question,VBYesNo+VBQuestion,WindowTitle)
    If Answer = vbYes then Message = "Yes" Else Message = "No"
Wscript.echo Message
```

NOTE

The `if...then...else` statement when used in a single line does not require the `End if` keywords.

Operators

A *variable* can be assigned a value using the = (equal to) assignment operator. Likewise, other VBScript operators can be used in your script to perform mathematical operations, comparison operations, logical operations, and concatenation operations. Table 2.4 outlines these VBScript operators.

TABLE 2.4 VBScript Operators

Operator Type	Description
Arithmetic Operators	Arithmetic operators are operators that can be used to perform mathematical calculations.
Comparison Operators	Comparison operators are operators that can be used for data and object testing equivalence.
Logical Operators	Logical operators can be used to build logical expressions and manipulate numbers at bit level.
Concatenation Operators	Concatenation operators can be used to concatenate strings. (It is like gluing two strings together.)

Arithmetic Operators

Arithmetic operators provide a means of performing mathematical operations, such as addition and subtraction, in your scripts. Table 2.5 lists mathematical operators in VB-Script and demonstrates their use.

Most of the operators listed in Table 2.5 are self-explanatory. However, there are a few that need further explanation, as listed:

- Exponentiation operator (`^`) is the same as raising a number to a certain power.
- Negation is making a number negative. This is done in VBScript by prefixing a minus (–) sign to the number.
- Remainder or Modulo (`MOD`) operator only returns the remainder from the division of two operands.
- Integer division is like rounding the result of a division; it omits the fraction from the result and returns only the integer portion. For example, `5/2` would return `2` and not `2.5`.

TABLE 2.5 Mathematical Operators

Operation	Operator	Example	Result
Addition	+	4 + 2	6
Subtraction	-	4 – 2	2
Multiplication	*	4 * 2	8
Division	/	4 / 2	2
Exponentiation	^	4 ^ 2	16
Negation	-	-(4)	–4
Integer Division	\	5 \ 2	2
Remainder	MOD	5 MOD 2	1

Comparison Operators

VBScript offers powerful operators that can be used to assign values to variables and perform arithmetic operations. VBScript also provides comparison operators that allow you to compare values for making decisions in your scripts, as described in Table 2.6.

Logical Operators

In your script, at times, you may want to ensure that more than two conditions are met before a task is accomplished. For example, consider the following code:

```
FirstName = inputbox("Enter first name")
LastName = inputbox("Enter last name")
If FirstName = "bobby" AND LastName = "malik" then
    Wscript.Echo "Name matched"
Else
    Wscript.Echo  "Name did not match"
End if
```

When you run this script and type `bobby` as the first name and `malik` as the last name, the script will display the `Name matched` message. This is because both the first name and the last name conditions were met (that is, the first name was equal to the literal `bobby` and the last name was equal to `malik`). Under all other circumstances, both the conditions will not be satisfied. For example, if you type `bobby` as the first name and `Malik` as the last name, only the first name condition is met and therefore, the script will echo the `Name did not match` message. This type of operation is made possible by using the `AND` operator that provides logical conjunction in VBScript.

Similarly, the VBScript also provides the `OR` operator that is used as the logical disjunction operator. For example, the following code would display `Name matched` if either of the two conditions is met.

TABLE 2.6 Comparison Operators

Operation	Operator	Returns (Examples)	
Equal to	=	Returns True if the values are equal. False if not.	
		Example	**Result**
		`10 = 5 * 2`	`True`
		`"Bob" = "bob"`	`False`
		`"Bob" = "Bob"`	`True`

		`strName = "bob"`
		`strName2 = "Bob"`
		`strName = strName2`
			`False`

Greater than	>	Returns `True` if the first value is greater than the second value	
		Example	**Result**
		`10 > 5 * 2`	`False`
		`2 > 1`	`True`
Less than	<	Returns `True` if the first value is less that the second value	
		Example	**Result**
		`10 < 5 * 2`	`False`
		`2 < 4`	`True`
Greater than or Equal to	>=	Returns `True` if the first value is greater than or equal to the second value	
		Example	**Result**
		`10 >= 5 * 2`	`True`
		`2 >= 4`	`False`
Less than or Equal to	<=	Returns `True` if the first value is less than or equal to the second value	
		Example	**Result**
		`10 <= 5 * 2`	`False`
		`2 <= 4`	`True`
Object Comparison	`Is`	Returns `True` if two objects have the same instance.	
		Example	**Result**

		`Set Obj1 = CreateObject(Wscript.Shell)`
		`Set Obj2 = CreateObject(Wscript.Shell)`
		`Obj1 is Obj2`
			`False`

		`Set Obj1 = CreateObject(Wscript.Shell)`
		`Set Obj2 = Obj1`
		`Obj1 is Obj2`
			`True`

```
FirstName = inputbox("Enter first name")
LastName = inputbox("Enter last name")
If FirstName = "bobby" OR LastName = "malik" then
    Wscript.Echo "Name matched"
Else
    Wscript.Echo  "Name did not match"
End if
```

For example, if you type `bobby` as the first name and `Malik` as the last name, the `Name matched` message is displayed. It is because at least one of the conditions (first name was equal to `bobby`) was met. Similarly, even if you type `joe` as the first name and `malik` as the last name, the script will echo the `Name matched` message, because the `LastName = "malik"` condition was met. It is only when neither of the conditions is met (that is, if you type `Bobby Malik` as the first and the last name) that the `Name did not match` message will be echoed by the script.

Remember that Bobby is not equal to bobby. Similarly Malik is not equal to malik, as previously explained in the "Comparison Operators" section.

Besides the commonly used `AND` and `OR` logical operators, VBScript also provides other logical operators, such as `NOT`, `EQV`, `XOR` and `IMP`. Table 2.7 lists all the logical operators provided by VBScript.

TABLE 2.7 Logical Operators

Operation	Operator	Returns (Examples)
Logical Conjunction	AND	Returns TRUE if all conditions are met.
Logical Disjunction	OR	Returns TRUE if either of the conditions is met.
Logical Negation	NOT	Returns TRUE if the negation condition is met.
Logical Exclusion	XOR	Evaluates when only one bit is set.
Logical Equivalence	EQV	Returns TRUE if all conditions are met. Also returns TRUE if all conditions are not met. For example, `1 = 1 EQV 2 = 2` will return TRUE and `1 = 2 EQV 2 = 1` will also return TRUE
Logical Implication	IMP	Returns TRUE if both expressions are true or if the right side expression is true. For example, the following will return TRUE `1 = 1 imp 2 = 2`

→

Operation	Operator	Returns (Examples)

		whereas the following will return FALSE
		`1 = 1 imp 2 = 1`
		`1 = 2 imp 2 = 1`

Concatenation Operators

It is possible to add two strings together in VBScript using the `&` concatenation operator. The following example illustrates how to add (glue) together two strings:

```
StringOne = "This is "
StringTwo = "an example of string concatenation"
Wscript.echo StringOne & StringTwo
```

Upon execution the script will echo `This is an example of string concatenation.` It is also possible to concatenate a string and integer in the same manner, as demonstrated in the following example:

```
StringOne = "User number: "
IntegerOne = 123
Wscript.echo StringOne & IntegerOne
```

When this script is executed, it produces the following result:

```
User Number: 123
```

Likewise, two integers can also be concatenated together, as shown in the following example:

```
IntegerOne = 1
IntegerTwo = 23
Wscript.echo IntegerOne & IntegerTwo
```

When executed, the script will produce 11 instead of 2 as the result.

In VBScript, you can also use the `+` (addition) operator to concatenate two strings as follows:

```
StringOne = "This is "
StringTwo = "an example of string concatenation"
Wscript.echo StringOne + StringTwo
```

However, the same cannot be used to concatenate two integers (*mathematical addition* will be performed if two integers are added using the `+` operator). A `Type Mismatch` error will also appear if a string is added to an integer (or vice versa), as in the following example:

```
StringOne = "User number: "
IntegerOne = 123
Wscript.echo StringOne + IntegerOne
```

At runtime this script will generate a `Type Mismatch` error, as shown in Figure 2.9.

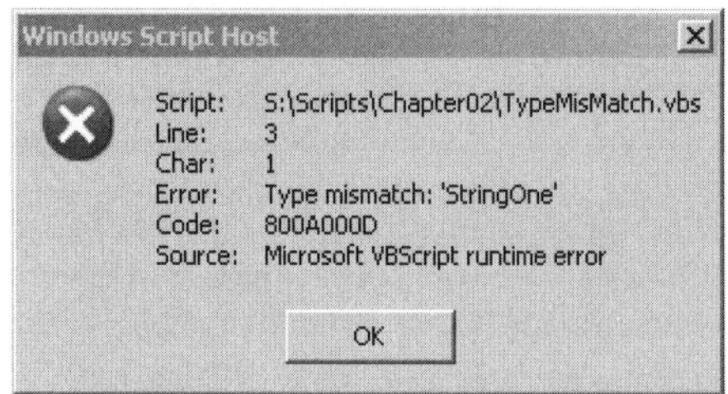

FIGURE 2.9 `Type Mismatch` error generates when a string and an integer value are added using the `+` operator.

Operator Precedence

There may be situations where more than one operation occurs in an expression. When VBScript encounters more than one operation in an expression, the operations are performed from left to right. However, VBScript follows certain rules; the arithmetic group operators are evaluated first, then concatenation, comparison, and lastly, logical operators.

Within each operator, the operations are set in the following order:

1. Arithmetic operation: ^, - ,(*, /), \, Mod,(+, -)
2. Concatenation operation: `&`
3. Comparison operation: =, <>, <, >, <=, >=, `Is`
4. Logical operation: `Not`, `And`, `Or`, `Xor`, `Eqv`, `Imp`

This order can be overridden by using parentheses. Operations in parentheses are evaluated before operations outside the parentheses, however, inside the parentheses follow the normal order of operations (that is, arithmetic…logical operation). For example, the following two statements look the same but produce different results.

- `ResultA = 1 + 2 * 4 + 2`
- `ResultB = (1+2) * (4+2)`

- `Wscript.echo ResultA & vbNewLine & ResultB`
- Upon execution the `ResultA` produces `11` and the `ResultB` produces `18`, as addition is forced in the second calculation with parentheses.

Collection

A *collection* is a group of objects of the same type. For example, `colFiles` in Listing 2.16 is the collection of the file objects of the c:\temp folder. Similarly, the `colSubFolders` in Listing 2.16 is the collection of the subfolder objects of the c:\temp folder.

LISTING 2.16 Example of Collection of Files and Folders

```
Dim objFs
Dim colFiles
Dim colSubFolders
Dim sFolderPath
sFolderPath = "c:\temp"
set objFs = CreateObject("Scripting.FileSystemObject")
    set objFolder = objFs.GetFolder(sFolderPath)
        set colFiles = objFolder.Files
        set colSubFolders = objFolder.SubFolders
    Wscript.echo "There are " & _
                  colFiles.Count & _
                   " files in " & _
                    sFolderPath
    Wscript.echo "There are " & _
                 colSubFolders.Count & _
                  " sub folders in " & _
                   sFolderPath
    set objFolder = nothing
    set colSubFolders = nothing
    set colFiles = nothing
    set objFs = nothing
```

On a collection, you can perform iteration (see next topic) and count the total number of objects in the collection. For example, to display the name of each file in a folder, do the following:

- Create a `FileSystemObject` object
- Connect to the folder using the `GetFolder` method (`GetFolder` method is covered under VBScript Runtime later in this chapter). The `GetFolder` method gets the collection of all files in the folder.
- For each file in the collection of files: echo the name of the file

Figure 2.10 describes the `FileName.wsf` script that echoes the total number of files in a given folder and the name of each file in the folder.

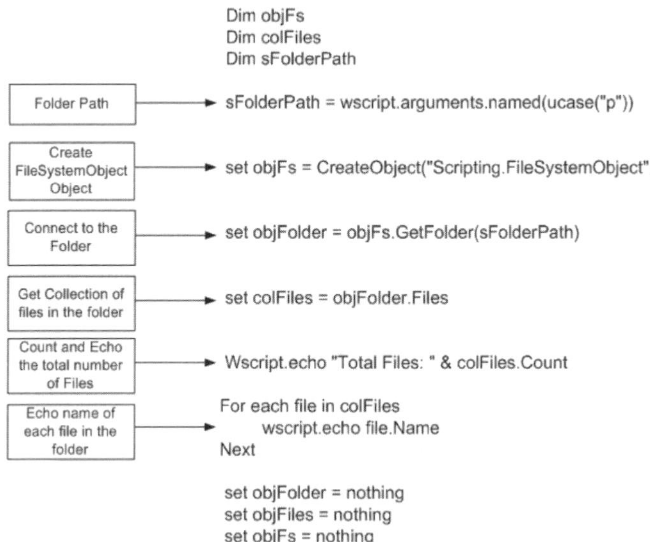

FIGURE 2.10 Echo total number of files and name of each file in a folder.

Complete `FileName.wsf` *script file is located on the CD-ROM at Scripts/Chapter02. The syntax for the script is* `FileCount.wsf /p:<Path to Folder>`

Iteration

To iterate (or loop), computers need instructions known as looping structures. Looping structures determine how many times a loop's statements will execute and on what condition the loop will end.

In VBScript, you can use three structures: `Do…loop`, `For…Next`, and `For each…next`. Using these structures, you can iterate (loop) to execute statements within the looping structures. For example, the script in Listing 2.17 counts and displays the total number of lines in the text file.

LISTING 2.17 Counts and Displays the Total Number of Lines in the Text File

```
CountLine = 0
Const FOR_READING = 1
    sFileName = wscript.arguments(0)
      set objFs = CreateObject("Scripting.FileSystemObject")
        set objFile = objFs.OpenTextFile(sFileName,FOR_READING)
          do while not objFile.AtEndOfStream
              objFile.ReadLine
                CountLine = CountLine + 1
          loop
      Wscript.Echo CountLine
```

Complete script is on the CD-ROM as `Listing2_16.wsf`.

Do...Loop Statement

The `Do...Loop` statement repeatedly executes a block of statements until the condition is met (becomes `TRUE`) or while a condition is met (is `TRUE`). For example, the script in Listing 2.15 loops through the text file until value of the `AtEndOfStream` property is set to `TRUE` by the `FileSystemObject` object. In other words, the `Do...Loop` statement repeatedly executes the `objFile.ReadLine`, `CountLine = CountLine + 1` statements until the `AtEndOfStream` is set to `TRUE` by the `objFile` object.

Syntax for the `Do...Loop` statement is as follows:

```
Do [{while | until} condition]
    [statements]
    [exit do]
    [statements]
Loop
```

For example, in the following `Do...Loop` loops until the value of `iCount = 100`

```
Dim iCount
iCount = 1
Do until iCount = 100
       iCount = iCount + 1
Loop
```

It can also have the following syntax:

```
Do
    [statements]
    [Exit do]
    [statements]
Loop [{while | until} condition]
```

For example, the following `Do...Loop` loops while the value of `iCount` is less than 100

```
Dim iCount
iCount = 1
Do
iCount = iCount + 1
Loop while iCount < 100
```

For...Next Statement

As you use the `Do...Loop` statement, you use the `For...Next` statement to repeatedly execute a block of statements. However, the `For...Next` statement is generally used where you want to execute a block of statements only a specified number of times. For example, the script in Listing 2.18 pads (prefixes) the data with `0` (zeros) to increase length of the data to `8` characters using the `For...Next` loop, if the length of the data is less than `8` characters:

LISTING 2.18 `For...Next` Loop Pads the Data with `0` (zeros)

```
Wscript.echo padding(10)
function padding(data)
    lendata = len(data)
  for i = 1 to (8 - lendata)
    pad = pad & 0
  next
   padding = pad & data
end function
```

ON THE CD

This script is stored on the CD-ROM as Padding.vbs in the scripts/chapter02 folder.

Following is the syntax of the `For...Next` statement:

```
For counter = start To end [Step step]
    [statements]
    [Exit for]
    [statements]
Next
```

By default the `For...Next` loop increments the counter by one. You can, however, override this by passing, as a parameter to the `For...Next` statement, the number of times to increment the counter. For example, by default (when you omit the `Step` parameter), the following will display all `6` numbers of the counter:

```
Counter = 0
For Counter = 1 to 6
    Wscript.Echo Counter
Next
```

And the following code will display only odd numbers (1,3,5) as the `Step` parameter is set to `2` (increment the counter by `2`) in the `For...Next` statement:

```
Counter = 0
For Counter = 1 to 6 Step 2
    Wscript.Echo Counter
Next
```

For Each...Next

Like other looping structures, `For each...Next` is another type of looping structure that can be used to iterate (or loop) to execute a block of statements. However, it is used only to iterate through each element of an array or a collection. For example, the following iterates each file in the file collection to display the name and the type of the file.

```
sFolderPath = "c:\"
  set objFs = CreateObject("Scripting.FileSystemObject")
  set objFolder = objFs.GetFolder(sFolderPath)
 set colFiles = objFolder.Files
For each objFile in colFiles
  Wscript.echo objFile.Name & ", " & objFile.Type
```

ON THE CD

Complete script is stored on the CD-ROM as `DisplayFileType.wsf` *at the scripts/ chapter02 folder.*

Following is the complete syntax for the `For each...Next` statement:

```
For each element In group
    [statements]
    [Exit for]
    [statements]
Next
```

Procedures

In VBScript, a script can be divided into logical parts called procedures. Procedures are blocks of code of a script that can be called from anywhere within the script using the `Call` statement. VBScript provides two types of procedures: `Sub` and `Function`.

Sub Procedures

`Sub` procedures wrap code within the `Sub...End Sub` keywords and can take arguments and use them within the procedures. For example, the code in Listing 2.19 calls a `Sub` procedure that calculates the number of days lapsed between two dates. The `LapsedDays` procedure takes the `StartDate` and the `EndDate` as parameters (that is, when calling the `LapsedDays` procedure you must pass the first and the second date that the code within the `sub...end sub` keywords uses to calculate the lapsed days).

LISTING 2.19 Display Number of Days Lapsed between Two Dates

```
StartDate = "01/01/2005"
EndDate = Now
Call LapsedDays(StartDate,EndDate)

Sub LapsedDays(StartDate,EndDate)
    DaysLapsed = DateDiff("d",StartDate,Enddate)
    MsgBox DaysLapsed & " days has lapsed since " & StartDate
End Sub
```

As a procedure is called, the script control is handed over to the procedure that is being called. It is only when `End Sub` keywords are encountered by VBScript that it continues to execute the next line of code as shown in Figure 2.11.

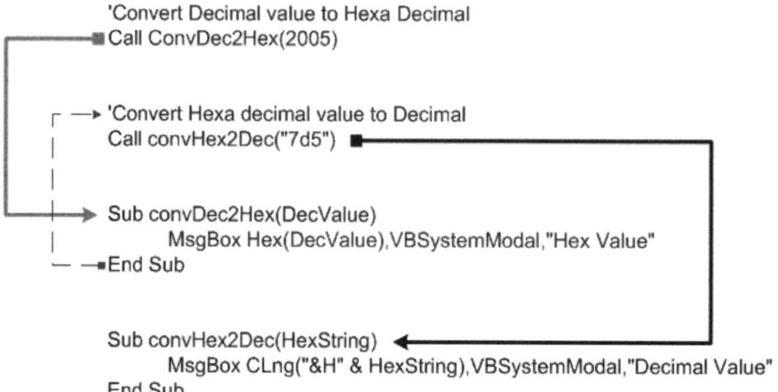

'Convert Decimal value to Hexa Decimal
Call ConvDec2Hex(2005)
'Convert Hexa decimal value to Decimal
Call convHex2Dec("7d5")
Sub convDec2Hex(DecValue)
MsgBox Hex(DecValue),VBSystemModal,"Hex Value"
End Sub
Sub convHex2Dec(HexString)
MsgBox CLng("&H" & HexString),VBSystemModal,"Decimal Value"
End Sub

FIGURE 2.11 Procedure control flow example.

NOTE

The code within the Sub *procedure is executed only when the* Sub *procedure is explicitly called. In Listing 2.19 the* Call LapsedDays(StartDate,EndDate) *calls the* Sub *procedure. If no call is made for the* Sub *procedure within the script (that is, if you remove the* Call LapsedDays<StartDate,EndDate> *statement from the script) the statements within the* LapsedDays Sub *procedure are ignored.*

In Figure 2.11, when VBScript encounters the Call convDec2Hex statement, it branches over to the convDec2Hex subprocedure. It processes all of the statements within the Sub...End Sub keywords before resuming the execution of the next statement in the script as denoted by the dotted line in the figure.

When VBScript encounters the next call statement, Call convHex2Dec, it again branches out to execute the statements within the convHex2Dec sub procedure. After all the statements within the convHex2Dec sub procedure are completely executed, the script ends (as there are no other lines of code for processing after the Call convHex2Dec statement).

Function Procedures

Like Sub procedures, Function procedures are also blocks of code grouped together between Function...End Function keywords. When called, Function procedures also execute the statements that are within the Function...End Function keywords. As with Sub procedures, Function procedures can also take parameters and process them within the procedure. However, Function procedures differ from the Sub procedures because they can return a value.

For example, as shown in Figure 2.12, when the Bytes2MB function in the script is called (and value in bytes is passed as the parameter), it calculates and returns the value in megabytes.

```
set objWMI = getobject("winmgmts:")

wqlLogicalDisk = "Select * from Win32_LogicalDisk " & _
                                    "Where DriveType=3"

Set colLogicalDisk = objWMI.ExecQuery(wqlLogicalDisk)

For each item in colLogicalDisk

  Wscript.Echo "Drive: " & Item.Name & _

               VBNewLine & "Drive Size: " & _

                        Bytes2MB(item.Size)  & " MB"
Next

Set objWMI = nothing
Set colLogicalDisk = nothing

Function Bytes2MB(iBytes)
      MbValue = round(iBytes /(1024^2),2)
      Bytes2MB = MbValue
End Function
```

Figure 2.12 Bytes2MB function procedure returns the size in MB value.

Usually `Function` procedures are referenced as `Functions` and `Sub` procedures are referenced as `Subs` (or subroutines).

NOTE

VBScript Built-in Functions

Other than writing your own custom functions, you can also use the intrinsic (built-in) functions in VBScript. VBScript provides several functions that you can use in your scripts to do string operations, date and time operations, conversions, mathematical operations, and boolean operations.

VBScript provides many intrinsic functions; however, in this book we will cover only specific functions that are most commonly used in the scripts.

NOTE

String Functions

VBScript provides several functions that you can use for string operations. Following are a few functions that you may frequently use within your scripts:

`InStr:` `Instr` (pronounced as "in string") function can be used to find out if a string contains another string or a character. If found, the function returns the position of the first occurrence of the string. For example, the following uses `Instr` function to identify if the "`\`" string is contained within the string "`C:\temp\MyFolder`":

```
Path = "C:\temp\MyFolder"
wscript.echo instr(Path,"\")
```

When run, the code returns `3` as the first position of the "`\`" character found within "`C:\temp\MyFolder`" string.

`Instr` has the following syntax:

```
InStr([start, ]string1, string2[, compare])
```

where:

Start: optional value that sets the starting position for each search. Default value is the first position of the string.

String1: required string value that is being searched.

String2: required value that you are searching for.

Compare: Optional numeric value that indicates the kind of comparison to use. If this value is set to `0` (the default value) VBScript will perform a binary comparison. Setting it to `1` will force VBScript to perform textual comparison.

`InstrRev:` While `Instr` searches a string or a character within another string from left to right, the `InstrRev` function searches from right to left. For example, the following (although similar to the `Instr` example), will return `8`:

```
Path = "C:\temp\MyFolder"
Wscript.echo InstrRev(Path,"\")
```

Like `Instr`, `InstrRev` also returns the position of the first occurrence of the string or the character, if found.

`Left:` The `Left` function in VBScript can be used to extract a specific number of characters from the left. For example, the following code extracts 3 characters from the left of the string to display the `C:\` drive letter in the path.

```
Path = "C:\temp\MyFolder
wscript.echo Left(Path,3)
```

Following is the syntax for the `Left` function:

```
Left (string, length)
```

`Right:` As `Left`, the `Right` function also returns a specific number of characters of a string. However, it returns the characters starting from the right of the string. For example, the following code displays `MyFolder` (`8` characters in length):

```
Path = "C:\temp\MyFolder"
wscript.echo right (Path,8)
```

The `Right` function has the following syntax:

```
Right (string, length)
```

`Mid:` VBScript also provides the `Mid` function that can be used to extract a specified number of characters from a string. However, unlike the `Right` and the `Left` functions, you must specify the starting position in the string. For example, the following code returns `8` characters (`MyFolder`) starting after the position of `\` (determined by the `InstrRev` function `+ 1`) character within the `Path`:

```
Path = "C:\Temp\MyFolder"
StartPosition = InstrRev(Path,"\") + 1
Wscript.echo Mid (Path, StartPosition, 8)
```

Following is the syntax for the `Mid` function:

```
Mid (string, start [, length])
```

`Len:` To determine a length of the string, you can use VBScript's `Len` function. The `Len` function returns an integer value that represents the length of a given string (including white spaces). For example, the following code displays the length of the string stored in the `Path` variable.

```
Path = "C:\temp\My Folder"
Wscript.echo Len (Path)
```

When the script is run, it returns an integer value of 17 (that is 16 actual characters and a space character)

The `Len` function uses the following syntax:

```
Len (string)
```

`Ltrim, Rtrim, Trim:` VBScript provides `LTrim`, `RTrim`, and `Trim` functions to remove the leading and trailing spaces within a string.

While the `LTrim` function returns the string after removing the leading spaces, the `RTrim` function returns the string after removing the trailing spaces. For example the following examples show how the string will be trimmed using these functions:

`LTrim` *Example:*

```
ServerNames = "      Server01,    Server01        "
Wscript.echo LTrim (ServerNames)
```

When the `LTrim code` is executed, it displays the output shown in Figure 2.13.

`RTrim` *Example:*

```
ServerNames = "      Server01,    Server01        "
Wscript.echo RTrim (ServerNames)
```

When the `RTrim` code is run it displays the output shown in Figure 2.14.

FIGURE 2.13 Result `LTrim` example.

FIGURE 2.14 Result `RTrim` example.

The `LTrim` and `RTrim` functions use the following syntax:

```
LTrim (string)
RTrim (string)
```

The `RTrim` and `LTrim` functions can be used together on a given string to strip both the leading and trailing spaces from a string. For example, to strip the leading and trailing spaces, the following example uses the `LTrim` function to remove the leading spaces and then uses the `RTrim` function to strip the trailing spaces from the string returned by the `LTrim` function:

```
ServerNames = "     Server01,     Server01       "
Wscript.echo RTrim( LTrim(ServerNames) )
```

Alternatively, you can also use `Trim` function in VBScript to do the same. The `Trim` function returns the string after removing both the leading and the trailing spaces, as shown in the following example:

`Trim` *Example:*

```
ServerNames = "     Server01,     Server01       "
Wscript.echo Trim (ServerNames)
```

Figure 2.15 shows the result generated by running the previous code.

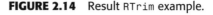

FIGURE 2.15 Result `Trim` example.

`UCase, LCase:` VBScript provides the `UCase` and the `LCase` functions that can be used in scripts to change the case of a string. For example, the following changes all the characters of the string to uppercase using the `UCase` function:

`UCase` *Example:*

```
Name = "john doe"
Wscript.echo UCase(Name)
```

When the code is executed, `john doe` is displayed as `JOHN DOE.` as shown in Figure 2.16. As `UCase` converts a given string to uppercase, the `LCase` function converts the given characters to lowercase characters. For example, the following code converts all characters from uppercase to lowercase characters. Figure 2.17 displays the converted characters.

FIGURE 2.16 Changes and displays the name to uppercase characters.

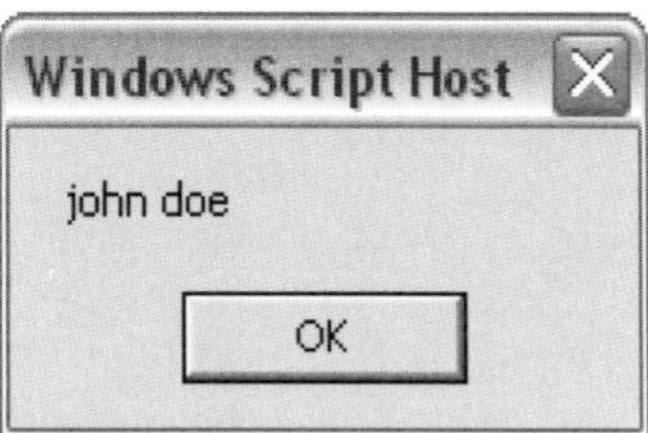

FIGURE 2.17 Changes and displays the name to lowercase characters.

`LCase` *Example:*

```
Name = "JOHN DOE"
Wscript.echo LCase(Name)
```

Both the `UCase` and the `LCase` functions convert all of the characters passed to the function. Therefore, `John Doe`, `john Doe`, `John Doe` (and all other combinations) when passed to the `UCase` function will always be returned as `JOHN DOE`. Similarly, the same when passed to the `LCase` function will always be returned as `john doe`.

Replace: The `Replace` function in VBScript can be used to search and replace a string within another string. The `Replace` function takes a string expression, a search string, the replace string arguments. Optionally it takes the start, count, and the compare arguments. The following example illustrates how to replace the C: drive letter with D: drive letter in a path using the `Replace` function.

```
Path = "C:\temp\MyFolder"
wscript.echo Replace (Path,"C:","D:")
```

The Replace function searches for a literal character(s) passed as the search string; that is, a search for C: is not same as searching c:. Therefore, it is best to convert the case of the string expression that you are searching and then search for the string of the same case, as the following example illustrates:

```
Path = "C:\temp\MyFolder"
wscript.echo Replace (LCase(Path),"c:","d:")
```

NOTE

If you use the LCase *or the* UCase *functions to covert the string in the replace function, the* replace *function will return the text in the case used. Therefore in the previous code, the script will return the value in all lowercase characters as* d:\temp\myfolder.

Split: VBScript provides the Split function that you can use to split a string value into multiple string values. The Split function splits a string value based on a character passed as the delimiter and, returns an array of string. Following is the syntax for the Split function:

```
Split (expression [, delimiter [, count [, compare]]])
```

The Split function takes expression as a required argument and delimiter, count, and compare as the optional arguments. It returns a zero-based, one-dimensional array of a specified number of elements containing the split string values (substrings of the string).

Each element in the array contains the text split based on the delimiter. For example, the following splits the server names based on the comma (,) delimiter:

```
ServerNames = "Server01,Server02,Server03,Server04"
Servers = Split(ServerNames, ",")
For each item in Servers
    Wscript.echo item
Next
```

By default the Split function returns all substrings of the string. To limit the number of substrings that the function should return, you can pass a number as the count argument. For example, if you pass 2 as the argument the Split function will split the expression passed to the function as follows:

1. First substring of the expression.
2. Rest of the substrings of the expression.

The following example shown in Listing 2.20, for instance, splits the Server01, Server02,Server03,Server04 string into two substrings (array of two elements); one containing Sever01 and the other containing Server02,Server03, Server04 values (substrings).

LISTING 2.20 `Split` Function Returns `2` Substring When `2` Is Passed as a `Count` Argument

```
ServerNames = "Server01,Server02,Server03,Server04"
  Servers = Split(ServerNames, ",", 2)
  For each item in Servers
        Wscript.echo item
Next
```

`Join:` `Join` function of VBScript does the opposite of the `Split` function; that is, it joins the array of substrings into a single substring. It takes a list (array of substrings) as a required argument and a delimiter as an optional argument as shown in the following syntax statement:

```
Join (list [, delimiter])
```

The following example uses the `Join` function to join the array of server names into a comma delimited string:

```
Dim ServerNames(5)
ServerNames(0) = "Server01"
ServerNames(1) = "Server02"
ServerNames(2) = "Server03"
ServerNames(4) = "Server04"
Wscript.echo Join(ServerNames,",")
```

By default the `Join` function uses space as a delimiter if the optional delimiter argument is not passed to the function. To ensure that no space is used while concatenating the substrings, you need to use two double quotes (double quote followed by another double quote) without space between them, as shown in the following example:

```
Dim Path(2)
Path(0) = "c:\"
Path(1) = "Scripts\VBScript Scripts"
Wscript.echo Join(Path,"")
```

The `Join` method is most useful when you need to display information stored in an array, as shown in the example in Listing 2.21:

LISTING 2.21 Script Displaying the Use of `Join` Function for Display

```
Dim objWMI, colItems
 set objWMI = GetObject("Winmgmts:root\Cimv2")
  set colItems = objWMI.ExecQuery("Select * from Win32_Printer")
   For each item in colItems
     Wscript.echo VBNewLine
     Wscript.echo "Printer = " & item.Name
     Wscript.echo "Paper names = " & Join(item.PrinterPaperNames, ",")
     Wscript.echo VBNewLine
```

```
    next
   set colItems = nothing
  set objWMI = nothing
```

When the script in Listing 2.21 is run with Cscript.exe, it produces output similar to that shown in Figure 2.18. The script displays the printer name and the printer paper names associated with the printer in a comma-delimited format (array of string values joined into a single string using the `Join` function).

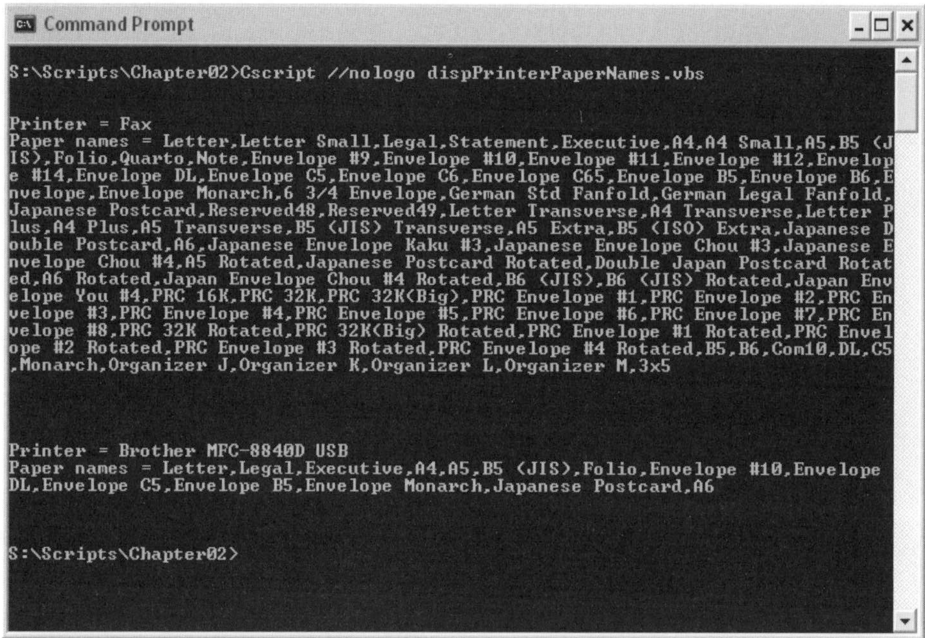

FIGURE 2.18 Output generated by running the code in Listing 2.21

`ASC:` `ASC` function in VBScript takes a string and returns the corresponding ANSI character code of the first letter in the string. For instance, in the following example, when the code is executed, it displays the number `83`; the ANSI number for `S` letter:

```
Wscript.echo ASC("SecurePassword")
```

The `ASC` function uses the following syntax:

```
ASC (string)
```

To convert every letter in the string, you can do the following:

- Pass the string to the `ASC` function. (This will convert the first letter of the string to ANSI character.)
- Loop through the rest of the letters using the `For Next` loop.
- Inside the loop, use the `MID` function to pass individual letters to the `ASC` function for conversion.

The following code illustrates how to use the `ASC` function (along with the `For Next` loop and the `MID` function) to convert and display each letter of the string to its corresponding ANSI number:

```
sPassword = Wscript.Arguments(0)
 AnsiPassword = Asc( sPassword )
    For i = 2 to Len(sPassword)
        AnsiPassword = AnsiPassword & " " & ASC( Mid(sPassword,i) )
    Next
Wscript.Echo VBNewLine, AnsiPassword
```

When the previous code is executed, it converts every letter of the password (passed to the script as an argument) into its corresponding ANSI value. As seen in Figure 2.19, when executed with Cscript shell, it displays the password as ANSI value.

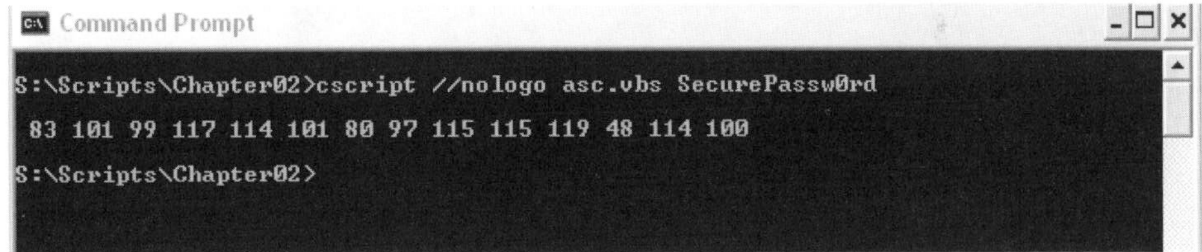

FIGURE 2.19 Letters passed as an argument to the script converted and displayed in ANSI number format.

`CHR:` The `CHR` function inVBScript does the opposite of the `ASC` function; it takes an ANSI number and returns the corresponding letter. The `CHR` function has the following syntax:

```
CHR ( charactercode )
```

In the following example the `CHR` function returns `S` character when the code is executed:

```
Wscript.echo CHR(83)
```

`StrComp:` Usually you would compare two integer values to determine if one value is greater than another value. However, there may be times that you need to compare two strings to determine if one string is less than another string.

To compare two strings, VBScript provides the `StrComp` function. It takes two strings, compares the two values and returns the values, as listed in Table 2.8.

TABLE 2.8 `StrComp` Return Values

If	StrComp Returns
String1 is less than *String2*	–1
String1 is equal to *String2*	0
String1 is greater than *String2*	1
String1 or *String2* is Null	`Null`

The following illustrates the use of the `StrComp` function:

```
Const TEXT_COMPARE = 1
Wscript.echo StrComp("Build Version 5.6.00.1", _
                     "MLIM BUILD 5.6.01.1", _
                               TEXT_COMPARE)
```

When the previous code is executed, it displays `-1` because *String1* is less than *String2* (that is (`"Build Version 5.6.00.1" is less than "Build Version 5.6.01.1"`).

Math Functions

Math functions included in VBScript enable you to perform operations on numbers in your scripts. Following are a few that you might find useful:

`Hex:` The `Hex` function converts a value to hexadecimal form and returns it in a string format. For example, the following converts a value returned by the `Err.Number` into hexadecimal value and returns it in a string format:

```
Wscript.echo "0x" & Hex(Err.Number)
```

NOTE

If a fractional value is passed as a parameter to the `Hex` function, it is first rounded to the nearest whole number before the function returns the string.

Int: The INT function returns the whole number piece of an argument. If the argument is negative, Int returns the first integer value that is less than or equal to the argument. For example, the following displays only the whole number of the total drive size:

```
Set objFs = CreateObject("Scripting.FileSystemObject")
  DiskSize = objFs.GetDrive("C:").TotalSize / (1024^3)
  Wscript.echo Int (DiskSize) & " GB"
Set objFs = nothing
```

Round: The Round function takes an integer value and returns a number rounded to a specified number of decimal places. For example, the following rounds the total size of the drive to two numbers of decimal places:

```
Set objFs = CreateObject("Scripting.FileSystemObject")
  DiskSize = objFs.GetDrive("C:").TotalSize / (1024^3)
     Wscript.echo Round (DiskSize, 2) & " GB"
   Set objFs = nothing
```

Conversion Functions

VBScript uses the variant type for all variables. However, in many cases, an argument of a certain type is required. For example, two variables can be added only if they have the Int (integer) sub type.

Addition of two strings will be concatenation and not a mathematical addition.

VBScript provides a number of functions that can be used in a script to change the subtype of a variable. Following are some of the conversion functions available in VBScript:

CStr: The CStr function takes an expression and converts and returns the expression in string subtype format. It has the following syntax:

```
Cstr (expression)
```

The following example converts an integer value to a string value before adding it to another string value:

```
Wscript.Echo "Server" + Cstr(1)
```

If the CStr *function is not used to convert the integer value to the string data type before adding it to a string value, VBScript will display a* Type Mismatch *error (error handling is covered in more detail later in this chapter).*

`CInt:` The `CInt` function converts an expression to integer subtype. It has the following syntax:

```
CInt ( expression )
```

The following example converts a string value to an integer value before performing a mathematical calculation:

```
Wscript.echo CInt (DiskSize) / (1024 ^ 2)
```

VBScript will generate a `Type Mismatch` error if you try and add an integer value to a string value; similarly, it will generate a `Type Mismatch` error if you use a string value in a mathematical calculation. Therefore, as a good practice, you should force convert the values to the integer type before using the value in a mathematical calculation.

`CDbl:` The `CDbl` function takes an expression and returns the value as a double subtype. The `CDbl` function uses the following syntax:

```
CDbl ( expression )
```

The following example illustrates how the `CDbl` function can be used to convert a value to a double subtype:

```
Yen = (105.12)
 Dollars = CDbl(Yen *  123.4532)
Wscript.echo Dollars
```

When this code is executed, it generates a number with double-precision, as shown in Figure 2.20.

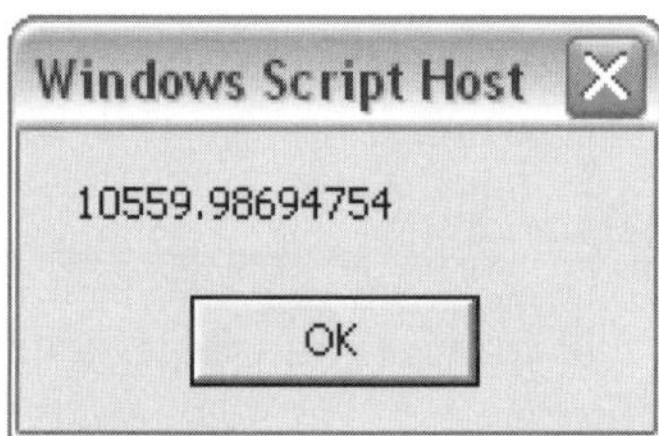

FIGURE 2.20 Double-precision arithmetic value returned by the `CDbl` function.

`CSng:` While the `CDbl` function returns the double-precision value, the `CSng` returns the single-precision value. It uses the following syntax:

```
CSng ( expression )
```

The following example illustrates how to convert a value to a single-precision value using the `CSng` function:

```
Yen = (105.12)
 Dollars = CSng(Yen *  123.4532)
Wscript.echo Dollars
```

When this code is executed, it generates a number with single-precision (note that there are only two numbers after the dot), as shown in Figure 2.21.

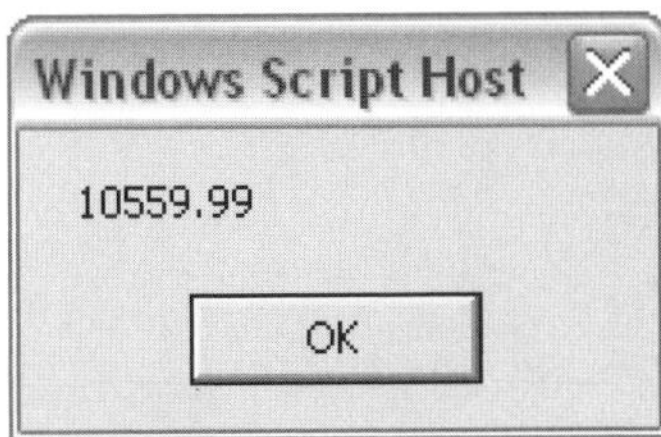

FIGURE 2.21 Single-precision arithmetic value returned by the `CSng` function.

`CByte:` The `CByte` function takes an expression and converts and returns an expression of byte subtype. The `CByte` function has the following syntax:

```
CByte ( expression )
```

`CLng:` The `CLng` takes an expression and converts and returns an expression of long subtype. The `CLng` function has the following syntax:

```
CLng ( expression )
```

For example, the following script converts the hexadecimal value to a decimal value using the `CLng` function and displays both the hexadecimal and the decimal values:

```
Dim HexValue
HexValue = 19
Wscript.Echo " Hex value = " & HexValue, VbNewLine, _
    "Decimal Value = " & CLng("&H" & HexValue)
```

`CDate:` The `CDate` function takes an expression and, converts and returns an expression of date subtype. For example, the following will convert the string `January 1, 2005` to `1/1/2005` date format.

```
sDate = "January 1, 2005"
Wscript.echo cDate(sDate)
```

`cDate` function has the following syntax:

```
CDate ( expression )
```

NOTE

VBScript provides the `TypeName` function that can be used to find out the subtype of a variable. For example, the following code displays the subtype of the variable before and after it is converted to a date format:

```
sDate = "January 1, 2005"
Wscript.echo TypeName(StringDate)
dtDate = cDate(StringDate)
Wscript.echo TypeName(dtDate)
```

Date and Time Functions

VBScript also provides several date and time functions that can be used in scripts to manipulate date and time, as shown:

`Date:` The `Date` function displays the current system date. It takes no parameters. The following example will display the current system date:

```
Wscript.echo Date
```

`Day:` The `Day` function returns the day as a numeric value between `1` and `31`. It takes date as an argument. The following code will display the day from the current system date.

```
Wscript.echo Day(Date)
```

`Month:` The `Month` function, similar to the `Day` function, returns the month of a given date as a numeric value. The following code will display the month from the current system date.

```
Wscript.echo Month(Date)
```

`Year:` As the `Month` and the `Day` functions, the `Year` function returns the year of a given date. The following code will display the year from the current system date.

```
Wscript.echo Year(Date)
```

`Weekday`: The `Weekday` function takes date and optionally a `firstdayofweek` argument and returns a numeric value representing the day of the week. The function defaults to Sunday, if the `firstdayofweek` is omitted. Table 2.9 lists the settings for the `firstdayofweek` argument.

TABLE 2.9 `firstdayofweek` Constants

Day	Numeric Value
System	0
Sunday	1
Monday	2
Tuesday	3
Wednesday	4
Thursday	5
Friday	6
Saturday	7

The following example illustrates the use of the `Weekday` function.

```
Wscript.Echo "Welcome! Today is " & DayOfWeek(Date)
Function DayOfWeek(dtDate)
    Select Case WeekDay(dtDate)
        Case 1 : DayOfWeek = "Sunday"
        Case 2 : DayOfWeek = "Monday"
        Case 3 : DayOfWeek = "Tuesday"
        Case 4 : DayOfWeek = "Wednesday"
        Case 5 : DayOfWeek = "Thursday"
        Case 6 : DayOfWeek = "Friday"
        Case 7 : DayOfWeek = "Saturday"
    End Select
End Function
```

`DateSerial:` The `DateSerial` function takes year, month, and day as arguments and returns the variant of subtype date. The year argument can be any year between `100` and `9999`. For example, the following returns the date subtype with `1/1/2005` value:

```
Wscript.Echo DateSerial (2005, 1, 1)
```

`DateValue:` The `DateValue` function takes a string argument containing a valid date and returns a date subtype. For example, the following converts the `Jan 1, 2005` to `1/1/2005` date subtype value.

```
Wscript.echo DateValue ("Jan 1, 2005")
```

`DateDiff:` The `DateDiff` function takes `interval`, two (first and second) dates and, optionally, `firstdayofweek` and `firstweekofyear` as arguments and returns the number of intervals between the two dates. For example, the following script displays the number of days difference between `1/1/2005` and the current system date based on the `d` (Day) interval:

```
Date1 = #1/1/2005#
Date2 = Date
Wscript.echo DateDiff("d", Date1, Date2)
```

The `DateDiff` function supports the intervals listed in Table 2.10.

TABLE 2.10 `Interval` Argument Values

Interval	Description
yyyy	Year
q	Quarter
m	Month
y	Day of year
d	Day
w	Week
ww	Week of year
h	Hour
n	Minute
s	Second

`DatePart:` The `DatePart` function takes `interval`, a date, optionally `firstweekofday` and `firstweekofyear` as arguments and returns a specified part of the given date.

For example, the following displays the quarter of the year in which the current system date is. For instance, if the date is `8/8/2005` then the `DatePart` function will return `3` (as in third quarter of the year):

```
Wscript.echo DatePart("q",Date)
```

`Time:` The `Time` function returns the current system time. It takes no arguments. The following will display the current system time:

```
Wscript.echo Time
```

Hour: The Hour function takes time as an argument and returns a number between 0 and 23, representing the hour of the day. The following will display the hour value of the current system time:

```
Wscript.echo hour(Time)
```

Minute: The Minute function retrieves the minute value out of a time value. The following will display the minute value of the current system time:

```
Wscript.echo Minute(Time)
```

Second: The Second function retrieves the second value out of a time value. The following will display the second value of the current system time:

```
Wscript.echo second(Time)
```

Now: The Now function retrieves the date and time of the current system. It does not take any arguments. The following will display the current date and time of the system:

```
Wscript.echo Now
```

Boolean Functions

Boolean functions always return a True or False value. They can be used to check for the truth of a condition. For example, if you want to ensure that a variable was initialized (is not Null) then you can use the isNull function to check the condition as follows:

```
Dim sName
If isNull(sName) then
   Wscript.Echo "Yes"
Else
   Wscript.echo "No"
End if
```

Typically a variable with null value is a variable that is not assigned a valid value.

In the previous example, since the sName variable is not initialized (no value is assigned), the script will display the Yes message when executed. If the sName variable isinitialized as shown in the following example, the script will echo the No message, denoting that the sName variable contains a value:

```
Dim sName
Dim sName = "Bob"
If isNull(sName) then
   Wscript.Echo "Yes"
Else
   Wscript.echo "No"
End if
```

Additionally, since VBScript has little built-in error checking (error handling is covered later in this chapter), *n* boolean functions can also be used to test data before passing it to a function.

For example, you can check if a value is `date` subtype before passing it to the `Datediff` function (VBScript will display a `Type Mismatch` error if a value other than the `date` subtype is passed to the function.) The following example illustrates the use of the `IsDate` function:

```
Date1 = #1/1/2005#
Date2 = Date
If isDate(Date1) and isDate(Date2) then
      Wscript.echo DateDiff("d", Date1, Date2)
End if
```

Boolean function can also be used to identify the data type. For example, the `isArray` boolean function in Listing 2.22 is used to identify if the data retrieved by reading the registry value is of array data type. (If the `isArray` function was not used to identify the data type, the script will generate a `Type Mismatch` error because the script will try to display array data as string data.)

LISTING 2.22 `isArray` Example

```
set wShell = createobject("wscript.shell")
     CONST   VALUE_NAME = _
             "HKLM\Software\Microsoft\Windows NT\" _
                     & "CurrentVersion\Winlogon\passwordexpirywarning"
           PassExpiryWarn = wShell.regread(VALUE_NAME)
             if isArray(PassExpiryWarn) then
                     Wscript.echo Join(PassExpiryWarn)
             else
                     Wscript.echo PassExpiryWarn
             End if
        Set wShell = nothing
```

Besides the `isNull`, `isDate`, and `isArray` boolean functions, VBScript also provides other functions that you can use in your scripts to test a condition. Table 2.11 lists these boolean functions included in VBScript.

TABLE 2.11 Boolean Functions

Function	Description

`isEmpty`	Has the variable been initialized?
	Example:
	`On Error Resume Next`
	`Dim Myname`
	`MyName = Wscript.Arguments(0)`
	`if isEmpty(Myname) then`
	`   MyName = "John Doe"`
	`End if`
	`Wscript.Echo MyName`

`isNumeric`	Is this a numeric value?
	Example:
	`Dim iDiskSize`
	`iDiskSize = Wscript.Arguments(0)`
	`If isNumeric(iDiskSize) then`
	`   Wscript.Echo idiskSize /1024 & " KB"`
	`Else`
	`   Wscript.Echo _`
	`         "Calculations can be performed on" & _`
	`                         " integer values only"`
	`End If`

`isObject`	Is this variable an object?
	Example:
	`On Error Resume Next`
	`Set objWMI = GetObject("Winmgmts:")`
	` if Err.Number = 0 and isObject(objWMI) then`
	` 'Do Something`
	`else`
	`  Wscript.Echo Err.Number & ": ",Err.Description`
	`end if`
	`Set objWMI = nothing`

`Inputbox` and `Msgbox` Functions

Although scripts are generally used for automation (that is, scripts are written to be run unattended and do not interact with the user), there may be instances where you may need to write a script to get or display information to the user. For interacting with the user, VBScript provides the following functions:

> **`Inputbox`:** VBScript provides the `Inputbox` function that can be used to get basic information from the user. The `Inputbox` takes the following seven arguments (other than the `Prompt` argument, all arguments are optional):

1. `Prompt`: This argument is a string containing the question (or the statement) that you want to display in the `Inputbox`.
2. `Title`: The string expression passed as the `Title` argument is displayed as the title of the `Inputbox`.
3. `Default`: This argument can be used to pre-populate the text box of the `Inputbox` with a value. If passed, it becomes the default value of the `Inputbox`.
4. `xPos`: The `xPos` argument specifies the horizontal position of the `Inputbox` in relation to the screen. For example, to position the `Inputbox` to the absolute left of the screen, you should pass `0` (zero) as the `xPos` argument.
5. `yPos`: The `yPos` argument specifies the vertical position of the `Inputbox` in relation to the screen. Pass `0` as the `yPos` argument to position the `Inputbox` to the top of the screen.
6. `Helpfile`: The string expression that identifies the help file to open when context sensitive help (F1 key is pressed) is used. Context argument must also be passed along with this argument.
7. `Context`: This argument is the numeric value that identifies the help context id appropriate for the help topic.

Practically speaking, it is too much work to create a context-sensitive help file. Therefore, `Helpfile` and the `Context` arguments are always omitted by the script programmers.

The `Inputbox` function has two major shortcomings: the text typed in the text box is displayed in clear text and therefore is not suitable for getting sensitive information such as a password; it is limited to only one textbox and, therefore `Inputbox` function must be called multiple times to get multiple information which can be very annoying for the user. If you need to interact with the user to get more than basic information, it is better to use other input options, such as an HTA script or an HTML, type form created using the `InternetExplorer.Application object`. (These options are covered later in this chapter.)

`Msgbox`: The `Msgbox` function included in VBScript can be used to display messages on the user's screen. For example, you can display the error message when it occurs using the `Msgbox` as follows:

```
On Error Resume Next
Err.Raise 1, "Msgbox_Err.vbs", "Msgbox Err message example"
If Err.Number <> 0 then
      Msgbox Err.Number & ", " & Err.Description
End if
```

The `Msgbox` function serves a dual purpose. It can be used to either display information or it can be used to ask a question that has definite answers (`Yes` and `No`; `Abort`, `Retry` and `Cancel`). For example, Figure 2.22 shows a message window that asks the user if the script should create a new text file. If the user clicks the `Yes` button, a new text file will be created and if the user chooses to click the `No` button, the script will exit without creating the text file.

By default, the `Msgbox` function displays the message passed to the function and waits for the user to click the `Ok` button as shown in Figure 2.23.

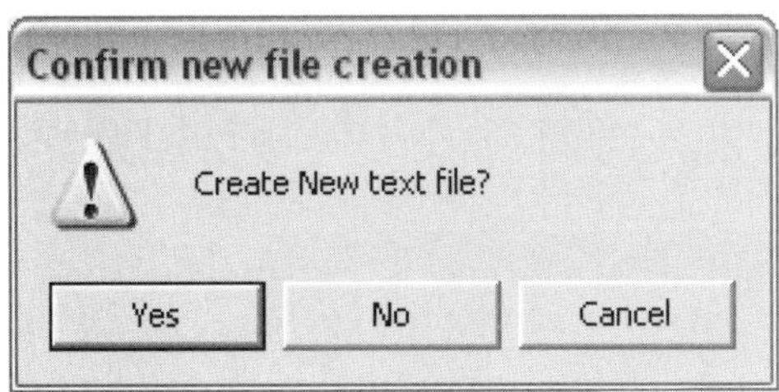

FIGURE 2.22 `Msgbox` asking the user if the script should create text file.

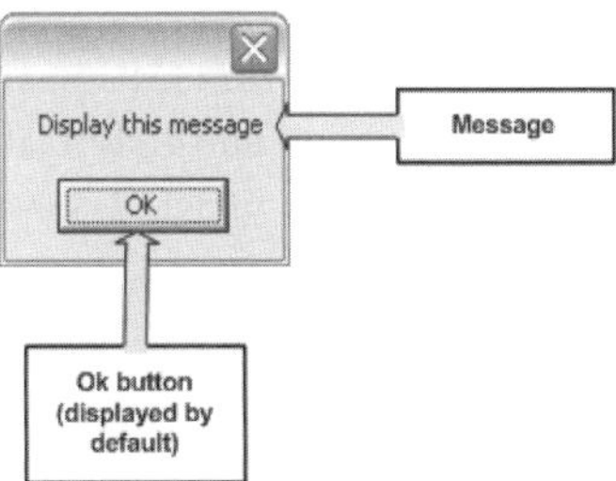

FIGURE 2.23 `Msgbox` window displayed with default options.

You can change the default behavior of the `Msgbox` window to display different function buttons, display an icon, such as a critical error (stop) icon, and the window title, as shown in Figure 2.24.

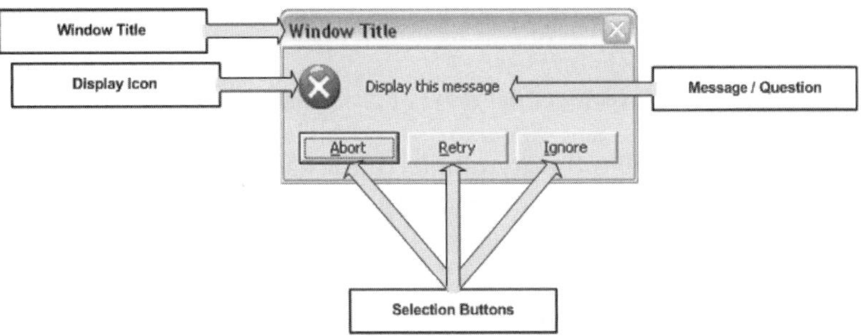

FIGURE 2.24 Customized message box window.

When the user clicks a button, the `Msgbox` function returns the value that indicates which button was clicked by the user. Based on the selection, you can take the appropriate action. For example, the following script asks the "`Are you the scripting guy?`" question and displays the `Yes` and `No` buttons along with the `Question` icon. The script, when executed, waits for the user to click a button and displays "`Yes`" or "`No`" in another `Msgbox` window based on the user's selection. Figure 2.25 shows the `Msgbox` window that asks the user "`Are you the scripting guy?`" question.

```
Question = "Are you the scripting guy?"
Windowtitle = "Confirm"
Answer = MsgBox (Question,VBYesNo+VBQuestion,WindowTitle)
Select case Answer
           case vbYes
                  Message = "Yes"
            case vbNo
                  Message = "No"
End Select
Wscript.echo Message
```

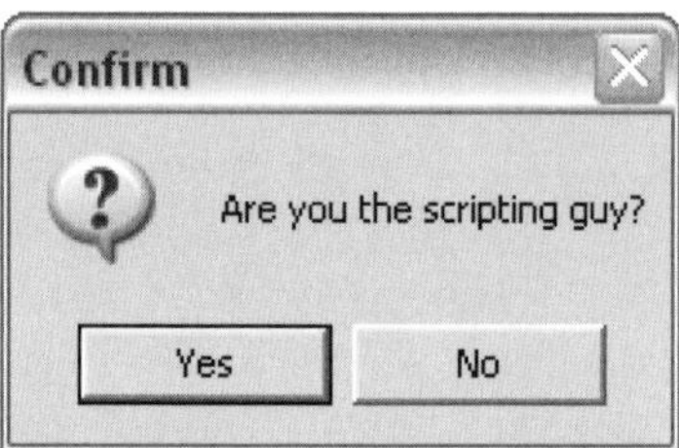

FIGURE 2.25 `Msgbox` window asking the user "Are you the scripting guy?" question.

The `Msgbox` function syntax is as follows:

```
MsgBox (prompt [, buttons] [, title] [, helpfile, context])
```

Table 2.12 describes the arguments of the `Msgbox` function and Table 2.13 lists VB-Script constants of the buttons for the `MsgBox` window.

TABLE 2.12 `Msgbox` Arguments

Parameter	Required / Optional	Default Value
Prompt	Required	No default value
Buttons	Optional	0 (`vbOkOnly`)
Title	Optional	Application name is placed in the title bar
Helpfile	Optional	No default value
Context	Optional (required if Helpfile is provided)	No default value

TABLE 2.13 VBScript Constants of Buttons for `Msgbox` Function

Constant	Value	Description
`vbOKOnly`	0	Display `OK` button only.
`vbOKCancel`	1	Display `OK` and `Cancel` buttons.
`vbAbortRetryIgnore`	2	Display `Abort`, `Retry`, and `Ignore` buttons.
`vbYesNoCancel`	3	Display `Yes`, `No`, and `Cancel` buttons.
`vbYesNo`	4	Display `Yes` and `No` buttons.
`vbRetryCancel`	5	Display `Retry` and `Cancel` buttons.
`vbCritical`	16	Display Critical Message icon.
`vbQuestion`	32	Display Warning Query icon.
`vbExclamation`	48	Display Warning Message icon.
`vbInformation`	64	Display Information Message icon.
`vbDefaultButton1`	0	First button is default.
`vbDefaultButton2`	256	Second button is default.
`vbDefaultButton3`	512	Third button is default.
`vbDefaultButton4`	768	Fourth button is default.
`vbApplicationModal`	0	Application modal; the user must respond to the message box before continuing work in the current application.
`vbSystemModal`	4096	System modal; all applications are suspended until the user responds to the message box.

Comments

Comments are lines of code that are ignored by the script engine (VBS or Jscript interpreters). Comments are means of including description of a code or the script within the script. For example, generally, the first line of code is a comment that describes the script and its purpose.

Generally, programmers write code and then add comments to the program. Although there is no specified approach that should be followed for writing comments, it is best to add a comment while writing the code; it saves you from duplicating the scripting efforts.

Comments can be included in VBScript using a single quote, as follows:

```
' This is a comment added to a script.
' It demonstrates the use of a single quote to include comments in a
  script
```

VBScript considers everything to the right of the single quote to be a comment. Therefore, the following code will generate a `Msgbox` syntax error (the string value, although inside two single quotes, is still considered a comment):

```
Msgbox ' This is a comment '
```

However, a single quote wrapped within a double quote is considered as string data. Therefore, the following code will not generate an error; the value, although within single quotes, is not considered as a comment.

```
MsgBox " ' This is not a comment ' "
```

When the script is run, it will display the string value along with the two single quotes, as shown in Figure 2.26.

FIGURE 2.26 Comment displayed along with the two single quotes.

You can also use the `REM` statement in VBScript to include comments in your scripts. For example, the following demonstrates how to use the `REM` statement to include a comment:

```
Rem This is a comment.
```

If the `REM` statement, however, follows other statements on the same line, it must be separated from other statements using a colon as shown in the following example:

```
Msgbox "This is not a comment" : REM This is a comment
```

Unless you need to insert more than a comment within two statements on the same line (such as, `Msgbox "This is not a comment" : REM This is a comment : MsgBox "Comment"`) there is no practical benefit of using the `REM` statement over the single quote method.

Comments are ways to include description to your scripts. As discussed later in the "Commenting" section of Chapter 3 of this book, comments play an important role in scripts; they provide better understanding of the script and the code snippets in the script. Therefore, it is good practice to include them in your scripts. However, you should be careful when including comments, as a lot of comments can bloat (increase the size of) your scripts.

Error Handling

Errors and bugs happen. No mater how good a programmer you are, errors and bugs still seem to occur. Part of the reason is that most scripts are created and tested in controlled environments, and fail when ported to a different environment. For example, a script created in the development environment may fail when ported to the production environment either because the user in the production environment may not have the required privileges, or a resource (a disk drive or a remote system) may not be available in the production environment.

Another reason for the scripts to have errors is because VBScript has very limited built-in error handling. For example, if you try to add a `string` type to an `integer` type data, VBScript will generate a `Type mismatch` error. If you mistype the syntax of a VBScript command (function, method, or property) VBScript will display a `Syntax error`.

VBScript expects such errors to be handled by the programmer of the script. Therefore, it is vital to understand the type of errors that occur in a script and how to rectify or handle these errors in your scripts. Generally, you can group the errors into three types: *Syntax Errors, Runtime Errors, and Logical Errors.*

Syntax Errors

Syntax errors happen when VBScript encounters an error during compilation of the code. These errors are generated because VBScript did not understand what it was to do with the command or a statement. For example, if you do not pass the `Prompt` (required parameter) argument to the `Msgbox` function, VBScript will throw a `Syntax error`, as shown in Figure 2.27.

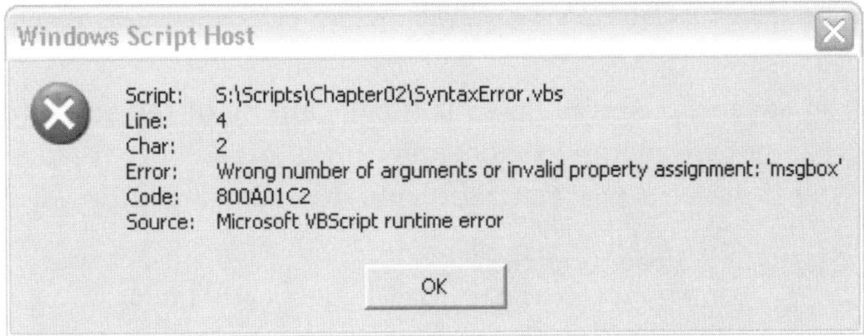

FIGURE 2.27 Syntax error message displayed by VBScript.

Since VBScript displays the error message with the line at which the error has occurred, syntax errors are easy to fix. All you have to do is look up the correct syntax in VBScript documentation (or search the Internet) and change it to the correct syntax (such as pass the required `Prompt` argument to the `Msgbox` function).

Runtime Errors

Runtime errors occur when VBScript attempts to execute a statement that is not allowed. For example, VBScript will generate the `Type mismatch` runtime error if you pass a string value to a function that expects a date or an integer subtype value. For example, the following statement will generate a runtime `Type Mismatch` error when it is executed by VBScript.

```
for i = 0 to "ten"
    wscript.echo i
next
```

NOTE

Even if a numeric value is wrapped inside quotes, VBScript interprets it as numeric for the purpose of calculation. Therefore, `"10"` *instead of* `"ten"` *will be considered a valid value and will not generate the* `Type mismatch` *error.*

Runtime errors halt the execution of the scripts. Therefore, in the previous code, when VBScript displays an error (because it attempted to execute a statement that was expecting a numeric value of `10` instead of the string value of `ten`), the script halts at the error message window. When the user clicks the `Ok` button (of the message widow), the script ends.

To handle runtime errors, you need to write code (normally, capturing the error using the `Err` object) so that VBScript does not halt and end the execution of the script when it encounters an error. For instance, to force the script to continue execution, even if it finds errors, you can add the `On Error Resume Next` statement at the beginning of your script.

`On Error Resume Next`, along with the `Err` object, allows you to correctly handle errors in your scripts. For example, if you are unsure that an object will be available when you create it, you can do the following to correctly handle the error that will be generated by the `CreateObject` method:

1. Add `On Error Resume Next` at the beginning of the script (or just before the `CreateObject` method statement)
2. After the `CreateObject` method, add the following lines:

```
If Err.Number <> 0 then
        Wscript.echo Err.number, Err.Description
        Wscript.Quit
End if
statements…
```

Figure 2.28 illustrates how a runtime error can be handled.

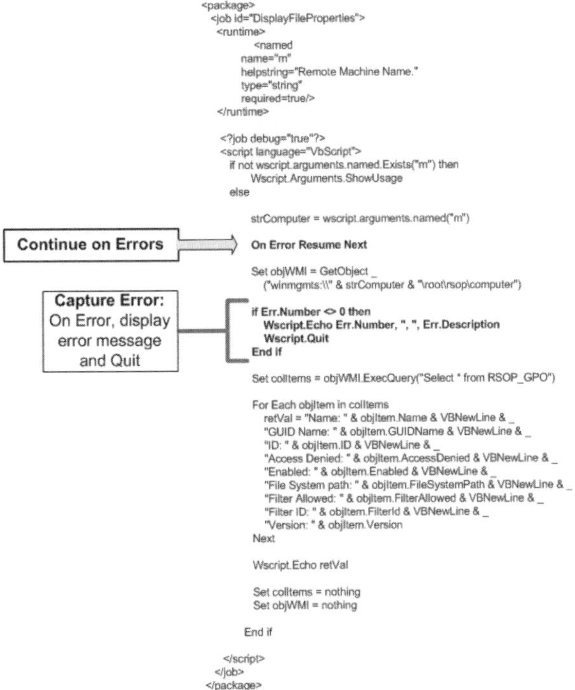


```
<package>
  <job id="DisplayFileProperties">
   <runtime>
         <named
       name="m"
       helpstring="Remote Machine Name."
       type="string"
       required=true/>
   </runtime>

   <?job debug="true"?>
   <script language="VbScript">
     if not wscript.arguments.named.Exists("m") then
         Wscript.Arguments.ShowUsage
     else

         strComputer = wscript.arguments.named("m")

         On Error Resume Next

         Set objWMI = GetObject _
           ("winmgmts:\\" & strComputer & "\root\rsop\computer")

         if Err.Number <> 0 then
           Wscript.Echo Err.Number, ", ", Err.Description
           Wscript.Quit
         End if

         Set colItems = objWMI.ExecQuery("Select * from RSOP_GPO")

         For Each objItem in colItems
           retVal = "Name: " & objItem.Name & VBNewLine & _
           "GUID Name: " & objItem.GUIDName & VBNewLine & _
           "ID: " & objItem.ID & VBNewLine & _
           "Access Denied: " & objItem.AccessDenied & VBNewLine & _
           "Enabled: " & objItem.Enabled & VBNewLine & _
           "File System path: " & objItem.FileSystemPath & VBNewLine & _
           "Filter Allowed: " & objItem.FilterAllowed & VBNewLine & _
           "Filter ID: " & objItem.FilterId & VBNewLine & _
           "Version: " & objItem.Version
         Next

         Wscript.Echo retVal

         Set colItems = nothing
         Set objWMI = nothing

       End if

   </script>
  </job>
</package>
```

FIGURE 2.28 Handling runtime errors illustration.

As shown in Figure 2.28, the `On Error Resume Next` statement is inserted just before the `Set` statement to ensure that the script will continue to run even if the script is unable to create the WMI object. The `If then` statement, included in the script after the `Set` statement, ensures that the error (if any) generated by calling the `Set` statement is captured and displayed as a custom error message, created by the programmer, instead of the error message displayed by VBScript.

When VBScript encounters an error, it displays the error message and terminates the execution of the script. This can be overridden by including the `On Error Resume Next` *statement in your script, either at the beginning of the script or just before the statement that you know (or think) will (or may) cause an error. However, since the* `On Error Resume Next` *statement hides the error messages and continues execution on error, it is the programmer's responsibility to add code to the script for capturing and displaying error messages.*

Logical Errors

Syntax and the runtime errors encountered by VBScript are easier to locate and fix because VBScript will display these errors as and when they occur. On the other hand, logical errors are difficult to trace and troubleshoot. For example, the `ComputerRole.wsf` script in Listing 2.23 always displays the computer role as `Standalone Workstation`, even when run against a remote computer or on a system other than a standalone workstation, such as a Windows 2000 server:

LISTING 2.23 `ComputerRole.wsf` Script with Logical Error

```
<package>
<job id="DisplayComputerRole">
  <runtime>
   <named
         name="m"
         helpstring="Remote Machine Name."
         type="string"
         required=true/>
   </runtime>
    <?job debug="true"?>
    <script language="VbScript">
      If not wscript.arguments.named.Exists("m") then
             Wscript.Arguments.ShowUsage
      Else
          strComputer = wscript.arguments.named("m")
          On Error Resume Next
          Set objWMI = GetObject("winmgmts://" & sComputerName)
          if Err.number <> 0 then
              Wscript.Echo Err.Number, Err.Description
               Wscript.Quit
          end if
          Set colItems = objWMI.instancesof("Win32_computersystem")
             for each item in colItems
              Wscript.echo Role(item.DomainRole)
             next
             Set colItems = nothing
             Set objWMI = nothing
        End if

         Function Role(Computerrole)
           select case Computerole
             case 0 : Role = "Standalone Workstation"
             case 1 : Role  = "Member Workstation"
             case 2 : Role  = "Standalone Server"
             case 3 : Role = "Member Server"
             case 4 : Role  = "Backup Domain Controller"
             case 5 : Role  = "Primary Domain Controller"
             case else : Role = "Unknown"
           end select
         End function
```

```
    </script>
  </job>
</package>
```

When the script is executed, it generates no errors but yet displays "Standalone Workstation" message for every system. This happens because of two reasons:

1. The strComputer variable is incorrectly passed as sComputer name to the GetObject statement. Because of this, the WMI object (Winmgmts:) always connects to the local system instead of the computer name passed as an argument to the script.
2. The Computerole variable name is passed to the Select Case statement instead of the Computerrole (with two r's) variable. Since, the Computerole variable is not initialized (that is, it is empty), VBScript interprets the variable's value to be 0, and therefore the Select Case statement always selects Case 0. Since the Select Case is always 0, the Role function always returns "Standalone Workstation" value.

Although, it was easy to identify the logical error in this script, it can be very difficult to identify these errors in a complicated script. Therefore, it is best practice to use the Option Explicit statement (covered earlier in the "Constants and Variables" section of this chapter) that forces declaration of the variables, thereby minimizing logical errors.

If you include the Option Explicit statement in your script and do not declare a variable, the script will display the Variable is Undefined error. This error will be displayed until all the variables in the script are declared. For example, if the following script is executed, the Variable is Undefined: <name of the variable> error will appear three times, as shown in Figures 2.29, 2.30, and 2.31.

```
Option Explicit
 Wscript.Echo VarOne, VarTwo, VarThree
```

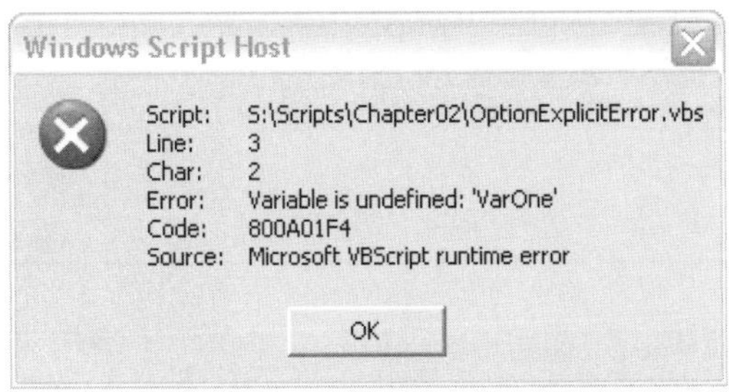

FIGURE 2.29 First Variable is Undefined error displayed by the script.

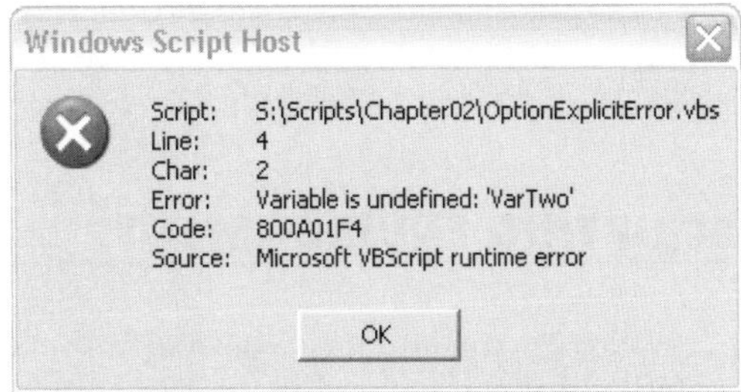

FIGURE 2.30 Second Variable is Undefined error displayed by the script. This error is displayed only after the first Variable is Undefined error has been corrected.

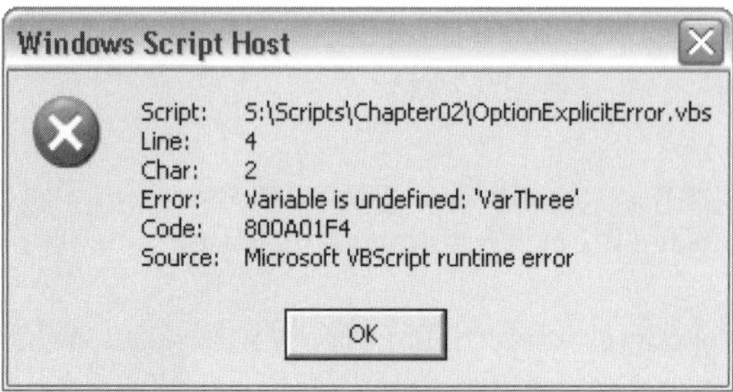

FIGURE 2.31 Third `Variable is Undefined` error displayed by the script. This error is displayed only after the first and second `Variable is Undefined` errors have been fixed.

VBScript will not display all undefined variables in a single error message, even if there is more than one undefined (not explicitly defined using the `DIM` statement) variables in the script. Instead VBScript will display the error messages in an iterative manner (that is, VBScript will display the next error, if any, only if the current undefined error is fixed).

Therefore, the error message displayed in Figure 2.30 will not be displayed by the script until `VarOne` is defined using the `DIM` statement as follows:

```
DIM VarOne
```

Similarly, the error in Figure 2.31 will not be displayed until both the `VarOne` and `VarTwo` variables are defined using the `DIM` statement, as follows:

```
Dim VarOne, VarTwo
```

NOTE

You can define the variables in a single `DIM` statement or multiple `DIM` statements. Refer to "Constants and Variables" section of this chapter.

SCRIPTING ENVIRONMENTS

VBScript is a language that requires a scripting environment to run in. For example, VBScript can be used in an ASP (Active Server Pages) that runs in the IIS server environment. Similarly, if included in HTML pages, VBScript runs in a browser, such as IE. The truth is that VBScript is an ActiveX® script engine that can provide scripting capability to any host that supports ActiveX scripting.

Since ASP scripting is out of the scope of this book, this topic will introduce you to the two scripting environments—Windows Script Host and Microsoft HTML Applications—that are most commonly used for systems administration scripts.

Windows Script Host (WSH)

Commonly known as WSH, Windows Script Host is a scripting environment that can support any ActiveX scripting language. By default, WSH supports the Microsoft VBScript and Jscript ActiveX languages. However, you can download and install other ActiveX languages, such as ActivePerl from ActiveState (*http://www.ActiveState.com*). After you successfully install ActivePerl, you can write and run Perl scripts in WSH.

WSH not only provides an environment to run the scripts, it also exposes ActiveX objects that you can use in your scripts to perform tasks, such as display currently logged-on username. For example, as shown in the following lines of code, using the `Wscript.Network` object inWSH you can get the currently logged-on username:

```
Dim objWshell
Set objWNet = Createobject("Wscript.Network")
Wscript.echo objWNet.UserName
Set objWNet = nothing
```

The current version (v5.6) in WSH, released along with Microsoft Windows XP® release, provides many enhancements over its previous version (v2.0). The current release now includes the following new features:

- You can remotely execute scripts
- New processes can be treated as objects
- Includes support for file inclusion
- Supports multiple languages within the same script
- Supports drag and drop
- Access to the current working directory through the `CurrentDirectory` method
- Enhanced security model
- Supports new WSF (Windows Script File) format that conforms to XML standards

Interfaces

WSH provides two interfaces—Wscript (Wscript.exe) and Cscript (Cscript.exe)—that can be used to execute scripts. Scripts executed with Wscript execute in the Windows environment, whereas scripts executed with Cscript execute as command-line scripts.

Cscript is designed for use from a command window (an MS-DOS window) and Wscript interfaces directly with the Windows GUI (graphical user interface), but there is very little difference between the two interfaces in terms of functionality. What differences there are will be covered later in this chapter.

Wscript: If you double-click a script file, by default the script is executed with Wscript. This is because a default installation of WSH sets the interface to Wscript. exe. This default script host can be changed to Cscript.exe by running the following command:

```
Wscript /H:Cscript
```

You can execute a script with Wscript by either double-clicking the script (if the host is set to Wscript.exe) or by running the script in the following manner:

```
Wscript C:\ScriptFolder\ScriptName.vbs
```

Wscript syntax is as follows:

```
Wscript ScriptName.Extension [options…]
```

Wscript supports the options listed in Table 2.14.

TABLE 2.14 Wscript.exe Options

Option	Description
//B	Batch mode. This suppresses script errors and prompts from being displayed. This is used when you want to suppress errors from displaying on the user's screen, such as a login script.
//D	Enable active debugging. This is used when you want to enable debugging in your scripts. Generally used by the developer of the script to capture bugs as they occur.
//E:engine	Use engine for executing script. By default if a .VBS or a .JS script is executed, it will invoke the appropriate (VBScript for .VBS and Jscript for .JS) scripts. For other scripts, such as Perl script, you can use this option.
//H:hostshell	Wscript.exe is the default host shell. This can be changed using this option. To set Cscript as the default host, use //H:Cscript, and to set Wscript as the default host, use //H:Wscript.
//I	Interactive mode (opposite of //B). This is the default mode. In the interactive mode, all script errors are displayed on the user's screen.
//Job:xxxx	Execute a WSF job. This is useful if you have a WSF file defined with multiple jobs (see WSF section for more details).
//Logo	Display logo (default). This option displays the following banner when the script is executed with Cscript.exe: `Microsoft (R) Windows Script Host Version 5.6 Copyright (C) Microsoft Corporation 1996-2001. All rights reserved.`

→

Option	Description
//Nologo	Prevents Cscript logo from displaying. No banner will be shown at execution time.
//S	Save current command-line options for this user.
//T:nn	Time out in seconds. Maximum time a script is permitted to run. You can use this to ensure that the script is ended if the operation is not completed within a time span.
//X	Execute script in debugger. This option is good for developers of the script to test the script by running it in the debugger.
//U	Use Unicode for redirected I/O from the console.

You can execute the Wscript from within the command window. However, since Wscript is GUI, the results will not be displayed in the command window; results will be displayed in a GUI-type window.

Cscript: Scripts executed with Cscript are like the Batch (.bat or .cmd) scripts that execute within a command window. Therefore, whenever a script is executed with Cscript, Cscript opens a command window (if not already open) and executes the script within that window.

CScript has the following syntax:

```
Cscript ScriptName.Extension [options…]
```

As Cscript supports the same switches as Wscript, the options listed in Table 2.14 are also valid for Cscript.

WSH Script Files

WSH supports three script file types: .VBS / .JS, and .WSF, as described:

- .VBS / .JS: The files that have the .VBS extension are the script files that contain the script written in VBScript language. On the other hand, .JS are scripts written in Jscript language.

VBScript or Jscript is a matter of personal choice. Programmers that are versed with C- or C++-type languages may feel more comfortable in using Jscript, and the VB programmers will feel at home with VBScript. Since this book is written for systems administrators that are interested in learning how to automate systems administration using VBScript, most scripts in this book will have the .vbs extension.

- .WSF: Windows Script File (.WSF), included in WSH Version 5.6, provides several enhancements over the .VBS and .JS script file formats. For example, .WSF files give you the capability of including code written in multiple languages, as shown in the following example:

```
<package>
   <job id=" MultiLanguage">
      <script language="VBScript">
    Dim objwNet
     sComputerName = Wscript.Arguments(0)
      Set objwNet = Wscript.CreateObject("Wscript.Network")
            if (sComputerName = objwNet.ComputerName) then
                    Wscript.Echo "This is your local computer"
            else
                    Wscript.echo "This is not your local computer name"
            end if
    Set objwNet = nothing
      </script>

     <Script language="jscript">
    var objwNet
    var sComputerName;
    var arguments = WScript.Arguments;
      objwNet = new ActiveXObject("Wscript.Network");
        sComputerName = arguments[0];
            if (sComputerName == objwNet.ComputerName)
               {
                WScript.Echo ("This is your local computer");
               }
               else
               {
                WScript.Echo ("This is not your local computer");
               };
     </Script>
   </job>
</package>
```

If you program in VBScript, support for multiple languages will allow you to use code written by programmers who may prefer writing scripts in Jscript language.

Another enhancement that the WSF files provide over other types of files is that they support file inclusion. For example, the following code includes the `functions.vbs` (`src="Functions.vbs"`) script file that provides the `WriteErr` subroutine to the script at runtime:

```
<package>
   <job id="IncludeExample">
      <script language="VBScript" src="Functions.vbs">
        On Error Resume Next
```

```
        Err.Raise 1, "WsfInclude.wsf", "WSF file include example"
      if Err <> 0 then Msgbox WriteErr, _
  VbOkOnly+VbCritical, _
  "Error:"
      </script>
   </job>
</package>
```

Besides providing the capability to run multiple languages and include files, WSF also provides better arguments handling capability. For instance, if you need to pass more than one argument a script, you must remember the arguments and the order in which the arguments should be passed. For example, if your `StopProcess.VBS` script takes two arguments, the first argument as the computer name and second argument as the name of the process that you want to stop, you must pass the arguments to the script in the order specified. The following shows how the arguments must be passed to the `StopProcess` script:

```
StopProcess <Computer Name> <Process Name>
```

If you forget the order of the arguments and reverse the arguments (that is pass the process as the first argument and the computer name as the second argument), the script will take the process name to be the computer name and the computer name to be the process name. For example, following is the incorrect order of the arguments:

```
StopProcess Process1 Computer1
```

As a result of passing the arguments out of order in the previous example, the script will fail unless you have a computer name called `Process1` that is running a `Computer1` process.

WSF can make the order of the arguments irrelevant, as it allows you to name the arguments for identification. For instance, in the following example, the `StopProcess.vbs` script that takes the `Computer` and `Process` as the arguments when converted to WSF can be called as follows:

```
StopProcess /Computer:<Computer Name> /Process:<Process Name>
```

Since the arguments are now named (`/Computer` and `/Process`), the order in which they are passed to the script becomes irrelevant. Moreover, you can use the `ShowUsage` method to make your scripts self-documenting.

WSF files support both the NAMED and UNNAMED arguments. Both are covered in this section.

WSF files also have another advantage; they conform to the eXtensible Markup Language (XML) file format. XML is a markup language, much like HTML, that was designed to describe data. However, unlike HTML, XML tags are not predefined (i.e., they are not specific HTML predefined tags, such as `<HTML>` or `<BODY>`); you must define your own tags. XML uses a Document Type Definition (DTD) or an XML schema to describe the data contained in the XML.

Microsoft defined the schema (collection of tags) used by WSF files. As XML schema is designed to be self-descriptive, XML makes WSF files easier to read, understand, and work with. WSF files have the following XML elements (element is another name for tag):

`<?Job?>` element: This specifies the attributes for error handling. It has the following syntax:

```
<?job error= "flag" debug= "flag" ?>
```

where `flag = True` or `False` value.

`XML` element: This must be the first element in the script file as it indicates that a file should be parsed as XML. The XML element has the following syntax:

```
<?XML version= "version" [standalone= "DTDflag"] ?>
```

where `version` is the string in the form of `n.n` specifying the XML level of the file. This is always 1.0.

`Description` element: Marks the descriptive text that is displayed when the `ShowUsage` method is executed or when the script is run with `/?` command-line switch. It can be added to the script, as follows:

```
<description>
     Description of the script.
</description>
```

`Example` element: The example element can be used to add example of the script usage. It can be added, as follows:

```
<example>
   Example: StopProcess /Computer:MyComputer /Process:RunningProcess
</example>
```

`Job` element: Marks the beginning and end of a job within WSF file. It can be added to the script file, as follows:

```
<job [id=JobId]>
   Job code
</job>
```

`Named` element: This element describes a named argument of the script. It can be added to the script, as follows:

```
<named
   Name= namedname
   Helpstring = helpstring
   Type = "string|boolean|simple"
   Required = Boolean
/>
```

`UnNamed` element: This element describes an unnamed argument of the script. It can be added to the script, as follows:

```
<unnamed
   Name= namedname
   Helpstring = helpstring
   many = boolean
   Required = Boolean or integer
/>
```

`Object` element: This is an alternate method of defining objects in WSF files that can be referenced in the script (that is, you can use this to create an object instead of creating it with the `CreateObject` or the `GetObject` methods):

```
<object
   id= "objID"
{classid = "clsid:GUID" | progid="progID"}
[events="hookevents"] />
```

`Package` element: If you have multiple jobs defined by the `<job>` element, it must be enclosed within the `package` element, as follows:

```
<package>
<job id=1>
   Job code
</job>
<job id=2>
   Job code
</job>
</package>
```

`Reference` element: While the object element can be used to define a new object, the `<reference>` element can be used to include a reference to an external type library. It can be added to the WSF file, as follows:

```
<reference
[object = "progID" | guid = "typelibGUID"]
[version="version"]/>
```

`Resource` element: The `<resource>` element isolates textual or numeric data that should not be hard-coded into a script. It can be added into the WSF file, as follows:

```
<resource id="resourceID">
   text or number
</resource>
```

Runtime element: The set of runtime arguments for a script are grouped together by the `<runtime>` element. It must be added to the script, as follows:

```
<runtime>
   <named attributes etc. />
   <unnamed attributes etc. />
   <example>Example text</example>
   ...
</runtime>
```

Script element: The `<script>` element contains the code for the script. It has two attributes: `language` and `src`. The `language` attribute defines the language that the code is written in (such as VBScript for VBScript language and Jscript for Jscript language), and the optional `src` element defines the source file to include. It can be added to the script, as follows:

```
<script language="language" src="strFile">
   Script code
</script>
```

Usage element: By default, when the `ShowUsage` method is called the WSF file displays the default usage of the script. However, you can override the usage message to display by adding the `<usage>` element in your script. It can be added to the script, as follows:

```
<usage>
   Usage display text
</usage>
```

Some of these elements are essential elements (such as `<script>` element) that are typically included in every script that runs VBScript or Jscript code. Other elements (such as `<?xml>` element) are optional elements. Figure 2.32 shows a typical WSF script file that includes most of these XML elements.

NOTE

WSF files provide many enhancements over the .VBS files, especially better handling of the parameters; therefore, most scripts in this book that take arguments are written as WSF scripts.

- WSH files are not script files in which you can write code; they are script text files that can be used to customize execution of one or more script files. A WSH file is created automatically when you set the properties of a script file.
- WSH files are a great way of customizing your script execution for specific groups or individuals. For example, you can create two WSH files for a single script that runs a script in batch or interactive mode.

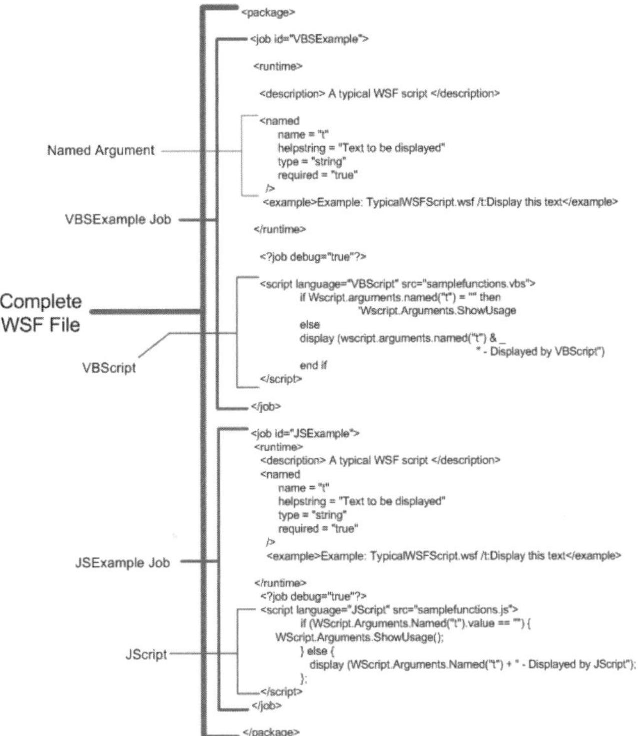

FIGURE 2.32 Typical WSF script file.

To create a .WSH file for a given script, do the following:

1. Right-click the script file in Windows explorer.
2. Click Properties on the Shortcut menus.
3. Choose the setting for the script.
4. Click OK to apply.

A WSH file with the same name as your script will be created. Following is an example of a typical .WSH file:

```
[ScriptFile]
Path=C:\Scripts\Chapter02\WsfMultiLang.wsf
[Options]
Timeout=10
DisplayLogo=1
Batchmode=0
```

NOTE

`Timeout`, `DisplayLogo`, and `Batchmode` are simply the command-line options for the environment. For example, executing the `WsfMultiLang.wsf` as `Cscript WsfMultiLang.wsf /t:10 /Logo /I` is similar to executing the WSH file.

WSH Built-in Objects

Every programming environment provides its own object model that developers can use to accomplish tasks. WSH is no different. WSH provides the following core set of objects that expose properties and methods that can be used in scripts to accomplish tasks such as map a network drive, execute a script on a remote system, set or retrieve Windows environment variables, etc.:

- `Wscript` object
- `WshShell` object
- `WshNetwork` object
- `WshController` object

`Wscript` *Object*

`Wscript` object is the root of the WSH object model. This object exposes several properties and methods that allow the programmer to:

- Link to external objects
- Retrieve the version of the scripting engine
- Retrieve the name and path information of the script file being executed
- Interact with the user

NOTE

The `WScript` object is automatically created and made available when you run a script with WSH. That is, you don't have to create it using `GetObject` or the `CreateObject` method.

`Wscript` object provides the following properties:

`Arguments` property: `Arguments` property returns the `WshArguments` object that contains the collection of arguments passed with the script upon execution. The collection begins with the zero as the first argument. The following code when saved as a script and run will display all arguments passed to the script:

```
Dim objArguments
Set objArguments = Wscript.Arguments
for each arg in objArguments
   wscript.echo arg
next
```

To pass an argument to a script, do the following:

```
CScript //NOLOGO ScriptName Argument1 Argument2 …
```

`BuildVersion` property: `Buildversion` property returns build version information in WSH. The following displays the build version of the installed WSH:

```
Wscript.echo "WSH build version is " & Wscript.BuildVersion
```

`Version` property: The `version` property returns the version of the script host. The following code when run will display the version number:

```
Wscript.Echo Wscript.Version
```

`FullName` property: Using the `FullName` property, you can retrieve the name and the complete path of the script host, as shown in the following example:

```
Wscript.echo Wscript.FullName
```

`Interactive` property: There are two WSH script modes: Batch and Interactive. In the Interactive mode, interaction with the user is enabled which allows the script to display messages on the user's screen and take input from the user. In Batch mode, however, this interaction is disabled.

`Interactive` property can be used to get or set the script mode. The following two examples illustrate the use of the `Interactive` property. The first example shows how to retrieve the `Interactive` property value and the second illustrates how to set the value to disable the interactive mode.

```
Wscript.echo Wscript.Interactive
Wscript.Interactive = false
```

`Name` property: The `Name` property can be used to retrieve the name of the script host. Including the following in your script will display the name at runtime:

```
Wscript.echo Wscript.Name
```

`Path` property: The `FullName` property can be used to get the complete path and the name of the script host. The `Name` property can be used to get only the name of the script host. The `Path` property can be used to retrieve the complete path to the script host. The following will display the complete path to the script host:

```
Wscript.echo Wscript.Path
```

`Script Name` property: The `ScriptName` property can be used to retrieve the name of the script being executed. For example, if you execute `getScriptName.vbs` that includes the following code, `getScriptName.vbs` will be displayed by the script:

```
Wscript.echo Wscript.ScriptName
```

`ScriptFullName` property: While the `ScriptName` property retrieves the name of the script being executed, `ScriptFullName` property retrieves the name along with the complete path to the script being executed. The following will display the complete path to the script along with the script filename:

```
Wscript.Echo Wscript.ScriptFullName
```

`StdIn` property: The `Stdin` property exposes the read-only input stream for the current script. For example, the following code waits for the user to type the computer name and press the Enter key. It then reads the input using the `Stdin.Readline()` method and displays the retrieved name of the operating system:

```
Wscript.echo "Computer Name:"
ComputerName = Wscript.stdin.ReadLine()
Set objWMI = GetObject("Winmgmts:")
Set objOS = objWMI.InstancesOf("Win32_OperatingSystem")
For each item in objOs
     Wscript.echo Item.Caption
Next
Set objOs = nothing
Set objWMI = nothing
```

`StdOut` property: The `StdOut` property exposes the write-only output stream for the current script. It can be used to write output to the console window. For example, you can replace the `Wscript.Echo` keywords with `Wscript.StdOut. Writeline` to write the output to the screen as follows:

```
Wscript.stdout.writeline "Computer Name:"
ComputerName = Wscript.stdin.ReadLine()
Set objWMI = GetObject("Winmgmts:")
Set objOS = objWMI.InstancesOf("Win32_OperatingSystem")
For each item in objOs
     Wscript.stdOut.writeline Item.Caption
Next
Set objOs = nothing
Set objWMI = nothing
```

The `StdOut` property also exposes the input stream of `Exec` object in WSH (covered later in this topic). For example, the following code executes a batch script that waits for the user to type in a machine name, passes it to the `pingcmd.cmd` batch file, and writes the output generated by the batch file to the Command window:

```
Dim sComputerName
Dim objStdIn, objwShell, objExec
Set objStdIn = Wscript.StdIn
 WScript.Echo " Enter Computer Name:"
  sComputerName =       objStdIn.Readline
    Set objwShell = CreateObject("Wscript.Shell")
      set objExec = _
  objwShell.Exec("pingcmd.cmd " & sComputerName)
          Do while not objExec.Stdout.AtEndofStream
           Result = Result & VBNewLine & objExec.StdOut.Readline
        loop
       Wscript.Stdout.writeline Result
    Set objStdIn = nothing
  Set objExec = nothing
Set objwShell = nothing
```

`StdErr` property: The `StdErr` property exposes the write-only error output stream of the current script. It can be used for error handling in your scripts. For example, the following code, when run, will pass the error message to the `StdErr` output stream:

```
On Error Resume Next
Err.Raise 1, "Msgbox_Err.vbs", "Msgbox Err message example"
if Err.Number <> 0 then
        Wscript.StdErr.WriteLine(ERr.Number & _
                                  ", " & Err.Description)
Else
        Wscript.StdOut.Writeline "No Error has occured"
End if
```

`Stdin`, `StdOut`, and `StdErr` properties are only available with `Cscript` script host. An `invalid handle` message will be displayed if a script containing either of these properties is executed with `Wscript script` host. Also, note that no error message will be displayed if the `On Error Resume Next` statement is used before the properties are used.

`Wscript` object provides the following methods:

`GetObject` method: Similar to `GetObject` method in VBScript, the `GetObject` method of `Wscript` object also retrieves an existing object with a specified `ProgID` (object's path identifier, such as `Wscript.Shell` is the identifier for the shell object in WSH), or creates a new one from a file. As with `GetObject` method in VBScript, `GetObject` in Wscript should be used when an instance of the object exists in memory. For example, the following gets an instance of `WMI` object using the `Winmgmts:` identifier:

```
Set objWMI = GetObject("Winmgmts:")
    if Err <> 0 then
        Wscript.Echo Err.Number & ", " & Err.Description
    else
        Wscript.Echo "Winmgmts: object created"
```

```
        end if
    Set objWMI = nothing
```

NOTE

The `GetObject` *method is successful because the WMI service is running, that is, the object already exists in the memory. If you stop and disable the WMI service and then execute the script, it will display an error message stating that the service is not started. By default the system attempts to start the WMI service before getting the object using the* `GetObject` *method.*

`CreateObject` method: As in VBScript, `Wscript` object also provides the `CreateObject` method that creates an instance of a COM (ActiveX Component Object Model) object. Using the `CreateObject` method, you can link to an external (to WSH) application. For example, the following code creates an instance of `Shell.Application` object, calls the `BrowseForFolder` method of the object, and opens the Explorer after the user chooses the folder to explore:

```
Set shell = Wscript.CreateObject("Shell.Application")
  set retval = Shell.BrowseForFolder(0, _
                "Select a folder to explore", 0,"C:\")
  shell.explore retval
set Shell = nothing
```

Although the `Wscript` object also provides the `CreateObject` method, it differs in syntax from `CreateObject` method in VBScript in syntax. The syntax for `Wscript` object is as follows:

```
Wscript.CreateObject(strProgramID,strPrfix)
```

Where the `strProgramID` (similar to the VBScript function) is the program identifier (such as `Shell.Application` is the program identifier for the file system object) and the `strPrefix` is the optional value indication for the function prefix. The prefix is used mostly when using events, which are covered later in this chapter. (See "Objects, Methods, and Properties" section of this chapter for `CreateObject` method in VBScript.)

`ConnectObject` method: The `ConnectObject` method binds the events of an object to the event handlers (sinks). After a call to the `ConnectObject` method, whenever an event occurs, WSH will look for a subroutine in the current executing script whose name is a concatenation of the `strPrefix` and the name of the event being fired. For example, the following code will create an instance of the `Word.Application` object, establish event handlers for the application object, open a new document, write text to the document, and save it as sample.doc. The application then closes when the `objWord.Quit` method is called. Upon quitting the `quit` event is fired that invokes the `Word_quit` subroutine that displays the `You are closing the Word application` message:

```
Dim objWord
  Set objwShell = WScript.CreateObject("WScript.Shell")
  Set objWord = Wscript.CreateObject("Word.Application")
  Set objDocument = objWord.Documents.Add
    Wscript.ConnectObject objWord,"word_"
      blnCancel = false
        objWord.Visible = true
          objDocument.Activate
            objWord.Selection.TypeText _
              "This is a word application started by a VBS Script"
                objDocument.SaveAs objWshell.CurrentDirectory _
                                                  & "\Sample.doc"
              Wscript.Sleep 1000
           objWord.Quit
          blnWord = true
        Do while blnWord
        Wscript.Sleep 5000
        loop
      Sub Word_Quit
      blnWord = false
       Wscript.echo "You are closing the Word application"
      End Sub
    Set objDocument = nothing
   Set objWord = nothing
 Set objwShell = nothing
```

`DisconnetObject` method: `DisconnetObject` method disconnects (unbinds) events of a connected object. Once the object has been disconnected, WSH will no longer respond to its events, although the object is still capable of firing events. In the following example, the `word_quit` event is not fired as the object is disconnected using the `DisconnectObject` method:

```
Dim objWord
  Set objwShell = WScript.CreateObject("WScript.Shell")
  Set objWord = Wscript.CreateObject("Word.Application")
  Set objDocument = objWord.Documents.Add
     Wscript.ConnectObject objWord,"word_"
      blnCancel = false
       objWord.Visible = true
          objDocument.Activate
            objWord.Selection.TypeText _
              "This is a word application started by a VBS Script"
                objDocument.SaveAs objWshell.CurrentDirectory _
                                                  & "\Sample.doc"
               Wscript.Sleep 1000
                      Wscript.DisconnectObject(objWord)
            objWord.Quit
          blnWord = true
        Do while blnWord
         Wscript.Sleep 5000
```

```
        loop
      Sub Word_Quit
      blnWord = false
      Wscript.echo "You are closing the Word application"
      End Sub
    Set objDocument = nothing
   Set objWord = nothing
 Set objwShell = nothing
```

`Echo` method: The Echo method provides your scripts the capability to output text (send message) to either a message box or to a command window. It outputs text to the command window when the script is run with Cscript and to the message box when the script is run with Wscript. The `Echo` method uses the following syntax:

```
Wscript.Echo [Arg1, Arg2, Arg3…]
```

If you want to only output text to the user's screen, it is best to use the `Echo` method instead of the `Msgbox` function. The `Echo` method can output to a message box or a console window based on the script shell the script was executed with as compared to the `Msgbox` function that can only output to a message box window.

`Quit` method: When there are no lines of code to execute, the script engine ends the script. However, you can also force end the script by calling the `Quit` method. The `Quit` method can return an optional error code. The method uses the following syntax:

```
Wscript.Quit ([intErrorCode])
```

If a script calls the `Quit` method, without the optional error code, as the last statement in the script, the script will end normally.

`Sleep` method: When called, the `Sleep` method suspends script execution for a specified length of time. Script execution is resumed after the wait period ends. The `Sleep` method has the following syntax:

```
Wscript.Sleep (inTime)
```

`intTime` argument of the `Sleep` method is the integer value that indicates the interval (in milliseconds) that the script remains inactive.

`WshShell` Object

`WshShell` object provides access to the native windows shell. It can be used to run programs locally, manipulate registry keys and values, create shortcuts (including URL shortcuts), access system folders, and manipulate system and user environment variables. `Wscript.Shell` is the unique identifier for the `WshShell` object. To create an instance of the `WshShell` object, do the following:

```
Set VariableName = WScript.CreateObject("WScript.Shell")
```

`WshShell` object provides the following properties:

`CurrentDirectory` property: The `CurrentDirectory` property returns the current working directory where the script being executed resides. For example, if you execute a script from C:\Scripts folder, the `CurrentDirectory` property will return `C:\Scripts`. The `CurrentDirectory` property can be called, as follows:

```
Dim objwShell
Set objwShell = WScript.CreateObject("WScript.Shell")
Wscript.Echo objwShell.CurrentDirectory
Set objwShell = nothing
```

`Environment` property: The `Environment` property takes `system` or `user` keywords as the location of the environment variable and returns the `WshEnvironment` object (that is, it returns the collection of the environment variable for the location). For example, the following code displays all the `system` variables within the collection returned by the `Environment` property:

```
Dim objwShell, objEnv
Set objwShell = CreateObject("Wscript.Shell")
  Set objEnv = objwShell.Environment("system")
    For each item in objEnv
      Wscript.echo item
    Next
  Set objEnv = nothing
Set objwShell = nothing
```

`SpecialFolders` property: The `SpecialFolders` property takes the name of a special folder and returns the `WshSpecialFolers` object (that is, it returns the collection of all the special folders, like desktop, favorites, fonts, MyDocuments, etc.). For example, the following code displays the collection of special folders returned by the `SpecialFolders` property:

```
Dim objwShell, objSP
 Set objwShell = CreateObject("Wscript.Shell")
  Set objSP = objwShell.SpecialFolders
     For each folder in objSP
      wscript.echo folder
     Next
  Set objwShell = nothing
 Set objSP = nothing
```

The `WshShell` object provides the following methods:

`AppActivate` method: The `AppActivate` method activates the application (that is, it brings focus to the application). It takes the title of the application (the title string of the application that you see in the task manager window) and returns a `Boolean` value that identifies if the method was successful or unsuccessful in setting the focus to the application. If the string title passed to the method is not found, then the method activates any application whose title string begins with *title* keyword. However, if no application with *title* keyword at the beginning of the title is found, the method tries to activate a window that has *title* keyword at the end of the string. It arbitrarily activates an application if more than one instance of the application name by title exists. In the following example, the script sets focus to the `Printers and Faxes` window and closes it by sending the `%FC` (`ALT+F+C` keys) to the window.

```
Dim objwShell
Set objwShell = CreateObject("Wscript.Shell")
  if objwShell.AppActivate("Printers and Faxes") then
   objwShell.SendKeys "%FC"
  End if
Set objwShell = nothing
```

`CreateShorcut` method: The `CreateShorcut` method takes the pathname of the shortcut to create a shortcut. It either returns `WshShortcut` object or the `WshURLShortcut` object. Simply calling the `CreateShortcut` method does not create the shortcut; you must call the `Save` method to write the changes to the disk. The following code will create the shortcut to the administrative tools and save it to the desktop folder of the `All Users` profile.

```
Dim objwShell
Dim AllUsersDesktop, sAllUsersStartMenu
 Set objwShell = CreateObject("Wscript.Shell")
  sAllUsersDesktop = objwShell.SpecialFolders("AllUsersDesktop")
   sAllUsersStartMenu = objwShell.SpecialFolders("AllUsersStartMenu")
    set objLink = _
      objWShell.CreateShortcut(sAllUsersDesktop & _
                                 "\Admin Tools.lnk")
         objLink.TargetPath = sAllUsersStartMenu & _
                          "\Programs\" & _
                                 "Administrative Tools"
         objLink.WindowStyle = 1
        objLink.IconLocation = "C:\WINDOWS\system32\main.cpl,10"
         objLink.Hotkey = "CTRL+SHIFT+A"
         objLink.Description = _
                "Shortcut to Administrative tools folder"
         objLink.WorkingDirectory = sAllUsersDesktop
         objLink.Save
     Set objLink = nothing
  Set objwShell = nothing
```

NOTE

This is similar to creating a Word or a text document that stores all changes that you make to the document in the memory and writes to the disk only when you save the document.

`ExpandEnvironmentString` method: The `ExpandEnvironmentString` method takes a name of the environment variable and returns its expanded value. For example, the following string expands the `%windir%` variable and passes it to the `BrowseFor` method in the script:

```
Dim objwShell
Set objwShell = CreateObject("Wscript.Shell")
 RootFolder = _
    objwShell.ExpandEnvironmentStrings("%windir%")
      Set objShell = CreateObject("Shell.Application")
         set retval = objShell.BrowseForFolder(0, _
              "Select a folder to explore", 0,RootFolder)
      objShell.explore retval
    Set retval = nothing
  set objShell = nothing
Set objwShell = nothing
```

`LogEvent` method: The `LogEvent` method adds an event entry to an event log file. It takes an integer value that represents the event type (Table 2.15 lists the event types), a string value containing the log entry text, and optionally, a string value indicating the name of the computer system where the event log is stored (if omitted the local computer name is used). The `LogEvent` method returns a `Boolean` value; a `True` value indicates that the log entry was successful and a `False` value indicates that the method failed to add the even log entry. The following code illustrates how to add an `ERROR` event entry to the event log:

```
On Error Resume Next
CONST SUCCESS = 0
CONST ERROR = 1
Set objwShell = Createobject("Wscript.Shell")
Err.Raise 1, "LogEvent.vbs", "LogEvent method example"
If Err.Number <> 0 then
      objwShell.LogEvent ERROR, Err.Number & ", " & Err.Description
Else
      objwShell.LogEvent SUCCESS, Wscript.ScriptName & _
                                         " script completed Successfully"
End if
Set objwShell = nothing
```

When the code is run, it adds an entry to the `Application` event log file. Figure 2.33 shows the event log entry created by the `LogEvent` method.

TABLE 2.15 Event Types

Type	Value
0	SUCCESS
1	ERROR
2	WARNING
4	INFORMATION
8	AUDIT_SUCCESS
16	AUDIT_FAILURE

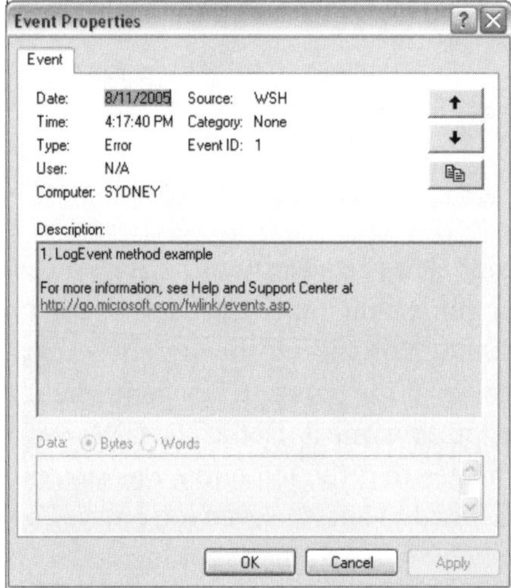

FIGURE 2.33 `Eventlog` entry created by the `LogEvent` method.

`Popup` method: `Wscript.Echo` and `Msgbox` are the most preferred methods for displaying information to the user. However, WSH also provides the `Popup` method that can be used to display messages. One advantage that the `Popup` method provides over the other two methods is that the message window created with the `Popup` method can be displayed for a specific period of time. For example, the following script waits 10 seconds for the user to click the `Yes` or `No` button before it closes:

```
Dim objwShell
  Dim sMsg
   sMsg = "Do you enjoy scripting?" & VbNewLine & VbNewLine & _
                "This message box will close in 10 seconds."
           Set objwShell = CreateObject("Wscript.Shell")
```

```
retVal = objwShell.Popup (sMsg, _
                          10, _
                          "Question:", _
                          4 + 32)
     Select Case retVal
           Case -1
                 sMsg = "You did not click any buttons"
           Case  6
                 sMsg = "You clicked the Yes button"
           Case  7
                 sMsg = "You clicked the No button"
     End Select
   Wscript.Echo sMsg
 Set objwShell = nothing
```

The `Popup` method has the following syntax:

```
intButton = _
      object.Popup (strText, [nSecondsToWait], [strTitle], [nType])
```

It takes the following arguments:

- `Object`: `WshShell` object
- `strText`: Message string that will be displayed in the `Popup` message box.
- `nSecondsToWait`: Maximum length of time the `Popup` message should be displayed. This argument is optional. If this value is zero or omitted, the message window remains visible until the user clicks a button in the message window.
- `strTitle`: The title for the message window. This argument is optional.
- `nType`: Numeric value that indicates the type of buttons (Table 2.16 lists the button types) and icons (Table 2.17 lists the icon types) that should be displayed in the message window. This argument is also optional.

TABLE 2.16 Button Types

Value	Description
0	Show OK button
1	Show OK and `Cancel` buttons
2	Show `Abort`, `Retry`, `Cancel` buttons
3	Show `Yes`, `No`, and `Cancel` buttons
4	Show `Yes` and `No` buttons
5	Show `Retry` and `Cancel` buttons

TABLE 2.17 Icon Types

Value	Description
16	Show "Stop Mark" icon
32	Show "Question Mark" icon
48	Show "Exclamation Mark" icon
64	Show "Information Mark" icon

The `Popup` message returns the following value:

- `IntButton:` An integer value indicating the button clicked by the user to dismiss the message window. Table 2.18 lists the values returned by the `Popup` method.

TABLE 2.18 `Popup` Message Return Values

Value	Description
1	OK button was clicked
2	Cancel button was clicked
3	Abort button was clicked
4	Retry button was clicked
5	Ignore button was clicked
6	Yes button was clicked
7	No button was clicked
–1	None of the buttons was clicked

`RegRead`, `RegDelete`, `RegWrite` methods: The `RegRead`, `RegDelete` and the `RegWrite` methods can be used to manipulate the windows registry. As the names suggest, `RegRead` is used to read the registry keys and values; `RegDelete` is used to delete a registry key or a value; and `RegWrite` is used to modify an exiting value or create a new registry key or value. The following code illustrates how to create, delete, and modify registry keys and values:

```
Dim objwShell, bKey
 Set objwShell = WScript.CreateObject("WScript.Shell")
   objwShell.RegWrite "HKLM\Software\CRM\",1
    objwShell.RegWrite "HKLM\Software\CRM\RegScript", _
                               Wscript.ScriptName, _
                                          "REG_SZ"
```

```
   bKey = objwShell.RegRead("HKLM\Software\CRM\")
    if bKey then
        WScript.Echo _
            objwShell.RegRead("HKLM\Software\CRM\RegScript")
    End if
     retVal = objwShell.Popup ("Delete registry keys?", _
                               5,"Confirm:",4 + 32)
      if retval = -1 or retVal = 6 then
          objwShell.RegDelete "HKLM\Software\CRM\RegScript"
          objwShell.RegDelete "HKLM\Software\CRM\"
      End if
Set objwShell = nothing
```

You can either use the abbreviated name for the root keys, such as HLKM for HKEY_LOCAL_MACHINE or use the full root key name.

The `RegRead` method has the following syntax:

```
Object.RegRead (strName)
```

It takes the following arguments:

- *`Object`*: `WshShell` object
- *`strName`*: String value indicating the registry key or value that you want to read.

You must use the trailing backslash (\) to read the Default registry key value.

The `RegDelete` value has the following syntax:

```
Object.RegDelete (strName)
```

It takes the following arguments:

- *`Object`*: `WshShell` object
- *`strName`*: String value indicating the registry key or value that you want to delete.

You must use the trailing backslash (\) to delete a registry key.

The `RegWrite` method has the following syntax:

```
Object.RegWrite (strName, anyValue [, strType])
```

It takes the following arguments:

- `Object`: `WshShell` object
- `strName`: String value indicating the registry key or value that you want to write.
- `anyName`: This argument can have three types of values:
    1. the name of the new key you want to create
    2. the name of the value that you want to add to an existing key
    3. the new value that you want to assign to an existing value name
- `strType`: String value indicating the type of data stored in the value.

`Run` method: The `Run` method executes a specified program as a new process. It takes command (the command for the program to execute) and optionally the window state of the program's window and a `Boolean` value that indicates whether the `Run` command should wait for the command to complete execution before continuing to the next statement in the script. A `True` value for the `Run` command to wait and a `False` value will suggest that the command should not wait before continuing to the next statement in the script.

The `Run` command has the following syntax:

```
Object.Run (strCommand, [intWindowStyle], [bWaitOnReturn])
```

Listing 2.24 shows the `RunProg.vbs` script that takes program name, window style, and wait state as arguments, and runs the program accordingly.

LISTING 2.24 `RunProg.vbs` Script

```
Dim objArgs, objwShell
Dim sProgramName, iWindowStyle, bWaitState
CONST SYNTAX_MSESSAGE = _
 "Syntax: Cscript RunProg.vbs <ProgramName> <WindowStyle> <WaitState>"
CONST ERROR_MESSAGE = "An Error occured running the program."
CONST ERROR_MESSAGE_TRYAGAIN =  "Please check the path and try again"
Set objArgs = Wscript.Arguments
if objArgs.Count <> 3 then
  Msgbox SYNTAX_MSESSAGE,VBOkOnly+VBCritical,"Error:"
 else
  sProgramName = objArgs(0)
   iWindowStyle = objArgs(1)
     bWaitState = objArgs(2)

  set objwShell = CreateObject("Wscript.Shell")
    retVal = objwShell.Run (sProgramName, iWindowStyle, bWaitState)
    if retVal <> 0 then
      Wscript.Echo ERROR_MESSAGE & VBNewLine & ERROR_MESSAGE_TRYAGAIN
  End if
  Set objwShell = nothing
```

```
end if
Set objArgs = nothing
```

`Exec` method: In addition to the `Run` method, `WshShell` object also provides the `Exec` method. Unlike the `Run` method, the `Exec` method returns `WshScriptExec` object. The `Exec` method provides status information of the script that executes along with access to the `StdIn`, `StdOut`, and `StdErr` streams.

In the following example, the `Exec` method is used to execute the `IExplore.exe` application. The `Exec` method returns the `WshScriptExec` (that is stored in the `objExec` variable) object that is then used to get the status of the running application. The script waits until the status is changed to other than `0`. When the user closes the Internet Explorer window, the `Exec` method returns a status of `1` that force-ends the wait. The script at the end displays the status before ending:

```
Dim sInternetExplorer,sSiteName
Dim objStdIn, objwShell, objExec
sInternetExplorer = "C:\Program Files\Internet Explorer\IExplore.exe "
Set objStdIn = Wscript.StdIn
 WScript.Echo " Enter Name of a website:"
  sSiteName =   objStdIn.Readline
    Set objwShell = CreateObject("Wscript.Shell")
     objwShell.Popup "Opening " & sSiteName,5
      set objExec = _
        objwShell.Exec(sInternetExplorer & sSiteName)
          Do while objExec.Status = 0
           Wscript.Sleep 1000
        loop
       Wscript.echo "Exec Status = " & objExec.Status
    Set objStdIn = nothing
  Set objExec = nothing
Set objwShell = nothing
```

`SendKeys` method: `WshShell` object provides the `SendKeys` method that can be used in a script to send keystrokes to an application as if the keys were typed on the keyboard attached to the system. `SendKeys` method can be useful in situations where you need to close a message dialog box that needs a response, such as a `MsgBox` window that is waiting for the user to click the `Ok` button. The following example illustrates how to use the `SendKeys` method to close an error message window displayed by a script:

```
Dim objwShell
  Set objwShell = CreateObject("Wscript.Shell")
    objwShell.Run "Msgbox_err.vbs",1,False
      Wscript.Sleep 500
         objwShell.AppActivate "Error:"
         Wscript.Sleep 500
      objwShell.SendKeys "{ENTER}"
  Set objwShell = nothing
```

`WshNetwork` ***Object***

WSH provides the `WshNetwork` object that exposes methods and properties that you can use in your scripts to work with networks and printers. `Wscript.Network` is the unique identifier for the `WshNetwork` object. To create an instance of the `WshNetwork` object, do the following:

```
Set VariableName = WScript.CreateObject("WScript.Network")
```

`WshNework` object has the following properties:

`ComputerName:` The `ComputerName` property retrieves the name of the computer (`NetBIOS` name). The following will display if the name of the computer matches the name passed as an argument to the `isLocal` custom function procedure:

```
<package>
   <job id="ComputerName Example">
     <runtime>
         <named
             name="m"
             helpstring="Machine Name."
             type="string"
             required=true/>
     </runtime>
      <?job debug="true"?>
      <script language="VbScript">
         if not wscript.arguments.named.Exists("m") then
                Wscript.Arguments.ShowUsage
         else

                strComputer = wscript.arguments.named("m")

                Wscript.Echo isLocal(strComputer)
         end if
        Function isLocal(sComputer)
           Set objwNet = CreateObject("Wscript.Network")
                if Ucase(objwNet.ComputerName) = UCase(sComputer) then
                        isLocal = "True"
                else
                        isLocal = "False"
                end if
           Set objwNet = nothing
        End Function
      </script>
   </job>
</package>
```

`UserName:` The `UserName` property retrieves the currently logged-on username. It does not take any arguments. The following example displays the currently logged-on username using the `UserName` property.

```
Dim objwNet
   Set objwNet = CreateObject("Wscript.Network")
   Wscript.Echo objwNet.UserName
 Set objwNet = nothing
```

The `UserName` property returns the currently logged-on use name even if the script is run under another user's context using the `RunAs` command. `RunAs` is covered in Chapter 1 and Chapter 3.

`UserDomain`: The `UserDomain` property retrieves the currently logged-on user's domain name. If the computer is not joined to the domain, or the user has logged in locally (that is, the user has logged in using the local user account rather than the domain user account) the property returns the local computer name as the domain name.

The following script displays the currently logged-on user's domain name:

```
Dim objwNet
   Set objwNet = CreateObject("Wscript.Network")
   Wscript.Echo objwNet.UserDomain
 Set objwNet = nothing
```

Using the `UserDomain` and the `UserName` properties, you can display the username in the `Domain\User` format as follows:

```
Dim objwNet
   Set objwNet = CreateObject("Wscript.Network")
   Wscript.Echo objwNet.UserDomain & "\" & _
                               objwNet.Username
   Set objwNet = nothing
```

When this script is executed, it will display the username and the domain name as shown in Figure 2.34.

FIGURE 2.34 Domain name and the username displayed in the `Domain\User` format.

Besides the properties, `WshNetwork` provides methods to manage printers and network connections.

Following are the methods that you can use in your scripts to list the currently mapped network drives, map a network drive, and disconnect a network drive:

`EnumNetworkDrives:` The `EnumNetworkDrives` method allows you to list the currently mapped network drivers. When called the method returns a collection of the currently mapped network drives. The returned collection is an array that associates the logical drive letter and with its associated UNC (Uniform Naming Convention) path. The logical drive letter (or the local name) is stored in the even array elements (such as 0,2,4) and the UNC path is stored in the odd array elements (such as 1,3,5). Figure 2.35 shows how the collection of three drives is stored in an array.

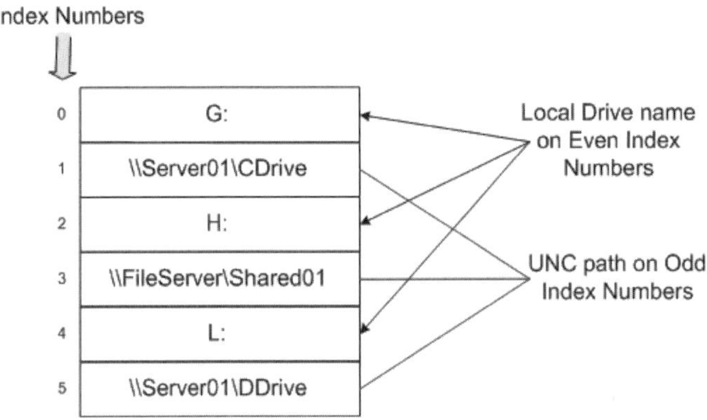

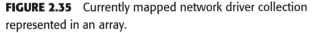

FIGURE 2.35 Currently mapped network driver collection represented in an array.

As two elements in an array constitute a single drive mapping, to display each drive mapping using a `For Next` loop you need to use `Step 2`, as shown in the following example:

```
Dim objwNet, colNetDrives
 Set objwNet = CreateObject("Wscript.Network")
   set colNetDrives = objwNet.EnumNetworkDrives
      for i = 0 to colNetDrives.Count -1 Step 2
             Wscript.Echo colNetDrives.item(i) , "=", _
                                     colNetDrives.item(i+1)
      next
   Set colNetDrives = nothing
set objwNet = nothing
```

When the previous code is executed, the script loops through each alternate element of the array to display the drive name and the UNC path using the `i` and `i+1` index numbers. Since the array always begins with `0` and the `Count` property always returns the total number of drives starting from one, you need to reduce one number (seen as `-1` in the code) from the total number of drives to avoid a `Subscript Out of Range` error.

`MapNetworkDrive:` Using the `MapNetworkDrive` method you can map a network drive. The `MapNetworkDrive` takes local name (local drive name), remote name (UNC path) and optional update profile as boolean (`True` or `False`), the username, and the password as the arguments. `MapNetworkDrive` has the following syntax:

```
object.MapNetworkDrive (strLocalName, strRemoteName, _
                        [bUpdateProfile], [strUser], [strPassword])
```

The `MapNetworkDrive.wsf` script in Listing 2.25 takes local name, UNC path, and optionally the update profile, username and the password; it maps the network drive based on the arguments passed to the script.

LISTING 2.25 `MapNetworkDrive.wsf` Script

```
<package>
   <job id="Map Network Drive">
    <runtime>
      <description> Map a network drive </description>
      <named
            name = "L"
            helpstring = "Local Drive name"
            type = "string"
            required = "true"
        />
      <named
            name = "R"
            helpstring = "UNC Path"
            type = "string"
            required = "true"
        />
      <named
            name = "I"
            helpstring = "Save to profile"
            type = "boolean"
            required = "false"
        />
      <named
            name = "U"
            helpstring = "Username (Domain\User)"
            type = "string"
            required = "false"
```

```
      />
    <named
          name = "P"
          helpstring = "Password for the user"
          type = "string"
          required = "false"
      />
      <example>
       Example: SetRemoteWSH /l:Q: /r:\\server\share /I+
      </example>

  </runtime>
    <?job debug="true"?>
    <script language="VBScript">
     if Wscript.arguments.named("l") = "" or _
        Wscript.arguments.named("r") = "" then
             Wscript.Arguments.ShowUsage
     else

         sLocalName = Wscript.Arguments.Named("l")
         sRemoteName = Wscript.Arguments.Name("r")

         bProfile = Wscript.Arguments.Name("i")
             if bProfile = "" then bProfile = False

         sUserName = Wscript.Arguments.Named("u")
         sPassword = Wscript.Arguments.Name("p")

         Set objwNet = CreateObject("Wscript.Network")
           if sUserName = "" then
            result = objwNet.MapNetworkDrive (sLocalName, _
                                              sRemoteName, _
                                              bProfile)
          else
            result = objwNet.MapNetworkDrive (sLocalName, _
                                              sRemoteName, _
                                             bProfile, _
                                              sUserName, _
                                              sPassword)
          end if
          if result = 0 then
             Wscript.Echo "The mapping was successful"
          else
             Wscript.Echo "Unable to map the network drive.", _
                                   VBNewLine, "Error: " & result
          end if
         Set objwNet = nothing
       end if

    </script>
  </job>
</package>
```

RemoveNetworkDrive: While MapNetworkDrive can be used to create new network mappings, RemoveNetworkDrive can be used to remove the network mappings. The RemoveNetworkDrive takes the name of the mapped network drive (such as Q:) and optionally the argument to force-delete the mapped drive and remove it from the users profile. RemoveNetworkDrive has the following syntax:

```
object.RemoveNetworkDrive(strName, [bForce], [bUpdateProfile])
```

The RemoveNetworkDrive.wsf script in Listing 2.26 takes the mapped network name argument to remove the network mapping. It optionally takes /F (force remove) and /I (remove from profile) values.

LISTING 2.26 RemoveNetworkDrive.wsf Script

```
<package>
<job id="Remove Network Drive">
<runtime>
  <description> Remove a mapped network drive </description>
  <named
        name = "L"
        helpstring = "Local Drive name"
        type = "string"
        required = "true"
    />
  <named
        name = "F"
        helpstring = "Force delete the drive"
        type = "boolean"
        required = "false"
    />
  <named
        name = "I"
        helpstring = "Save to profile"
        type = "boolean"
        required = "false"
    />

    <example>
       Example: RemoveNetworkDrive /l:Q: /F- /I+
    </example>

    </runtime>
      <?job debug="true"?>
      <script language="VBScript">
       if Wscript.arguments.named("l") = "" then
             Wscript.Arguments.ShowUsage
       else
```

```
            sLocalName = Wscript.Arguments.Named("l")
            bForce = Wscript.Arguments.Name("f")
              if bForce = "" then bForce = False

            bProfile = Wscript.Arguments.Name("i")
              if bProfile = "" then bProfile = False

            sUserName = Wscript.Arguments.Named("u")
            sPassword = Wscript.Arguments.Name("p")

            Set objwNet = CreateObject("Wscript.Network")

               result = objwNet.RemoveNetworkDrive (sLocalName, _
                                       bForce, _
                                       bProfile)
             if result = 0 then
              Wscript.Echo "The mapping was successfully removed"
             else
              Wscript.Echo "Unable to remove the network drive.", _
                                VBNewLine, "Error: " & result
             end if
             Set objwNet = nothing
              end if

        </script>
      </job>
    </package>
```

EnumPrinterConnections: `WshNetwork` object exposes the `EnumPrinterConnections` method that returns the information of the currently installed printer mappings. The `EnumPrinterConnections` method has the following syntax:

```
objPrinters = object.EnumPrinterConnections
```

The `EnumNetworkConnections` does not take any arguments, and like `EnumNetwork-Drives`, it returns a collection. The collection is as an array that associates the- network printer local names with their associated UNC names. Therefore, as in `EnumNetwork-Drives`, the local name for the printer is stored in the even array elements (such as elements `0`, `2`, `4`) and the UNC path is stored in the odd array elements (such as `1`, `3`, `5`). Figure 2.36 shows how the collection of three printer connections is stored in an array.

Similar to the `EnumNetworkDrives`, as two elements in an array constitute a single drive mapping, to display each drive mapping using a For `Next` loop you need to use `Step 2`, as shown in the following example:

```
Dim objwNet, colPrinterCons
 Set objwNet = CreateObject("Wscript.Network")
   set colPrinterCons = objwNet.EnumPrinterConnections
```

```
    for i = 0 to colPrinterCons.Count -1 Step 2
     Wscript.Echo colPrinterCons.item(i) , "=", _
                           colPrinterCons.item(i+1)
    next
   Set colPrinterCons = nothing
set objwNet = nothing
```

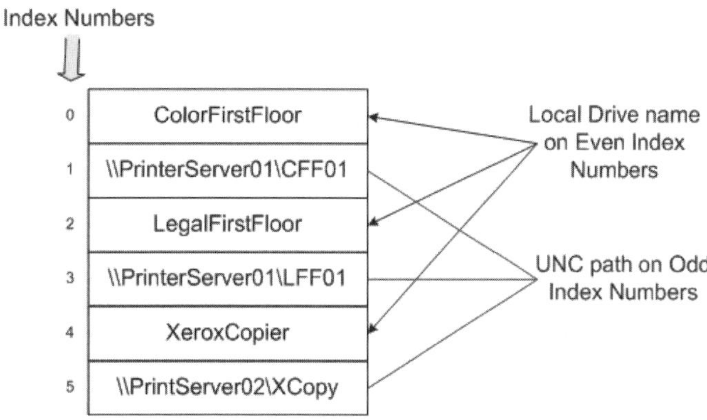

FIGURE 2.36 Current printer connections collection represented in an array.

When the previous code is executed, the script loops through each alternate element of the array to display the local name of the printer and the corresponding UNC path using the `i` and `i+1` index numbers. Because the array always begins with `0`, and the `Count` property always returns the total index number of elements starting from one (for example, a count of 5 would mean total of 5 elements of `1` thru `5`), you need to reduce one number (seen as `-1` in the code) from the total index numbers to avoid a `Subscript Out of Range` error.

`AddPrinterConnection:` The `AddPrinterConnection` takes local printer name (`strLocalName`) and UNC name (`strRemoteName`) as arguments to add a remote MS-DOS-based printer connection. Optionally, you can also specify if the connection information should be updated in the profile. You also optionally provide the username (`strUser`) and the user password (`strPassword`) to use when establishing a printer connection. If the username and password arguments are passed to the method, the method will use this username and password combination to connect to the remote system instead of connecting using the currently logged-on user's credentials.

```
AddPrinterConnection has the following syntax:
object.AddPrinterConnection ( strLocalName, _
                              strRemoteName _
                             [,bUpdateProfile] _
                              [,strUser] _
                                [,strPassword] )
```

The following example illustrates how to add a printer connection using the `AddPrinterConnection` method:

```
Dim objwNet
 Dim RemoteMachine, RemotePrinter
   RemoteMachine = "sydney"
     RemotePrinter = "BrotherFax"
     Set objwNet = CreateObject("WScript.Network")
   objwNet.AddPrinterConnection "LPT1", _
                              "\\" & RemoteMachine _
                              & "\" & RemotePrinter
   Set objwNet = nothing
```

When you run the previous code, an MS-DOS printer connection is created as shown in Figure 2.37.

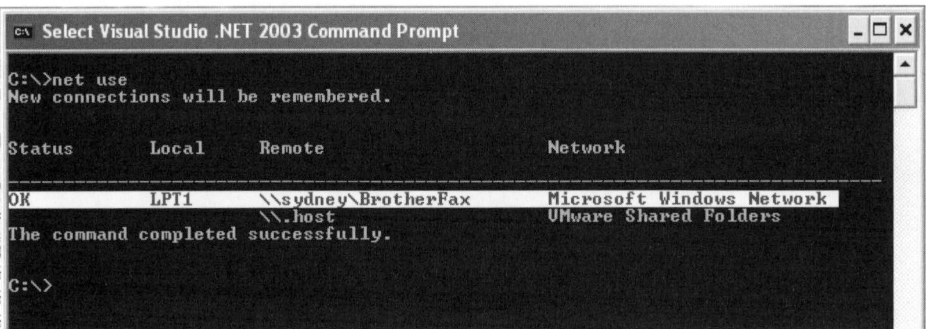

FIGURE 2.37 MS-DOS printer connection shown in a command window.

If you use `AddPrinterConnection` *to add a printer, no information will be displayed in the Printers and Faxes Windows special folder. To view the connections, you can type* `net use` *in the command-prompt window.*

`AddWindowsPrinterConnection:` The `AddWindowsPrinterConnection` takes only the printer path (`strPrinterPath`) to add a Windows-based printer connection, unlike the `AddPrinterConnection` method. This method is like adding a printer locally using the control panel in Windows. Another difference between the `AddPrinterConnection` and `AddWindowsPrinterConnection` is that the `AddWindowsPrinterConnection` allows you to add a printer without directing the printer to a specific port (such as LPT1). If the `AddWindowsPrinterConnection` fails to establish a connection, an error similar to the one shown in Figure 2.38 is generated.

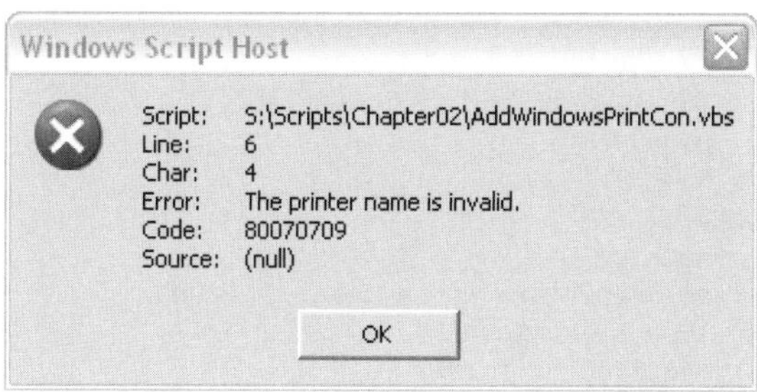

FIGURE 2.38 Error generated if the `AddWindowsPrinterConnection` fails to establish a connection.

The `AddWindowsPrinterConnection` method has the following syntax:

```
object.AddWindowsPrinterConnection (strPrinterPath)
```

The following example illustrates how to use the `AddWindowsPrinterConnection` to add a new printer connection to the computer:

```
Dim objwNet
 Dim RemoteMachine, RemotePrinter
   RemoteMachine = "Atlanta"
     RemotePrinter = "Xerox"
     Set objwNet = CreateObject("WScript.Network")
   objwNet.AddWindowsPrinterConnection _
                          "\\" & RemoteMachine _
                            & "\" & RemotePrinter
 Set objwNet = nothing
```

`RemovePrinterConnection:` Using the `RemovePrinterConnection` method you can remove an existing printer connection. It takes the name of the printer (Local name such as `LPT1` for MS-DOS printer connection or the UNC name, such as `\\printserver\printer` for Windows printer connection) as a required argument. It takes force delete and update profile as optional arguments. Following is the syntax for the `RemovePrinterConnection` method:

```
object.RemovePrinterConnection(strName, [bForce], [bUpdateProfile])
```

The code in the following example when executed removes a printer connection passed as an argument to the script:

```
<package>
 <job id="Remove Network Drive">
<runtime>
<description> Remove a mapped network drive </description>
<named
     name = "L"
     helpstring = "Local Drive name"
     type = "string"
     required = "true"
  />
<named
     name = "F"
     helpstring = "Force delete the drive"
     type = "boolean"
     required = "false"
  />
<named
     name = "I"
     helpstring = "Save to profile"
     type = "boolean"
     required = "false"
  />
  <example>
     Example: RemovePrinterCon /l:Xerox /F- /I+
  </example>

</runtime>
<?job debug="true"?>
<script language="VBScript">
if Wscript.arguments.named("l") = "" then
     Wscript.Arguments.ShowUsage
else
    sLocalName = Wscript.Arguments.Named("l")
    bForce = Wscript.Arguments.Named("f")
        if bForce = "" then bForce = False
    bProfile = Wscript.Arguments.Named("i")
        if bProfile = "" then bProfile = False
         Set objwNet = CreateObject("Wscript.Network")

         result = objwNet.RemovePrinterConnection ( _
                                sLocalName, _
                                bForce, _
                                bProfile)
         if result = 0 then
          Wscript.Echo "The printer was successfully removed"
         else
          Wscript.Echo "Unable to remove the printer.", _
                            VBNewLine, "Error: " & result
```

```
        end if
       Set objwNet = nothing
      end if
    </script>
  </job>
</package>
```

To remove a connection using this script you can do the following:

- Remove an MS-DOS printer connection:

```
RemovePrinterCon /L:LPT1
```

- Remove a Windows printer connection:

```
RemovePrinterCon /L:\\PrintServer\Printer
```

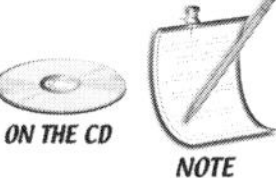

`RemovePrinterCon.wsf` script file is located on the CD-ROM at Scripts\Chapter02. The script takes three parameters: `/L`, `/F` and `/I`. `/L` is the required parameter that takes the local name of the printer connection. `/F`, optional parameter, takes a boolean value that you can use to force-delete the printer. `/I`, optional parameter, takes a boolean value that you can use to update the user profile. Double-clicking the script will display these options.

`SetDefaultPrinter`: Besides providing the ability to create and delete printers, `WshNetwork` object also provides you the `SetDefaultPrinter` method that you can use to set the role of the printer to a default printer for the user.

For example, if you have two printers on your computer—color and black and white (BW)—and you generally print to the BW printer, you can set the BW printer to be the default printer so all applications print to the BW printer using the following script:

```
<package>
   <job id="Remove Network Drive">
    <runtime>
      <description> Remove a mapped network drive </description>
      <named
            name = "L"
            helpstring = "Local Drive name"
            type = "string"
            required = "true"
        />

        <example>
         Example: SetDefaultPrinter /l:Xerox
        </example>
```

```
        </runtime>
          <?job debug="true"?>
          <script language="VBScript">
        if Wscript.arguments.named("l") = "" then
                        Wscript.Arguments.ShowUsage
                else

            sLocalName = Wscript.Arguments.Named("l")

            Set objwNet = CreateObject("Wscript.Network")

               result = objwNet.SetDefaultPrinter ( _
                                                sLocalName)
             if result = 0 then
                Wscript.Echo sLocalName & _
    " printer has been set as default printer"
             else
                Wscript.Echo "Unable to set " & sLocalName & _
                                " printer as the default printer.", _
                                          VBNewLine, "Error: " & result
             end if
              Set objwNet = nothing
             end if

          </script>
      </job>
    </package>
```

The `SetDefaultPrinter` takes the local printer name (`strPrinterName`) as the only argument. Following is the syntax for `SetDefaultPrinter` method:

```
object.SetDefaultPrinter(strPrinterName)
```

The `SetDefaultPrinter` *method sets any printer as a default printer, whether it is a local printer (installed and attached locally on the system) or a network printer.*

`WshController` Object

Prior to WSH v5.6, you could only run scripts locally (that is, run a script to accomplish a task on the same system where you execute the script). With WSH v5.6 you can run a script on a remote system (that is, run a script on the remote system to accomplish tasks on a remote system) using the `WshContoller` object.

`WshController` is the unique identifier for the `WshController` object. To create an instance of the `WshContoller` object, do the following:

```
Set VariableName = WScript.CreateObject("WshController")
```

WshController object has no properties and the following method:

CreateScript method: The CreateScript method allows execution of a script on a remote (target) system. It takes a script name (such as C:\MinimizeAll. vbs) as a required argument and a remote machine name as an optional argument (if the remote machine name is omitted, the script will execute on the local computer).

If you are running WSH Version 5.6.6626 that ships with Internet Explorer 6 and Windows XP, the target script (such as MinimizeAll.vbs shown in Listing 2.27) will be copied to the remote computer's memory and then executed from the memory. In later versions of WSH, such as included with Windows Server 2003, the target script (such as MinimizeAll.vbs shown in Listing 2.27) will be copied to the temporary directory of the account that is used to execute the script on the remote computer. The script will then be executed with the security settings for the remote computer and the temporary directory.

To execute a script on a remote computer (called the target computer), you need:

1. A script that needs to be run on a target computer: namely, the target script.
2. A script that will execute the target script on the remote computer: namely, the host script.

You also must set up the environment as follows:

1. Make sure both computers (local and target) are running WSH v5.6.
2. Add the following string registry value (REG_SZ) named Remote to HKey_Local_Machine\Software\Microsoft\Windows Script Host\Settings registry key. Set its value to 1 to enable remote WSH and 0 to disable it.
3. Add the remote user that will execute the host script to the local Administrators group on the remote computer.

TIP

Any member of the local Administrators group can remotely execute a script. This potentially is a security risk. Also, running your scripts as an Administrator is not the most secure method of executing the scripts. Because of the security concerns, WshController *is not a practical method of remotely executing scripts. To securely execute scripts on a remote system, you can use the* Create *method of* Win32_process *class in WMI instead.*

ON THE CD

NOTE

You can use the SetRemotewsh.wsf *script included on the CD-ROM to enable and disable remote WSH.*

After the environment setup is complete, you can execute the script (such as `ExcRemoteScript.wsf`—known as the host script—shown in Listing 2.27) to remotely execute the target script (such as `MinimizeAll.vbs`) on a remote system.

Figure 2.39 shows how the host script (`ExecRemoteScript.wsf`) seen in Listing 2.27 executes the target script (`MinimizeAll.vbs`) on a remote system to minimize all open windows on the remote system's desktop.

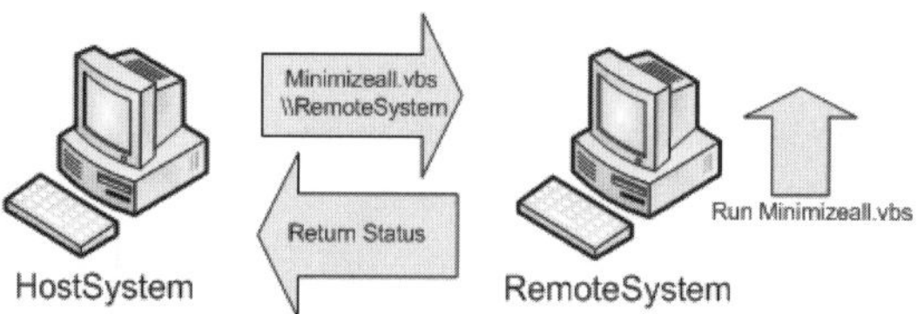

FIGURE 2.39 `ExecRemoteScript.wsf` executing a script on a remote (target) computer.

LISTING 2.27 Executes `MinimizeAll.vbs` Script on a Remote Machine Passed as an Argument to the Script

```
<package>
   <job id="RemoteMinAll">
    <runtime>
      <description>
Minimize all desktop windows on a remote system
      </description>
      <named
            name = "m"
            helpstring = "Remote machine name"
            type = "string"
            required = "true"
        />
        <example>Example: ExecRemoteScript /m:RemoteMachineName</example>
    </runtime>
    <?job debug="true"?>
    <script language="VBScript">
    if Wscript.arguments.named("m") = "" then
      Wscript.Arguments.ShowUsage
    else
      Dim objController, objRemoteScript
      Set objController = WScript.CreateObject("WSHController")
       Set objRemoteScript = objController.CreateScript("minimizeall.vbs", _
       Wscript.Arguments.named("m"))
       Wscript.ConnectObject objRemoteScript, "Remote_"
       objRemoteScript.Execute
        Do While RemoteScript.Status <> 2
            WScript.Sleep 100
```

```
          Loop
         Set objRemoteScript = nothing
        Set objController = nothing
      end if
      </script>
    </job>
</package>
```

The CreateScript method returns a handle of an instance of a WshRemote object. The WshRemote object allows you to remotely administer the computer systems on a computer network. It exposes the following methods and properties that you can use to start, terminate, or get status and errors of the script executed by the CreateScript method:

Error property: The Error property of WshRemote object returns the WshRemote Error object (it is the same as the Err object returned by the script, when it is run on the local system). The WshRemoteError object provides properties, such as Number (as in Err.Number), Description (as in Err.Description), and Source (as in Err.Source) that you can use to get the information on the error that occurred in a script that was run on the target system. Additionally, WshRemote Error object also exposes the Line and the SourceText properties that provide additional information about the error in the remote script.

Status property: The WshRemote object's Status property provides the status of the script being executed on the target computer. For example, the script in Listing 2.27 (earlier in this chapter) loops until the remote script stops running, that is, the status property returns 2.

When called, the Status property returns one of the values listed in Table 2.19.

TABLE 2.19 WshRemote Object's Status Properties Return Values

Return Value	Numeric Value	Description
NoTask	0	The remote script object has been created but not executed.
Running	1	The remote script object is currently executing.
Finished	2	The remote script object has finished running.

Execute method: WshRemote object's Execute method starts an execution of the remote object. When the Execute method is called, it fires the Start event (see following note) of the WshRemote object.

As the name suggests, an event is something that occurs on a system when you do something or something happens on the system. For example, if you execute notepad.exe on your computer, you fire a execute event. When your system receives the execute event, it loads the notepad.exe application into the memory that fires the load memory event. Loading the notepad.exe into the memory creates a new process that generates the new process event. When you close the notepad.exe application, then it fires the `End` event.

`Terminate` method: The `Execute` method starts the execution of a script, and the `Terminate` method force-kills (ends) the remote object.

`Terminate` method should be used as the last resort because the application terminated by calling the `Terminate` method will not end gracefully. If a program does not end gracefully, the system may not release memory used by the program, causing a memory leak (memory blocked for the terminated application but not used by the system).

HTML APPLICATIONS (HTAs)

WSH provides very limited functionality for building GUI (graphical user interface) type applications. For example, if you need to display a welcome message to the user, you are limited to displaying the message only in a standard text format, using either the `Msgbox` method, `PopUp` method, or the `Wscript.Echo` method.

Moreover, it is also not possible to display additional messages on the user's screen without popping up additional message windows in addition to the text formatting limitation; that is, you cannot format text for display, such as increase or decrease the size of the text being displayed. For instance, the script in Listing 2.28 to display the welcome message, current date and the free diskspace on the C:\ drive, will pop up three message windows—first for the welcome message, second for today's date and the third free space on the user's C:\ drive—when run with Wscript.

LISTING 2.28 Sample Script That Displays Multiple Message Windows

```
Option Explicit
Dim objFs
Dim objwNet
Dim sUserName
 Set objFs = CreateObject("Scripting.FileSystemObject")
 Set objwNet = CreateObject("Wscript.Network")

 sUserName = objwNet.UserName
  Wscript.Echo "Welcome " & sUserName
```

```
    Wscript.Echo "Today" & "'" & "s Date is: " & _
                                Month(now) & _
                             "/" & Day(now) & _
                                "/" & Year(now)
    Wscript.Echo ShowFreeSpace("c:\")
 Set objFs = nothing
 Set objwNet = nothing

Function ShowFreeSpace(drvPath)
  Dim objdrive, s
  Set objdrive = objFs.GetDrive(objFs.GetDriveName(drvPath))
    s = s  & FormatNumber(objdrive.FreeSpace/(1024^2), 0)
    s = "Your C: Drive has " & s & " Mbytes Free Space"
  ShowFreeSpace = s
End Function
```

Figure 2.40 shows the three message boxes that will appear on the screen if the script is run using Wscript.

Windows Script Host
Welcome Bobby
OK
Windows Script Host
Today's Date is: 9/3/2005
OK
Windows Script Host
Your C: Drive has 114,926 Mbytes Free Space
OK

FIGURE 2.40 Message windows displayed if the `WelcomeUser.vbs` script is run with Wscript.

By running the `WelcomeUser.vbs` script with Cscript instead of Wscript, however, you can avoid the pop-up messages (pop-up messages can be very annoying since they require the user to click `Ok` to continue) shown in Figure 2.40. Running the script with Cscript will display the messages in a command window instead of the pop-up message boxes. Figure 2.41 shows how the message will be displayed if executed with Cscript.

Command Prompt
S:\Scripts\Chapter02>cscript /nologo welcomeuser.vbs
Welcome Bobby
Today's Date is: 11/27/2005
Your C: Drive has 108,239 Mbytes Free Space
S:\Scripts\Chapter02>

FIGURE 2.41 Messages displayed in the command window if the `WelcomeUser.vbs` script is run with Cscript.

NOTE

If the `MsgBox` method is used instead of the `Wscript.Echo` method, message boxes similar to the ones shown in Figure 2.40 will appear on the user's screen even if you run the script with `Cscript`. See earlier in this chapter to learn about `MsgBox` function.

You can overcome the GUI limitations by creating an HTA script instead of a .VBS script that you can run with MSHTA.EXE shell. For example, you can convert the `WelcomeUser.vbs` script into HTA script to make it more interactive and user friendly. Listing 2.29 shows the `WelcomeUser.hta` script code.

NOTE

By default when you double-click an HTA file, it executes with `MSHTA.EXE` shell.

LISTING 2.29 `WelcomeUser.hta` Script

```
<html>
<!-----------------------------------------------------
WelcomeUser.hta
------------------------------------------------------>
<head>
<HTA:APPLICATION
     ID="WelcomeUserHTA"
     APPLICATIONNAME="Welcome User HTA Script"
     SCROLL="no"
     SINGLEINSTANCE="yes"
     WINDOWSTATE="normal"
     BORDER="thick"
     BORDERSTYLE="normal"
     MAXIMIZEBUTTON="yes"
     MINIMIZEBUTTON="yes"
        INNERBORDER="yes"
     SYSMENU="yes" />
<title>Welcome User HTA Script Example</title>

<style>
body
{ background-color:#ffffff; font-family:Arial;
  font-size: 8pt; margin-top:5px; margin-left:5px;
  margin-right:5px; margin-bottom:5px; }
</style>

<script type="text/vbscript">
Option Explicit
   Dim objFs
   Dim objwNet
   Dim sUserName

Sub Window_Onload
    Window.ResizeTo 400,130
     Set objFs = CreateObject("Scripting.FileSystemObject")
      Set objwNet = CreateObject("Wscript.Network")
```

```
        sUserName = objwNet.UserName
        Welcome.innerHTML = _
            "<B>Welcome</B> " & _
            "<Font face='Arial,Helvetica' color='gray' Size='4'>" _
                                            & sUserName & "</Font>"
        CurrentDate.innerHTML = _
            "<Font face='Arial,Helvetica' color='Blue' Size='2'>"  _
                                & "Today" & "'" & "s Date is: " & _
                                                    Month(now) & _
                                                    "/" & Day(now) & _
                                                    "/" & Year(now) & _
"</Font>"
             DisplayDriveInformation

End Sub

Sub DisplayDriveInformation
    FreeSpace.innerHTML = ShowFreeSpace(TypicalFrm.DrivePath.Value)
End Sub

Function ShowFreeSpace(drvPath)
   Dim objdrive, s
    Set objdrive = objFs.GetDrive(objFs.GetDriveName(drvPath))
     s = s  & FormatNumber(objdrive.FreeSpace/(1024^2), 0)
      s = "<Font size=2>Your <B>C:</B> Drive has " & _
          "<b>" & s & "</b> Mbytes Free Space</font>"
   ShowFreeSpace = s
End Function

Sub Window_OnUnload
     Set objFs = nothing
     Set objwNet = nothing
End Sub
</script>
</head>
<body>
<!----------------------------------------------------
Format the HTA using standard HTML
----------------------------------------------------->
 <CENTER>
  <Form name="TypicalFrm">
    <Table border=0 cellpadding=1 cellspacing=2
                        bgcolor="#eeeeee" width="100%">
        <TR bgcolor="#ffffff">
            <TD>
                <div id="Welcome"
                           style= "width:100%; height:100%;"></div>
            </TD>
        </TR>
        <TR bgcolor="#ffffff">
```

```
            <TD>
                <div id="CurrentDate"
                          style= "width:100%; height:100%;"></div>
            </TD>
        </TR>
        <TR bgcolor="#ffffff">
            <TD>
                <input type="hidden" name="DrivePath" value="C:\">
                <div id="FreeSpace"
                          style= "width:100%; height:100%;"></div>
            </TD>
        </TR>
     </Table>
   </Form>
 </CENTER>
</body>
</html>
```

When the `WelcomeUser.hta` file is executed, it displays a user-friendly HTML-style window as shown in Figure 2.42.

Welcome User HTA Script Example
Welcome Bobby
Today's Date is: 9/3/2005
Your C: Drive has 114,893 Mbytes Free Space

FIGURE 2.42 User-friendly HTML-type window displayed when `WelcomeUser.hta` is run.

Introduction

Besides the Windows Script Host (WSH) shell, you can also use HTML Applications to develop and run administrative scripts. HTML Applications, commonly known as HTAs, are full-fledged applications that leverage the power of Internet Explorer—its object model, performance, rendering power, protocol support, and channel-download technology—without enforcing the strict security model and user interface of the browser. Figure 2.43 shows a typical HTA application that when run displays the HTML type content in a browser window, as shown in Figures 2.44 and 2.45.

NOTE

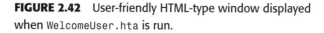

HTML is a big topic in itself; therefore, it is beyond the scope of this book. A good source for a beginner to learn HTML is http:// www.w3.org *and* http://www.w3schools.com/. *To learn more about DHTML (Dynamic HTML) coding you can visit* http:// msdn.microsoft. \com.

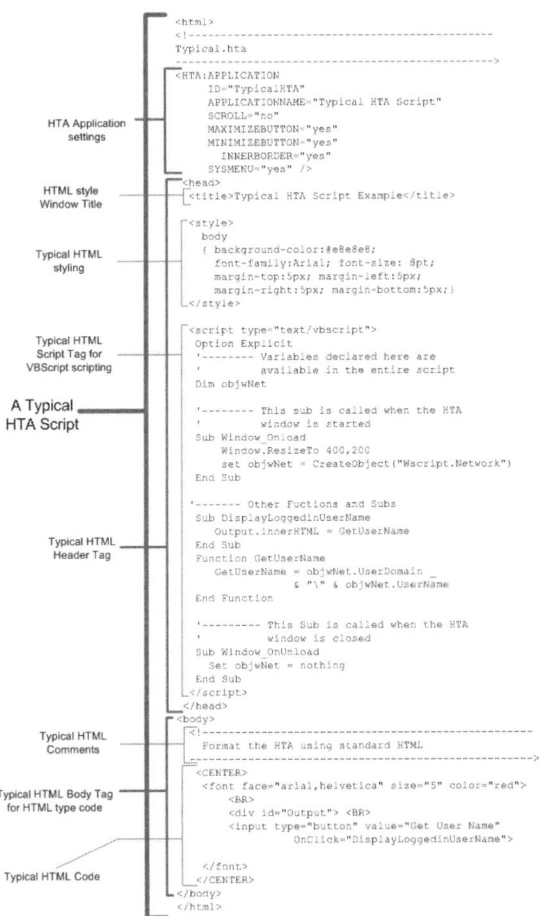


```
<html>
<!--------------------------------------------------
Typical.hta
-------------------------------------------------->
<HTA:APPLICATION
     ID="TypicalHTA"
     APPLICATIONNAME="Typical HTA Script"
     SCROLL="no"
     MAXIMIZEBUTTON="yes"
     MINIMIZEBUTTON="yes"
       INNERBORDER="yes"
     SYSMENU="yes" />
 <head>
 <title>Typical HTA Script Example</title>

 <style>
   body
   { background-color:#e8e8e8;
     font-family:Arial; font-size: 8pt;
     margin-top:5px; margin-left:5px;
     margin-right:5px; margin-bottom:5px;}
 </style>

 <script type="text/vbscript">
  Option Explicit
  '-------- Variables declared here are
  '         available in the entire script
  Dim objwNet

  '-------- This sub is called when the HTA
  '         window is started
  Sub Window_Onload
      Window.ResizeTo 400,200
      set objwNet = CreateObject("Wscript.Network")
  End Sub

 '------- Other Fuctions and Subs
  Sub DisplayLoggedinUserName
     Output.innerHTML = GetUserName
  End Sub
  Function GetUserName
     GetUserName = objwNet.UserDomain _
                 & "\" & objwNet.UserName
  End Function

  '--------- This Sub is called when the HTA
  '          window is closed
  Sub Window_OnUnload
    Set objwNet = nothing
  End Sub
 </script>
 </head>
<body>
  <!---------------------------------------------------
   Format the HTA using standard HTML
  --------------------------------------------------->
  <CENTER>
   <font face="arial,helvetica" size="5" color="red">
       <BR>
       <div id="Output"> <BR>
       <input type="button" value="Get User Name"
                 OnClick="DisplayLoggedinUserName">

   </font>
  </CENTER>
</body>
</html>
```

FIGURE 2.43 A typical HTA script.

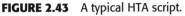

FIGURE 2.44 Typical script when run shows the HTML-type window displaying a button.

FIGURE 2.45 HTML-type output displayed in a window after the button (displayed in Figure 2.44) is clicked.

Creating an HTA

Creating an HTA is simple; you can write an HTML page and save it with .hta extension. For example, do the following to create a simple HTML file using Notepad and then change the extension (from .html) to .hta.

1. Open the Notepad.exe application
2. Type the following in the Notepad window

```
<html>
<head>
    <title>Simple HTML file</title>
</head>
<body>
    <center>
            <font size="5">This is a simple html file</font>
    </center>
</body>
</html>
```

3. Save the file as Simple.html.
4. Double-click the file to view the html page.
5. Rename the file from Simple.html to Simple.hta.
6. Double-click Simple.hta to view the HTML page, as shown in Figure 2.46.

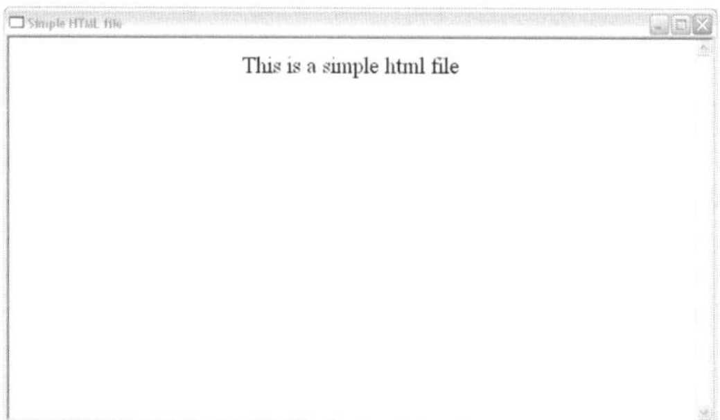

FIGURE 2.46 HTML code in Simple.hta file executed as HTML application.

Although HTAs are like HTML files, they do have HTA-specific functionality such as the `HTA:Application` tag and properties that tell the HTAs how to behave as an application. The `HTA:Application` tag provides a limited set of attributes that you can use in HTAs to control a number of things: from border style to the program icon and its menu. Table 2.20 lists the attributes that can be set and retrieved using the `HTA:Application` tag.

TABLE 2.20 `HTA:Application` Attributes

Attribute	Property	Description
ApplicationName	Object.ApplicationName	Sets or retrieves the name of the HTA.
Border	Object.Border	Sets or retrieves the type of window border of the HTA.
BorderStyle	Object.BorderStyle	Sets or retrieves the style set for the content border within the HTA window.
Caption	Object.Caption	Sets or retrieves a boolean value that indicates whether the window is set to display a title bar or caption, for the HTA.
Caption	Object.CommandLine	Retrieves the argument used to launch the HTA.
ContextMenu	Object.ContextMenu	Sets or retrieves whether the context menu is displayed when the right mouse button is clicked.
Icon	Object.Icon	Sets or retrieves the name and location of the icon specified in the HTA.
InnerBorder	Object.InnerBorder	Sets or retrieves whether the inside 3D border is displayed.
MaximizeButton	Object.MaximizeButton	Sets or retrieves a boolean value that indicates whether a `Maximize` button is displayed in the title bar of the HTA window.
MinimizeButton	Object.MinimizeButton	Sets or retrieves a boolean value that indicates whether a `Minimize` button is displayed in the title bar of the HTA window.
Navigable	Object.Navigable	Sets or retrieves whether linked documents will be loaded in the main HTA window or in a new browser window.
Scroll	Object.Scroll	Sets or retrieves whether the scroll bars are displayed.
ScrollFlat	Object.ScrollFlat	Sets or retrieves whether the scroll bar is 3D or flat.
Selection	Object.Selection	Sets or retrieves whether the content can be selected with the mouse or keyboard.
ShowInTaskbar	Object.ShowIntaskbar	Sets or retrieves a value that indicates whether the HTA is displayed in the Microsoft Windows taskbar.

→

Attribute	**Property**	**Description**
`SingleInstance`	`Object.SingleInstance`	Sets or retrieves a value that indicates whether only one instance of the specified HTA can run at a time.
`SysMenu`	`Object.SysMenu`	Sets or retrieves a boolean value that indicates whether a system menu is displayed in the HTA.
`Version`	`Object.Version`	Sets or retrieves the version number of the HTA.
`WindowState`	`Object.WindowState`	Sets or retrieves the initial size of the HTA window.

It is not essential to include the `HTA:Application` tag in an HTA script. However, it provides functionality that can help you control the look and feel, and the functionality of the HTA. For example, you can disable the `right click` menu by setting the `ContextMenu` setting to false and/or set the icon for the script by setting the `Icon` property.

Properites can be set in the HTA by simply including the `HTA:Application` tag in the `HEAD` HTML tag as shown in Listing 2.30.

LISTING 2.30 Defining HTA Behavior Using `HTA:Application` Tag

```
<HTML>
<HEAD>
   <HTA:APPLICATION
     ID="objHTA"
     APPLICATIONNAME="HTA Application Name"
     SCROLL="no"
     SINGLEINSTANCE="yes"
     WINDOWSTATE="normal"
     BORDER="thick"
     BORDERSTYLE="normal"
     MAXIMIZEBUTTON="yes"
     MINIMIZEBUTTON="yes"
     INNERBORDER="yes"
     SELECTION="no"
     SYSMENU="yes"
     WINDOWSTATE="maximized"
     VERSION="1.0.0.1"
/>
</HEAD>
<BODY>
</BODY>
</HTML>
```

HTA:Application tag requires a closing tag. There are two ways you can close a tag:

1. `<HTA:Application …></HTA:Application>`
2. `<HTA:Application … />`

The `HTA:Application` tag is also considered an object for the purpose of scripting. It can be used to retrieve the properties of the HTA. To retrieve the properties of the HTA you can use the `HTA:Application` object's `ID` property as shown in Listing 2.31.

LISTING 2.31 Retrieving HTA Properties

```
<HTML>
    <HEAD>
        <HTA:APPLICATION
                    ID="objHTA"
                    APPLICATIONNAME="Retrieve HTA Properties" />
         <Script Language="VBS">
           Document.write "<B>HTA Application Name: </B>" & _
                          objHTA.ApplicationName & "<BR>"
            Document.write "<B>HTA Window State: </B>" & _
                                           objHTA.WindowState
        </Script>
    </HEAD>
<BODY>
</BODY>
</HTML>
```

When this script is run, it displays the name of the application set in the `APPLCATIONAME` property and the default window state retrieved from the `WINDOWSTATE` property of the `HTA:Application` tag shown in Figure 2.47.

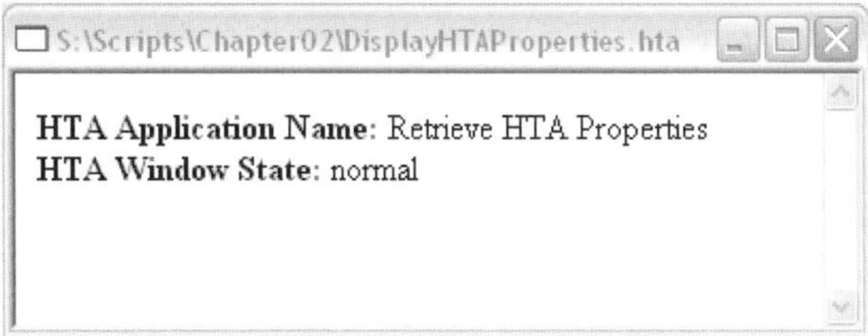

FIGURE 2.47 `APPLICATIONNAME` and `WINDOWSTATE` properties retrieved and displayed in an HTA.

One of the shortfalls of HTAs is that they do not provide a simple method of handling command-line arguments. However, they do provide the `CommandLine` property that retrieves the entire command-line command (as it was typed on the command line). For example, if you type the

```
htacommandline.hta /u:user1 /p:password1
```

command at the command prompt to execute the script in Listing 2.32 the script will display the entire command line as you had typed it. Figure 2.48 shows the command typed at the command prompt:

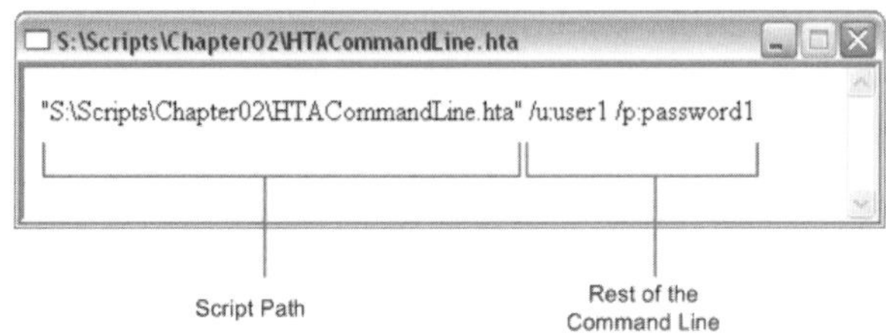

FIGURE 2.48 Command line used to execute `HTACommandLine.hta` script displayed by retrieving the `CommandLine` property of the HTA.

LISTING 2.32 `HTACommadLine.hta` Script

```
<HTA:APPLICATION ID="oHTA"
   APPLICATIONNAME="Sequencer"
     BORDERSTYLE="normal"
     CAPTION="yes"
     MAXIMIZEBUTTON="no"
     MINIMIZEBUTTON="yes"
     SHOWINTASKBAR="no"
     SINGLEINSTANCE="no"
     SYSMENU="yes"
     VERSION="1.0"
     WINDOWSTATE="normal"
  />
<script language="VBScript">
 Sub Window_OnLoad
      sCommandLine = oHTA.CommandLine
      document.write sCommandLine
 End Sub
</script>
```

Parsing Script Path from the Command Line

Generally, if you create a `.VBS` or `.WSF` script and run it with WSH, you can use the `WshArguments` object in your code to parse the arguments passed to the script. To do the same for an HTA file, you have to write code to parse the command line and the arguments.

However, before you can parse the arguments, you must separate the script path included in the command line retrieved using the `CommandLine` property from the rest of the command line. The code in Figure 2.49 shows how to parse and display the script path from the command line.

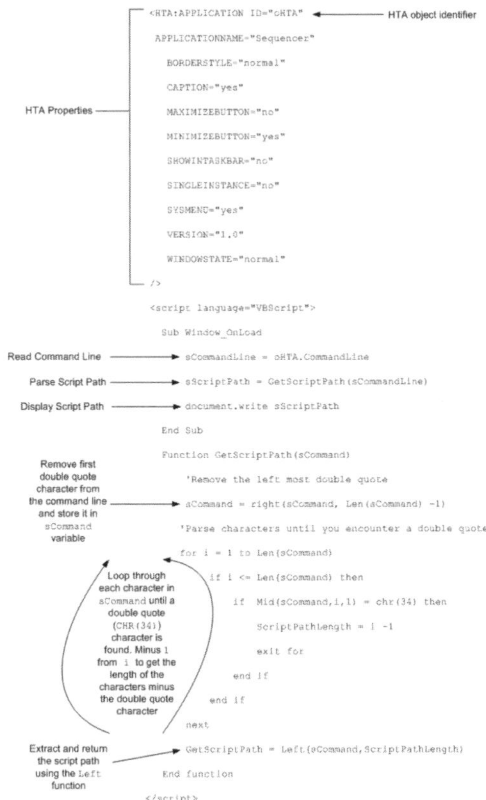

FIGURE 2.49 `ParseScriptPath.hta` **script details.**

If you execute the script shown in Figure 2.49 in the following manner:

```
C:\>ParseScriptPath.hta /u:user1 /p:password1
```

the script will display the parsed script path from the command line as follows:

```
C:\ParseScriptPath.hta
```

The command line returned by the `CommandLine` *property always includes the full path to the script. For example, if you execute the* `ParseScriptPath.hta` *from C:\Scripts folder, the* `CommandLine` *property will return it as* `C:\Scripts\ParseScriptPath.hta`*.*

As seen in Figure 2.49, the `GetScriptPath` custom function is used to retrieve the script path from the complete command line. The script path is always within the start and the end double quote (") characters.

To extract the script path from the command line, you must get the characters within these two double quotes. To do this the `GetScriptPath` function does the following

1. The function begins by removing the first character from the left of the command line (the double quote that you don't need) and stores the remaining command line in the `sCommand` variable using the following command:

```
sCommand = right(sCommand, Len(sCommand) -1)
```

2. To parse the script path from the rest of the command line stored in the `sCommand` variable, the script loops through each remaining character in the command line until it encounters a double quote (CHR(34)) to calculate the length of the characters (that constitute the script path) to extract from the left of the command line as shown in the following code:

```
for i = 1 to Len(sCommand)
     if i <= Len(sCommand) then
         if  Mid(sCommand,i,1) = chr(34) then
             ScriptPathLength = i -1
             exit for
         end if
     end if
next
```

3. The `Left` function is used to extract the number of characters that constitute the command line and the extracted value is retuned by the function as shown in the following:

```
GetScriptPath = Left(sCommand,ScriptPathLength)
```

The returned value from the `GetScriptPath` custom function is then displayed using the following code:

```
document.write sScriptPath
```

Parsing Arguments from the Command Line

Since HTA has no object that parses arguments passed at the command line, you must build your own logic to retrieve the arguments passed to an HTA. As seen in the previous section ("Parsing Script Path from the Command Line"), you must write code to extract the script path from the command line. Similarly, as seen in Figure 2.49, the script parses the username and the password passed as arguments at the command line. To extract the username and password, the script does the following:

1. Removes the left-most character (the double quote)
2. Gets the complete script path using the `GetScriptPath` function
3. Removes the script path and the double quote that immediately follows the script path, and stores the remaining characters of the command line into the `sParameters` variable using the following:

```
'Remove the Script path from sCommand.
'Also remove the double quote following the Script Path
sParameters = Replace(sCommandLine,sScriptPath & CHR(34),"")
```

4. Trims the leading and trailing spaces from the command line using the `Trim` function as follows:

```
sParameters = Trim(sParameters)
```

5. The script then displays the script path and the remaining portion of the command line using the following:

```
document.write sScriptPath & "<BR>" & sParameters
```

Working with Arguments

Once you have separated the script path and the rest of the command line characters (arguments passed at the commad line), it is easy to work with the arguments. However, it is up to the programmer to handle the arguments. For example, if your script syntax requires you to pass the username and password as an argument, then you must write code to parse such parameters. The script in Listing 2.33 is an example of a script that expects the user to pass the username and the password in the following format:

```
C:\>HTACommandLine_full.hta /u:User1 /p:Password1
```

LISTING 2.33 Parsing Command Line Arguments Example

```
<HTA:APPLICATION ID="oHTA"
   APPLICATIONNAME="Sequencer"
      BORDERSTYLE="normal"
      CAPTION="yes"
      MAXIMIZEBUTTON="no"
      MINIMIZEBUTTON="yes"
      SHOWINTASKBAR="no"
      SINGLEINSTANCE="no"
      SYSMENU="yes"
      VERSION="1.0"
      WINDOWSTATE="normal"
/>
<script language="VBScript">
```

```
'Global variables
Dim sUserName
Dim sPassword
 Sub Window_OnLoad
   sCommandLine = oHTA.CommandLine
    sScriptPath = GetScriptPath(sCommandLine)
     'Remove the Script path from sCommand.
     'Also remove the double quote following the Script Path
      sParameters = Replace(sCommandLine,sScriptPath & CHR(34),"")
        sParameters = Trim(sParameters)
       document.write sScriptPath & "<BR>" & sParameters
      ParseParameters sParameters
    document.write "<BR>" & sUserName & ", " & sPassword
 End Sub

 Function GetScriptPath(sCommand)
   'Remove the left most double quote
   sCommand = right(sCommand, Len(sCommand) -1)
    'Parse characters until you encounter a double quote
    for i = 1 to Len(sCommand)
       if i <= Len(sCommand) then
           if  Mid(sCommand,i,1) = chr(34) then
               ScriptPathLength = i -1
               exit for
           end if
       end if
    next
   GetScriptPath = Left(sCommand,ScriptPathLength)
 End function

 Sub ParseParameters(sPara)
  if sPara = "" then exit sub
   arrParas = Split(sPara," ")
     for j = 0 to ubound(arrParas)
           arrParam = Split(arrParas(j),":")
             Select Case arrParam(0)
               Case "/u"
                    sUserName = arrParam(1)
               Case "/p"
                    sPassword = arrParam(1)
             End Select
       next
 End Sub
</script>
```

When the script in Listing 2.33 is executed with the username and password passed as arguments, the script does the following:

1. Script declares the variables using the `DIM` statement and calls `Window_OnLoad` function

2. Retrieves and stores the command line information to the sCommandLine variable
3. Calls `GetScriptPath` function and passes the `sCommandLine` variable as the argument
4. The `GetScriptPath` function separates the script name from the arguments
5. The script next cleans up the parameters (arguments) returned by the `GetScriptPath` function
6. Displays the script path and the arguments.
7. `ParseParameters` function is called that separates the script path and rest of the command line arguments. It is used to extract the values of the `/u` and `/p` arguments. To separate the script path from the rest of the command line, the `ParseParameters` function uses the `Split` method. in VBScript (`Split` function is covered earlier in the "VBScript Built-in Functions" section of this chapter)
8. Displays the values as `User1`, `Password1`

Converting VBS Script to an HTA

You can convert your VBScript scripts into HTA script by either simply copying and pasting the code from VBScript to an HTA or by renaming your existing `.VBS` extension to `.HTA` in VBScript script. However, before you copy the VBScript code and paste it into an HTA, you must consider the following:

1. The VBScript code must be placed within the `<Script>…</Script>` tags; only the code within these tags is considered script code.
2. The language for the `<Script>` tag is set as VBS or VBScript shown as follows:

   ```
   <script language="VBScript">
   ```

   or

   ```
   <script language="VBS">
   ```

   By default the script language is set to Jscript.
3. Replace each `Wscript.Echo` statement with `Document.Write` statement. Since the `Wscript.Echo` is exposed by WSH as a native WSH object (that is, you do not explicitly create the object using the `CreateObject` or the `GetObject` methods) and the HTAs are not run with Wscript or Cscript shell, this method is unavailable in an HTA script.

All methods and properties exposed by WSH and used in the scripts as `Wscript.method` (such as `Wscript.Echo`) or `Wscript.Property` (such as `Wscipt.FullName`) are unavailable in HTA scripts. In other words, any method or property that begins with the keyword `WScript` is unavailable in HTAs. However, do not confuse this with the WSH objects (such as `Wscript.Shell`, `Wscript.Network`, `WshController`.,..) that you use in your VBS scripts. These can still be used in the HTAs as they are considered as external objects.

For example, to convert the `UpTime.vbs` VBScript script, you can do the following:

1. Create a new text file with `.hta` extension. (For example, `UpTime.hta`)
2. Open the HTA text file and type the following

```
<script language="VBScript">
```

3. Type (or copy and paste) the code from `UpTime.vbs` into `UpTime.hta` after the `<Script>` tag as shown below:

```
<Script language="VBScript">
Dim StartDate, EndDate, DateTime
Dim objWMI, colEventLog, item
EndDate = Now()
' Create a new datetime object
Set dateTime = CreateObject("WbemScripting.SWbemDateTime")
Set objWMI = GetObject("Winmgmts:")
Set colEventLog = _
       objWMI.ExecQuery( _
                   "Select TimeGenerated from win32_NTLogEvent" & _
                               " where LogFile = 'System' and " & _
                               "EventCode = 6005")
For each item in colEventLog
    DateTime.Value = item.TimeGenerated
    StartDate = DateTime.GetVarDate
    Exit For
Next
    Call UpTime(cDate(StartDate),EndDate)
     Set objWMI = nothing
     Set colEventLog = nothing
      'Calculate and display the computer up time
Sub UpTime(StartDate,EndDate)
    LapsedDays = DateDiff("d",StartDate,Enddate)
    Document.write "The computer has been up for " & _
LapsedDays & " days"
End Sub
```

4. Type `</Script>` tag as the last line in the HTA as shown below:

```
<Script language="VBScript">
Dim StartDate
...
...
End Sub
</Script>
```

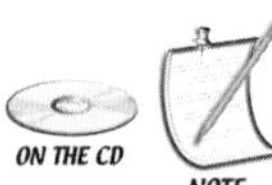

`UpTime.vbs` is available on the CD-ROM at Scripts\Chapter02. You can copy and paste the code from this script to the HTA instead of typing the code.

5. Replace the `Wscript.Echo` with `Document.Write` in the following line:

```
Document.write "The computer has been up for " & LapsedDays & " days"
```

6. Save the text file
7. Double-click the HTA to run it.

Simple scripts like this are easy to convert from VBScript to HTA. However, a complicated script may require additional changes (such as writing code to parse the command line arguments) that may force you to write a lot more code than you have written to create the VBScript script. Nevertheless, where you need your scripts to interact with the users, the GUI functionality of the HTAs makes them more desirable than VBScript scripts.

VBSCRIPT RUNTIME OBJECTS

VBScript runtime objects provide three important functionalities that neither VBScript nor WSH provide natively. For example, both VBScript and WSH cannot be used to manage Windows files and folders, or provide dictionary-type encrypt files.

FileSystemObject

The `FileSystemObject` provides objects that you can use in your script to create text files, create files and folders, delete files and folders, and get information on drives, folders and files of the Windows file system. Table 2.21 lists the objects of the `FileSystemObject`.

TABLE 2.21 `FileSystemObject` Objects

Object	Description
`FileSystemObject`	Contains methods and properties that can be used to, in general, manipulate files and folders. For example, the `FileExists` method can be used to check if a file exists before opening it for reading.
`Drive`	Provides methods and properties that can be used to retrieve information on physical and logical drives on the system.
`File`	Provides methods and properties that can be used to query information on files (such as file name, date created etc.) and create, delete or move files.
`Folder`	Provides methods and properties that can be used to query information on folders (such as folder name, date created, etc.) and create, delete, or move folders.
`TextStream`	Provides methods and properties that can be used to read or write to the text files.

`FileSystemObject` Object

The `FileSystemObject` object is the parent object to the rest of the objects (`Drive`, `File`, `Folder`, and `TextStream`). The `FileSystemObject` object can be created as follows:

```
Set object = CreateObject("Scripting.FileSystemObject")
```

The `object` is the variable name that will store the newly created object and `"Scripting.FileSystemObject"` is the unique identifier of the `FileSystemObject` object. The `FileSystemObject` object has no properties and provides the following methods:

`FileExists:` The `FileExists` method takes a file path (including the file name) as an argument, verifies if the file exists and returns a `Boolean` value; `True` if the file exists and `False` if the file does not exist. The following example determines if the script file exists in the specified path. It displays the file exists message if the `FileExists` method returns a `True` value, otherwise it displays the `file not found` message:

```
Dim objFs
CONST FILE_PATH = "C:\Scripts\FileExists.vbs"
Set objFs = CreateObject("Scripting.FileSystemObject")
If objFs.FileExists(FILE_PATH) then
        Wscript.Echo FILE_PATH & " file exists"
Else
        Wscript.Echo FILE_PATH & " file not found"
End If
Set objFs = nothing
```

`FolderExists:` The `FolderExists` method takes a folder path (including the folder name) as an argument, verifies if the folder exists and returns a `Boolean` value; `True` if the folder exists, and `False` if the folder does not exist. In the following example, the script determines if C:\Scripts folder exists and accordingly displays the `folder exists` or the `folder not found` message:

```
Dim objFs
CONST FOLDER_PATH = "C:\Scripts"
Set objFs = CreateObject("Scripting.FileSystemObject")
If objFs.FolderExists(FOLDER_PATH) then
        Wscript.Echo FOLDER_PATH & " folder exists"
    Else
            Wscript.Echo FOLDER_PATH & " folder not found"
    End If
    Set objFs = nothing
```

`DriveExists:` The `DriveExists` method takes a drive name as an argument, verifies if the drive exists and returns a `Boolean` value; `True` if the drive exists and `False` if the drive does not exist. The following script determines if the C drive exists on the system and displays the drive `exists` or the drive `does not exist` message based on the `True` or the `False` value returned by the `DriveExists` method:

```
Dim objFs
CONST DRIVE = "C"
Set objFs = CreateObject("Scripting.FileSystemObject")
If objFs.DriveExists(DRIVE) then
         Wscript.Echo DRIVE & " exists"
Else
         Wscript.Echo DRIVE & " does not exist"
End If
Set objFs = nothing
```

`BuildPath:` The `BuildPath` method can be used to append a folder name to an existing path. It takes the path and a name (that you want to append to the existing path) as the argument and returns the new path as the string value, as shown in the following example:

```
Dim objFs
CONST EXISTING_PATH = "C:\Scripts"
Set objFs = CreateObject("Scripting.FileSystemObject")
  Wscript.Echo objFs.BuildPath( _
                               EXISTING_PATH, _
                               "Registry Scripts")
Set objFs = nothing
```

The `BuildPath` method returns `C:\Scripts\Registry Scripts` string value. The `BuildPath` method only builds the path from the strings passed as the parameter; it does not validate that the path exists; to check if the path exists, you can use the `FolderExists` method (covered earlier in this section).

`GetAbsolutePathName:` `GetAbsolutePathName` method can be used to get the complete and unambiguous path from the root of the drive for the specified path. It takes path specification (such as `GetAbsolutePathName.vbs`) as an argument. It returns the complete path from the specification. For instance, the following example gets the absolute path to the Chapter02 folder.

```
Dim objFs
 CONST FILE_PATH = "GetAbsolutePathName.vbs"
Set objFs = CreateObject("Scripting.FileSystemObject")
 Wscript.Echo objFs.GetAbsolutePathName(FILE_PATH)
Set objFs = nothing
```

The script, when executed returns `S:\Scripts\Chapter02\AbsolutePathName .vbs` as the absolute path.

`GetBaseName:` The `GetBaseName` method takes the file path (including the name of the file) and returns the name of the file minus the file extension. In the following example, the `GetBaseName` method returns `GetBaseName` string value, the base name of the `GetBaseName.vbs` file name:

```
Dim objFs
CONST FILE_PATH = "S:\Scripts\Chapter02\GetBaseName.vbs"
 Set objFs = CreateObject("Scripting.FileSystemObject")
   Wscript.Echo objFs.GetBaseName(FILE_PATH)
Set objFs = nothing
```

GetDriveName: The GetDriveName method can be used to retrieve the name of the drive from a given path. For example, the following code when executed will return S: as the drive name:

```
Dim objFs
CONST FILE_PATH = "S:\Scripts\Chapter02\GetBaseName.vbs"
    Set objFs = CreateObject("Scripting.FileSystemObject")
   Wscript.Echo objFs.GetDriveName(FILE_PATH)
Set objFs = nothing
```

GetExtenstionName: While GetBaseName method can be used to retrieve the base name of the file, GetExtensionName method can be used to retrieve the extension name of the file. For example, when the following code is executed it returns vbs as the extension name of the file:

```
Dim objFs
 CONST FILE_PATH = "S:\Scripts\Chapter02\GetBaseName.vbs"
  Set objFs = CreateObject("Scripting.FileSystemObject")
 Wscript.Echo objFs.GetExtensionName(FILE_PATH)
Set objFs = nothing
```

GetParentFolderName: The GetParentFolderName method can be used to retrieve the name of the parent folder of a file or a folder. The GetParentFolderName takes a path as an argument and returns the path to the parent folder as a string value. For example, when the following code is executed it returns the parent folder of the GetParentFolderName.vbs script:

```
Dim objFs
 sPath = Wscript.ScriptFullName
   Set objFs = CreateObject("Scripting.FileSystemObject")
  Wscript.Echo objFs.GetParentFolderName(sPath)
Set objFs = nothing
```

GetTempName: The GetTempName method returns a randomly generated temporary folder or a file name. It does not take any arguments. The following example illustrates how to get a temporary name as string:

```
Dim objFs
   Set objFs = CreateObject("Scripting.FileSystemObject")
  sTempPath = objFs.GetTempName
 Wscript.Echo sTempPath
Set objFs = nothing
```

`GetTempName` function returns a temporary name that you can use to create a file or a folder. The returned name has the .tmp extension.

`GetSpecialFolder:` The `GetSpecialFolder` method returns an object of a Windows special folder, such as the Windows folder (where the Windows operating system files are located) or the System folder (where the system files for the operating system are located).

The `GetSpecialFolder` method takes special folder constant values as an argument. Table 2.22 lists the constants and their corresponding values.

TABLE 2.22 Constants for the `GetSpecialFolder` Object

Constant	Value	Description
`WindowsFolder`	0	Path to the Windows files (for example, C:\windows). Same as in `%windir%` environment variable.
`SystemFolder`	1	Path to the system files of the windows operating system (for example, C:\windows\system32).
`TempFolder`	2	Path to the folder that holds the temporary files (for example, C:\temp). Same as in `%tmp%` environment variable.

When calling the `GetSpecialFolder` method, you pass one of the constants (seen in Table 2.22), as shown in the following example:

```
CONST WindowsFolder = 0
CONST SystemFolder = 1
CONST TempFolder = 2
Dim objFs
Set objFs = CreateObject("Scripting.FileSystemObject")
sWindowsFolder = objFs.GetSpecialFolder(WindowsFolder)
sSystemFolder = objFs.GetSpecialFolder(SystemFolder)
sTempFolder = objFs.GetSpecialFolder(TempFolder)
Wscript.Echo "Windows Folder: " & _
                                sWindowsFolder & _
                                      vbNewLine & _
                                   "System Folder: " & _
                                      sSystemFolder & _
                                             vbNewLine & _
                                         "Temp Folder: " & _
                                                sTempFolder

Set objFs = nothing
```

`CreateFolder:` The `CreateFolder` method can be used to create a new folder. It takes a string as the name of the folder to create and returns a folder object of the newly created folder, as shown in the following example:

```
Dim objFs
  sFolderPath = "C:\Scripts"
   Set objFs = createobject("scripting.filesystemobject")
    Set objFolder = objFs.CreateFolder(sFolderPath)
        Wscript.Echo objFolder.Path & _
                                   " Created at: " & _
                                     objFolder.DateCreated
      Set objFolder = nothing
    Set objFs = nothing
```

`CreateTextFile`: The `CreateTextFile` method creates a new text file. It takes `Filename` as a required argument and, `Overwrite` and `Unicode` as optional parameters. The `CreateTextFile` method creates the text file by the name passed as the `Filename` argument. It overwrites a file with the name passed as the `Filename` if the `Overwrite` argument is set to `True`. By default the `CreateTextFile` method creates the text file as ASCII that can be overridden, to create a Unicode file, by passing a `True` value as the `Unicode` argument. The following code illustrates the use of the `CreateTextFile` method:

```
Dim objFs
 CONST FOLDER_PATH = "C:\Windows"
  CONST OUT_FILE_NAME = "Executables.txt"
  Set objFs = CreateObject("Scripting.FileSystemObject")
  Set objFile = objFs.CreateTextFile(OUT_FILE_NAME,True)
   Set objFolder = objFs.GetFolder(FOLDER_PATH)
    Set objFiles = objFolder.Files
    if objFiles.Count > 0 then
     For each File in objFiles
      if LCase(objFs.GetExtensionName(File.Path)) = _
                                                     "exe" then
               objFile.Writeline File.Path _
                                   & ", " & File.DateCreated
        end if
       Next
     else
       objFile.Writeline "No files found in " & _
                                                    Folder_Path
     end if
          objFile.Close
       Set objFile = nothing
     Set objFiles = nothing
    Set objFolder = nothing
  Set objFs = nothing
Wscript.Echo "All Done!"
```

This script is saved on the CD-ROM as `CreateNewTextFile.vbs` in the Scripts\Chapter02 folder.

`OpenTextFile`: While the `CreateTextFile` method creates a new file, the `OpenTextFile` method opens an existing text file for reading or appending. The `OpenTextFile` method has the following syntax:

```
OpenTextFile(Filename[, IOMode[, Create[, Format]]])
```

where `Filename` is the name of the file to open; `IOMode` is the input output mode (`Read`, `Write`, and `Append` mode), the `Create` argument specifies whether the method should create a new file if the file (specified in the `Filename` argument) does not exist, and the `Format` argument specifies the format (`Unicode`, `ASCII`, or whatever is the system default) the file should be opened in.

For example, the following code demonstrates how to append logging information to a text file. The script opens the text file, for appending, if it already exists or creates a new file, if the file does not exist:

```
Dim objFs
  CONST FOR_READ = 1
  CONST FOR_WRITE = 2
  CONST FOR_APPEND = 8
  CONST FILE_NAME = "StartStop.log"
   Set objFs = CreateObject("Scripting.FileSystemObject")
     Set objFile = objFs.OpenTextFile(FILE_NAME, _
                                       FOR_APPEND, True)
       objFile.Writeline "Log Started at: " & now
         Wscript.Sleep 5000
       objFile.WriteLine "Log Ended at: " & now
    Set objFile = nothing
   Set objFs = nothing
```

The `OpenTextFile` method opens a text file only if there is some content in the text file. It displays `Input past end of file` error (as shown in Figure 2.50) if the file does not contain any content.

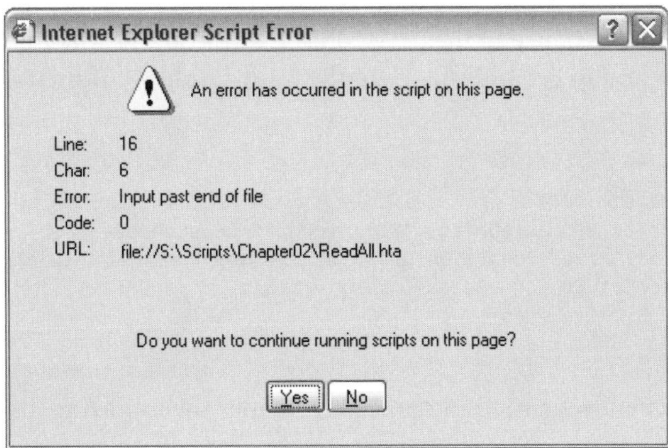

FIGURE 2.50 `Input past end of file` error.

Therefore, it is best to check if the size of the text file is greater than zero (0) before opening the file using the `OpenTextFile` method, as shown in the following example:

```
Dim objFs
  CONST FOR_READ = 1
  CONST FOR_WRITE = 2
  CONST FOR_APPEND = 8
  CONST FILE_NAME = "StartStop.log"
   Set objFs = CreateObject("Scripting.FileSystemObject")
   If objFs.GetFile(FILE_NAME).Size > 0 then
    Set objFile = objFs.OpenTextFile(FILE_NAME, _
                                    FOR_READ)
     Wscript.Echo objFile.ReadAll
   Else
     Wscript.Echo "The file does not contain any content"
   End If
    Set objFile = nothing
   Set objFs = nothing
```

There are other methods (such as `copyfile`, `deletefile`, and `movefile`) that are exposed as the part of the `FileSystemObject` object. Since these objects are also exposed as part of the `FileSystemObject` object's sub objects (the `Drive`, `File`, and `Folder` objects), we will discuss them when we discuss the sub objects.

Drive Object

The `Drive` object exposes methods and properties that you can use in your scripts to retrieve information about the drives attached to a system. The `Drive` object is a sub object of the `FileSystemObject` object. Therefore, there is no unique identifier that you can use to create a `Drive` object using the `CreateObject` or the `GetObject` method as you create the `FileSystemObject`. Instead you use the `GetDrive` method of the `FileSystemObject` to get an instance of the `Drive` object. For example, the following code calls the `GetDrive` method to get an instance of the `C:` drive object. It then displays the total size of the drive.

```
Dim objFs
 sDriveName = "C:"
   Set objFs = CreateObject("Scripting.FileSystemObject")
    Set objDrive = objFs.GetDrive(sDriveName)
      Wscript.Echo round(objDrive.TotalSize / (1024^2)), "MB"
    Set objDrive = nothing
Set objFs = nothing
```

The `Drive` object has no methods; it provides the following properties, however:

`AvailableSpace:` The `AvailableSpace` property returns space available to the user on a specified drive. It returns an integer value in bytes that can be converted to kilobytes or megabytes, as shown in the following example:

```
Dim objFs
 sDriveName = "C:"
   Set objFs = CreateObject("Scripting.FileSystemObject")
    Set objDrive = objFs.GetDrive(sDriveName)
      Wscript.Echo _
          round(objDrive.AvailableSpace / (1024^2)), "MB"
    Set objDrive = nothing
Set objFs z= nothing
```

`DriveLetter:` The `DriveLetter` property returns the drive letter that represents the drive. The following example illustrates the use of the `DriveLetter` property:

```
Dim objFs
 sDriveName = "C:\"
   Set objFs = CreateObject("Scripting.FileSystemObject")
    Set objDrive = objFs.GetDrive(sDriveName)
      Wscript.Echo objDrive.DriveLetter
    Set objDrive = nothing
Set objFs = nothing
```

`DriveType:` The `DriveType` property returns the type of the specified drive as a numeric value. Table 2.23 lists the types returned by the property:

TABLE 2.23 Drive Types Returned by the `DriveType` Property

Value	Drive Type
0	Unknown
1	Removable
2	Fixed
3	Network
4	CD-ROM
5	RAM

The following example illustrates how to list the types of drives on a system:

```
On Error Resume Next
Dim objFs
  Set objFs = CreateObject("Scripting.FileSystemObject")
    For i = Asc("a") to Asc("z")
      Set objDrive = objFs.GetDrive(Chr(i) & ":")
       if objDrive.IsReady then
            Wscript.Echo Chr(i) & ":", "-", _
                       GetDriveType(objDrive.DriveType)
       end if
         Set objDrive = nothing
```

```
    next
   Set objFs = nothing

Function GetDriveType(iDriveType)
  if iDriveType = "" then exit function
   Select Case iDriveType
     Case 1 : rValue = "Removable"
     Case 2 : rValue = "Fixed"
     Case 3 : rValue = "Network"
     Case 4 : rValue = "Cd-Rom"
     Case 5 : rValue = "Ram"
       Case else : rValue = "UnKnown"
   End Select
  GetDriveType = rValue
End Function
```

`FileSystem:` The `FileSystem` property returns the type of file system in use for the specified drive. For example, the following script displays the type of file system of the C:\ drive:

```
Dim objFs
 sDriveName = "C:\"
   Set objFs = CreateObject("Scripting.FileSystemObject")
    Set objDrive = objFs.GetDrive(sDriveName)
      Wscript.Echo objDrive.FileSystem
    Set objDrive = nothing
Set objFs = nothing
```

`FreeSpace:` The `FreeSpace` property returns the amount of free space available to the user in the specified drive or the network share. It returns the value in bytes that you can convert to megabytes, as shown in the following example:

```
Dim objFs
 sDriveName = "C:"
   Set objFs = CreateObject("Scripting.FileSystemObject")
    Set objDrive = objFs.GetDrive(sDriveName)
      Wscript.Echo _
           round(objDrive.FreeSpace / (1024^2)), "MB"
    Set objDrive = nothing
Set objFs = nothing
```

NOTE

Generally, `FreeSpace` property will return the same value as the `AvailableSpace` property. It will list a different value only if the system supports quota.

`IsReady:` The `IsReady` property returns a `Boolean` value (`True` or `False`) that can be used to determine if the drive is ready. For example, a CD-ROM drive with no media inserted into the drive is considered as not ready as the following script illustrates:

```
Dim objFs
 sDriveName = "D:"
   Set objFs = CreateObject("Scripting.FileSystemObject")
    Set objDrive = objFs.GetDrive(sDriveName)
     If objDrive.isReady then
       Wscript.Echo _
           round(objDrive.FreeSpace / (1024^2)), "MB"
     End If
    Set objDrive = nothing
Set objFs = nothing
```

`Path:` The `Path` property can be used to retrieve the path of the specified drive. For example, the following script displays the drive path of the C drive name:

```
Dim objFs
 sDriveName = "C"
   Set objFs = CreateObject("Scripting.FileSystemObject")
    Set objDrive = objFs.GetDrive(sDriveName)
      Wscript.Echo Ucase(objDrive.Path)
    Set objDrive = nothing
Set objFs = nothing
```

The `Path` property is a common property for `Drive`, `File`, and `Folder` objects that can be used to retrieve the path to a `file`, `folder` or a `drive`.

`SerialNumber:` The `SerialNumber` property can be used to retrieve the decimal serial number used to uniquely identify the disk volume. The `SerialNumber` property can be used, as shown in the following example:

```
Dim objFs
 sDriveName = "C:"
  Set objFs = CreateObject("Scripting.FileSystemObject")
    Set objDrive = objFs.GetDrive(sDriveName)
      Wscript.Echo objDrive.SerialNumber
    Set objDrive = nothing
Set objFs = nothing
```

`ShareName:` The `ShareName` property retrieves the share name of a specified drive. It returns a zero-length string if the drive is not shared. The following script when executed will display the share name of the C: drive:

```
Dim objFs
 sDriveName = "C:"
  Set objFs = CreateObject("Scripting.FileSystemObject")
    Set objDrive = objFs.GetDrive(sDriveName)
      sShareName = objDrive.ShareName
      If Len(sShareName) > 0 then
       Wscript.Echo UCase(sShareName)
```

```
      Else
       Wscript.Echo sDriveName & " drive is not  shared"
      End if
    Set objDrive = nothing
Set objFs = nothing
```

`TotalSize:` The `TotalSize` property returns the total space of a drive or a network share. It returns the value in bytes. To display the returned value in megabytes, you can divide the bytes with $(1024)^2$ (that is, 1024*1024), as shown in the following example:

```
On Error Resume Next
Dim objFs
  Set objFs = CreateObject("Scripting.FileSystemObject")
    For i = Asc("a") to Asc("z")
      Set objDrive = objFs.GetDrive(Chr(i) & ":")
       if objDrive.IsReady then
            Wscript.Echo Chr(i) & ":", "(" & _
                Round(objDrive.TotalSize / (1024^2)), _
                  "MB)"
       end if
         Set objDrive = nothing
    next
   Set objFs = nothing
```

`VolumeName:` The `VolumeName` property retrieves the volume name of a specified drive. It returns a zero-length string if a drive does not have a volume name. The following script when executed will display the volume names of each of the drives that exist on the local system (including the mapped network drives):

```
On Error Resume Next
Dim objFs
  Set objFs = CreateObject("Scripting.FileSystemObject")
    For i = Asc("a") to Asc("z")
      Set objDrive = objFs.GetDrive(Chr(i) & ":")
       if objDrive.IsReady then
            Wscript.Echo Chr(i) & ":", "(" & _
                                    objDrive.VolumeName & ")"
       end if
         Set objDrive = nothing
    next
   Set objFs = nothing
```

`RootFolder:` The `RootFolder` property returns a folder object representing the root folder of a specified drive. The following example illustrates the use of the `RootFolder` property:

```
On Error Resume Next
Dim objFs
  Set objFs = CreateObject("Scripting.FileSystemObject")
    For i = Asc("a") to Asc("z")
      Set objDrive = objFs.GetDrive(Chr(i) & ":")
       if objDrive.IsReady then
            set objFolder = objDrive.RootFolder
                Wscript.Echo objFolder.Path
            Set objFolder = nothing
       end if
         Set objDrive = nothing
    next
   Set objFs = nothing
```

File and Folder Objects

Both the `File` and the `Folder` objects of the `FileSystemObject` object exposes methods that can be used to create, delete, or move a file or a folder. While the `File` object provides the information on files, the `Folder` object provides information regarding the folders. A property, for example `DateCreated` property, can be used to get information on both the folders and files.

Both the `File` and the `Folder` objects, like the `Drive` object, are also sub objects of the `FileSystemObject` object. Therefore, there is no unique identifier that you can use to create the `File` or the `Folder` object.

You use the `GetFolder` method of the `FileSystemObject` to get an instance of the `Folder` object. For example, the code in Listing 2.34 calls the `GetFolder` method to get an instance of the `C:\Documents and Settings` folder object. It then displays the short name (in `8.3` naming format) of the folder.

LISTING 2.34 Retrieving `ShortName` Property of the `Folder` Object

```
Dim objFs
 CONST FOLDER_PATH = "C:\Documents and Settings"
   Set objFs = CreateObject("Scripting.FileSystemObject")
    Set objItem = objFs.GetFolder(FOLDER_PATH)
      Wscript.Echo objItem.ShortName
    Set objItem = nothing
Set objFs = nothing
```

Like the `GetFolder` method is used to get an instance of the `Folder` object, the `GetFile` method is used to get an instance of the `File` object. For example, the code in Listing 2.35 calls the `GetFile` method to get an instance of a `File` object. It then displays the short name (using the same `ShortName` property shown in Listing 2.35) of the file.

LISTING 2.35 Retrieving `ShortName` Property of the *File* Object

```
Dim objFs
 CONST FILE_PATH = "C:\windows\WINHLP32.EXE"
   Set objFs = CreateObject("Scripting.FileSystemObject")
    Set objItem = objFs.GetFile(FILE_PATH)
      Wscript.Echo objItem.ShortName
    Set objItem = nothing
Set objFs = nothing
```

Figure 2.51 shows the differences in the code between Listing 2.34 and Listing 2.35.

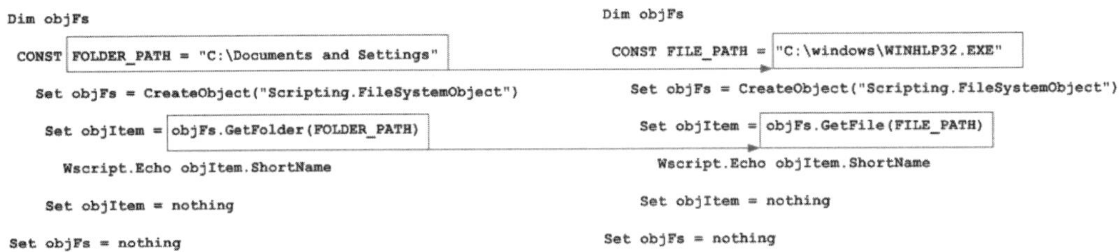

FIGURE 2.51 Differences between the code in Listing 2.34 and Listing 2.35.

The `File` and the `Folder` objects support the following methods:

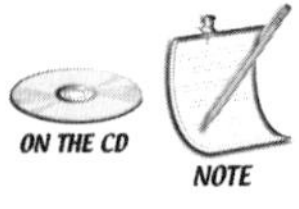

NOTE

The following examples are on only the `Folder` object. However, in Scripts\Chapter02 folder on the CD-ROM you will find examples for the `Folder` and the `File` object for the common methods and properties. The `Folder` examples are saved as `Folder<action>.vbs` (e.g., `FolderCopy.vbs`) and the `File` examples are saved as `File<action>.vbs` (e.g., `FileCopy.vbs`)

`Copy:` The `Copy` method can be used to make a copy of a specified folder. When the method is called it copies the folder and all of its contents from one specified location to the other specified location. The `Copy` method has the following syntax:

```
Object.Copy ( destination [, overwrite ] )
```

The `Copy` method takes the destination folder as the required parameter and a `Boolean` (`True` or `False`) value as the optional argument. A `True` value will overwrite the existing files and folders (even if they are marked as read-only) and a `False` will not overwrite the existing files or folder. If the optional overwrite value is not passed, the files and folder are overwritten. In the following example the script uses the `Copy` method to make a copy of C:\Temp folder:

```
Dim objFs
 sFromFolderPath = "C:\temp"
 sToFolderPath = "C:\Temp2"
   Set objFs = CreateObject("Scripting.FileSystemObject")
    Set objItem = objFs.GetFolder(sFromFolderPath)
      Result = objItem.Copy (sToFolderPath)
        if Result = 0 then
          Wscript.Echo "Folder copy completed successfully"
        else
         Wscript.Echo "Unable to copy folder"
        end if
    Set objItem = nothing
Set objFs = nothing
```

`Delete:` The `Delete` method can be used to delete an existing folder. The `Delete` method takes an optional `Boolean` value that can be used to force delete the folder. Passing a `True` value will force delete the folder and files (all files and subolders including the ones marked as read-only). A `False` value will not delete the read-only files and folders. By default the `Delete` method will not delete the files and folders marked as read-only, as in the following example:

```
On Error Resume Next
Dim objFs
 sFolderPath = "C:\temp2"
  Set objFs = CreateObject("Scripting.FileSystemObject")
    Set objItem = objFs.GetFolder(sFolderPath)
      objItem.Delete
        if Err = 0 then
          Wscript.Echo sFolderPath & _
                       " deleted successfully"
        else
          Wscript.Echo "Error deleting " & _
                        sFolderPath, Err.Description
        end if
    Set objItem = nothing
Set objFs = nothing
```

`Move:` The `Move` method can be used to move the folder from one location to another. When the `Move` method is called it moves the folder and all of its contents to the specified location. It takes the destination path as the required argument. The following example illustrates its use:

```
Dim objFs
 sFromFolderPath = "C:\temp"
 sToFolderPath = "C:\Temp2"
   Set objFs = CreateObject("Scripting.FileSystemObject")
    Set objItem = objFs.GetFolder(sFromFolderPath)
      Result = objItem.Move (sToFolderPath)
        if Result = 0 then
```

```
            Wscript.Echo "Folder moved successfully"
          else
            Wscript.Echo "Unable to move folder"
          end if
      Set objItem = nothing
  Set objFs = nothing
```

The `Folder` and `File` objects also provide properties that can be used to get information about the folder, such as `DateCreated`, `DateLastModified`, `DateLastAccessed`, `IsRootFolder`, `Drive`, `Name`, `Path`, `ParentFolder`, `ShortName`, `ShortPath`, `Size`, and `Attributes`, as listed in Table 2.24.

TABLE 2.24 Properties of the `Folder` and `File` Objects

`DateCreated`	The `DateCreated` property returns the date and time the specified folder was created.
	Example:
	`Dim objFs`
	` sFolderPath = "C:\temp"`
	`   Set objFs =  CreateObject("Scripting.`
	`   FileSystemObject")`
	`    Set objFolder = objFs.GetFolder(sFolderPath)`
	`      Wscript.Echo objFolder.DateCreated`
	`    Set objFolder = nothing`
	`Set objFs = nothing`

`DateLastModified`	The `DateLastModified` property returns the date and time the specified folder was last modified.
	Example:
	`Dim objFs`
	` sFolderPath = "C:\temp"`
	`   Set objFs = CreateObject("Scripting.`
	`   FileSystemObject")`
	`    Set objFolder = objFs.GetFolder(sFolderPath)`
	`      Wscript.Echo objFolder.DateLastModified`
	`    Set objFolder = nothing`
	`Set objFs = nothing`

`DateLastAccessed`	The `DateLastAccessed` property returns the date and time the specified folder was last accessed.
	Example:
	`Dim objFs`
	` sFolderPath = "C:\temp"`
	`   Set objFs = CreateObject("Scripting.`
	`   FileSystemObject")`
	`    Set objFolder = objFs.GetFolder(sFolderPath)`
	`      Wscript.Echo objFolder.DateLastAccessed`
	`    Set objFolder = nothing`
	`Set objFs = nothing` →

`Drive`	The `Drive` property returns the drive letter of the drive on which the specified folder resides. For example, the following code when executed will return `C:` as the C:\Temp folder resides on the C: drive:
	Example:
	`Dim objFs`
	` sFolderPath = "C:\temp"`
	`  Set objFs = CreateObject("Scripting.`
	`  FileSystemObject")`
	`    Set objFolder = objFs.GetFolder(sFolderPath)`
	`      Wscript.Echo objFolder.Drive`
	`    Set objFolder = nothing`
	`Set objFs = nothing`

`Name`	The `Name` property returns the name of the specified folder.
	Example:
	`Dim objFs`
	` sFolderPath = "C:\temp"`
	`  Set objFs = CreateObject("Scripting.`
	`FileSystemObject")`
	`    Set objFolder = objFs.GetFolder(sFolderPath)`
	`      Wscript.Echo objFolder.Name`
	`    Set objFolder = nothing`
	`Set objFs = nothing`

`Path`	The `Path` property returns the path to the specified folder.
	Example:
	`Dim objFs`
	` sFolderPath = "C:\Documents and Settings"`
	`  Set objFs = CreateObject("Scripting.`
	`  FileSystemObject")`
	`    Set objFolder = objFs.GetFolder(sFolderPath)`
	`      Wscript.Echo objFolder.Path`
	`    Set objFolder = nothing`
	`Set objFs = nothing`

`ParentFolder`	The `ParentFolder` property returns the `Folder` object of the parent folder of the specified folder or file. For example, the following code when executed will return the name of the parent folder by retrieving the `Name` property of the parent folder of s:\Scripts\Chapter02 folder:
	Example:
	`Dim objFs`
	` sFolderPath = "s:\Scripts\Chapter02"`
	`  Set objFs = CreateObject("Scripting.`
	`  FileSystemObject")`
	`   Set objFolder = objFs.GetFolder(sFolderPath)`
	`    Set objParentFolder = objFolder.ParentFolder`
	`      Wscript.Echo objParentFolder.Name` →

```
        Set objParentFolder = nothing
      Set objFolder = nothing
  Set objFs = nothing
```

`ShortName`	The `ShortName` property returns the name of the folder in 8.3 naming convention.
	Example:
	`Dim objFs`
	` CONST FOLDER_PATH = "C:\Documents and Settings"`
	`   Set objFs = CreateObject("Scripting.`
	`   FileSystemObject")`
	`    Set objFolder = objFs.GetFolder(FOLDER_PATH)`
	`      Wscript.Echo objFolder.ShortName`
	`    Set objFolder = nothing`
	`Set objFs = nothing`

`ShortPath`	The `ShortPath` property returns the name of the folder in 8.3 naming convention.
	Example:
	`Dim objFs`
	` CONST FOLDER_PATH = "C:\Documents and Settings"`
	`   Set objFs =`
	`CreateObject("Scripting.FileSystemObject")`
	`    Set objFolder = objFs.GetFolder(FOLDER_PATH)`
	`      Wscript.Echo objFolder.ShortPath`
	`    Set objFolder = nothing`
	`Set objFs = nothing`

`Size`	The `Size` property returns the current size of the specified folder. The size is the total size of all the files and folders in the specified folder.
	Example:
	`Dim objFs`
	` CONST FOLDER_PATH = "C:\Documents and Settings"`
	`   Set objFs =`
	`CreateObject("Scripting.FileSystemObject")`
	`    Set objFolder = objFs.GetFolder(FOLDER_PATH)`
	`      Wscript.Echo _`
	`         Round(objFolder.Size / (1024^2)), "MB"`
	`    Set objFolder = nothing`
	`Set objFs = nothing`

`Attributes`	The `Attributes` property, unlike the other properties is a read/write property (that is, you can both retrieve and set the attributes of a folder). The `Attributes` property when queried returns the attributes (such as `ReadOnly`, `Hidden`, `System`, and so on) of the specified folder. The `Attributes` property has the following syntax: →

`object.Attributes [= newattributes]`	The `object` is the `Folder` object and the `newattributes` argument is the set of attributes that you want to set. The `newattributes` argument can have any of the following values or any logical combination of the following values:

Constant	Bit Value	Description
Normal	0	Normal File. No attributes are set.
ReadOnly	1	ReadOnly file.
Hidden	2	Hidden file.
System	4	System file.
Volume	8	Disk drive volume label.
Directory	16	Folder or a Directory.
Archive	32	File has changed since the last backup.
Alias	64	Link or Shortcut.
Compressed	128 (in Windows XP, you may see this bit as 2048)	Compressed file.

The following example makes all the folders in c:\temp folder as read-only.

Example:

```
Dim objFs
 CONST FOLDER_PATH = "C:\temp"
   Set objFs =
CreateObject("Scripting.FileSystemObject")
    Set objFolder = objFs.GetFolder(FOLDER_PATH)
      Set Folders = objFolder.subFolders
 For each Folder in Folders
   set objSubFolder = objFs.GetFolder(Folder.Path)
   if objSubFolder.Attributes and 1 then
          'Do nothing. The file is already read only
   else
    objSubFolder.Attributes = _
                        objSubFolder.Attributes + 1
   end if
        Set objSubFolder = nothing
        Next
      Set Folders = nothing
    Set objFolder = nothing
Set objFs = nothing
```

In addition to the properties listed in Table 2.24, the `Folder` object also provides properties listing in Table 2.25.

TABLE 2.25 Properties of the `Folder` Object

Method	Description

`Files`	The `Files` property returns the collection of all the files in the specified folder. You can iterate through the collection to get the properties of the files in the collection. For example, the following code when executed will echo the total number of files in the collection returned by the `Files` property, and then iterate through the collection to echo the file name and the size of each file in the C:\temp folder.
	Example:
	`Dim objFs`
	`CONST FOLDER_PATH = "C:\temp"`
	`  Set objFs = CreateObject("Scripting.FileSystemObject")`
	`   Set objFolder = objFs.GetFolder(FOLDER_PATH)`
	`    Wscript.Echo objFolder.Files.Count`
	`     For each File in objFolder.Files`
	`       Wscript.Echo File.Name, _`
	`     Round(File.Size / (1024^2)), "MB"`
	`     next`
	`   Set objFolder = nothing`
	`Set objFs = nothing`

`SubFolders`	The `SubFolders` property returns the collection of subfolders within the specified folder. You can iterate through the collection to get the properties of the subfolder in the collection. For example the following code when executed will echo the total number of subfolders in the collection returned by the `SubFolders` property, and then iterate through the collection to echo the name and the date created of each folder in the C:\Windows folder.
	Example:
	`Dim objFs`
	`CONST FOLDER_PATH = "C:\temp"`
	`  Set objFs = CreateObject("Scripting.FileSystemObject")`
	`   Set objFolder = objFs.GetFolder(FOLDER_PATH)`
	`    Wscript.Echo objFolder.SubFolders.Count`
	`     For each Folder in objFolder.SubFolders`
	`       Wscript.Echo Folder.Name, _`
	`     Round(Folder.Size / (1024^2)), "MB"`
	`     next`
	`   Set objFolder = nothing`
	`Set objFs = nothing`

`IsRootFolder`	The `IsRootFolder` returns a boolean value which indicates if the specified folder is a root folder or not. A `True` value indicates that it is a root folder and `False` indicates otherwise.

→

Method	Description

	Example:
	`Dim objFs`
	` sFolderPath = "C:\temp"`
	`   Set objFs =`
	`CreateObject("Scripting.FileSystemObject")`
	`    Set objFolder = objFs.GetFolder(sFolderPath)`
	`     if objFolder.IsRootFolder then`
	`      Wscript.Echo sFolderPath, "is a root folder"`
	`     else`

TextStream Object

The `TextStream` object is the most commonly used object of the `FileSystemObject` object as it allows you to work with text files. The `TextStream` object provides methods that you can use in your scripts to read and write to text files. For example, the code in Listing 2.36 creates a new text file and writes the name and size of each of file in the C:\temp folder to the created text file.

LISTING 2.36 Create a Text File and Write the Name and Size of Each File in C:\temp Folder to the Text File

```
Dim objFs
CONST FOLDER_PATH = "C:\temp"
CONST OUT_FILE_NAME = "FileInformation.txt"
 Set objFs = CreateObject("Scripting.FileSystemObject")
   Set objFile = objFs.CreateTextFile(OUT_FILE_NAME)
     Set objFolder = objFs.GetFolder(FOLDER_PATH)
       objFile.WriteLine "Total Files: " & _
                          objFolder.Files.Count
       For each File in objFolder.Files
        objFile.WriteLine File.Name & ", " & _
            Round(File.Size / (1024^2)) & " MB"
       Next
      objFile.Close
    Set objFile = nothing
  Set objFolder = nothing
 Set objFs = nothing
```

The `TextStream` object provides methods to read and write to the files, but it does not provide the methods to create a new text file or open an existing text file. You must use `CreateTextFile` and `OpenTextFile` methods (covered earlier in the chapter) of the `FileSystemObject` object, as shown in Listing 2.36.

The `CreateTextFile` and the `OpenTextFile` methods return the `TextStream` object. Once you have the object, you can read or write to the text files using the following methods and properties of the `TextStream` object:

`ReadAll`: The `ReadAll` method allows you to read all the contents of the opened file at once. It returns the entire content of the text file as a string. The example in Listing 2.37 illustrates how to use the `ReadAll` method:

LISTING 2.37 Code `ReadAll` Method Illustration

```
    <script language="VBS">
Private Sub Window_OnLoad
      FileContent.Disabled = true
End Sub
Sub ReadFile
Dim objFs
CONST FOR_READING = 1
sFilePath = FilePath.Value
   Set objFs = CreateObject("Scripting.FileSystemObject")
    if objFs.FileExists(sFilePath) then
      Set objFile = objFs.OpenTextFile(sFilePath,FOR_READING)
          FileContent.Value = objFile.ReadAll
          FileContent.Disabled = False
          objFile.Close
      Set objFile = nothing
    else
      Document.Write "Unable to open file " & sFilePath
    end if
    Set objFs = nothing
End Sub
</script>
<Body>
      <input type="File" name="FilePath">
      <input type="Button" OnClick="Readfile" value="Get File Content">
      <br>
      <textarea rows="25" cols="85"
                    name="FileContent" value=""></textarea>
</Body>
```

In the example in Listing 2.37, the ReadAll.hta script can be used to open a selected text file and display its contents in the text box, as shown in Figure 2.52.

`Read`: The `Read` method can be used to read a specific number of characters from the file. The `Read` method takes number of characters as an argument and returns the string value. The following example illustrates how to read 10 characters from a given text file:

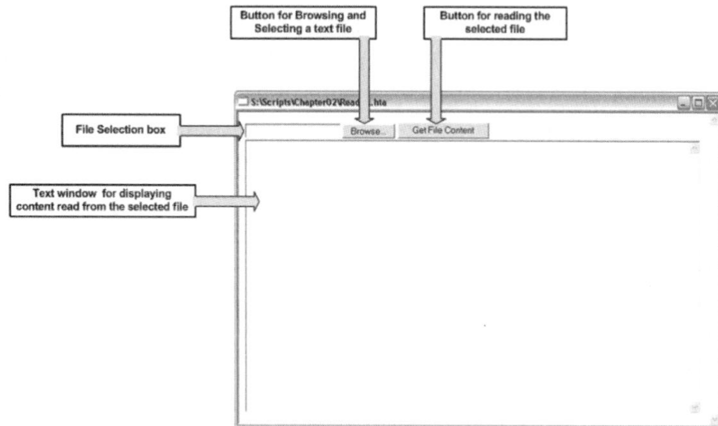

FIGURE 2.52 `ReadAll.hta` script reads the contents of a text file using the `ReadAll` method and displays the contents of the file in a text box.

```
<script language="VBS">
Sub ReadFile
Dim objFs
CONST FOR_READING = 1
sFilePath = FilePath.Value
   Set objFs = CreateObject("Scripting.FileSystemObject")
    if objFs.FileExists(sFilePath) then
        Set objFile = objFs.OpenTextFile(sFilePath,FOR_READING)
          sFileContent = objFile.ReadAll
            if Len(sFileContent) >= 10 then
                  result.innerhtml = objFile.Read(10)
            else
                  result.innerhtml = "There are only " & _
Len(sFileContent) & _
                 " characters in the text file"
        end if
          objFile.Close
        Set objFile = nothing
    else
        result.innerhtml = "Unable to open file " & sFilePath
    end if
End Sub
</script>
<Body>
        <input type="File" name="FilePath">
        <input type="Button" OnClick="Readfile" value="Get File
Content">
        <div id="result">
</Body>
```

NOTE

If the number of characters in the text file is less than the number passed to the `Read` *method (for example, if you pass 10 to the* `Read` *method and the file only contains 5 characters), the script will generate an* `Input past end of file` *error. Therefore, the code in this example checks to see if the total number of characters are equal to or greater than 10 characters before attempting to read the content.*

`ReadLine:` The `ReadLine` method reads an entire line from the text file. For example, the following reads a line of the text file:

```
Dim objFs
CONST FOR_READING = 1
CONST FILE_NAME = "YouCanDeleteThisFile.txt"
 Set objFs = CreateObject("Scripting.FileSystemObject")
   if objFs.FileExists(FILE_NAME) then
        if objFs.GetFile(FILE_NAME).Size > 0 then
          Set objFile = objFs.OpenTextFile(FILE_NAME,FOR_READING)
            Wscript.Echo objFile.ReadLine
          objFile.Close
          Set objFile = nothing
        else
          Wscript.Echo "The " & FILE_NAME & " is empty"
        end if
   else
        Wscript.Echo FILE_NAME, "does not exit"
   end if
 Set objFs = nothing
```

When you run the script it reads only the first file of the text file. To read the next line (or all the content line by line) you must loop through the text file as the example in Listing 2.38 illustrates.

LISTING 2.38 `ReadLineByLine.hta` **Script Demonstrates How to Read Each Line and Display the Lines**

```
    <script language="VBS">
Sub ReadFile
    Dim objFs
    Dim Count
    Count = 1
    CONST FOR_READING = 1
    sFilePath = FilePath.Value
     Set objFs = CreateObject("Scripting.FileSystemObject")
      if objFs.FileExists(sFilePath) then
         if objFs.GetFile(sFilePath).Size > 0 then
          Set objFile = _
             objFs.OpenTextFile(sFilePath,FOR_READING)
           Do while not objFile.AtEndOfStream
             sLine = sLine & "<br>" & _
                        Count & "." & VBTab & _
                                  objFile.ReadLine
```

```
                Count = Count + 1
        loop
              result.innerhtml = sLine
                objFile.Close
             Set objFile = nothing
      else
                    result.innerhtml = "The " & _
                            sFilePath & " is empty"
        end if
  else
          result.innerhtml =  sFilePath & _
                                   " does not exit"
  end if
 Set objFs = nothing
End Sub
</script>
<Body>
    <input type="File" name="FilePath">
        <input type="Button" OnClick="Readfile" value="Get File Content">
        <Div id="result">
</Body>
```

To read and display lines (with line numbers) using `ReadLinebyLine`.hta script shown in Listing 2.38, you can do the following:

1. Double-click `ReadLinebyLine.hta`
2. Click on the Browse button to browse for a text file to open
3. Select a text file to open and click Ok
4. Click the `Get File Content` button to read and display the contents of the text file that you selected in Step 3

When the `Get File Content` button is clicked, `ReadFile` *sub* procedure is invoked. The code within the `ReadFile` *sub* procedure opens the text file and does the following steps, as shown in Figure 2.53.

1. It creates an instance of the `FileSystemObject` object.
2. Next it checks to see if the file exists.
3. It then checks to ensure that the file contains data.
4. Next, the script opens the text file by calling the `OpenTextFile` method.
5. After the file is open, the script calls the `Do While…loop` statement ensuring that the script loops through each line in the opened text file until the end of file is reached (that is, the `AtEndOfStream` property returns a true value; `AtEndOfStream` is covered in the properties section of the `TextStream` object).
6. Within the `Do while…loop` statement the script reads each line of the text file and stores it in the `sLine` variable, as shown in Figure 2.53.

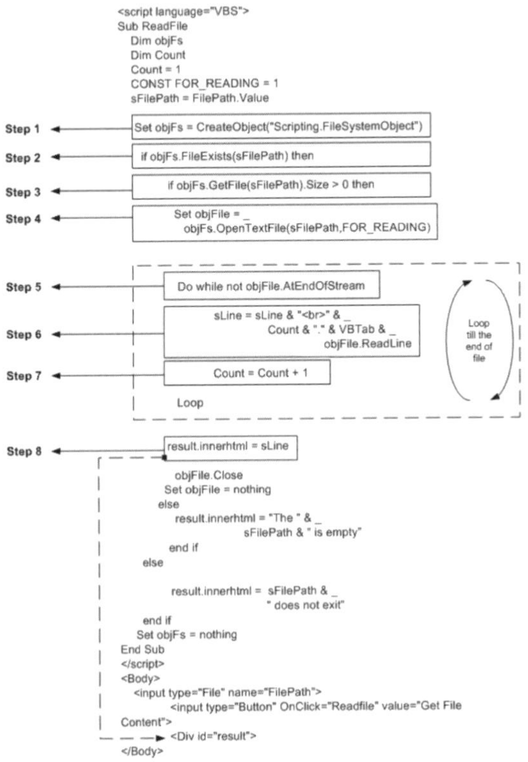

<script language="VBS">
Sub ReadFile
Dim objFs
Dim Count
Count = 1
CONST FOR_READING = 1
sFilePath = FilePath.Value
Step 1
Set objFs = CreateObject("Scripting.FileSystemObject")
Step 2
if objFs.FileExists(sFilePath) then
Step 3
if objFs.GetFile(sFilePath).Size > 0 then
Step 4
Set objFile = _
objFs.OpenTextFile(sFilePath,FOR_READING)
Step 5
Do while not objFile.AtEndOfStream
Step 6
sLine = sLine & "<br>" & _
Count & "." & VBTab & _
objFile.ReadLine
Step 7
Count = Count + 1
Loop
Loop till the end of file
Step 8
result.innerhtml = sLine
objFile.Close
Set objFile = nothing
else
result.innerhtml = "The " & _
sFilePath & " is empty"
end if
else
result.innerhtml = sFilePath & _
" does not exit"
end if
Set objFs = nothing
End Sub
</script>
<Body>
<input type="File" name="FilePath">
<input type="Button" OnClick="Readfile" value="Get File
Content">
<Div id="result">
</Body>

FIGURE 2.53 Steps of the `ReadFile` method in `ReadLinebyLine.hta` script.

7. It also adds the line count (in `Count` variable) to the line so the display can include the line numbers.
8. After reading the entire file, line-by-line, the script displays the result in an HTML format.

`Skip:` At times you may want to skip reading a few characters. To do so, you can use the `Skip` method. The `Skip` method takes an integer value as number of characters to skip. For example, the following code skips every other character (one character, beginning with the first character) to display alternate (odd) numbers stored in the Numbers.txt text file:

```
Dim objFs
CONST FOR_READING = 1
CONST FILE_NAME = "Numbers.txt"
 Set objFs = CreateObject("Scripting.FileSystemObject")
```

```
    if objFs.FileExists(FILE_NAME) then
         if objFs.GetFile(FILE_NAME).Size > 0 then
           Set objFile = objFs.OpenTextFile(FILE_NAME,FOR_READING)
             Do while not objFile.AtEndOfStream
               objFile.Skip(1)
               Wscript.Echo objFile.Read(1)
             Loop
           objFile.Close
           Set objFile = nothing
         else
           Wscript.Echo "The " & FILE_NAME & " is empty"
         end if
    else
         Wscript.Echo FILE_NAME, "does not exist"
    end if
  Set objFs = nothing
```

The script will generate an error if the number of characters to skip is greater than the number of characters in the line.

`SkipLine:` The `Skip` function skips a number of specified characters and the `SkipLine` method skips the next line in the text stream. The following example displays how to read every alternate line in the text file:

```
Dim objFs
CONST FOR_READING = 1
CONST FILE_NAME = "Numbers2.txt"
 Set objFs = CreateObject("Scripting.FileSystemObject")
   if objFs.FileExists(FILE_NAME) then
        if objFs.GetFile(FILE_NAME).Size > 0 then
          Set objFile = objFs.OpenTextFile(FILE_NAME,FOR_READING)
            Do while not objFile.AtEndOfStream
              Wscript.Echo objFile.ReadLine
objFile.SkipLine
            Loop
          objFile.Close
          Set objFile = nothing
        else
          Wscript.Echo "The " & FILE_NAME & " is empty"
        end if
   else
        Wscript.Echo FILE_NAME, "does not exit"
   end if
 Set objFs = nothing
```

`Write:` The `Write` method takes a string value and writes it to the text file. For example, as illustrated in Listing 2.39, you can write information to a file using the `Write` method.

LISTING 2.39 Write Data to a Text File Using `Write` Method

```
<script language="VBS">
Dim objFs
CONST FOR_READING = 1
Private Sub Window_OnLoad
      FileContent.Disabled = true
      Save.Disabled = true
      Set objFs = CreateObject("Scripting.FileSystemObject")
End Sub
Sub ReadFile
sFilePath = FilePath.Value
if sFilePath = "" then
      Msgbox "You must specify a file name.",VBOkOnly+VBCritical
              Exit Sub
End if
    if objFs.FileExists(sFilePath) then
      Set objFile = objFs.OpenTextFile(sFilePath,FOR_READING)
          FileContent.Disabled = False
          Save.Disabled = False
          FileContent.Value = objFile.ReadAll
          objFile.Close
      Set objFile = nothing
    else
      Document.Write "Unable to open file " & sFilePath
    end if
End Sub
Sub EnableSave
   Save.Disabled = False
End Sub
Sub SaveFile
      set objFile = objFs.CreateTextFile(FilePath.Value,true)
      objFile.write FileContent.value
      objFile.Close
      set objFile = nothing
      Document.write FilePath.Value & _
" <font color=green>successfully saved</font>"
End Sub
Sub Window_OnUnload
    Set objFs = nothing
End Sub
</script>
<Body>
      <input type="File" name="FilePath">
      <input type="Button" OnClick="Readfile" value="Get File Content">
      <br><textarea rows="25" cols="85"
           name="FileContent" value=""
                    OnChange="EnableSave"></textarea>
      <br><input type="button" name="save"
OnClick="SaveFile" Value="Save">
</Body>
```

The `Write.hta` script shown in Listing 2.39 can be used to open and edit and save (write to the text file) an existing text file, using the `Write` method as follows:

1. Double-click the `Write.hta` script to launch it
2. Click on the `Browse` button to browse for a text file
3. Select a text file and click the `OK` button
4. Click on `Get File Content` button
5. Edit the text as needed
6. Click on the `Save` button to save the changes

When the `Save` button is clicked, the `OnClick` event calls the `SaveFile` method. The `SaveFile` method creates a file with the same name that was opened for editing and writes the changed content from the `TextArea` to this newly created file before closing the file.

`Writeline:` The `Writeline` method, like the `Write` method, also writes the text passed as an argument into the text file. However, along with the text, the `WriteLine` method also writes the new line character marking the end of a line (similar to writing a text and hitting the enter key). For example, using the `Writeline` method you can write messages, one per line, to a log file for tracing and troubleshooting. The example in Listing 2.40 demonstrates how to write a *sub* procedure that you can call over and over again in your scripts to write logging information, line by line, into a text file.

LISTING 2.40 `WriteLine` Method Used for Logging Information to a Text File

```
Option Explicit
Dim objFs, objwShell
Dim objFolder, File
Dim sWindowsFolder
CONST OUTPUT_LOG_FILE_NAME = "WriteLine.log"
CONST WINDOWS_FOLDER = 0
CONST FOR_APPEND = 8

  Set objFs = CreateObject("Scripting.FileSystemObject")
    sWindowsFolder = objFs.GetSpecialFolder(WINDOWS_FOLDER)
      WriteLog OUTPUT_LOG_FILE_NAME, _
                   "Script Started at: " & now
      WriteLog OUTPUT_LOG_FILE_NAME, _
                        "Getting System Folder"
       Set objFolder = objFs.GetFolder(sWindowsFolder)
        if Err <> 0 then
       WriteLog OUTPUT_LOG_FILE_NAME, _
             "Unable to get Windows Folder : " & _
                          "Error: " & Err.number _
                               & ", " & err.Description
```

```
      end if
   WriteLog OUTPUT_LOG_FILE_NAME, _
          objFolder.Files.Count & _
             " files found in " & _
                       sWindowsFolder
   For each File in objFolder.Files
  WriteLog "Files.txt", _
     File.Name & ", " & _
       File.DateCreated _
          & ", " & File.Size
   Next
      WriteLog OUTPUT_LOG_FILE_NAME, "Clearing Memory"
    Set objFolder = nothing
  WriteLog OUTPUT_LOG_FILE_NAME, _
     "Script ended at: " & Now
 Set objFs = nothing
Sub WriteLog(FileName,msg)
  Dim objFile
     Set objFile = objFs.OpenTextFile( _
                  FileName,FOR_APPEND, True)
  objFile.WriteLine msg
    objFile.Close
  Set objFile = nothing
End Sub
```

When the `Writeline.vbs` script shown in Listing 2.40 is run, the `WriteLog` method is called again and again, as shown in Figure 2.54. The `WriteLog` method when called opens (or creates) the text file passed as the `FileName` argument, and appends the message passed as the `msg` argument using the `WriteLine` method. The script creates two files, Files.txt that contains the file information from the c:\Windows folder and the Writeline.log that contains the logging information similar to the following:

```
Script Started at: 9/17/2005 5:04:19 PM
Getting System Folder
166 files found in C:\WINDOWS
Clearing Memory
Script ended at: 9/17/2005 5:04:21 PM
```

The `WriteLine.log` may also contain error information if an error is encountered by the script while creating the `FileSystemObject` object, as shown in Figure 2.54.

`WriteBlankLines:` To write a blank line to a text file, you can call the `WriteLine` method and pass two double quotes as follows:

```
Object.WriteLine ""
```

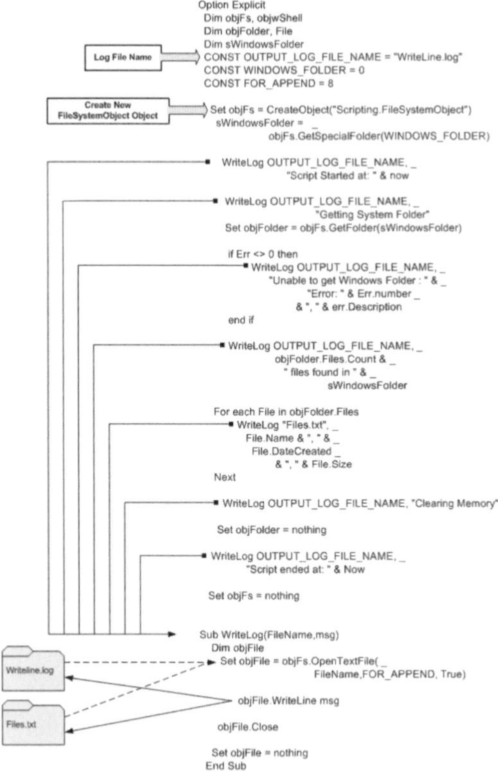
Option Explicit
Dim objFs, objwShell
Dim objFolder, File
Dim sWindowsFolder
Log File Name
CONST OUTPUT_LOG_FILE_NAME = "WriteLine.log"
CONST WINDOWS_FOLDER = 0
CONST FOR_APPEND = 8
Create New FileSystemObject Object
Set objFs = CreateObject("Scripting.FileSystemObject")
sWindowsFolder = _
objFs.GetSpecialFolder(WINDOWS_FOLDER)
WriteLog OUTPUT_LOG_FILE_NAME, _
"Script Started at: " & now
WriteLog OUTPUT_LOG_FILE_NAME, _
"Getting System Folder"
Set objFolder = objFs.GetFolder(sWindowsFolder)
if Err <> 0 then
WriteLog OUTPUT_LOG_FILE_NAME, _
"Unable to get Windows Folder : " & _
"Error: " & Err.number _
& ", " & err.Description
end if
WriteLog OUTPUT_LOG_FILE_NAME, _
objFolder.Files.Count & _
" files found in " & _
sWindowsFolder
For each File in objFolder.Files
WriteLog "Files.txt", _
File.Name & ", " & _
File.DateCreated _
& ", " & File.Size
Next
WriteLog OUTPUT_LOG_FILE_NAME, "Clearing Memory"
Set objFolder = nothing
WriteLog OUTPUT_LOG_FILE_NAME, _
"Script ended at: " & Now
Set objFs = nothing
Sub WriteLog(FileName,msg)
Dim objFile
Set objFile = objFs.OpenTextFile(_
FileName,FOR_APPEND, True)
objFile.WriteLine msg
objFile.Close
Set objFile = nothing
End Sub
Writeline.log
Files.txt

FIGURE 2.54 The working of the `Writeline.vbs` script described.

However, using this method you can add only one line at a time. To add more than one blank line to the text file, you can use the `WriteBlankLines` method. The `WriteBlankLines` method has the following syntax:

```
Object.WriteBlankLines(lines)
```

`Object` is the `FileSystemObject` and the lines is the integer value that denotes how many blank lines `WriteBlankLines` method should write to the text file. For example, the code in Listing 2.41 writes two blank lines to the text file after every line:

LISTING 2.41 `WriteBlankLines` Example

```
    set objFs = CreateObject("scripting.FileSystemObject")
set objFile = objFs.CreateTextFile("WriteBlankLines.txt")
  for i = 0 to 10
     objFile.WriteLine "This line is followed by two blank lines"
     objFile.WriteBlankLines 2
```

```
    next
  objFile.Close
 Set objFile = nothing
set objFs = nothing
```

When the code in Listing 2.41 is executed, it writes 10 lines of text, each followed by two blank lines.

Dictionary Object

Earlier in the "Variables and Arrays" section you learned about arrays. Arrays allow you to store multiple values in a single variable. Each value is stored into an area (known as element) that is marked with an index number. Using these index numbers you can retrieve or set the value of an element. For example, in the following example, `Days(0)` retrieves the first value (that is Monday) in the array and `Days(4)` retrieves the 5th value (that is Friday) in the `Days` array.

```
Days = Array("Monday","Tuesday","Wednesday", _
         "Thursday","Friday","Saturday","Sunday")
WScript.Echo Days(0)
WScript.Echo Days(4)
```

One of the limitations of the arrays is that you have to look into each element of an array to find a value that you are looking for. For example, to check if a name (`MEXICO`) exists in an array (`Countries`), you must search through the array as shown in the following example:

```
Countries = Array("US","GERMANY","ENGLAND", _
            "CANADA","MEXICO","CHINA", _
            "INDIA","SOUTH AMERICA","JAPAN")
Found = False
for each Country in Countries
   if Country = "MEXICO" then
    Wscript.Echo "MEXICO", "found"
    Found = True
   End if
next
if Not Found then Wscript.Echo "MEXICO", "not found"
```

This makes arrays unsuitable for situations that require you to search for a value in a large array.

For such situations, you can use the `Dictionary` object. A `Dictionary` object is like an associative array that is composed of a collection of keys and a collection of values where each key is associated with one value. The `Dictionary` object has the following unique identifier:

```
Scripting.Dictionary
```

You can create a `Dictionary` object using the `CreateObject` method as show in the following code:

```
Set objDict = CreateObject("Scripting.Dictionary")
```

The `Dictionary` object provides the following methods:

`Add:` The `Add` is one of the three ways of adding `key` and `value` pair information to the `Dictionary` object. It has the following syntax:

```
Object.Add (Key, Value)
```

The *`Object`* is the `Dictionary` object and the `key` is the key associated with the `Value`. Following is an example of the `Add` method:

```
Set objDict = CreateObject("Scripting.Dictionary")
    objDict.Add "Server01","Domain1"
      objDict.Add "Server02","Domain2"
         objDict.Add "Server03","Domain1"
        objDict.Add "Server04","Domain1"
     objDict.Add "Server05","Domain2"
  Wscript.Echo objDict("Server04")
       Set objDict = nothing
```

You can also add the `key` and `value` pair in the following manner:

```
objDict("Server01") = "Domain1"
```

`Items:` The `Items` method can be used to retrieve a collection of items in an array format. The `Items` method has the following syntax:

```
Object.Items ()
```

You can list all values of the keys by calling the Items method, as shown in the following example:

```
Set objDict = CreateObject("Scripting.Dictionary")
     objDict.Add "Server01","Domain1"
       objDict.Add "Server02","Domain2"
         objDict.Add "Server03","Domain1"
            objDict.Add "Server04","Domain1"
            objDict.Add "Server05","Domain2"
       arrItems = objDict.Items
    For each value in arrItems
       Wscript.Echo value
    Next
  Set objDict = nothing
```

`Keys:` While the `Items` method returns an array of items (values) in the dictionary, the `Keys` method returns an array of keys in the dictionary. It has the following syntax:

```
Object.Items ()
```

Following illustrates how to lists all the keys in the dictionary:

```
Set objDict = CreateObject("Scripting.Dictionary")
     objDict.Add "Server01","Domain1"
       objDict.Add "Server02","Domain2"
         objDict.Add "Server03","Domain1"
            objDict.Add "Server04","Domain1"
            objDict.Add "Server05","Domain2"
       arrItems = objDict.keys
    For each key in arrItems
       Wscript.Echo key
    Next
  Set objDict = nothing
```

`Exists:` When you add a key that already exists in the dictionary (for example, if you add `Server01` twice to the dictionary), you will receive an error as shown in Figure 2.55.

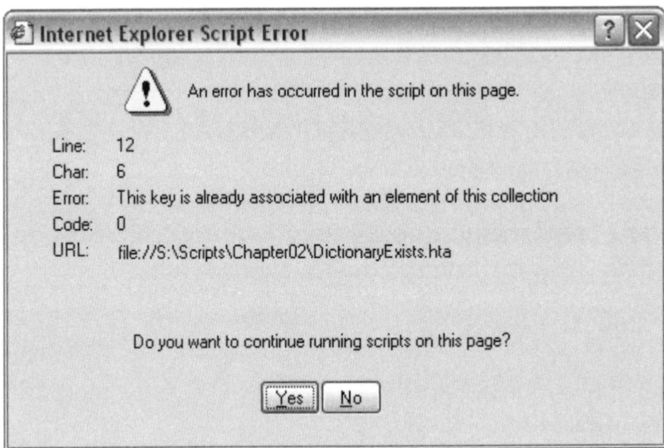

FIGURE 2.55 Error message displayed when the key being added to the `Dictionary` object already exists in the dictionary.

To avoid such errors, you can use the `Exists` method to ensure that the key does not exist in the dictionary before adding the `key` and `value` pair. The `Exists` method returns a `True` if the key already exists in the dictionary, and `False` if the key does not exist in the dictionary. The `Exists` method has the following syntax:

```
bReturn = objDict.Exists(Key)
```

The example in Listing 2.42 illustrates how to use the `Exists` method to verify if the key exists in the dictionary. If the key being added already exists in the dictionary, the script displays the key already exists message; otherwise it simply adds the key to the dictionary and displays all key and value combinations, as shown in Figure 2.56.

FIGURE 2.56 `DictionaryExists.hta` script in action.

LISTING 2.42 `DictionaryExists.hta` Script Illustrates Use of the `Exists` Method

```
   <script language="vbs">
Dim objDict
Sub Window_OnLoad
  window.resizeto 300,300
  Set objDict = CreateObject("Scripting.Dictionary")
End Sub
Sub AddKey
  if objDict.Exists(dictKey.value) then
      msgbox dictKey.value & "  already exists"
      exit sub
  end if
   objDict.Add dictKey.value, dictvalue.value
   arrKeys = objDict.Keys
   for i = 0 to objDict.Count -1
        DisplayDictionary = DisplayDictionary & _
                          arrKeys(i) & _
                          ", " & objDict.item(arrKeys(i)) _
                          & "<br>"
   next
   result.innerhtml = DisplayDictionary
End Sub
```

```
   Sub Window_OnUnload
      Set objDict = nothing
   End Sub
    </script>
  <body>
      <table width=100% border=0
          bgcolor=#eeeeee cellspacing=1 cellpadding=1 >
         <tr bgcolor=#ffffff >
             <th>Key</th><td><input type=text name=dictKey></td></tr>
         <tr bgcolor=#ffffff >
             <th>Value</th><td><input type=text name=dictvalue></td></tr>
         <tr bgcolor=#ffffff > <td colspan=2 >
             <input type=Button Value="Add Value" OnClick=AddKey>
         </td></tr>
         </table>
         <br><br>
         <div id=result>
  </body>
```

`Remove:` To remove a `key` and `value` pair from the dictionary, you can use the `Remove` method. It has the following syntax:

```
Object.Remove (Key)
```

The `Object` is always the `Dictionary` object and the `key` is the key that you want to remove from the dictionary.

The example in Listing 2.43 illustrates how to remove a `key` and `value` pair from the dictionary.

LISTING 2.43 `Remove` **Method Illustration**

```
Set objDict = CreateObject("Scripting.Dictionary")
  objDict.Add "Server01","Domain1"
    objDict.Add "Server02","Domain2"
      objDict.Add "Server03","Domain1"
         objDict.Add "Server04","Domain1"
            objDict.Add "Server05","Domain2"
          objDict.remove "Server03"
         arrKeys = objDict.Keys
     for i = 0 to objDict.Count -1
       Wscript.Echo arrKeys(i) & _
                     ", " & objDict.item(arrKeys(i))
     next
 Set objDict = nothing
```

When the script in Listing 2.43 is executed, it adds `Server01` through `Server05` to the dictionary and then removes `Server03` using the `Remove` method. The script then loops through the dictionary to display the `key` and `value` combination.

RemoveAll: While the Remove method removes a single key and value combination, the RemoveAll method removes all the key and value combinations in the dictionary. It has no arguments. Following is the syntax for the RemoveAll method

```
Object.RemoveAll()
```

The following example illustrates how to remove all the key and value combinations from the dictionary:

```
Set objDict = CreateObject("Scripting.Dictionary")
objDict.Add "Server01","Domain1"
  objDict.Add "Server02","Domain2"
    objDict.Add "Server03","Domain1"
       objDict.Add "Server04","Domain1"
          objDict.Add "Server05","Domain2"
      objDict.RemoveAll
       Wscript.Echo "The Dictionary has " & _
                     objDict.Count & _
                       " number of keys"
Set objDict = nothing
```

Besides these methods the Dictionary object also provides the following properties:

Count: The Count property returns the number of key and value pairs that are in the dictionary. For example, in the following example, the Count property returns 5 as the total number of key and value combination, as shown in Figure 2.57.

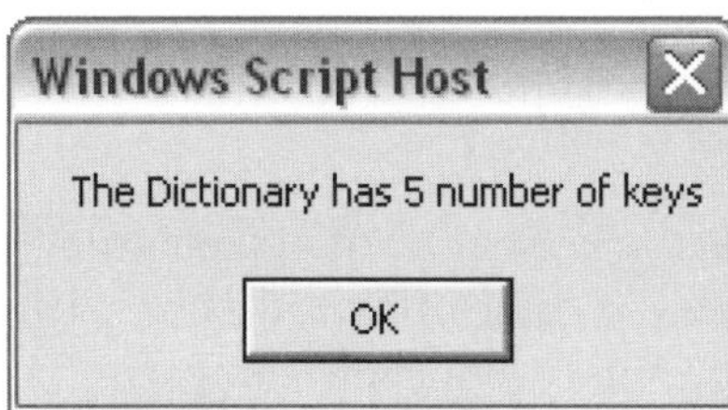

FIGURE 2.57 DictionaryCount.vbs script displaying the total number of key and value combinations returned by the Count property.

Item: The Item property can be used to retrieve or set a specific item, that is, the value associated with the key in a dictionary. You must pass the key to set or retrieve when calling the Item property. The Item property has the following syntax:

```
Object.Item(key) [ = newitem ]
```

The `Object` in the syntax is the `Dictionary` object. The `key` is the key that you want to set or retrieve and `newitem` (within the square brackets) is the optional item value that you can associate with the specified key. For example, as shown in Listing 2.44, the `Server01`, `Server02` and `Server03` values are associated with `Domain1`, `Domain2`, `Domain1` values, respectively.

LISTING 2.44 Key Value Association Example

```
Set objDict = CreateObject("Scripting.Dictionary")
  objDict.Item("Server01") = "Domain1"
    objDict.Item("Server02") = "Domain2"
      objDict.Item("Server03") = "Domain1"
  Wscript.Echo objDict.Item("Server02")
Set objDict = nothing
```

`Key:` Unlike the `Item` property that can be used to both set and retrieve the `value` associated with a `key`, the `Key` property can be only used to set the `key` in the `Dictionary`. The `Key` property has the following syntax:

```
Object.Item(key) = newitem
```

The following example demonstrates how to set the `Server01` key to `Server04` using the `Key` property:

```
Set objDict = CreateObject("Scripting.Dictionary")
  objDict.Item("Server01") = "Domain1"
    objDict.Item("Server02") = "Domain2"
      objDict.Item("Server03") = "Domain1"
    objDict.Key("Server02") = "Server04"
  Wscript.Echo objDict.Item("Server04")
Set objDict = nothing
```

`CompareMode:` The `CompareMode` property sets and retrieves the comparison mode of the `Dictionary` object. A value of `1` sets the comparison mode to text and `0` to binary mode. When in the binary mode, the comparison is case sensitive. For example, in the following example the method will return no value when you retrieve the `server01` key rather than the `Server01` key as compared to when the comparison mode is set to text.

```
Set objDict = CreateObject("Scripting.Dictionary")
 objDict.CompareMode = 0
  objDict.Item("Server01") = "Domain1"
    objDict.Item("Server02") = "Domain2"
      objDict.Item("Server03") = "Domain1"
  Wscript.Echo objDict.Item("server01")
Set objDict = nothing
```

Script Encoder

Scripts are easy to create and read because they are stored in a text file. Generally, it is ok to leave them in the clear text state in the text files for everyone to open and read them. However, there may be times when you want to restrict users from reading your scripts. For such situations, you can use the Script Encoder tool.

The Script Encoder is a command-line tool that you can use to encrypt your final script before release. However, before you can use the Script Encoder tool, you must download it from msdn.microsoft.com/scripting (*http://msdn.microsoft.com/library/default.asp?url=/downloads/list/webdev.asp*) Web site. It is a free download.

Once you have downloaded and installed the Script Encoder tool, you can use the Screnc.exe file to encrypt your scripts. The `Screnc.exe` has the following syntax:

```
SCRENC [/s] [/f] [/xl] [/l defLanguage ] [/e defExtension] InputFile Out-
putFile
```

Table 2.26 describes the options of the Screnc.exe command.

TABLE 2.26 Screnc.exe Options

Part	Description
/s	Optional argument. Switch that specifies that the Script Encoder is to work silently, that is, produce no screen output. If omitted, the default is to provide verbose output.
/f	Optional argument. Specifies that the input file is to be overwritten by the output file. Note that this option destroys your original input source file. If omitted, the output file is not overwritten.
/xl	Optional argument. Specifies that the @language directive is not added at the top of .ASP files. If omitted, @language directive is added for all .ASP files.
/l defLanguage	Optional argument. Specifies the default scripting language (Jscript® or VBScript) to use during encoding. Script blocks within the file being encoded that do not contain a language attribute are assumed to be of this specified language. If omitted, Jscript is the default language for HTML pages and scriptlets, while VBScript is the default for active server pages. For plain text files, the file extension (either .js or .vbs) determines the default scripting language.
/e defExtension	Optional argument. Associates the input file with a specific file type. Use this switch when the input file's extension doesn't make the file type obvious, that is, when the input file extension is not one of the recognized extensions, but the file content does fall into one of the recognized types. There is no default for this option. If a file with an unrecognized extension is encountered and this option is not specified, the Script Encoder fails for that unrecognized file. Recognized file extensions are .asa, .asp, .cdx, .htm, .html, .js, .sct, and .vbs.
InputFile	Required argument. The name of the input file to be encoded, including any necessary path information relative to the current directory.
OutputFile	Required argument. The name of the output file to be produced, including any necessary path information relative to the current directory.

The Script Encoder utility supports the following script types

ASP: This format consists of a text active server page containing valid HTML and embedded scripting blocks within `<SCRIPT> ... </SCRIPT>` tags or `<% ... %>` tags. Applications that use this format include Microsoft® Internet Information Server (IIS). Recognized file extensions are .asp, .asa, and .cdx.

HTML: This format consists of a text file that contains valid HTML along with embedded script blocks. Applications using this scripting format include Microsoft FrontPage®, Microsoft Visual InterDev™ and virtually all Web designers and browsers. Recognized file extensions are .htm and .html.

Plain text: This format consists of a text file that contains only script with no surrounding tags. Applications using scripting format include Windows® Script Host (WSH) and Microsoft Outlook®. Recognized file extensions are .js and .vbs, which are changed to .jse and .vbe, respectively, after encoding.

Scriptlet: This format consists of a text file that contains valid scriptlet code within `<SCRIPT> ... </SCRIPT>` tags. Recognized file extensions are .sct and .wsh.

To encode your script (for example `MyScript.vbs`) you can do the following:

1. Open a command window
2. Change the Script Encoder directory (by default the Script Encoder is installed in the Program Files folder)
3. Type the following command

```
c:\> Screnc.exe c:\scripts\Myscript.vbs c:\scripts\Myscript.vbe
```

The script encoder will take `MyScripts.vbs` script, and output the encoded script to `MyScript.vbe`.

The Script Encoder encrypts all text in the script file. To encrypt only the code and leave the description header unencrypted, you can include the following tag after the description in your script:

```
'**Start Encode**
```

The tag must be typed exactly as shown.

All text after this tag will be encrypted by the Script Encoder. The following code when encrypted will only encrypt the code and not the script description:

```
'This is script description and will not be encoded
'**Start Encode**
Wscript.Echo "This is encrypted code"
```

After encryption the file will look like the following:

```
'This is script description and will not be encoded
'**Start
Encode**#@~^LQAAAA==@#@&@#@&q/1DkaYc3m4W~J:trd,k/,nx1DXaOnN,mKNnJaA0AAA==^#~@
```

ScriptEncodeSample.vbe included on the CD-ROM is the encrypted script that was generated from ScriptEncodeSample.vbs also included on the CD-ROM in the Scripts\Chapter02 folder.

Running the encoded file is simple; you run it as you run the .vbs script with Cscript.exe or Wscript.exe script hosts. You can also encrypt HTML applications and the WSF files using the same method. Listing 2.45 shows a sample encoding of a HTA script.

LISTING 2.45 Encode Sample HTA Script (see "HTML Application" section of the chapter)

```
<html>
<!--------------------------------------------------------
ScriptEncodeSample.hta
--------------------------------------------------------->
<HTA:APPLICATION
      ID="ScriptEncodeSampleHTA"
      APPLICATIONNAME="Script Encode Sample HTA Script"
      SCROLL="no"
      SINGLEINSTANCE="yes"
      WINDOWSTATE="normal"
      BORDER="thick"
      BORDERSTYLE="normal"
      MAXIMIZEBUTTON="yes"
      MINIMIZEBUTTON="yes"
         INNERBORDER="yes"
      SYSMENU="yes" />
<head>
     <title>Script Encode Sample</title>
     <script language="vbscript">
         'This is script description and will not be encoded
         '**Start Encode**
         Sub Window_OnLoad
             Document.Write "This is encrypted text"
         End Sub
    </script>
</head>
 <body>
 </body>
</html>
```

You would encode the sample script in Listing 2.45 using the Script Encoder utility by following the following steps:

1. Add the `'**Start Encode**` from where you want the code to be encoded (must be within the `<script>…</script>` tags)
2. Save the changes and rename the file from `ScriptEncodeSample.hta` to `ScriptEncodeSample.htm`.
3. Run Script Encoder command to encode the script as follows:

```
screnc ScriptEncodeSample.htm ScriptEncodedSample.htm
```

4. Rename the script from `ScriptEncodeSample.htm` to `ScriptEncodedSample.hta` and from `ScriptEncodedSample.htm` to `ScriptEncodedSample.hta`
5. Run `ScriptEncodedSample.hta` as you run any other HTML application.

The encoded script `ScriptEncodedSample.hta` looks like the following after it has been encoded:

```
<html>
<!-------------------------------------------------------
ScriptEncodeSample.hta
-------------------------------------------------------->
<HTA:APPLICATION
      ID="ScriptEncodeSampleHTA"
      APPLICATIONNAME="Script Encode Sample HTA Script"
      SCROLL="no"
      SINGLEINSTANCE="yes"
      WINDOWSTATE="normal"
      BORDER="thick"
      BORDERSTYLE="normal"
      MAXIMIZEBUTTON="yes"
      MINIMIZEBUTTON="yes"
      INNERBORDER="yes"
      SYSMENU="yes" />
<head>
     <title>Script Encode Sample</title>
     <script language="VBScript.Encode">
          'This is script description and will not be encoded
          '**Start Encode**#@~^bgAAAA==@#@&P~,P,PP,?!8PqkUNKhm6
SWm[@#@&PP,~~P,P,P~P9G1Eh+
ORqDrO PJP4b/~kk~ x^MXaY+9PDn6DJ@#@&,P~~,PP,3x9P?!8@#@&,P,PhsAAA==^#~@</scri
pt>
</head>
 <body>
 </body>
</html>
```

Notice that the `language` property of the `<script>` tag is changed to `VBScript.Encode` from `VBScript`.

WINDOWS SCRIPT COMPONENTS

The more scripts you write, the more you realize that you use the same `Functions` and `Sub` procedures in your scripts over and over again. For example, you may use the `WriteLog` (shown earlier in Listing 2.40) `Sub` procedure in every script that you write to provide for logging and debugging in your scripts.

Usually, you would use the copy and paste method to copy the common functions from an existing script to the script that you are creating. Over a period of time, you may even create a text file for the common functions, like `commonfunctions.txt`. You would then copy the common functions and `Sub` procedures from this common text file. This all is good, but copying common functions and `Sub` procedures to every script bloats the script. Besides, it is prone to human errors. To overcome this problem you can use the Windows Script Components.

Windows Script Components (commonly known as WSC files) are text files that behave like an ActiveX component (COM object). Similar to an ActiveX component (such as the `FileSystemObject`), WSCs also have a unique identifier and must be created using the `CreateObject` method. For example, the following will create a new ActiveX component

```
Set objCommon = CreateObject("MyComponent")
```

Like the ActiveX components, WSCs provide methods and properties that can be used in your scripts. In essence they are like custom reusable ActiveX components that you can create using a text editor.

You can create WSC using any scripting language that supports Microsoft ActiveX scripting interfaces, such as VBScript, Jscript, PerlScript and Python languages. WSC supports both common COM components and DHTML behavior. Some of the benefits of using WSC are that they are text files and therefore they are small in size and efficient. Also, they are easy to create, maintain and deploy and use in scripts. For example, you can create WSCs in a text editor and use it in your scripts as you use any other ActiveX object, such as the `FileSystemObject` object the following steps demonstrate:

1. Open Notepad.exe (or a text editor of your choice).
2. Type the following in the text file

```
<?xml version="1.0"?>
<component>

<registration
    description="MyComponent"
    progid="MyComponent"
    version="1.00"
    classid="{9bc85335-7f45-4466-bdb1-040a8d5f7c63}"
>
```

```
</registration>
<public>

    <method name="WriteLog">
            <prameter name="FileName"/>
            <prameter name="Msg"/>
    </method>
</public>
<script language="VBScript">
<![CDATA[
  Sub WriteLog(FileName,msg)
   Dim objFs
    Dim objFile
     Set objFs = CreateObject("Scripting.FileSystemObject")
       Set objFile = objFs.OpenTextFile( _
                    FileName,FOR_APPEND, True)
    objFile.WriteLine msg
      objFile.Close
    Set objFile = nothing
  End Sub

]]>
</script>
</component>
```

3. Save the file as MyComponent.wsc and close the text editor.
4. Right-click on the file and select `Register` from the menu, as shown in Figure 2.58. Registration will display the message shown in Figure 2.59.

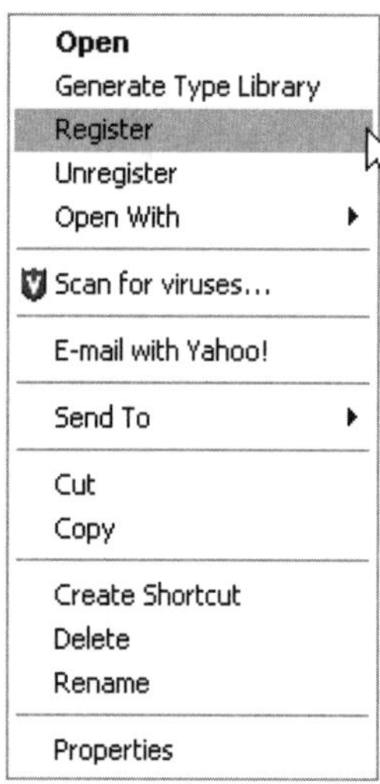

FIGURE 2.58 Right-click menu; select `Register` from the menu to register the component.

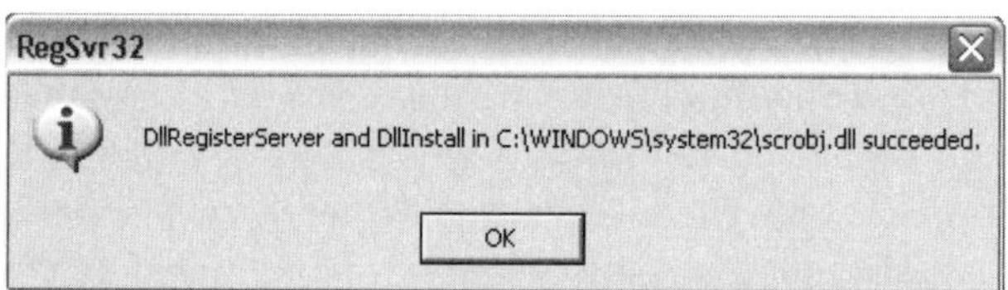

FIGURE 2.59 Message displayed when the script component is registered successfully.

5. Open Notepad.exe (or a text editor of your choice).
6. Type the following in the text editor window

```
CONST sFileName = "WriteLogComponent.log"
  Set objMyComponent = CreateObject("MyComponent")
    objMyComponent.WriteLog sFileName, "Log started at: " & now
      objMyComponent.WriteLog sFileName, _
           "This log was created by using" & _
               " the WriteLog method of the MyComponent component"
        Wscript.Sleep 5000
    objMyComponent.WriteLog sFileName, "Log Ended at: " & now
  Set objMyComponent = nothing
Save the file as WriteLogComponent.vbs
Run WriteLogComponent.vbs script  using Wscript or Cscript
Open WriteLogComponent.log file (it will be created in the same folder
where the WriteLogComponent.vbs script is located). The log file should
contain the contents similar to the following:
Log started at: 9/26/2005 9:07:38 PM
This log was created by using the WriteLog method of the MyComponent
component
Log Ended at: 9/26/2005 9:07:43 PM
```

A WSC file can be registered as COM component. However, it needs to be registered only once. Unlike DLL files that require you to unregister and re-register the DLL before the changes in the code are exposed for use in the scripts, WSC files do not require the file to be re-registered; the changes are available the next object is created.

An easy method of creating WSCs is by using the Windows Script Component Wizard. You can download and install the free WSC wizard from Microsoft's Web site (*http://msdn.microsoft.com/library/default.asp?url=/downloads/list/webdev.asp*). After you have installed the wizard, you can start the wizard from the startup menu located in Microsoft Windows Script program group. The wizard contains 6 steps, described as follows:

Step 1: The first step of the wizard allows you to define Windows Script Component object settings. Figure 2.60 shows the options that you have on this page.

Step 2: Step 2 allows you to do the following:

- Select a language for the WSC (such as VBScript, Jscript or other, like PerlScript).
- Select the options to support DHTML behavior.
- Select the options for debugging and error checking (if debugging and error checking is not enabled, errors generated by the component will not be passed to the calling scripts (that is, the component will run silently). The errors will appear to be generated by the calling script).

Figure 2.61 displays the options on the Step 2 page of the wizard.

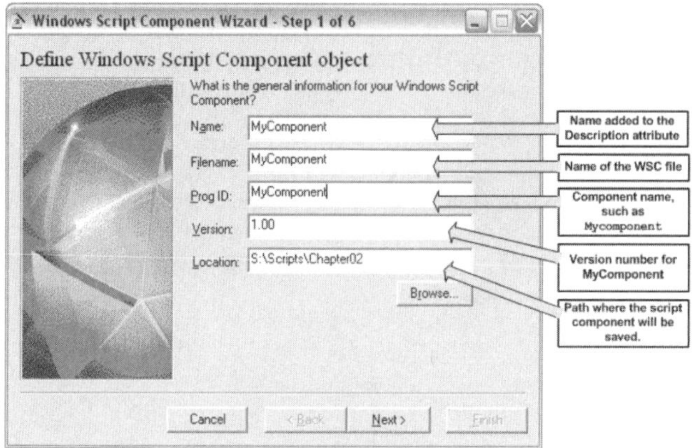

FIGURE 2.60 Step 1 of the WSC Wizard.

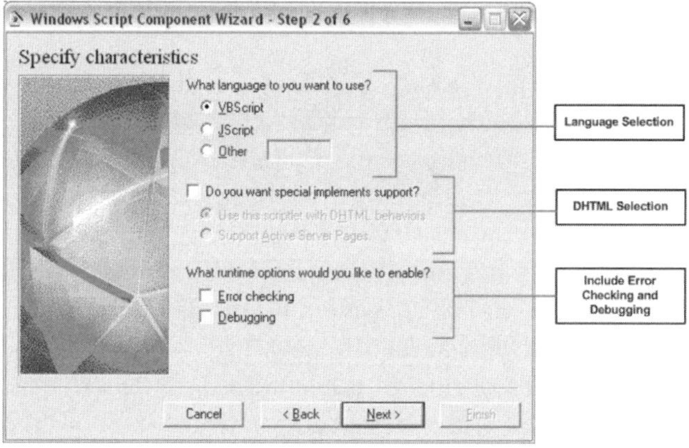

FIGURE 2.61 Step 2 of the WSC Wizard.

Step 3: Step 3 allows you to add properties to the WSC file. For example, you can add the `OutLogFile` property (as shown in Figure 2.62) that defines the output log file (how to create and use a WSC property is described later in this section). Figure 2.62 shows the Step 3 wizard page.

Step 4: Step 4 allows you to add methods to the WSC file. For example, you can add the `WriteLog` method (as shown in Figure 2.63) that you can call in your scripts to write information to a text file (how to create and use a WSC method is described later in this section). Figure 2.63 shows the Step 4 wizard page.

FIGURE 2.62 Step 3 of the WSC Wizard.

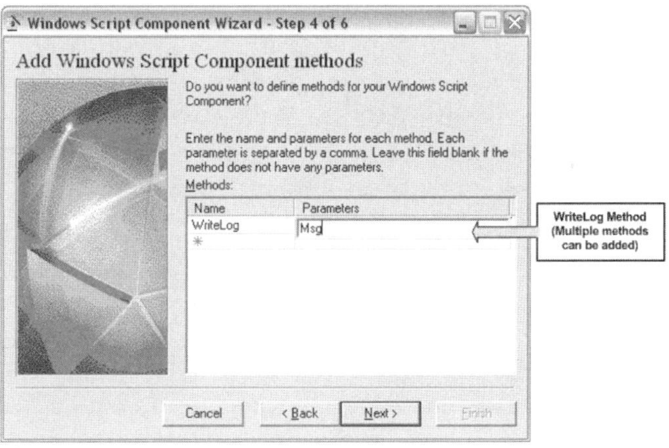

FIGURE 2.63 Step 4 of the WSC Wizard.

Step 5: Step 5 allows you to add events to a WSC file. Events can be added using the `<event>` tag (explained later in this chapter) or the `<attach>` tag (explained later in this chapter). Figure 2.64 shows the Step 5 wizard page.

Step 6: Step 6 displays the contents that will be written to the WSC file. This step allows you to review the contents and a chance to go back and change, add, or remove contents as needed. Figure 2.65 shows the Step 6 wizard page. You can click the `Back` button to return to Step 5 or click the `Finish` button to save the WSC file.

After you click the `Finish` button, the wizard saves the WSC file and displays the `Success` (or the `Failure`) message.

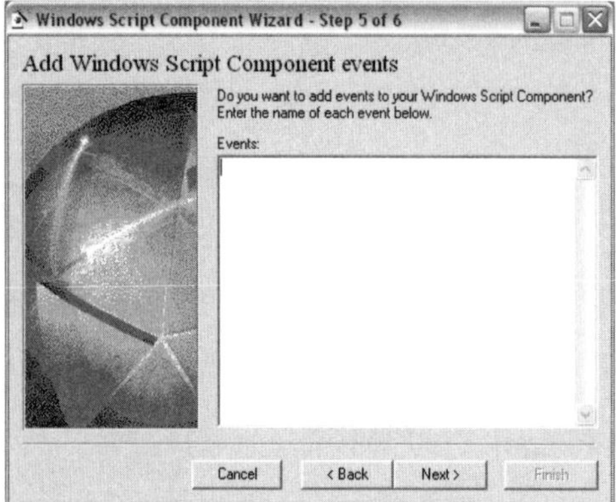

FIGURE 2.64 Step 5 of the WSC Wizard.

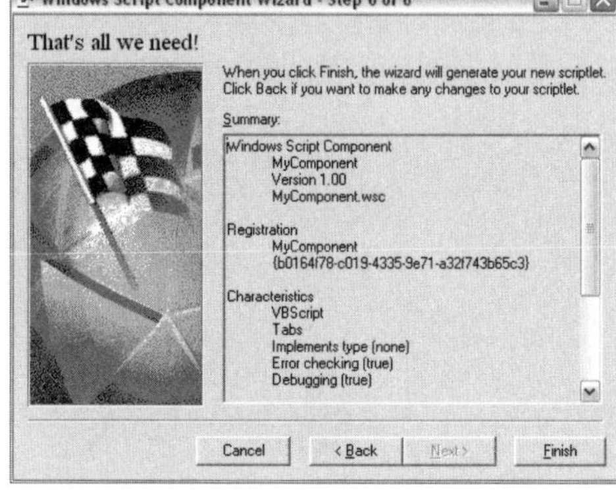

FIGURE 2.65 Step 6 of the WSC Wizard.

WSC XML Elements

WSCs, like WSF files conform to the XML format. For example, similar to the WSF files, every tag such as `<script>` must have the closing tag such as `</script>`. The starting tag must match the ending tag. For example, if the starting tag is `<script>` the ending tag cannot be anything other than `</script>`. The following does not conform to the XML standards because the `<script>` tag does not match the `<body>` tag:

```
<script>
      ...
      <body>
...
</script>
</body>
```

Following is the correct tag formation

```
<script>
...
</script>
<body>
...
</body>
```

The tag names are case sensitive and therefore the end tag name must be an exact string match of the starting tag (that is, `<Script>` would not match `</script>` or `</SCript>` tags). The following two examples illustrate unmatched and matched tags, respectively.

Unmatched Tag:

```
<Script>
...
</script>
```

Matched Tag:

```
<Script>
...
</Script>
```

NOTE

Elements (tags) in WSC examples contained in this book are generally in lower case.

WSC provides several XML elements that you can use to create a WSC file. Table 2.27 describes these elements.

TABLE 2.27 WSC XML Elements

Method	Description
`<?component?>`	Can be used to specify the attributes of error handling in WSC files.
`<?XML?>`	If included, indicates that the file must be parsed as an XML file.
`<comment>`	Can be used to include comments in WSC file. Text within this `<comment>`...`</comment>` is ignored at runtime.
`<component>`	Encloses the definition for a component. Multiple components can be defined within the `<package>`...`</package>` element.
`Package`	Can be used to enclose multiple components in a WSC file.
`<implements>`	Can be used to specify additional COM interface handlers. For example, ASP implement allows you to access the Internet Information Services Active Server Pages model, such as Response object.
`<object>`	This can be used to create objects that can be referenced by a script without using the `CreateObject` method. The objects are created as global objects and are available for use within the WSC files.
`<public>`	All methods, properties and events that are exposed by the WSC are wrapped within this element.

`<method>`	Can be used to declare a method of the component. Arguments of the `<method>` element can be defined in the `<parameter>`...`</parameter>` sub elements. For example, the following defines two parameters of the `WriteLog` method:
	`<method name="WriteLog">`
	`    <parameter name="LogFileName"/>`
	`    <parameter name="Msg"/>`
	`</method>`

→

Method	Description
`<property>`	Can be used to declare a property of the component.
`<event>`	Can be used to declare a custom event that can be fired within a component.
`<reference>`	Can be used to include a reference to an external type library. Referencing the object within the script component allows you to use the constants defined in the type library. For example, the following reference when included in the component will allow you to use the WMI constants, such as `WbemAuthenticationLevelDefault, wbemErrAccessDenied:` `<reference object="WbemScripting.SWbemLocator"/>`

`<registration>`	This can be used to define the name that is to be used to register the component as the COM component. For example, the following will register the component (defined within a `<component>` element) as SWAT.1.0 component.
	`<registration`
	`     description="common script component"`
	`     progid="SWAT.1.0"`
	`     version="1.00"`
	`     classid="{5d5c1b28-faca-4fe6-8c76-571d91dd2111}"`
	`/>`
	
	After the component is registered you can use it in your scripts by creating an instance of the object as follows:
	`set objSwat = CreateObject("SWAT.1.0")`

`<resource>`	Can be used to avoid hard coding textual data within the script component. For example, the following will allow you to reference the `Scripting.FileSystemObject` textual data defined in the `<resource>` element within the component
	`<resource id="FSObject">`
	`   Scripting.FileSystemObject`
	`</resource>`

Besides the XML elements, WSC also provides the following three functions that you can use within your script components:

`GetResource:` The `GetResource` function can be used to retrieve the value defined with the `<resource>` element. For example, the following gets the `Scripting.FileSystemObject` text defined in the `FSObject` resource to create a new instance of the `FileSystemObject`:

```
<component>
   <registration
```

```
    description="common script component"
    progid="SWAT.1.0"
    version="1.00"
    classid="{5d5c1b28-faca-4fe6-8c76-571d91dd2111}"
   />
<public>
    <method name="WriteDate">
            <Parameter name="LogFile"/>
    </method>
</public>
<resource id="FSObject">Scripting.FileSystemObject</resource>
<script language="VBScript">
    Function WriteDate(LogFile)
      Set objFs = CreateObject(GetResource("FSObject"))
        Set objFile = objFs.OpenTextFile(LogFile,8,true)
          objFile.Write Now()
        objFile.Close
          Set objFile = nothing
         Set objFs = nothing
    End Function
</script>
</component>
```

`fireEvent`: The `fireEvent` function can be used to invoke a custom event from WSC to the host application (script that is calling the functions exposed by WSC component). For example, the following invokes the `NoFileExists` event if the output log file that needs to be appended does not exist:

```
<?xml version="1.0"?>
<component>
<?component error="true" debug="true"?>
<registration
    description="fireEvent example"
    progid="FireEvent.Example"
    version="1.00"
    classid="{9bc85335-7f45-4466-bdb1-040a8d5f7c64}"
/>
<public>
    <property name="OutLogFile" get put />
    <method name="WriteLog">
            <parameter name="Msg"/>
    </method>
    <event name="NoFileExists" dispid="22"/>
</public>
<script language="vbscript">
<![CDATA[
    Dim OutLogFile
    Sub WriteLog(Msg)
      CONST FOR_APPEND = 8
       Set objFs = CreateObject("Scripting.FileSystemObject")
            if not objFs.FileExists(OutLogFile) then
                    fireEvent("NoFileExists")
```

```
                else
                   set objFile = objFs.OpenTextFile(OutLogFile,FOR_APPEND)
                        objFile.WriteLine Msg
                        objFile.Close
                end if
           Set objFs = nothing
        End Sub
        Function get_OutLogFile
                get_OutLogFile = OutLogFile
        End Function
        Sub put_OutLogFile(p)
                OutLogFile = p
        End Sub
]]>
</script>
</component>
```

The FireEvent event of the FireEvent.Example component can be used by the host application as the following script demonstrates:

```
set objFireEvent = _
    wscript.createobject("fireEvent.Example","eventname_")
      objFireEvent.OutLogFile = "test.txt"
        objFireEvent.writelog NOW()
         set objFireEvent = nothing
  Sub eventname_NoFileExists
      Wscript.echo objFireEvent.OutLogFile & " does not exist."
  End Sub
```

When the script is run, it sets the OutLogFile property of the FireEvent.Example component. After setting the output log file, the script attempts to log information to the log file by calling the WriteLog method.

The first thing after creating the FileSystemObject object, the WriteLog method calls the FileSystemObject object's FileExists method to check if the file exists. If the file exists, the file is opened and the information is written to the text file. However, if the file does not exist, an event is fired by calling the fireEvent function that the component passes to the calling script. Upon receiving the event information, the script calls the eventname_NoFileExists sub procedure that displays the file does not exist message on the user's screen. The script ends when the user closes the message window. Figure 2.66 shows this relationship between the host script and the WSC component.

CreateComponent: Generally, each component in the WSC file must be registered to expose the methods and properties of the component. Using the CreateComponent function however, you can create an instance of another component, defined within the WSC file, without registering the other component. For example in Listing 2.46, the WSC component includes two components—Parent and Child—and only the Parent component is registered as Component.Parent.

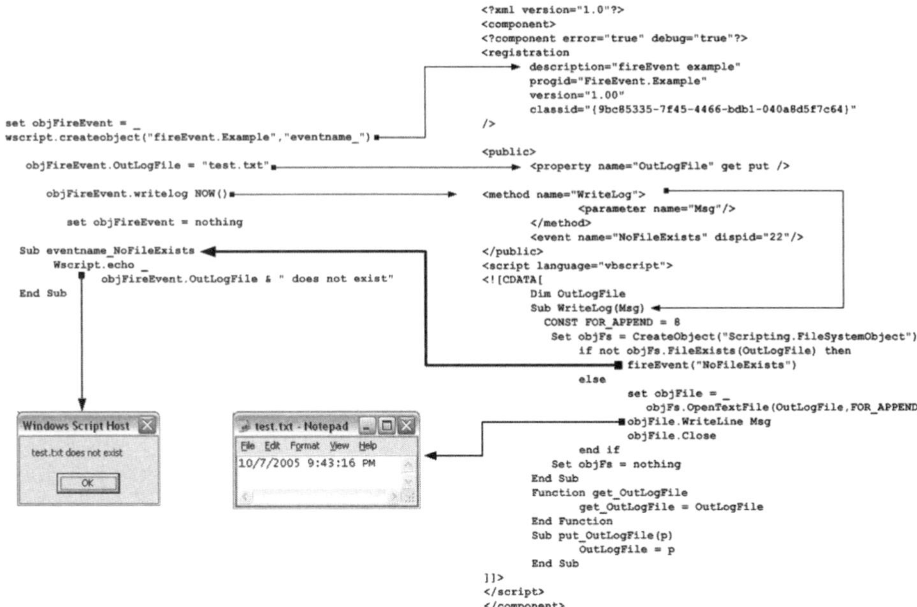

FIGURE 2.66 Event handling relationship between the host script and the WSC component.

LISTING 2.46 WSC File with Multiple Components

```
<?XML version="1.0"?>
<package>
<component id="Parent">
<?component error="true" debug="true"?>
<registration progid="Component.Parent"/>
<public>
   <property name="WriteLog"/>
</public>
<script language="VBScript">
<![CDATA[
       Dim WriteLog
       Set WriteLog = createComponent("Child")
   ]]>
</script>
</component>

<component id="Child">
<?component error="true" debug="true"?>
<registration progid="Component.Child"/>
<public>
   <method name="WriteLine" />
   <method name="WriteBlankLines"/>
</public>
```

```
<script language="VBScript">
<![CDATA[
   Function WriteLine(OutFileName,Msg)
       set objFs = CreateObject("Scripting.FileSystemObject")
       msgbox OutFileName
       Set objFile = objFs.OpenTextFile(OutFileName,8,True)
       objFile.WriteLine Msg
       objFile.Close
       set objFile = Nothing
       set objFs = Nothing
   End Function
   Sub WriteBlankLines(OutFileName,iLines)
       set objFs = CreateObject("Scripting.FileSystemObject")
       Set objFile = objFs.OpenTextFile(OutFileName,8,True)
       objFile.WriteBlankLines iLines
       objFile.Close
       set objFile = Nothing
       set objFs = Nothing
   End Sub

]]>
</script>
</component>
</package>
```

In Listing 2.46, the `Parent` component exposes the `WriteLog` property. The `WriteLog` property when called creates the `Child` component using the `CreateComponent` function. The `CreateComponent` function returns to the `WriteLog` property the `Child` component object that indirectly (through the `WriteLog` property of the `Parent` component) exposed the `WriteLine` and `WriteBlankLines` methods of the `Child` component that you can use in your scripts. The script in Listing 2.47 shows how to use the `WriteLine` and `WriteBlankLines` methods through the `Parent` component.

LISTING 2.47 Calling Script Illustrates the Use of `CreateComponent` Function in WSC

```
CONST OUT_FILE_NAME = "temp.log"
 Set objParent = CreateObject("Component.Parent")
    Set objWriteLog = objParent.WriteLog
       objWriteLog.WriteLine OUT_FILE_NAME,"Testing"
         objParent.Writelog.WriteBlankLines OUT_FILE_NAME, 2
       objWriteLog.WriteLine OUT_FILE_NAME, "After blank lines"
    Set objWriteLog = nothing
 Set objParent = nothing
```

Figure 2.67 shows the relationship of the calling script (see Listing 2.47) and the `Parent` and `Child` components packaged in one WSC file. The dotted lines in the figure denote the indirect relationship to the object from the host script and the solid lines denote a direct relationship from the host file to the WSC and relationship between the two components (`Parent` and `Child`) within the WSC components.

FIGURE 2.67 Relationship of the host script and the WSC file with `Parent` and `Child` components.

MICROSOFT XML DOCUMENT OBJECT MODEL (MSXML DOM)

eXtensible Markup Language (XML) is an important component of Microsoft Scripting Technologies. As seen earlier in this chapter, many important Microsoft Scripting Technologies, such as Windows Script File (WSF) and Windows Script Component (WSC) are based on XML. Besides these technologies, Microsoft also provides Microsoft XML (MSXML) Document Object Model (DOM) that you can use in your scripts to read and write XML documents.

DOM is an exact representation of the XML document in the memory. For example, the following XML document is represented as is (as you see in the file) in the memory:

```
<Servers>
    <Name>Server01</Name>
    <Name>Server02</Name>
</Servers>
```

MSXML DOM is a COM object that allows you to manipulate the DOM documents. For example the following code will read and echo all values in the `<Name>` and `</Name>` tags:

```
Set objXml = CreateObject("MSXML2.DOMDocument")
  objXml.Load "First.xml"
    Set objServers = objXml.SelectSingleNode("/Servers")
       For each objChild in objServers.ChildNodes
        Wscript.Echo objChild.Text
       Next
   Set objServers = nothing
Set objXml = nothing
```

As seen in this example, MSXML DOM object can be created using the `CreateObject` method. MSXML DOM can be created using the rental-threaded or the free-threaded model. The rental-threaded model can be created using `MSXML2.DOMDocument` unique identifier and the free-threaded model can be created using the `MSXML2.FreeThreaded-DOMDocument` unique identifier. Both models have identical behavior (that is, they both provide the same methods and properties and can be used in the same manner in the scripts); however, the rental-threaded model provides better performance because the parser does not have the overhead of managing multiple concurrent threads.

In most cases you would use the rental-threaded model as it provides better performance. However, there may be instances where you want to use the free-threaded model (rarely in case of scripts). For example, where the DOM object is created once and accessed by multiple users, such as an Active Server Pages (ASP) page accessed by multiple users, it would be best to create a free-threaded DOM object and store it in an application variable so that each user gets an instance of the same object rather than a new instance of the rental-threaded DOM object. To learn more about DOM object performance, you can read the following article: http://msdn.microsoft.com/library/default.asp?url=/library/en-us/dnexxml/html/xml02212000.asp

XML Document Format

The only requirement of an XML document is that it must be well formed; that is, it conforms to XML standards. For example, the following is a well-formed XML document:

```
<SERVERS>
    <SERVER ID="1" STATUS="on">
            <NAME>Server01</NAME>
            <DOMAIN>Domain1</DOMAIN>
            <LOCATION>New York</LOCATION>
    </SERVER>
    <SERVER ID="2" STATUS="on">
            <NAME>Server01</NAME>
```

```
            <DOMAIN>Domain2</DOMAIN>
            <LOCATION>New Jersey</LOCATION>
    </SERVER>
    <SERVER ID="3" STATUS="on">
            <NAME>Server01</NAME>
            <DOMAIN>Domain3</DOMAIN>
            <LOCATION>New England</LOCATION>
    </SERVER>
    <SERVER ID="4" STATUS="on">
            <NAME>Server01</NAME>
            <DOMAIN>Domain4</DOMAIN>
            <LOCATION>New Hampshire</LOCATION>
    </SERVER>
    <SERVER ID="5" STATUS="on">
            <NAME>Server01</NAME>
            <DOMAIN>Domain5</DOMAIN>
            <LOCATION>New Mexico</LOCATION>
    </SERVER>
</SERVERS>
```

A document is well formed if, at the minimum, it adheres to the following rules:

1. The start and the end tags are same; that is, if the start tag is `<MAIN>` then the end tag should be `</MAIN>`
2. The start and the end tags must match the case; that is, if the start tag is `<MAIN>` (all capital letters) the end tag must be `</MAIN>` (all capital letters); for instance the end tag cannot be `</main>` (all lowercase characters) or `</Main>` (combination of upper- and lowercase characters)
3. The start and end tags must be nested correctly; for example, `<main>…<server>…</main></server>` tags are not nested correctly since the starting and the end tags do not match. Correct nesting should be `<main><server>…</server></main>` where the start tag matches the end tag

Element

An XML document consists of tags known as elements (commonly known as nodes). An element is something that describes a piece of data (`<machinename>` tag may define the name of the machine). An element is governed by the following:

1. It is delimited by the < (less than) and > (greater than) tags.
2. Every element must have a matching closing tag that begins with < followed by / and ends with >. For example, the closing tag for `<MAIN>` is `</MAIN>`.
3. Elements are case sensitive; that is, `<Main>` element is not same as `<main>` or `<MaiN>` elements.

4. Elements must be properly nested. For example, `<main>…<server>…</main> </ server>` tags are not nested correctly since the starting and the end tags do not match. Correct nesting should be `<main><server>…</server></main>` where the start tag matches the end tag.
5. There can be only one root element in a document; other elements can be within this root element. The root element is technically known as the document element.
6. An element can contain other elements. The element that contains elements is known as the parent element and the elements within the parent element are known as the child elements (or children) as seen in Figure 2.68.

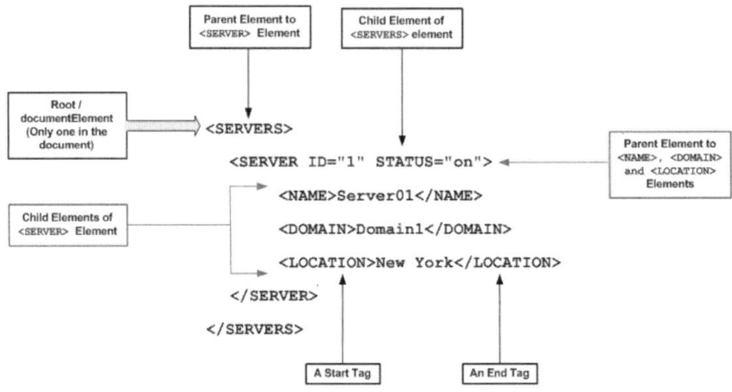

FIGURE 2.68 A typical XML document with root, parent, and child nodes.

7. There can be data within the start and end tags (`<Start>Data</Start>`).
8. Single tags can be used as empty tags; however, an empty tag must have a `/` (forward slash) before `>` (less than character) (for example, `<machinename/>`)

Table 2.28 lists some examples of elements:

TABLE 2.28 WSC XML Elements

Example	Description
`<Main></Main>`	Start and end tags
`<Main/>`	Empty tag
`<Server Status="off" />`	Empty tag that contains an attribute (attributes are explained in the next topic)
`<user>John Doe</user>`	Start and end tags that contain data

Attributes

Attributes are like helpers to the elements that are used to further explain the tag. For example, in the following XML file, each `<Server>` tag has the `STATUS` tag that provides additional information (that the server is `off` or `on`) about the server:

```
<Servers>
<Server STATUS="off">
    <name>Server01</>
</Server>
<Server STATUS="on" />
    <name>Server02</>
</Server>
<Server STATUS="on"/>
    <name>Server03</>
</Server>
</Servers>
```

If Attributes are used in the XML files, the following rules must be adhered to:

1. Attributes are case sensitive (therefore it is best to use the same case (upper or lower) to define the same attribute for each element of the same type)

For example, `STATUS` (all uppercase characters) is used in the last example. It makes retrieving the attribute values much easier, because only `[@STATUS="on"]` can be used to retrieve the element instead of multiples for each attributes. How to retrieve information is covered later in this section.

2. Attribute value must be enclosed within two double quotes
3. Attributes must be defined inside the start element before the `>` or `/>` symbols
4. There must be at the minimum one space between two attributes

Figure 2.69 shows a typical element with attributes.

Creating an XML file Using MSXML DOM

You can use the `FileSystemObject` to create an XML document. For example, the following code when run creates the XML document shown in Listing 2.48:

```
Dim ObjFs, ObjFile
  CONST FILE_NAME = "Servers.XML"
   XML_DATA = "<SERVERS>" & _
          "<SERVER>SERVER01</SERVER>" & _
          "<SERVER>Server02</SERVER>" & _
          "</SERVERS>"
   Set objFS = CreateObject("Scripting.FileSystemObject")
```

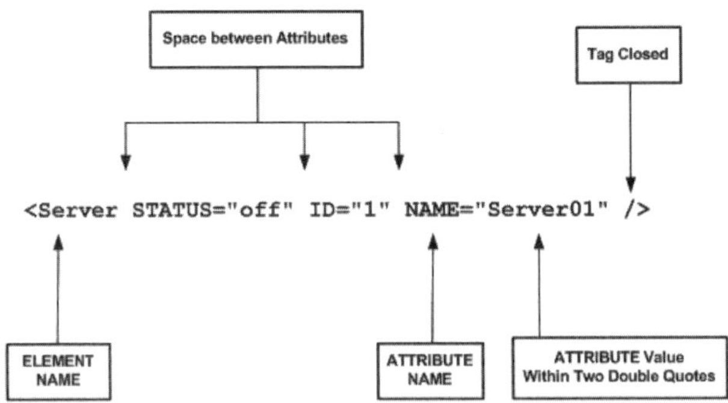

FIGURE 2.69 A typical element with attributes.

```
        Set objFile = objFs.CreateTextFile(FILE_NAME)
           objFile.Write XML_DATA
           objFile.Close
        Set objFile = nothing
     Set objFs = nothing
```

LISTING 2.48 `Servers.XML` File Definition

```
<SERVERS>
    <SERVER>SERVER01</SERVER>
    SERVER>Server02</SERVER>
 </SERVERS>
```

Alternatively, the XML file in Listing 2.48 can also be created using methods and properties exposed by the `MSXML2.DOMDocument` object, as shown in the following example:

```
Dim ObjXML
  CONST FILE_NAME = "Servers.XML"
   XML_DATA = "<SERVERS>" & _
          "<SERVER>SERVER01</SERVER>" & _
          "<SERVER>Server02</SERVER>" & _
          "</SERVERS>"
      Set objXML = CreateObject("MSXML2.DOMDocument")
    objXML.LoadXML XML_DATA
  objXML.Save FILE_NAME
Set objXML = nothing
```

Although you can manipulate an XML file as a text file using the `FileSystemObject`, it is, however, easier to work with XML documents using the MSXML DOM because it provides specific properties and methods (such as `LoadXML`, `CreateAttribute`, `CreateElement` covered in the next topic) that you can use to manipulate the XML document and its elements (nodes) and attributes.

Validating an XML File

After creating an XML file, you can validate that the XML file is well formed by simply opening it with IE. If the XML file is well formed, IE will display the XML data in the manner shown in Figure 2.70.

IE will display an error message if the XML file is not well formed. For instance, the closing tag `</SERVERS>` is missing from the XML file that causes the parser to display the error message shown in Figure 2.71.

Besides using IE to validate an XML file, you can also open the XML document with `MSXML2.DOMDocument` object's `Load` method to determine if the XML document is well formed. The following code can be used to validate an XML document:

```
Dim objXML
CONST XML_FILE = "Servers.xml"
 Set objXML = CreateObject("MSXML2.DOMDocument")
  objXML.Load XML_FILE
   if objxml.parseError.errorCode <> 0 then
    Wscript.Echo "Error Validating " & XML_FILE & _
                         VBNewLine & objXML.parseError.reason & _
                           VBNewLine & "Line # " & objXML.parseError.Line & _
                           VBNewLine & "Position # " &
objXML.parseError.LinePos
    Wscript.quit
   end if
 Wscript.Echo objXml.xml
Set objXML = nothing
```

FIGURE 2.70 Well-fomed `Servers.XML` file displayed with IE.

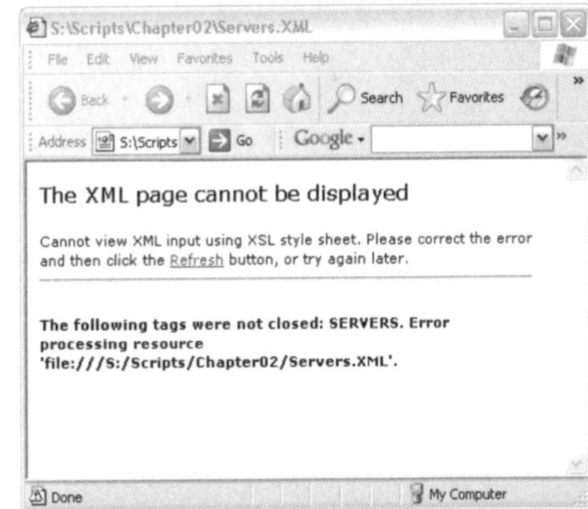

FIGURE 2.71 Error message displayed because the `Servers.XML` file is not well formed.

When the previous code is run, it will either display the XML data or an error, as shown in Figure 2.72.

Windows Script Host
Error Validating Servers.xml
The following tags were not closed: SERVERS.
OK

FIGURE 2.72 XML file error displayed if the document is not well formed.

Reading an XML File

To read an XML document, you must open it using MSXML DOM object's `Load` method. The `Load` method can be used to load an XML file into memory for reading and writing. It has the following syntax:

```
booleanValue = objXml.Load (XMLFile)
```

The `Load` method takes URL or a name (including path) of an XML file as the only argument. It returns a `Boolean` (`TRUE` if successful, `FALSE` if unsuccessful) value indicating if the method was able (or unable) to load the specified XML file. The following `Load.vbs` script loads the First.xml file and displays the content of the XML file, as shown in Figure 2.73:

```
Set objXml = CreateObject("MSXML2.DOMDocument")
  objXml.Load "First.xml"
    Wscript.Echo objXml.xml
Set objXml = nothing
```

Windows Script Host
<Servers>
<Name>Server01</Name>
<Name>Server02</Name>
</Servers>
OK

FIGURE 2.73 XML data displayed by `Load.vbs` script.

Besides displaying the entire content of the XML file, you can also search (matching a pattern) and read a single element or read multiple nodes of the same kind; you can use SelectSingleNode method to get a single node or use SelectNodes method to get multiple nodes of the same kind.

SelectSingleNode method retrieves the first instance of the node that matches the specified pattern. For example, the following retrieves the first <Name> node in the First.xml file and displays the data within the node (that is, displays Server01):

```
Set objXml = CreateObject("MSXML2.DOMDocument")
  objXml.Load "First.xml"
    Set objServer = objXml.SelectSingleNode("/Servers/Name")
    Wscript.Echo objServer.Text
    Set objServerName = nothing
Set objXml = nothing
```

SelectSingleNode takes the XPath (explained in the next section) query string as an argument and returns the first node object found by matching the query, as shown in the previous example. Once you have the node object, you can use several properties and methods to manipulate the node and the data within the node. For instance, the ParentNode property can be used to retrieve the parent node object of the returned object, as shown in the following example:

```
Set objXml = CreateObject("MSXML2.DOMDocument")
  objXml.Load "First.xml"
    Set objServer = objXml.SelectSingleNode("/Servers/Name")
    Set objServerParent = objServer.ParentNode
        Wscript.Echo objServerParent.NodeName
    Set objServerParent = nothing
   Set objServerName = nothing
Set objXml = nothing
```

Similarly, you can also use the ChildNodes property to retrieve all child nodes of the returned object. For example, the following code when executed displays the number of child nodes of the <Servers> node of the First.xml file:

```
Set objXml = CreateObject("MSXML2.DOMDocument")
  objXml.Load "First.xml"
    Set objServer = objXml.SelectSingleNode("/Servers")
    Set objServerChildren = objServer.ChildNodes
       Wscript.Echo objServerChildren.Length
    Set objServerParent = nothing
   Set objServerName = nothing
Set objXml = nothing
```

The ChildNodes property returns a collection of all the child nodes of the specified node that can be used to enumerate through the child nodes to display the text contained in each child node by looping through the collection, as shown in the following example:

```
Set objXml = CreateObject("MSXML2.DOMDocument")
  objXml.Load "First.xml"
    Set objServer = objXml.SelectSingleNode("/Servers")
    Set objServerChildren = objServer.ChildNodes
      For each child in objServerChildren
          Wscript.Echo Child.Text
      Next
    Set objServerParent = nothing
   Set objServerName = nothing
Set objXml = nothing
```

You also use the `FirstChild` property to get the first child node of the node object returned by the `SelectSingleNode` method, as shown in the following example:

```
Set objXml = CreateObject("MSXML2.DOMDocument")
  objXml.Load "First.xml"
    Set objServer = objXml.SelectSingleNode("/Servers")
    Set objServerFirstChild = objServer.FirstChild
      Wscript.Echo objServerFirstChild.Text
    Set objServerFirstChild = nothing
    Set objServer = nothing
Set objXml = nothing
```

While the `SelectSingleNode` can be used to retrieve the first node that matches the query pattern, `SelectNodes` returns the list of the nodes that match the query pattern. For example in the following script, `SelectNodes` retrieves all the `<Name>` nodes found in the `<Servers>` node:

```
Set objXml = CreateObject("MSXML2.DOMDocument")
  objXml.Load "First.xml"
    Set objServerName = objXml.SelectNodes("/Servers/Name")
    For i = 0 to objServerName.Length -1
            Wscript.Echo objServerName(i).text
    Next
    Set objServerName = nothing
Set objXml = nothing
```

In addition to retrieving a node, child nodes and the text of the node, you can also retrieve the attributes and its values. You can use the `Attributes` property to get the collection of all the properties of a node. For example, consider the following XML file with attributes defined for the `<SERVER>` nodes that the script in Listing 2.49 reads and displays:

```
<SERVERS>
    <SERVER ID="1" NAME="Server01" LOCATION="New York">
    <SERVER ID="2" NAME="Server01" LOCATION="New Jersey">
    <SERVER ID="3" NAME="Server01" LOCATION="New Mexico">
    <SERVER ID="4" NAME="Server01" LOCATION="New England">
    <SERVER ID="5" NAME="Server01" LOCATION="New Hampshire">
</SERVERS>
```

LISTING 2.49 `EnumAttributes.vbs` Script That Displays Each Attribute's Value

```
    Set objXml = CreateObject("MSXML2.DOMDocument")
      objXml.Load "ServersSample.xml"
    Set objServer = objXml.SelectNodes("/SERVERS/SERVER")
      For i = 0 to objServer.Length -1
              Set objAttrib = objServer(i).Attributes
                For each Attrib in objAttrib
                      Wscript.Echo Attrib.Name & " = " & Attrib.Text
                Next
              Set objAttrib = nothing
      Next
    Set objServerName = nothing
Set objXml = nothing
```

While the `Attributes` property can be used to retrieve all attributes of a node, the `GetAttribute` method can be used to retrieve a single attribute by name. The `GetAttribute` method takes the name of the attribute to retrieve as an argument and returns its value. In the following example the `GetAttribute` method is used to retrieve the value of the `NAME` attribute.

```
Set objXml = CreateObject("MSXML2.DOMDocument")
  objXml.Load "ServersSample.xml"
    Set objServer = objXml.SelectNodes("/SERVERS/SERVER")
    For i = 0 to objServer.Length -1
            Wscript.Echo objServer(i).GetAttribute("NAME")
    Next
    Set objServerName = nothing
Set objXml = nothing
```

Search XML Document Using XPath

XML Path Language is a general purpose language that can be used to navigate (query / filter) through XML documents. It can be used to search for a specific node (or nodes) within the XML document by querying for specific nodes or attributes.

XPath defines a path to a specific part of the XML document. For example, `/SERVERS/SERVER` defines a path to the `SERVER` nodes within the `SERVERS` node in the following XML document:

```
<SERVERS>
    <SERVER/>
    <SERVER/>
</SERVERS>
```

XPath represents an XML document as an inverted tree of nodes. It identifies the nodes of the XML document based on their type, name and values, in addition to the relationship of a node to the other nodes (such as Parent node, Child node, Sibling node) in the XML document. XPath returns one of the following objects:

- Node set
- Boolean
- Number
- String

For example, the query `/SERVERS/SERVER[@ID="1"]` returns the `<SERVER>` node whose `ID` attribute equals `1`. XPath is supported only by `SelectSingleNode` and `SelectNodes` methods of the MSXML DOM. The following example illustrates how to use `SelectSingleNode` method to display the value of the `LOCATION` attribute of the `<SERVER>` node whose `ID` is equal to `1`:

```
Set objXml = CreateObject("MSXML2.DOMDocument")
  objXml.Load "ServersSample.xml"
    Set objServer = objXml.SelectSingleNode("/SERVERS/SERVER[@ID='1']")
    Wscript.Echo objServer.GetAttribute("LOCATION")
    Set objServerName = nothing
Set objXml = nothing
```

XPath expressions can be absolute (starting from the root of the XML document) or relative (starting from the currently selected node). The following is an example of an absolute path:

```
/SERVERS/SERVER[@ID="2"]/NAME
```

The following is an example of a relative path

```
SERVER[@ID="2"]/NAME
```

of the following XML document

```
<SERVERS>
    <SERVER ID="1">
            <NAME>NewYork02</NAME>
    </SERVER>
    <SERVER ID="2">
            <NAME>NewYourk01</NAME>
    </SERVER>
</SERVERS>
```

Following are examples of some basic XPath expressions:

Current Context: `./` denotes the current context. For example, `./SERVER` refers to all the `<SERVER>` nodes in the current context as illustrated in the following example:

```
Set objXml = CreateObject("MSXML2.DOMDocument")
  objXml.Load "ServersSample.xml"
    Set objRootNode = objXml.SelectSingleNode("/SERVERS")
```

```
        Set objServer = objRootNode.SelectNodes("./SERVER")
      Wscript.Echo objServer.Length
        Set objServer = nothing
      Set objRootNode = nothing
Set objXml = nothing
```

When the script is executed it displays `5` as the number of `<SERVER>` nodes within the `<SERVERS>` node.

Document Root: `/` denotes the root of the document. For example, the following displays the number of elements in the document root:

```
Set objXml = CreateObject("MSXML2.DOMDocument")
  objXml.Load "ServersSample.xml"
    Set objRootNode = objXml.SelectSingleNode("/")
    Wscript.Echo objRootNode.ChildNodes.Length
      Set objRootNode = nothing
Set objXml = nothing
```

Recursive Descent: Every element can be substituted with `/`. For example, typing `//SERVER` is equal to typing `/SERVERS/SERVER`. In this example, the first `/` is for the root and the second `/` is for the `SERVERS` element. The following illustrates how to retrieve the `SERVER` element of the `SERVERS` element with the `ID` attribute value of `1`:

```
Set objXml = CreateObject("MSXML2.DOMDocument")
  objXml.Load "ServersSample.xml"
    Set objServer = objXml.SelectSingleNode("//SERVER[@ID='1']")
    Wscript.Echo objServer.NodeName
      Set objServer = nothing
Set objXml = nothing
```

You can create more complex expressions by combining these simple expressions and using the various XPath operators and special characters shown in Table 2.29.

This book covers only the basic parts of the XPath language. A complete discussion on XPath is beyond the scope of this book. You can get more information on XPath from http://Msdn.Microsoft.com.

Adding Elements and Element Value

Elements can be added to XML documents using MSXML DOM object's `CreateElement` method. The `CreateElement` method takes a string (name of the element) as a parameter to create the element in an existing element (or the `documentElement`). It returns the newly created element as an object. The `CreateElement` method has the following syntax:

```
set objNewNode = objXml.CreateElement(ElementName)
```

TABLE 2.29 XPath Operators and Special Characters

Operator	Description
/	Child operator; selects immediate children of the left-side collection. When this path operator appears at the start of the pattern, it indicates that children should be selected from the root node.
//	Recursive descent; searches for the specified element at any depth. When this path operator appears at the start of the pattern, it indicates recursive descent from the root node.
.	Indicates the current context.
..	The parent of the current context node.
*	Wildcard; selects all elements regardless of the element name.
@	Attribute; prefix for an attribute name.
@*	Attribute wildcard; selects all attributes regardless of name.
:	Namespace separator; separates the namespace prefix from the element or attribute name.
( )	Groups operations to explicitly establish precedence.
[ ]	Applies a filter pattern.
[ ]	Subscript operator; used for indexing within a collection.
+	Performs addition.
-	Performs subtraction.
div	Performs floating-point division according to IEEE 754.
*	Performs multiplication.
mod	Returns the remainder from a truncating division.

The `objNewElement` is the variable that will hold the new element object returned by the `CreateElement` method. The `objXml` is the `documentElement` (root of the document) in which the element is created. The `ElementName` is the name of the element to be created. For example, the following statement will create the <SERVER> element in the XML document:

```
set objNewNode = objXml.CreateElement("SERVER")
```

The `CreateElement` method only creates a new element for the XML document and must be appended as a child element to either the root element or some other element in the document. The newly created element can be appended as a child element of a node using the `AppendChild` method. The `AppendChild` method appends the newly created element as the last element of the node you are trying to append to. For example, the `CreateElement.vbs` script shown in Figure 2.74 creates a new <SERVER> node and appends it to the <SERVERS> node as the last child element.

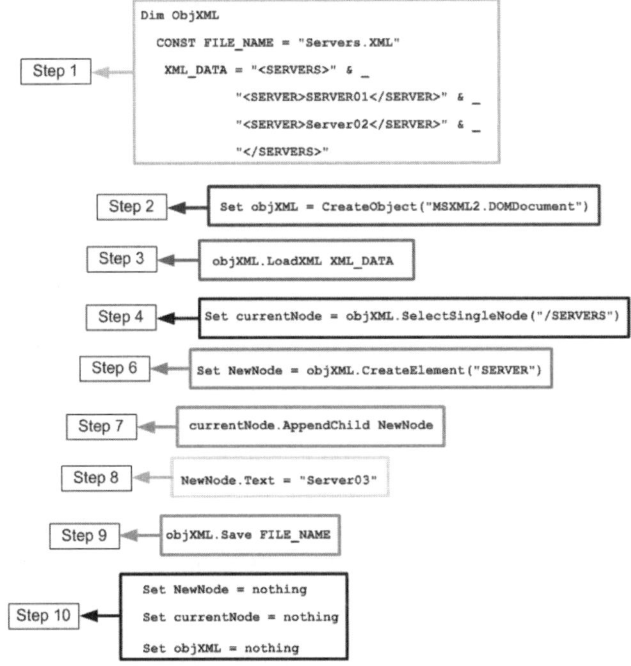

FIGURE 2.74 `CreateElement.vbs` script steps.

When the `CreateElement.vbs` script shown in Figure 2.74 is executed, it will do the following step-by-step:

1. Initialize the variables and constants including the initial XML elements
2. Create an `MSXML2.DOMDocument` object and store it in `objXml` variable
3. Load the initialized XML data from the `XML_DATA` constant
4. Get the `<SERVERS>` root element that will be the parent to the `<SERVER>` element that will be created and store it in the `currentNode` variable
5. Create the `<SERVER>` element using the `CreateElement` method and store it in the `NewNode` variable
6. Append the newly created element to the `currentNode` (the `<SERVERS>` node)
7. Add text to the newly created element
8. Save the XML file
9. Release memory used by the script

Adding Attributes and Setting Attribute Value

Like elements, attributes can also be appended to elements using the `MSXML2.DOMDocument` object methods and properties. Attributes can be appended by calling the `CreateAttribute` method.

The `CreateAttrbute` method takes a string (attribute name) as an argument and returns the newly created attribute as an object. `CreateAttribute` method has the following syntax:

```
set objNewAttrib = objXml.CreateAttribute(AttrbuteName)
```

Like the `CreateElement` method, the `CreateAttribute` method also only creates the attribute in the memory for the XML document. To attach the attribute (created using the `CreateAttribute` method) to an element, you must first get the attributes of the element using the `Attributes` property as follows:

```
Set objCurrentAttribs = objCurrentNode.Attributes
```

After retrieving the attributes of the current element (node) you can add the newly created Attribute using the `SetNamedItem` method as follows:

```
objCurrentAttribs.SetNamedItem objNewAttrib
```

Once the newly created attribute is appended to the element, you can save the XML file. However, this will only set an empty attribute (attribute with no value). To set the value of the attribute, you can use the `Text` property of the attribute object as follows:

```
objNewattrib.Text = "On"
```

The script in Listing 2.50 is the complete code that illustrates how to add the `STATUS` attribute with `On` value for each `<SERVER>` node in the following XML document:

```
<SERVERS>
    <SERVER>Server01</SERVER>
    <SERVER>Server02</SERVER>
    <SERVER>Server03</SERVER>
</SERVERS>
```

LISTING 2.50 `CreateAttribute` Script

```
Dim ObjXML
CONST FILE_NAME = "Servers.XML"
 XML_DATA = "<SERVERS>" & _
        "<SERVER>SERVER01</SERVER>" & _
        "<SERVER>Server02</SERVER>" & _
        "</SERVERS>"
      Set objXML = CreateObject("MSXML2.DOMDocument")
       objXML.LoadXML XML_DATA
```

```
                Set currentNode = objXML.SelectSingleNode("/SERVERS")
                  For each objChild in currentNode.ChildNodes
                     Set NewAttrib = _
                          objXml.CreateAttribute("STATUS")
                        Set currentAttribs = objChild.Attributes
                      currentAttribs.SetNamedItem NewAttrib
                     NewAttrib.Text = "On"
                  Next
              Set currentNode = nothing
           objXML.Save FILE_NAME
         Set objXML = nothing
```

Changing Attribute Value

The value of an attribute can be set in several ways. However, the easiest method is to use the `SetAttribute` method to set a new value to the attribute. For example, the following script changes the value of the `STATUS` attribute to `Off` from `On`:

```
Dim objXML
CONST XML_FILE = "Servers.xml"
 Set objXML = CreateObject("MSXML2.DOMDocument")
  objXML.Load XML_FILE
    Set objRoot = objXML.SelectSingleNode("/SERVERS")
      For each objChild in objRoot.ChildNodes
      objChild.SetAttribute "STATUS","Off"
    Set objStatusAttrib = nothing
      Next
    objXML.Save XML_FILE
   Set objRoot = nothing
 Set objXML = nothing
```

The attribute value is changed using the `SetAttribute` method. The `SetAttribute` method takes the attribute `name` and the attribute `value` as arguments. It sets the value of the attribute if it exists, and creates the attribute (and sets the value) if the attribute does not exist.

Changing Element Value

To change the value of an existing element, you can either use the `Text` property or the `NodeValue` property. The example in Listing 2.51 illustrates how to set the value of an element using the `Text` property and the example in Listing 2.52 illustrates how to set the element value using the `NodeValue` property.

LISTING 2.51 Using `Text` Property to Set Element Value

```
       Dim objXML
CONST XML_FILE = "Servers.xml"
i = 5
```

```
Set objXML = CreateObject("MSXML2.DOMDocument")
 objXML.Load XML_FILE
   Set objRoot = objXML.SelectSingleNode("/SERVERS")
     For each objChild in objRoot.ChildNodes
        objChild.Text = "Server0" & i
        i = i + 1
     Next
   objXML.Save XML_FILE
  Set objRoot = nothing
Set objXML = nothing
```

LISTING 2.52 Using `NodeValue` Property to Set Element Value

```
      Dim objXML
CONST XML_FILE = "Servers.xml"
i = 5
 Set objXML = CreateObject("MSXML2.DOMDocument")
  objXML.Load XML_FILE
    Set objRoot = objXML.SelectSingleNode("/SERVERS")
      For each objChild in objRoot.ChildNodes
         objChild.NodeValue = "Server0" & i
         i = i + 1
      Next
    objXML.Save XML_FILE
   Set objRoot = nothing
 Set objXML = nothing
```

Removing a Node or an Attribute

To remove an attribute from a node, MSXML DOM object provides the `RemoveAttribute` method. The `RemoveAttribute` method takes the name of the attribute as the only argument. It has the following syntax:

```
objCurrentNode.RemoveAttribute AttributeName
```

For example, the code in Listing 2.53 removes the `STATUS` attribute from all `<SERVER>` nodes in the `Servers.XML` file.

LISTING 2.53 Remove Attribute Example

```
Dim ObjXML
CONST FILE_NAME = "Servers.XML"
XML_DATA = "<SERVERS>" & _
        "<SERVER>SERVER01</SERVER>" & _
        "<SERVER>Server02</SERVER>" & _
        "</SERVERS>"
   Set objXML = CreateObject("MSXML2.DOMDocument")
      objXML.LoadXML XML_DATA
        Set currentNode = objXML.SelectSingleNode("/SERVERS")
           For each objChild in currentNode.ChildNodes
              objChild.RemoveAttribute "STATUS"
```

```
            Next
        Set currentNode = nothing
    objXML.Save FILE_NAME
    Set objXML = nothing
```

It is simple to remove an attribute from an element, however it is a bit more complex to remove a node from the XML file. It is because there is only one attribute in an element with the name that you want to remove but there may be several nodes with similar names. For example, it is simple to remove the `STATUS` attribute from the `<SERVER>` elements because there is only one `STATUS` attribute per element. On the other hand, because there are multiple `<SERVER>` nodes in the XML file, it is not as simple calling a `removeNode` method to remove a `<SERVER>` node; you must first identify which `<SERVER>` the node to remove before attempting to remove the node.

Removing a node is not as simple as passing the name of the node to a method for removing it from the XML file, therefore the MSXML DOM object does not provide a `removeNode` *method.*

The following code demonstrates how to remove a `<SERVER>` node from the Servers.XML file that we created earlier in this section:

```
Dim objXML
CONST XML_FILE = "Servers.xml"
Set objXML = CreateObject("MSXML2.DOMDocument")
  objXML.Load XML_FILE
    Set objRoot = objXML.SelectSingleNode("/SERVERS")
      For each objChild in objRoot.ChildNodes
    if UCase(objChild.Text) = "SERVER01" then
       objRoot.removeChild objChild
    End if
      Next
    objXML.Save XML_FILE
   Set objRoot = nothing
 Set objXML = nothing
```

In the previous example (when the script is executed), the script loops through each child node of the `<SERVERS>` node, compares the node value of each `<SERVER>` node and removes the child node of the `<SERVERS>` if the node value matches `SERVER01`.

To remove the node, the script calls the `removeChild` method. The `removeChild` method takes the child node object as an argument and returns the removed node as an object. It has the following syntax:

```
Set RemovedNode = objParentNode.removeChild objChild
```

1. `RemoveNode` in the syntax is the variable that will store the returned removed child node. `ObjParentNode` in the syntax is the object of the parent node from which the child node (`objChild`) is being removed using the `removeChild` method.
2. XML documents work great as short databases that can be easily searched and manipulated using MSXML DOM object model. Part II of this book extensively uses MSXML DOM object model to manipulate XML documents. Part II of the book will show you the practical use of the XML documents in scripts.

WINDOWS MANAGEMENT INSTRUMENTATION (WMI)

Web-based Enterprise Management (WBEM) is an IT industry initiative that focuses on developing a standard technology for accessing management information in an enterprise environment. WMI is Micrsoft's implementation of the WBEM standard. WMI uses one of the WBEM's core Common Information Model (CIM) standards to represent systems, applications, networks, devices, registry, services, and other management components. WMI can be used to automate Windows administration tasks in an enterprise environment.

WMI comes pre-installed with all Windows versions except Windows NT 4.0 and below operating systems. However, a free download is available for Windows NT, Windows 98/95 at *http://Microsoft.Com/downloads* (you must download and install it on the system, before you can use WMI-based scripts on these older systems).

NOTE

Although the WMI core component for Windows NT and Windows 95/98 can be downloaded and installed, it only provides limited functionality. To learn more on this see the WMI documentation.

WMI Providers

Systems can be managed through the WMI application programming interface (API). Using WMI APIs scripts can get and set static information maintained in the CIM repository and dynamic information maintained by the various types of providers.

WMI providers provide data to WMI that can be queried using WMI APIs. For example, the Win32 provider provides hardware and software information through Win32 APIs. Similarly, the Active Directory provider maps Active Directory objects to WMI that can be used in the scripts by accessing the Lightweight Directory Access Protocol (LDAP). Besides these providers, WMI also provides the following standard providers:

BizTalk Provider: Can be used to access the BizTalk administration object represented by WMI classes.

Cooked Counter Provider: This high-performance provider can be used to retrieve cooked (calculated) monitoring information. The Cooked Counter provider supplies cooked classes that allow scripts to obtain cooked performance data.

Performance Monitoring Provider: While the Cooked Counter provider returns cooked (calculated) monitoring information, the Performance Monitoring provider returns the monitoring information in its raw format (as returned by the operating system).

DFS Provider: The Distributed File System (DFS) provider provides for DFS administration through WMI classes.

DNS Provider: The DNS provider can be used to manage and configure Domain Name System (DNS) servers.

Disk Quota Provider: The Disk Quota provider allows you to manage disk quota settings through scripts.

Eventlog Provider: The Eventlog provider can be used to manage event log entries and event log files using scripts.

Internet Information Server (IIS) Provider: The IIS provider exposes programming interfaces for IIS server management. Using the IIS provider you can configure IIS servers and Web sites.

IP Route Provider: The IP Route provider can be used to get IP routing table information.

Job Object Provider: This read-only provider provides access to data about named kernel job objects; it does not report unnamed kernel job objects.

Microsoft Network Load Balancing (NLB) Provider: This provider allows you to automate management of Microsoft NLB. It provides several WMI classes that can be used for managing NLB.

Ping Provider: The provider provides status information provided by the standard *Ping* command. It can be used to ping a system to know its current status on the network.

Policy Provider: The Policy provider provides extensions to group policy through WMI classes, permitting refinements in the application of policy. Policies can be set using the WMI Query Language (WQL) and reside in the Active Directory.

Power Management Event Provider: The Power Management Event provider supplies information to the Win32_PowerManagementEvent class to describe power management events that result from power state changes.

Reporting Services Provider: Defines classes that allow you to automate the management of the Report Server and the Report Manager.

Security Provider: The Security provider can be used to retrieve and change the security settings of the accounts and file system.

Server Cluster: Defines a set of WMI classes that can be used to automate Microsoft cluster server management.

Session Provider: The Session provider can be used to manage network sessions and connections.

Shadow Copy Provider: The Shadow Copy provider can be used for storage volume management.

System Registry Provider: The System Registry provider can be used to retrieve and modify system registry keys and values.

Terminal Services Provider: The Terminal Services provider allows the scripts to manage the Terminal Services environment.

TrustMon Provider: The TrustMon provider provides access to information about domain trusts.

View Provider: The View provider creates new instances and methods based on instances of other WMI classes.

WDM Provider: Windows Driver Model (WDM) provider provides scripts access to the classes, instances, methods, and events of the hardware drivers that conform to the WDM.

Win32 Provider: This most commonly used WMI provider can be used for Windows system management.

Windows Installer Provider: The Windows Installer provider provides acces to information collected from Windows installer compliant applications and makes Windows Installer procedures available remotely. It can be used to retrieve information and deploy Windows Installer compliant packages.

Windows Product Activation: The Windows Product Activation provider can be used to administer Windows Product Activation (WPA) in Windows.

Since WMI in itself is a vast topic, a complete dicussion on WMI is beyond the scope of this book. Only specific classes of specific providers will be discussed in this book. For instance, not all classes exposed by the Win32 provider will be discussed. There are several good books are available, such as those by Alain Lisior, to learn more about WMI.

WMI Classes and Namespaces

WMI exposes systems management through classes. These classes map to system components, such as hard disk, processor, memory, operating system, network, services, etc. The classes provide methods and properties that can be used to read and write information to the system components on a local or remote system. Win32 WMI class is the most commonly used class for systems administration. There are several Win32 classes that can be used to manage the hardware, software, and the Windows operating system. For instance, as seen in the following example, the `Win32_OperatingSystem` class provides the `Caption` property that when queried retrieves the name of the operating system:

```
set objWMI = GetObject("Winmgmts:")
set objOpSys = objWMI.ExecQuery( _
"Select Caption from Win32_OperatingSystem")
       For each os in objOpSys
                Wscript.Echo os.Caption
       Next
   set objOpSys = nothing
set objWMI = nothing
```

Similarly, the computer name can also be retrieved using the `Name` property that is exposed by the `Win32_ComputerSystem` class. The following example illustrates how to use WMI to retrieve the local computer name:

```
set objWMI = GetObject("Winmgmts:")
   set objCs = objWMI.ExecQuery( _
                "Select Name from Win32_ComputerSystem")
       For each cs in objCs
                Wscript.Echo cs.Name
           Next
       set objCs = nothing
    set objWMI = nothing
```

WMI classes are organized into logical groups using namespaces. For example, the Win32 classes are grouped into the `Cimv2` namespace. Similar to a directory structure that has a drive (such as C:) as the top level folder within which all other folders reside, in WMI, all namespaces are a part of the `Root` top level namespace by default within which all namespaces reside.

Before you can use the WMI classes, you need to know the object path. For example, the following is a complete path to the `CIMV2` namespace that groups together the Win32 classes by default:

```
\\ComputerName\Root\Cimv2
```

The `ComputerName` in the object path can be the NetBIOS name of the local or the remote computer. `Root\Cimv2` is the path to the `Cimv2` namespace that is the part of the `Root` (top level) namespace.

Connecting to WMI

To manage systems tasks using WMI, you must first connect to the `SWbemServices` object for the namespace you want to query. For example, the following connects to the `Root\Cimv2` namespace on a remote computer with the `Florida` NetBIOS name:

```
set objWMI = Getobject("Winmgmts:\\Florida\Root\Cimv2")
```

You can either use a WMI moniker (as shown in the previous example) or use the WMI locator object to connect, query, and administer systems using WMI. WMI monikers can be created using the `GetObject` method and the WMI Locator object using the `CreateObject` method.

A WMI moniker has one mandatory and two optional components, as shown in Figure 2.75. The mandatory component is the prefix `"Winmgmts:"` (the colon and quotes are the part of the name). One optional component, as seen in Figure 2.75 is the security settings which can include the impersonation level, authentication level, authenticating authority, and security privilege. The second optional component is the object path (as discussed earlier in this topic), which might be a path to a remote computer, WMI namespace, or Win32 class.

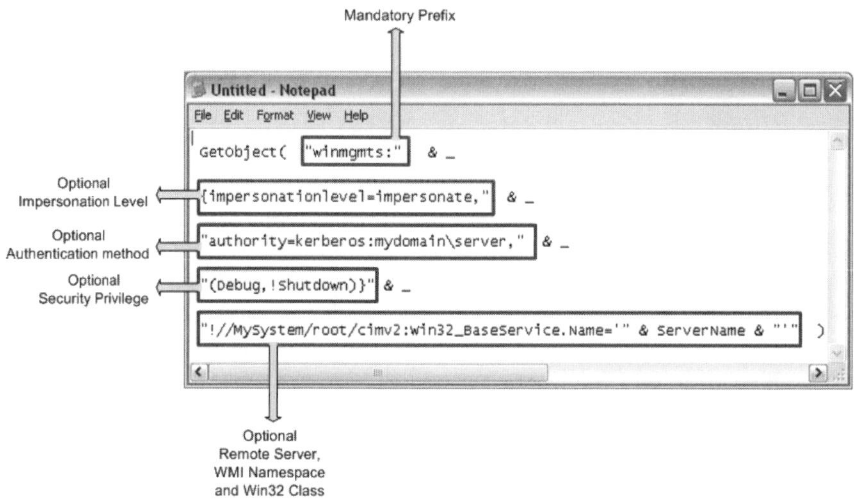

FIGURE 2.75 WMI moniker.

The WMI locator object on the other hand requires you to create the object and then call the `ConnectServer` method to connect to the WMI service, as shown in the example in Listing 2.54.

LISTING 2.54 WMI Object Locator Example

```
set objLocator = CreateObject("WbemScripting.SWbemLocator")
Set objWMI = objLocator.ConnectServer
set objOpSys = objWMI.ExecQuery( _
"Select Caption from Win32_OperatingSystem")
    For each os in objOpSys
        Wscript.Echo os.Caption
    Next
set objOpSys = nothing
set objWMI = nothing
set objLocator = nothing
```

The `ConnectServer` method takes the eight optional arguments and returns the `SWbemServices` object that is bound to the namespace specified in the optional `strNameSpace` (if not specified, the default namespace set in the `Hkey_local_Machine\Software\Microsoft\Wbem\Scripting\Default Namespace` registry value is used) argument. Following is the syntax of the `ConnectServer` method:

```
set objWMI = ConnectServer                (
  [ strServer = "." ],
  [ strNamespace = "" ],
  [ strUser = "" ],
  [ strPassword = "" ],
  [ strLocale = "" ],
  [ strAuthority = "" ],
  [ iSecurityFlags = 0 ],
  [ objwbemNamedValueSet = 0 ]
)
```

Table 2.30 lists and describes each `ConnectServer` argument.

TABLE 2.30 `ConnectServer` Method Arguments

Operator	Description
`strServer`	The `strServer` in the syntax can be the NetBIOS name (or IP Address) of the remote or local system.
`strNameSpace`	The `strNamespace` argument can be used to pass the namespace that you want the object bound to. For example, the following would bound the `Cimv2` namespace: `Root\Cimv2`
`strUser`	The `strUser` argument can be used to pass the user id to connect as. It can be in the Domain\UserName format.
`strPassword`	The `strPassword` can be used to pass the password for the user id specified in the `strUser` argument.
`strLocale`	The `strLocale` argument can be used to specify the lacalization code.

→

Operator	Description
strAuthority	The strAuthority can be used to set the authentication method. It takes Kerberos or NTLMDomain strings as the arguments, if passed.
iSecurityFlags	The iSecurityFlags can be used to pass flag values. A value of 0 causes the call to ConnectServer method to return only after the connection to the server is established. Whereas a value of 128 guarantees the call to return in 2 minutes or less which prevent your program from hanging indefinitely if the connection cannot be established successfully.
objwbemNamedValueSet	The objwbemNamedValueSet is generally left blank. However, if used it can only be SWbemNamedValueSet object that is used to provide additional information to the provider.

Besides the ConnectServer method, the locator object also exposes the Security_ property that can be used to read or set the security settings for the locator object. For example.The following example demonstrates how to set the AutheticationLevel (to packet level), ImpersonationLevel (to impersonate), and the Privileges (to debug) of the locator object.

```
CONST wbemAuthenticationLevelPkt = 4
CONST wbemImpersonationLevelImpersonate = 3
 set objLocator = CreateObject("WbemScripting.SWbemLocator")
  Set objWMI = objLocator.ConnectServer
   objWMI.Security_.AuthenticationLevel = wbemAuthenticationLevelPkt
     objWMI.Security_.ImpersonationLevel = _
                                wbemImpersonationLevelImpersonate
      objWMI.Security_.Privileges.AddAsString _
                                     "SeDebugPrivilege", True
          set objOpSys = objWMI.ExecQuery( _
                   "Select Caption from Win32_OperatingSystem")
                       For each os in objOpSys
                            Wscript.Echo os.Caption
                       Next
   set objOpSys = nothing
  set objWMI = nothing
set objLocator = nothing
```

SUMMARY

This chapter is the heart of the book. In this chapter you learned about the various Microsoft scripting technologies that you can use to automate systems management. The rest of the book is set up to show you how to implement these technologies to practical solutions. In this chapter you learned the VBScript language and how to create and run scripts in different environments. This chapter also covered new technologies such as MSXML DOM. It included practical examples that use combinations of various Windows scripting tecnologies to create a solution.

The next chapter, Chapter 3, delves into standardizing scripts and code. It gives you an insight of how and what to standardize in your scripts to make them easier to create, read, and maintain.

3 Scripting Standards

In This Chapter

- Introduction to scripting standards
- Why standardize?
- Naming standards
- Coding standards
- Script attributes
- Securing passwords
- Running scripts
- Testing scripts
- Debugging scripts

This chapter introduces you to good practices, techniques, and guidelines that you can use to develop scripting standards best suitable for you and your organization. Figure 3.1 illustrates a template of good practices covered in this chapter.

INTRODUCTION TO SCRIPTING STANDARDS

Project Management Institute (PMI) (*http://www.PMI.org*) establishes project management standards and guidelines; Distributed Management Task Force (*http://www.DMTF.org*) defines the Common Information Model (CIM) (WMI is Microsoft's implementation of CIM) standards. Similarly, World Wide Web Consortium (W3C) (*http://www.W3.org*) outlines the Web specifications and guidelines. However, there is no such body that outlines specifications or standards for scripting for Windows administration. Therefore, you must develop your own scripting standards that satisfy the good practice needs of you and your organization.

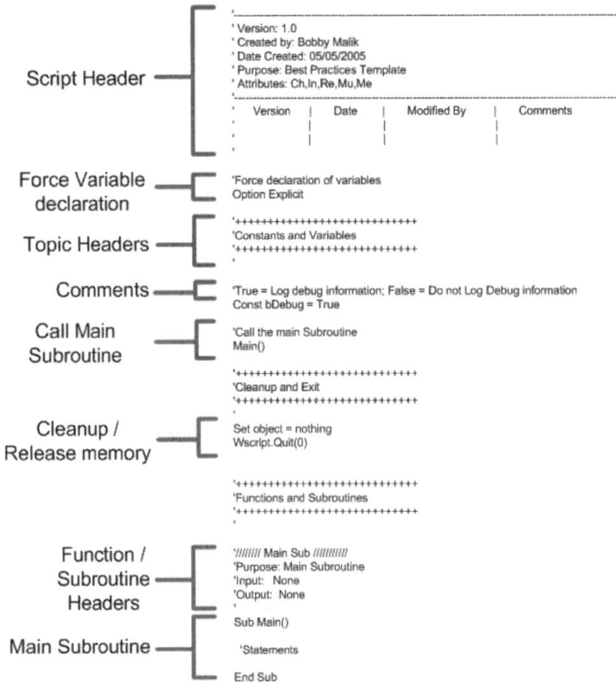

FIGURE 3.1 Good practices example.

There are several standards that you may want to form—starting from how to name the script files to how to run a script. Some standards you may adopt from your existing organizational programming standards, and others you may have to write from scratch.

For example, your organization may state that only specific comments should be included within the code to limit the size of the program, as shown in Listing 3.1.

LISTING 3.1 Example of Specific Comment

```
'True = Overwrite existing file; False = Do not overwrite existing file
Const bOverwrite = True
```

On the other hand, there may not be a standard that defines the length or the position of the comment, and you may have to formalize them. Similarly, there may be a standard defined for indenting your code, as shown in Figure 3.2, but there may not be a standard to define if you should use a TAB or a SPACE to indent your code.

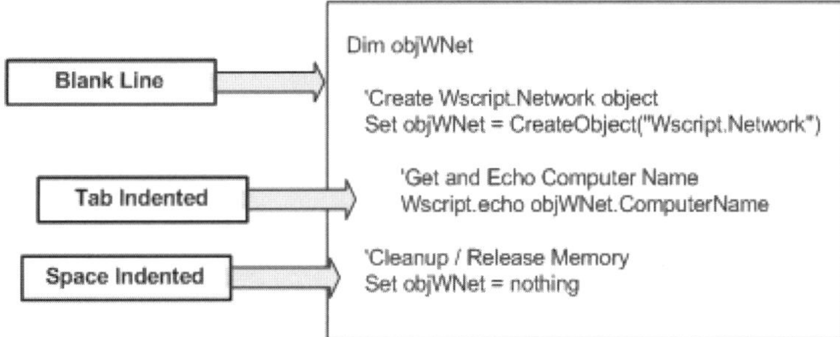

FIGURE 3.2 Example of indented code.

WHY STANDARDIZE?

If you are like most administrators, you may be thinking Why standardize? After all, standardization is yet another set of rules that you would need to follow (we all know that indenting your script would increase the time to write the script, and adding comments to your script would make your scripts larger). But imagine if this book wasn't formatted using standard English, that is, it did not follow any rules of written English and contained no punctuation; the book would have lines written as:

```
thisisabookonscriptingandautomationforwindowsitcoversseveralmicrosoftwindow-
stechnologiesandcontainsmanypracticalscriptingexamples
```

Can you read these lines? Do you wonder why? Simple, it is because the lines are not formatted and do not follow any of the rules of written English. If formatted correctly, as per English standards, the text should look as shown in Listing 3.2.

LISTING 3.2 Good Paragraph Formatting

```
     This is a book on scripting and automation for windows.  It covers several
  Microsoft Windows technologies and contains many practical scripting examples.
```

Similarly, a poorly formatted script may not be readable or understandable (even to you, if you happen to open the script after a lapsed period of time). For example, the script in Figure 3.3 is not formatted, that is, the code in the script is not indented for clarity and the variable names are not meaningful, making the script difficult to read and understand.

While it is necessary to format your code to make it readable and understandable, it is also vital that you format the results produced by a script. For example, the script in Figure 3.3, when run, does not format the output, making the output less readable and understandable, as seen in Listing 3.3.

```
set v1=createobject("scripting.filesystemobject")
set v2=v1.getfile("c:\windows\system32\wscript.exe")
set v3=v1.createtextfile("this is a file")
d1=true
if d1=true then
v3.write v2.name
d2=false
if d2=false then
v3.write v2.type
if d3=true then
v3.writeline v2.size
end if
end if
d4=5
if d4=5 then
v3.write v2.path
end if
end if
```

FIGURE 3.3 Bad code formatting example.

LISTING 3.3 Non-Formatted Output Generated by the Script in Figure 3.3

```
WSCRIPT.EXEApplicationC:\WINDOWS\SYSTEM32\WSCRIPT.EXE
```

It is not only necessary to format your code and the output generated by the script, it is also essential to appropriately name your script files. For example, if you name the script listed in Figure 3.3 as `ascript.vbs`, the name will not tell you what you created the script for. Therefore, it is essential to name your scripts in a more meaningful way, such as naming the script listed in Figure 3.3 as `BadFormattingExample.vbs`. That name immediately lets you know that this script was created as an example for bad formatting, which is more meaningful than naming the script `ascript.vbs`. Table 3.1 lists the scripting standards, explained in detail later in this chapter.

TABLE 3.1 Scripting Standards

Standard	Description	Example
Naming	Discusses the naming standards, such as name should not contain any spaces, should not be more than 16 characters, etc.	`setLegalText.vbs`
Coding	Defines standards for coding, including naming variables, including comments, indenting the code, structure of the scripts, and setting the default values	Include Script Headers Use i as a prefix for variables that hold integer-type value

→

Standard	Description	Example
Script Attributes	Discusses the categorization options, i.e., categorizing the scripts based on what the script does: does it run on a single system or a multiple system, do you run it only once or multiple times on scheduled basis, do you run the script unattended or interactively, etc.	`Ro`, `Un`, `On`, `Si`, `Lo`
Passwords	Discusses usage of passwords in scripts, such as non-interactive passwords or interactive passwords. Also describes encrypting for storage and using Script Store for encrypted storage and how to use certificates for encryption and decryption	Passed on command line In-Script passwords stored encrypted using Script Store
Running Scripts	Discusses options for running your scripts including using the type of shell to run your scripts	Run with `Cscript.exe /Nologo` option
Testing Scripts	Discusses how to prepare your environment for testing your scripts and how to create test cases for testing script functionality	Test Case 1: Check if a folder was created. Test Case 2: Check if a folder was deleted successfully.

NAMING STANDARDS

"To name your scripts right, important it is."

It is how Master Yoda (from *Star Wars*) would put it; and rightly so. If you think of it, if names were not important, then why would you have a name, and more so a meaningful one? Wouldn't you be called *6@%* or *1* or *soandso?* When was the last time some one addressed you as *I*? Hopefully, never.

Likewise, it wouldn't be meaningful if you name your scripts: `onescript.vbs` or `script1.vbs` or `myscript.vbs`. Therefore, it is important to create some naming standards that provide you consistency in naming your scripts and help you in identifying them. At the minimum a name should provide a clear understanding of what the script does or what you created it for, such as `DisplayMessage.vbs` or `calcLapsedDays.vbs`. Table 3.2 provides few guidelines that you can use to build your script naming standards upon.

TABLE 3.2 Script File Naming Standards

Standard	Description	Example

Meaningful Name	Give your script files a meaningful name. (A name that describes in brief what the script was created for or what it does.) As discussed before, a script at the minimum should display the purpose for which it was created.	`DispMsg.vbs`
		`DisplayMessage.vbs`
		`getFolderProp.vbs`
		`StartService.vbs`
		`StopService.vbs`

→

Standard	**Description**	**Example**

No Spaces	Script filename should not contain any spaces. (Including spaces in your script file name may require you to include the command in quotation marks. This can lead to confusion as a minimum of three quotation marks must be used to start and three to end.)	`DisplayMessage.vbs`
		`getFolderProp.vbs`
		`StartService.vbs`
		`StopService.vbs`

Special Characters	The filenames should not contain special characters excepting hyphen (`-`) and underscore (`_`).	`Display-Message.vbs`
		`Display_Message.vbs`
		`get-OSName.vbs`

Maximum 20 Characters	Maximum characters of a file name should not exceed 20 characters. (Keep it as short and meaningful as possible.)	`SoftwareInventory.vbs` `getFolderPath.vbs`
Capitalize First letter	Whenever possible, you should capitalize the first letter of each word used to form a filename.	`FolderPath.vbs` `ServiceStatus.vbs`

`get/set` Prefix	If a script only gets information, i.e., it only reads information, you should use `get` as a prefix. Whereas if a script gets information	`getFileProperties.vbs`
		`getFolderPath.vbs`
		`setServiceStart`

`Mode.vbs`	and sets values or configuration, then you should use `set` as a prefix.	

Version	You should include the version information as a suffix to the script name. Do not include periods (dots) as part of the name to separate the version information.	`getServiceInfo10.vbs`
		`StopService2001.vbs`
		`CreateFolderVer2_0.vbs`

CODING STANDARDS

Although it is most important to follow coding standards, by and large, they are the most difficult standards to follow since they require organization and self discipline. For example, if you were to ask two programmers working for an organization that has no defined coding standards, what naming convention they use for the variables in their programs, you would probably find that they both use different naming conventions. For instance, the first programmer may name the `debug` variable that holds `Boolean` value as `blnDebug` and the second programmer may name the same variable as `b_Debug` or simply as `D`.

It is relatively easier to live with insignificant and irrelevant file names, than to try and understand 100 lines of code that is poorly written and formatted; it may be worth your while to concisely define coding standards and to faithfully and consistently follow them.

Naming Variables and Constants

Standardizing the variable names is as important as standardizing the script names. Standardizing variable names will help you to reduce logical and runtime errors that may be caused because of a wrong type passed to a function.

If you name your variables correctly, it will be easier for you to identify the type of value that you should store in a variable. If you know the type of data stored in the variable, you will then pass the right data to the function, thereby greatly reducing your chances of introducing a runtime error.

Table 3.3 lists the variable naming conventions that you may use for naming your variables in the script.

TABLE 3.3 Variable Naming Standards

Prefix	Variable Value Type	Example
i	Integer	iCount
s	String	sName
b	Boolean	bDebug
dt	Date Time	dtNow
lng	Long	lngLongValue
dbl	Double	dblValue
arr	Arrays	arrMachines(100), arrMachines("A","B")

Special Variables

You may use a single character for special variables that are required in the "for next" loops, as shown:

```
i = 0
For i = 0 to 10
    Statement
      j = 0
      For j = 0 to 10
         Statement
      Next
Next
```

Constants

As a general rule, it is good to name your constants in all uppercase characters and separate each in the name by an underscore, as shown in the examples below:

```
CONST HKEY_LOCAL_MACHINE = &H0000008
CONST GLOBAL_MESSAGE = _
"Do not run this script if not authorized"
CONST FOR_READING = 8
```

Naming Functions, Subroutines, and Classes

Because functions and subroutines usually do something, wherever possible you should use `get` or `set` as a prefix to the name of the function or the subroutine. For example, you should use `setWinsAddress()` name for the function (or subroutine) that sets the Wins server address of a given machine; similarly you should use `getWinsAddress()` name for the function (or subroutine) that you use to retrieve the Wins server address. It is also fine to use other words such as `calc` if the function or the subroutine calculates a value. For example, a function that converts `MB` value to `GB` may be named `calcSize()`.

You should use `cls` as prefix to the class names. Here is an example of the class name

```
Class clsLogData
End Class
```

You should also use `Class_Initialize` and `Class_Terminate` private subroutines to set defaults and create objects for a class that cleans up the memory.

Commenting

It is good practice to add comments in your scripts that define what a piece of code does; it helps in better understanding the code. It is also good practice to embed, at the top of your script, script-relevant information such as the author's name, the date the script was created, the purpose of the script, how to run the script, all prerequisites of the script, and the legal notice (copyright). Including such information in your scripts helps the reader in knowing who created it; what the script accomplishes, how to use the script, and if he is authorized to run the script.

Header Information

Many organizations follow the standard of including (at the beginning of the document) header information as a brief summary that describes the contents of the document. This provides the reader an insight on the document, helps him decide if it is of relevance to him, and if he should (or should not) read the document. Following the same principle you can create and add the relevant script information as a header in your scripts. At a minimum, the header should contain the following information:

Version: Defines the version of the script when it was first created.

Created By: Defines the name of the creator author of the script. (It is good practice to include the full name of the creator author).

Purpose: Explains in brief the purpose of the script. For example, "Best Practices Template."

Attributes: This describes the script attributes. (Script attributes are explained later in this chapter.) For example, `Ro,In,Re,Mu,Me`.

History: This explains the history of the script, including version increments, date when the script was last modified, who modified the script, and what was modified in the script as seen in Figure 3.4.

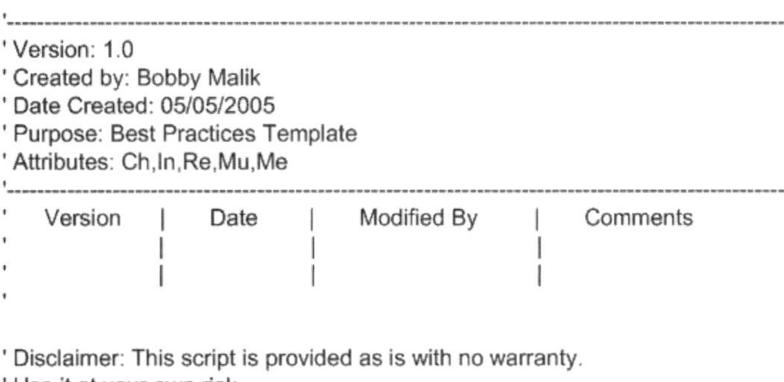

```
'--------------------------------------------------------------------------------
' Version: 1.0
' Created by: Bobby Malik
' Date Created: 05/05/2005
' Purpose: Best Practices Template
' Attributes: Ch,In,Re,Mu,Me
'--------------------------------------------------------------------------------
'   Version   |   Date   |   Modified By   |   Comments
'             |          |                 |
'             |          |                 |
'

' Disclaimer: This script is provided as is with no warranty.
' Use it at your own risk.
```

FIGURE 3.4 Example of script history.

Code Comments

The script header provides information about the script, whereas code comments provide information on the code snippet (or a line of code). It is generally a good practice to include comments in your code that provide more details about a line(s) of code. For example, the code in Listing 3.4 describes the `bDebug` constant and the values that you can set for this constant.

LISTING 3.4 Example of a Code Comment

```
'True = Log debug information; False = Do not Log Debug information
Const bDebug = True
```

Code comments should, however, be descriptive but concise. For example, the following comment does not provide any additional information about the code, as compared to the comment included in Listing 3.4. The comment in Listing 3.4 describes the values that you can set for the `bDebug` constant. It clarifies that setting the value of the `bDebug` constant to `True` will enable debug logging, and setting the same to `False` will disable it.

```
'Debugging Information
Const bDebug = True
```

Condition Standards

Although the condition standards may not be as important to standardize as other standards such as comments, nevertheless, if standardized they can make your code easier to read, understand, and troubleshoot.

Loops

It is important that you refrain from using open-ended loops, such as

```
Do
        Statement
        If (Condition) then exit do
Loop
```

You should instead use

```
Do while (Condition)
        Statement
Loop
```

It is easier to read and understand the second example. It also provides better control.

If Then Else

Avoid using single line if then else statements. For example, you should avoid using the following:

```
If condition then if condition then statement else statement
```

Although the previous code works fine, it can be confusing. The code should be modified as follows:

```
If condition then
        if condition then
                statement
        else
                statement
      end if
end if
```

Formatting Code

Formatting your code is like formatting your document. Generally, a well-formatted document is easier to read and understand. For example, it is easier to read and understand the paragraph shown in Listing 3.5, as it is well formatted for readability. The first line of the paragraph is indented an additional tab away from the left margin of the document (as compared to the rest of the lines in the paragraph), marking a beginning of the paragraph; first letter of each line is capitalized to mark the beginning of a line; a period (dot) is used to denote that a line has ended; and a question mark at the end of the last line tells the reader that this is a question and not a statement.

LISTING 3.5 Well-Formatted Paragraph

```
    This is an example of a well-formatted paragraph. The first line of the
paragraph is indented with an additional tab (four spaces) away from the rest
of the lines. The first character of each line is capitalized and each line
ends with a full stop or a question mark. Do you agree?
```

While a well-formatted document is easy to read, follow, and understand, a poorly formatted document can cause a headache to the reader trying to read and understand it. Similarly, poorly formatted code is hard to read and understand.

Consider the examples in Listing 3.6 and Listing 3.7. They are identical in content and perform the same task. Note the [...] notations in the first example. These indicate code statements that are so long that the lines can't be read on a typical display without scrolling across.

LISTING 3.6 Unformatted Code

```
sub savetext(objxml)
set objclasses = objxml.selectnodes("/MAIN/CLASS")
for each objclass in objclasses
objSwat.writelog outputlogfile, vbnewline & "**** " & objclass.attribu [...]
set objprops = objclass.selectnodes("PROPERTIES")
for each prop in objprops
if prop.haschildnodes then
for each childnode in prop.childnodes
childnodename = childnode.nodename
childnodetext = childnode.text
if childnodetext = "" then childnodetext = "N/A"
objswat.writelog outputlogfile, childnodename & " = " & childnodetext
next
end if
next
set objprops = nothing
next
set objclasses = nothing
end sub
```

LISTING 3.7 Formatted Code

```
Sub SaveText(objXml)
    Set objClasses = objXml.SelectNodes("/MAIN/CLASS")
    for each objClass in objClasses
       objSwat.Writelog OutputLogFile, VBNewLine & "**** " & _
                       objClass.Attributes.getNamedItem("NAME").text
        Set objProps = objClass.SelectNodes("PROPERTIES")
            for each Prop in objProps
                if Prop.HasChildNodes then
                    for each childNode in Prop.ChildNodes
                       ChildNodeName = childNode.NodeName
                       ChildNodeText = childNode.text
                       if ChildNodeText = "" then ChildNodetext = "N/A"
                       objSwat.writelog OutputLogFile, _
                                    ChildNodeName & " = " & ChildNodeText
                    next
                end if
            next
       set objProps = nothing
    next
    Set objClasses = nothing
End Sub
```

Although the code in Listing 3.6 and Listing 3.7 is the same and accomplishes the same task (that is save information to an XML file), there is a clear visual difference in the two listings. The code in Listing 3.7 is well formatted; therefore, it is readable and understandable. If you were to maintain this code, which code (the code in Listing 3.6 or the code in Listing 3.7) would you prefer to maintain? Also, if you were the author of this code, and were to review it after some time (for instance, a few months), which code (the code in Listing 3.6 or the code in Listing 3.7) would you prefer to have written?

NOTE

You format your code purely for aesthetics (that is, to make it readable and easier to understand). Formatting your code does not provide any functional enhancements to your scripts (that is, a well-formatted script does not run faster or slower, compared to an unformatted script); however, it makes the code easier to read, understand, and maintain.

Indenting

One of the methods of formatting your code is to indent it. Indenting your code as you write makes reading code much easier. Generally you indent for each loop structure or a conditional structure. A common convention is to indent your code with a tab or a space. For instance, an indented code snippet may look like this:

```
Do while
    Statement
      If (Condition) then
          Statement
```

```
        End if
          Statement
        Statement
    Loop
```

Not all text editors treat tabs the same. Therefore it is best to use spaces to separate the code. A tab generally equals four spaces.

You can indent your code as you like. In fact, every programmer has her own rules for indenting the code. However, if one were to categorize code indenting, it could be categorized as straight and curved indenting.

Straight indenting: Under straight indenting, all statements that fall within the main statement have the same indentation. Straight indenting is the easiest type of indenting and is very common. Figure 3.5 is an example of straight indenting.

Curved indenting: Curved indenting resembles an inverse C. You indent every line of code by adding a space (or multiple spaces) until you have written half (or almost half) of the lines of code within a structure. The rest of the code you indent by removing a space from every line of code. Figure 3.6 illustrates an example of curved indenting that forms an inverse C structure.

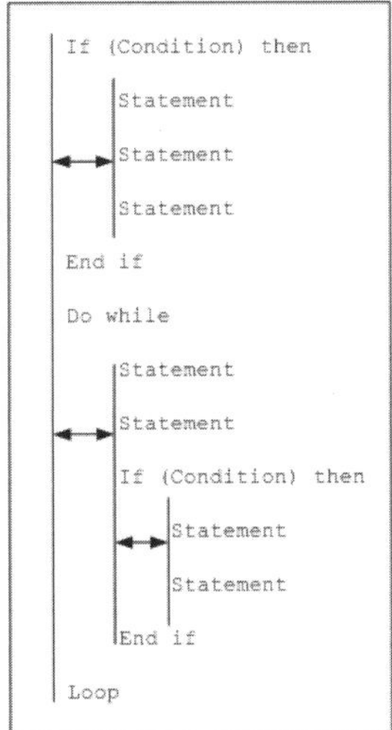

FIGURE 3.5 Straight-line indenting example.

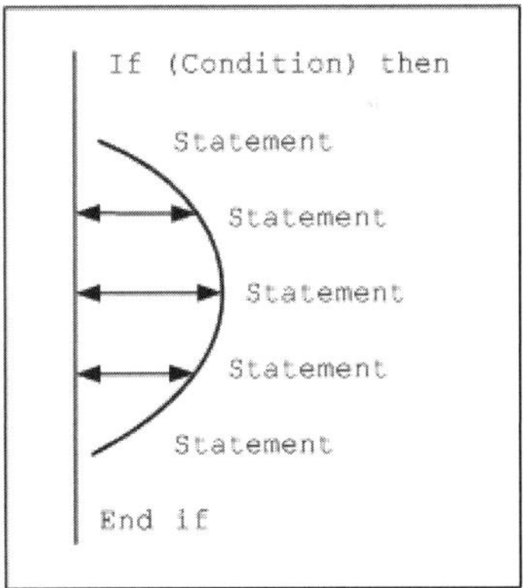

FIGURE 3.6 Curved indenting example.

Another form of curved formatting resembles an inverse Z, as shown in the following example:

```
If (Condition) then
  Statement
    Statement
      Statement
       Statement
         Statement
End if
```

Linebreaks

There is a limitation to how many characters a text editor can display in a line before the editor wraps the text to the next line. Although wrapped text may be good to read, wrapped code is not. For instance in Figure 3.7 the comment text wrapped into the next line is readable; however, the code looks confusing.

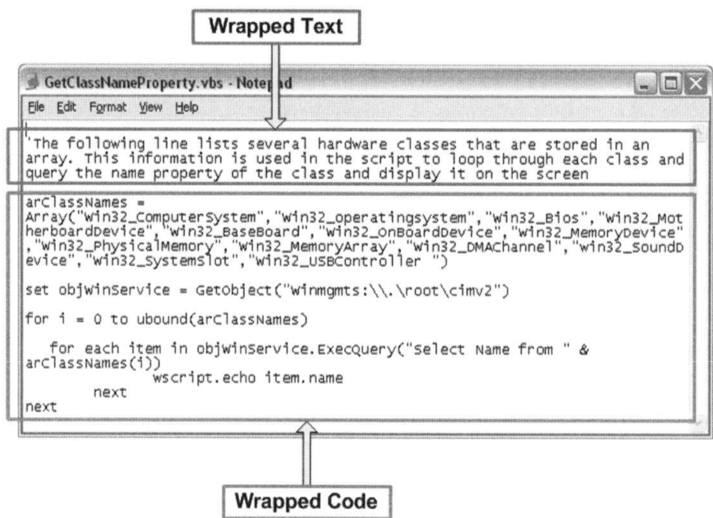

FIGURE 3.7 Illustrates an example of wrapped text and wrapped code.

Both the code and the comment text in Figure 3.8 are, however, readable. The single comment line is broken into multiple comment lines and the code lines (generally longer than 50 characters) are broken into parts (multiple lines) using the underscore (_) character. In VBScript, the underscore followed by a carriage return, signals that the line is continued onto the next line.

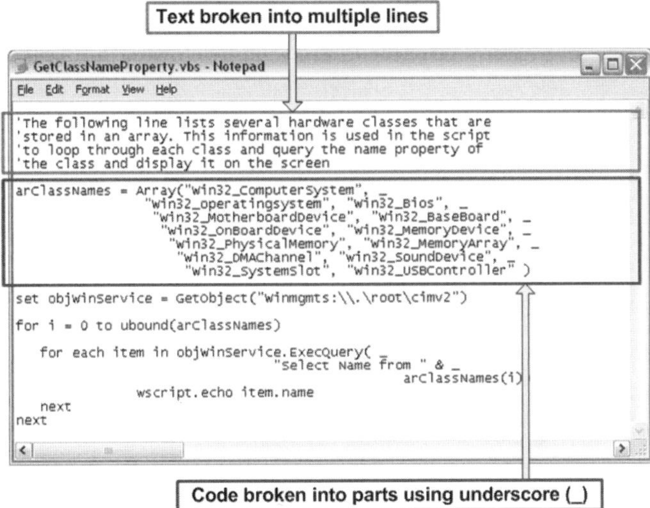

FIGURE 3.8 Illustrates an example of linebreak.

Notepad.exe, on a typical display monitor, displays about 80 characters on a single line before wrapping the text to the next line. Therefore, as a rule of thumb, you should break the lines in sets of 50 characters.

Be careful while breaking your line. You should insert breaks only at logical points. For example, the `"select * from win32_service where DisplayName = 'Alerter'"` statement should be broken as

```
"select * from win32_service " & _
        "where DisplayName = 'Alerter'"
and not as
"select * from win3" & _
        "2_Service wh" & _
         "ere DisplayName = 'Alerter'"
```

Blank Lines

When you write a document, you generally leave a blank line between two paragraphs. It helps the reader in identifying that a paragraph has ended and a new paragraph has begun. The same principle can be applied for code formatting. It is good practice to leave a blank line between two code constructs. This helps the reader in easily identifying the group of code that belongs together. Figure 3.9 illustrates use of blank lines to separate code constructs.

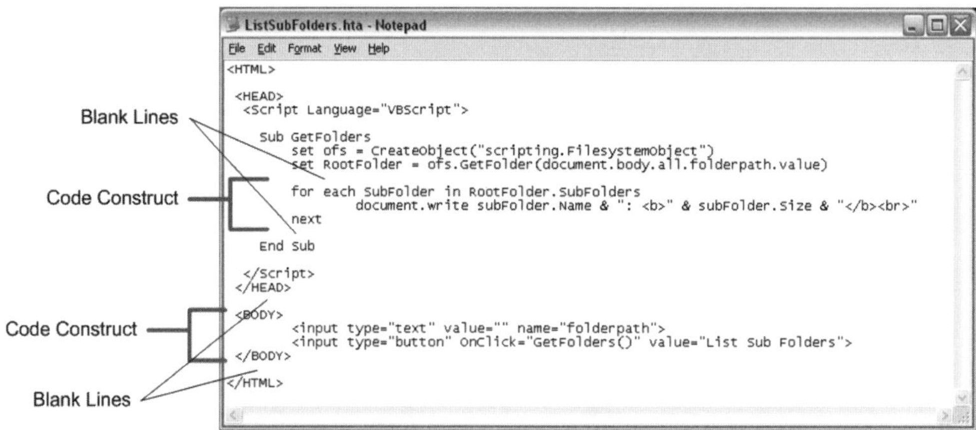

FIGURE 3.9 Illustrates uses of blank lines.

SCRIPT ATTRIBUTES

There are scripts that you run on the local system to retrieve information, such as the script in Listing 3.8 that retrieves the name of the computer. These types of scripts have low impact on the system, that is, they have little or no chance of crashing your system. Such scripts can be described as *read-only* scripts that are run on a *single system* and have *low impact* on your system.

LISTING 3.8 Read-Only Script, Run on a Single System That Has Low Impact on the System

```
Option Explicit
 Dim objWNet
   Set objWNet = CreateObject("Wscript.Network")
      Wscript.echo objWNet.ComputerName
   Set objWNet = nothing
```

Complete script is included on the CD-ROM.

On the other hand, there are scripts that you run to change settings of multiple systems, such as changing the Subnet Mask of the IP Address on all systems in your network. These scripts have major impact on your environment; that is, incorrectly setting the values can potentially bring down your entire environment. Such scripts you can describe as *change* scripts that are run on *multiple systems* and have *high impact* on the environment.

NOTE

There is always an impact of running a script. For example, the script in Listing 3.4 could potentially hang your system if the Windows API call (made by `Wscript.Network` *object) waits indefinitely to return the requested information that drives your CPU utilization to 100 percent. You can also potentially cause your system to crash by introducing a never-ending loop that consumes additional memory on every loop, commonly known as memory leak.*

If you know in advance the type of script and the risk associated with running the script, you would plan accordingly for any known damages or outages caused by running a high-risk script. For example, you may have resources on standby for manually changing the Subnet Mask in the environment, if the script does not function correctly or incorrectly sets the Subnet Mask by running the script. Knowing that it is a high-impact script, you may also double or triple check your script and test it by running against a single system before running against the entire environment. At the same time, you may run a script that has low impact and is run on (or against) a single system with ease, knowing the fact that it is low impact to the environment or the system, such as the script listed in Listing 3.8.

Besides a script being read-only or change-type that may be run on a single or multiple systems, a script may run in unattended (batch mode) or interactive (that is, the script requires user interaction) mode. It is also important to add an attribute that defines if the script should run interactively or unattended. For example, you would not run an interactive script, such as shown in Listing 3.9, on a scheduled basis because it would stop and wait for the user to input file path information before continuing.

LISTING 3.9 Interactive Script That Lists All Subfolders under a Given Folder

```
Set objFs = CreateObject("Scripting.FileSystemObject")
   sFolderPath = inputBox("Enter a path to the folder")
     Set objFolder = objFs.GetFolder(sFolderPath)
      if objFolder.SubFolders.Count <> 0 then
         for each objSubFolder in objFolder.SubFolders
             wscript.echo objSubFolder.Name
         next
      end if
```

ON THE CD

Complete script is included on the CD-ROM.

Defining Script Attributes

It is important to define the script attributes of a script. It is also important to standardize the location and the order of these attributes (that is, where the attributes comment should appear in the script and the order in which the attributes should be defined). For example, you may include the attributes (in the order shown) in the header of the script, as shown in Figure 3.10. Table 3.4 lists the attributes (in the order of precedence) and their descriptions.

TABLE 3.4 Script Attributes and Description

Precedence	Attribute	Description
1	Ro / Ch	Read Only / Change
2	Un / In	Unattended / Interactive
3	On / Re	Once / Repetitive
4	Si / Mu	Single / Multiple systems
5	Lo / Me / Hi	Low, Medium / High impact

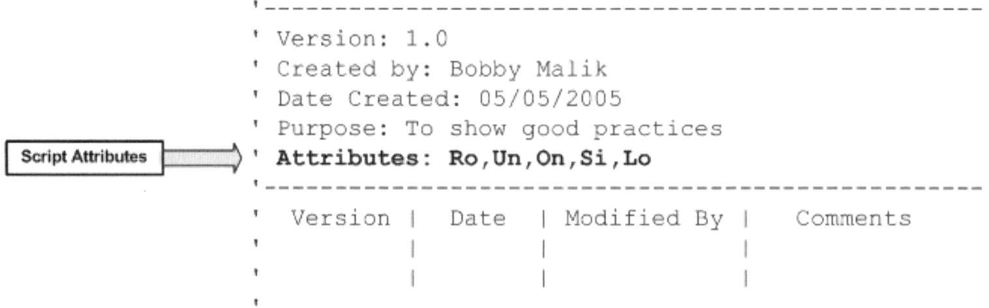

Script Attributes
'---
' Version: 1.0
' Created by: Bobby Malik
' Date Created: 05/05/2005
' Purpose: To show good practices
' Attributes: Ro,Un,On,Si,Lo
'---
' Version | Date | Modified By | Comments
' | | |
' | | |
'

FIGURE 3.10 Show script attributes.

SECURING PASSWORDS

After locking your door to your house, do you leave the key hanging on the door? On a similar note, would you want to secure data using logon accounts and leave the passwords in your scripts in clear text for everyone to see? If you do, and your security admin (or the security administration team) comes to know that you have included a password in a script in clear text, it most likely will raise a red flag, you would have to answer to your management why you did so, and would likely be asked to remove it and use a more secured method.

In most large organizations, there are rules for creating passwords, like: a password should be at least 8 characters long; at the least it must contain an uppercase, a lowercase and a special character; it must be changed once in 45 days. These rules are for your passwords that you type daily to logon to your system and access your organization's network.

Having passwords provides security; they protect your personal and organization's data. They ensure that only authorized persons have access to the protected data. Therefore, an organization generally mandates that you do not write down your password on paper, and more so, that you do not stick that password on your monitor. Likewise, you should develop a standard that defines the use of passwords in your scripts, such as:

Do not store passwords in scripts: Do not include passwords in your scripts, and more so, leave it there in clear text. If you do, ensure that you secure your script using ACLs (Access Control Lists are permissions, such as Read / Write / Delete, that you can use to secure your files and folders stored on a disk formatted as NTFS <NT file system>).

Encrypt your scripts: If it is essential that you store the password in your script, then you should consider encrypting your scripts using Microsoft Script Encoder, at the minimum.

Encrypt with Microsoft CryptoAPI: Another option for encrypting your passwords for storing and retrieval is to use certificates (self generated or obtained from a Public Certificate Authority, such as Verisign). Using certificates, you can encrypt the password that can be decrypted only if the certificate is installed for the user running the script.

Use secure input methods: Do not use `Inputbox` method in VBScript to obtain passwords. (The password in not hidden as you type it in the `Inputbox`, making it visible to prying eyes.) Use an Internet Explorer–type window (Internet Explorer includes a password text field that hides the text as you type) or use the `GetPassword()` method of `ScriptPW.Password` object (available in Windows XP and above only) to securely get passwords at runtime.

Using ACLs

As a rule of thumb, you should not store passwords in clear text in your scripts. If however, for any reason, you must store the password in a script, at the minimum, you should store the script on an NTFS partition and secure the script with appropriate permissions. Best practice would be to create a single group, add all users that you want to grant access to this group and grant permissions to the group instead of individual users. Using this methodology, you can easily monitor (using security audit event logs) the use of the script. Figure 3.11 shows the sample of NTFS permissions granted to the `ScriptUsers` group.

Using Microsoft Script Encoder

In Chapter 2, we discussed how to encrypt your scripts using Microsoft Script Encoder. If your scripts contain passwords, at the minimum, you should encrypt your scripts using Script Encoder. Figure 3.12 shows you the script encoded with Script Encoder.

This is not a foolproof method of securing your scripts. Encrypting your scripts and securing your script with ACLs will provide you more robust security.

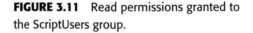

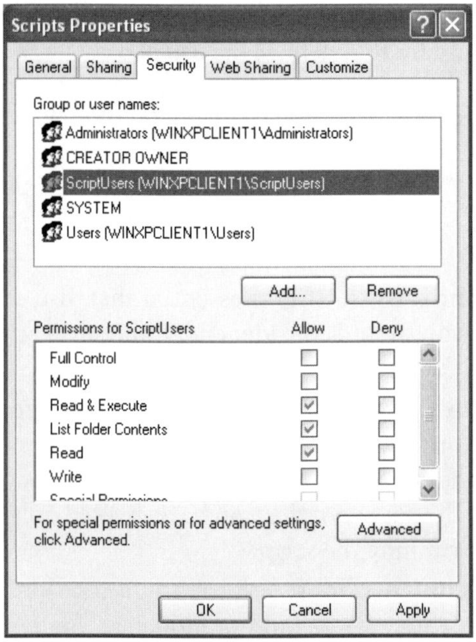

FIGURE 3.11 Read permissions granted to the ScriptUsers group.

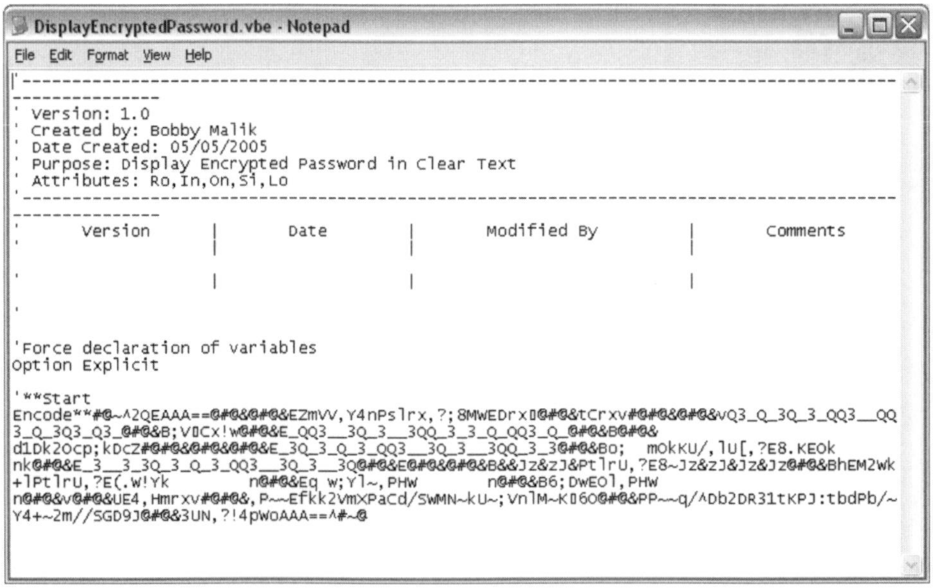

FIGURE 3.12 Script encoded with Microsoft Script Encoder.

Using Microsoft CryptoAPI

Earlier, access to Microsoft CryptoAPI was limited to programs, such as Visual Basic, that could leverage the Windows API. With the introduction of CAPICOM (the Microsoft ActiveX® control), Microsoft provided a COM interface to the Microsoft CryptoAPI.

CAPICOM exposes CryptoAPI functions that enable you to integrate digital signing and encryption functionality into your scripts. Using CAPICOM you can:

- Digitally sign and verify digitally signed data
- Search for a certificate and display its information
- Check certificate properties
- Encrypt and decrypt data with a password
- Encrypt and decrypt data using public keys and certificates

Script Store uses the userID and password as the password to encrypt and securely store your scripts.

Using Certificates to Secure Your Password

CAPICOM allows you to use a certificate to sign and encrypt the data. Once encrypted, the data can be decrypted only if the certificate (that was used to encrypt the data) is installed on the system and the user running the script has access to both the public and the private keys. For example, if `User1` is logged on to the computer, the certificate must be installed in the Certificate Authority of `User1`, as shown in Figure 3.13.

CAPICOM uses industry standard Public Private Key Infrastructure (PKI). Using the Public Key, you can only encrypt the data; to decrypt the data, however, the user must have access to the private key paired with the public key used to encrypt the data.

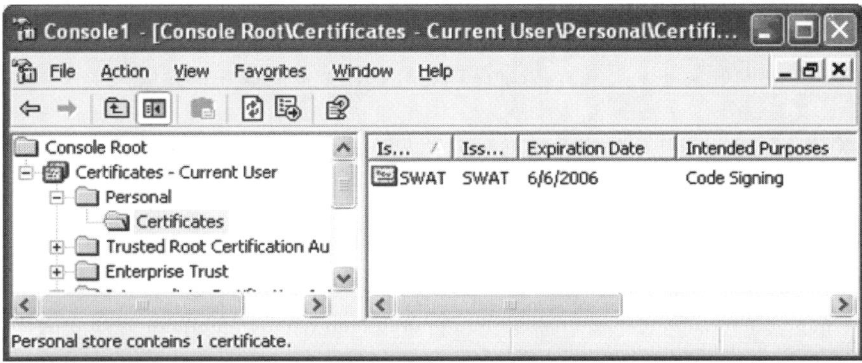

FIGURE 3.13 Certificate installed for the current user.

To use a certificate, you must first obtain a certificate. You can a obtain a certificate either from a Certificate Authority (CA), such as Verisign, by submitting a request (you can obtain a certificate as an individual or as an organization) or generate a personal certificate using Windows PKI. As certificate validates an identity, such as you, the CA issues you a certificate only after it has satisfactorily identified and validated your identity.

Certificates issued by Public Certificate Authorities are not free (that is, you will have to pay a fee to obtain the certificate). To obtain more information on the process and the cost associated with obtaining a certificate, you can visit *http://www.Verisign.com* or *http://www.thwate.com.*

For testing your scripts, however, you can generate a certificate using the Certification Authority Server included with Windows 2000 and Windows 2003 server. Certificate Authority Server is not installed on the server by default; you must add it from the Add and Remove Programs in the Control Panel (installing and configuring the Certificate Server is out of the scope of this book). After successfully installing the Certificate Server service, you can use the Certificate Authority MMC snap-in to create a new certificate. (You can read the Microsoft Knowledge Base article *http://support.microsoft.com/default.aspx?scid=kb;en-us;272555* to learn how to install certificate services in a non-Active Directory Environment and issue certificates.)

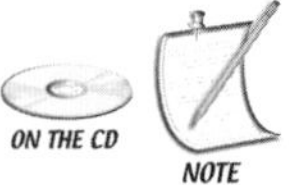

The CD-ROM includes a `SWAT.pfx` *certificate that you can import. You should install the certificate only on a test machine and use the certificate only for testing the scripts included with this book.*

Once you have obtained the certificate, you can use it to encrypt the data using CAPICOM. For encrypting data using a certificate, CAPICOM provides `CAPICOM.Certificate` and `CAPICOM.EnvelopedData` objects. Using these objects, you can import the certificate and encrypt content.

Certificate Object

The `CAPICOM.Certificate` object exposes the `Load` method that imports the certificate (SWAT.pfx) file. Listing 3.10 lists the syntax for the `Load` method.

LISTING 3.10 Load Method Syntax

```
Load ( ByVal FileName as String, _
     [ ByVal Password as String ], _
     [ ByVal KeyStorageFlag as CAPICOM_KEY_STORAGE_FLAG ], _
     [ ByVal KeyLocation as CAPICOM_KEY_LOCATION ] )
```

Name of the certificate (passed as `FileName` parameter) is the only required parameter of the `Load` method (that is, you must provide the certificate name, including the path to the certificate, when calling the `Load` method). Other parameters (`Password`, `KeyStorage-`

Flag and KeyLocation) are optional parameters (that is, the parameters are ignored if no value is passed). However, if the certificate requires a password, as the SWAT.pfx (included in CD-ROM) certificate requires, you must pass it as a parameter while calling the Load method, as shown in the following example:

```
objCertificate.load "SWAT.pfx","password"
```

EnvelopedData Object

The EnvelopedData object provides the following properties and methods that allow you to encrypt and decrypt your data:

Algorithm Property: This property allows you to set the encryption algorithm and the key length. (The algorithm property takes algorithm object as a value that contains the algorithm and the key length.) For example, the following code sets the encryption algorithm to 3DES and the key length to 256-bit keys.

```
Const CAPICOM_ENCRYPTION_ALGORITHM_3DES      = 3
Const CAPICOM_ENCRYPTION_KEY_LENGTH_128_BITS = 3
objEnvelopedData.Algorithm.Name = _
                        CAPICOM_ENCRYPTION_ALGORITHM_3DES
objEnvelopedData.Algorithm.KeyLength = _
                           CAPICOM_ENCRYPTION_KEY_LENGTH_128_BITS
```

You can directly pass 3 as a value to the ObjEnvelopedData.Algorithm.Name property and the ObjEnvelopedData.Algorithm.KeyLength property. However, setting constants and using the constant names to the ObjEnvelopedData.Algorithm.Name and the Obj EnvelopedData.Algorithm.KeyLength property will make your script more readable.

Content Property: This property contains the actual content (clear text) that needs to be encrypted. The following line illustrates how to set the content property:

```
objEnvelopedData.Content = "Encrypted Password"
```

Recipients Property: This property retrieves the collection of the recipients of the encrypted data. It takes the Recipients object as a value. Using the Add method of the Recipients object, you add the certificate that you imported using the Load method as the following code demonstrates:

```
objEnvelopedData.Recipients.Add(objCertificate)
```

Encrypt Method: As the name states, this method encrypts the data contained in the Content property using a session key that it generates. It then envelopes the encrypted content for each recipient by encrypting the session key with each recipient's public key and returns the BLOB that contains the encrypted contents and the session keys as an encoded string. As shown in Listing 3.11, after setting the properties of the `EnvelopedData` object, you can use the `Encrypt` method to encrypt data contained in the `Content` property.

LISTING 3.11 Encryption Script. Echo's Encrypted Data

```
Const CAPICOM_ENCRYPTION_ALGORITHM_3DES      = 3
Const CAPICOM_ENCRYPTION_KEY_LENGTH_128_BITS = 3
Const CAPICOM_ENCRYPTION_KEY_LENGTH_MAXIMUM = 0
Set objEnvelopedData = CreateObject("CAPICOM.EnvelopedData")
Set objCertificate = CreateObject("Capicom.Certificate")
objEnvelopedData.Algorithm.Name = _
               CAPICOM_ENCRYPTION_ALGORITHM_3DES
objEnvelopedData.Algorithm.KeyLength = _
               CAPICOM_ENCRYPTION_KEY_LENGTH_MAXIMUM
objCertificate.load "SWAT.pfx","password"
objEnvelopedData.recipients.add(objCertificate)
objEnvelopedData.Content = "Encrypted Password"
wscript.echo "Encrypted data = " & objEnvelopedData.encrypt
```

The code for this listing is on the CD-ROM as `EncryptData.vbs` *in Scripts\Chapter03.*

While you can use the `Load` method to temporarily import the certificate and use the imported certificate to encrypt data, you must install the certificate on the system (for the user running the script) before you can decrypt the data. When you attempt to decrypt data, and you do not have the certificate installed, you will receive an error message, as shown in Figure 3.14.

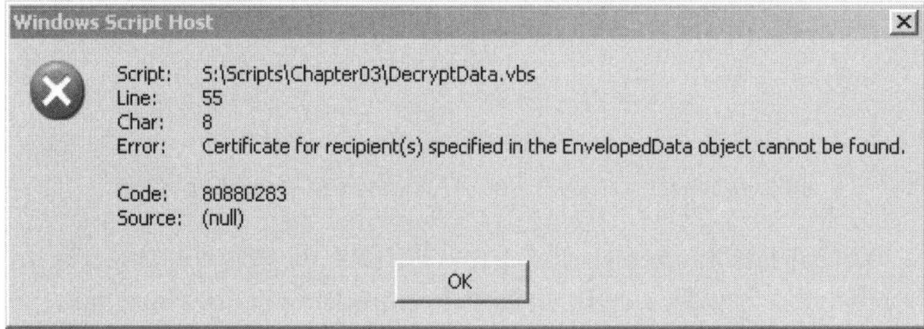

FIGURE 3.14 Error message displayed if the certificate is not installed on the system for the user running the script.

To install a certificate (for example, to install the SWAT certificate included with this book), do the following:

1. Logon as the user that will use the certificate, such as User1.
2. Double-click the Certificate (SWAT.pfx). The Certificate Import Wizard should start.
3. Click Next to continue.
4. Select the File to import (the path should already include Swat.pfx).
5. Click Next to continue.
6. Type in `password` (without quotes, in lowercase) in the password text box. Make sure that the `Mark this key as exportable` option is not checked. (You do not want the private key to be exportable.). Click Next.
7. Select `Place all certificates in the following store`; click on the Browse button, select Personal, and click OK; click Next, followed by Finish to complete the import.

To validate that the certificate has been imported, you can do the following:

- Click on Start => Run and type MMC. (This should open a new MMC Console window.)
- Select Add/Remove Snap-in from the File menu, as shown in Figure 3.15.

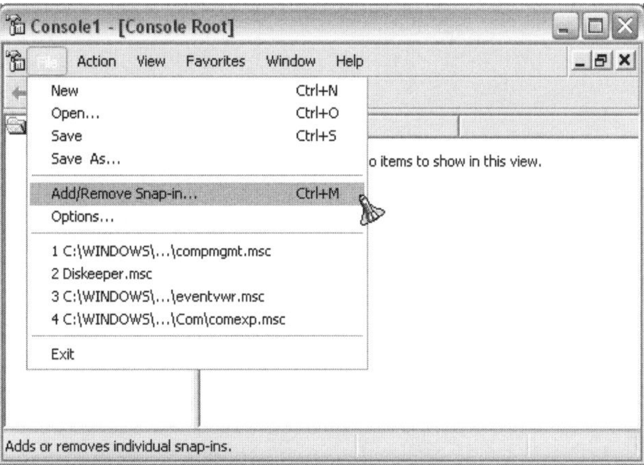

FIGURE 3.15 Add/Remove Snap-in menu item.

- In the Add/Remove Snap-in window, click the Add button to bring up the Add Standalone Snap-in.
- Select the Certificate item in the Add Standalone Snap-in window, as shown in Figure 3.16, and click the `Add` button.
- In the Certificates Snap-in window select My user account, as shown in Figure 3.17.

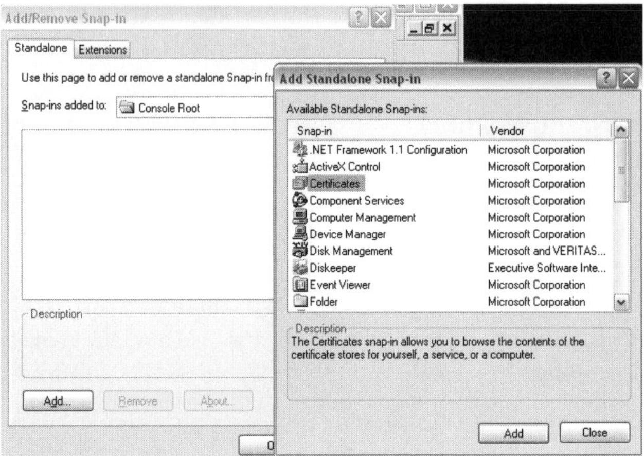

FIGURE 3.16 Select Certificate in the Add Standalone Snap-in window.

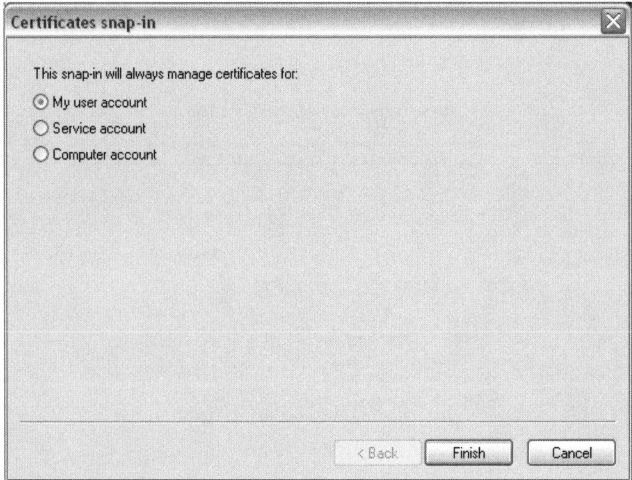

FIGURE 3.17 Select My user account in the Certificates Snap-in window.

- Click Finish to close the Certificate Snap-in window; click the `Close` button to close the Add Standalone Snap-in window and click the `Ok` button to close the Add/Remove Snap-in window.
- Navigate to the Certificate, as seen in Figure 3.18.
- Double-click the SWAT (certificate shown in the right window of the MMC console, shown in Figure 3.18) to view the installed certificate, as shown in Figure 3.19. Note that the certificate shows that the user has access to the private key.

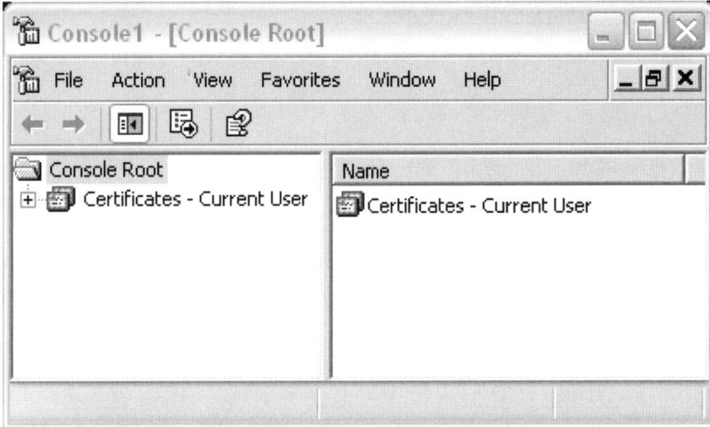

FIGURE 3.18 MMC console with Certificates Snap-in.

FIGURE 3.19 Installed SWAT Certificate that shows that the user has access to the private key.

If the certificate is installed and the user has access to the private key, it is simple to decrypt the data. All you have to do is call the `Decrypt` method and pass the encrypted data as the parameter. CAPICOM does the rest for you. Listing 3.12 lists the code that reads the encrypted data from a text file and echoes the decrypted data on the user's screen.

LISTING 3.12 Decrypt Data using CAPICOM

```
set objFs = createobject("scripting.FilesystemObject")
Set objFile = objFs.OpenTextFile("output.txt")
encrypteddata = objFile.readall
Set objEnvelopedData = CreateObject("CAPICOM.EnvelopedData")
objEnvelopedData.Decrypt(EncryptedData)
wscript.echo objEnvelopedData.content
```

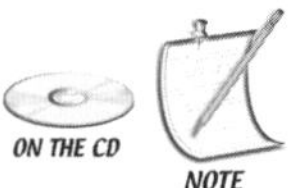

The code for this listing is on the CD-ROM as `Scripts\Chapter03\DecryptData.vbs`*. The* `EncryptedPassword.txt`*, that the script decrypts, is also included on the CD-ROM.*

Using the Microsoft CryptoAPI technology, you can safely encrypt and store the password in a text file that your script can decrypt at runtime. Using CAPICOM to encrypt your password is safer than embedding the password in your scripts and encrypting them using Microsoft Script Encoder, as the user must have the certificate, install it, and have access to both the private and public keys.

Using Secure Input Methods

Using `Inputbox` method in VBScript to get the password from the user is not a safe method of getting the password because the text that the user types in the text box is visible in clear text. Instead, to safely get a password from the user, you can use the following:

`GetPassword()` method: If you have Windows XP or Windows 2003, you can use the `GetPassword` method of the `ScriptPW.Password` object. The `GetPassword` method allows the user to safely type in the password in a command-prompt window, as shown in Figure 3.20.

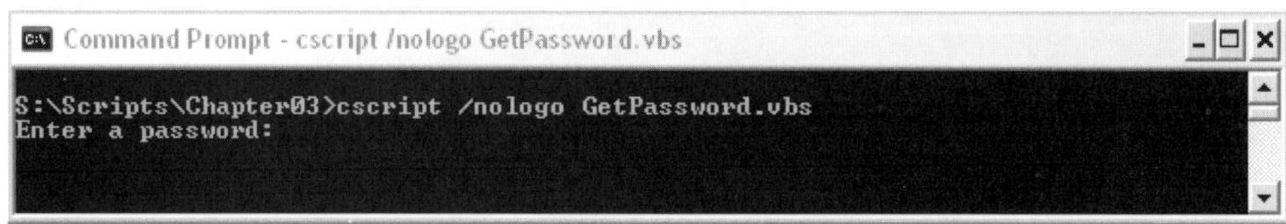

FIGURE 3.20 `GetPassword` method prompting the user to input a password.

If you like running your scripts with Cscript.exe, you will find this to be the easiest method of safely getting the password from the user. Listing 3.13 is an example of the `GetPassword` method.

LISTING 3.13 Example of `GetPassword` Method

```
Wscript.stdout.write "Enter a password:"
Set oPW = CreateObject("ScriptPW.Password")
password = oPW.GetPassword()
Wscript.stdout.writeblanklines(2)
wscript.echo password
```

The code for this listing is on the CD-ROM as `GetPassword.vbs`.

Internet Explorer (IE) object: HTML allows you to create an input text box that hides the text that the user enters. Using Internet Explorer object, you can create and display an HTML page that the user can use to securely provide you the password as shown in Figure 3.21.

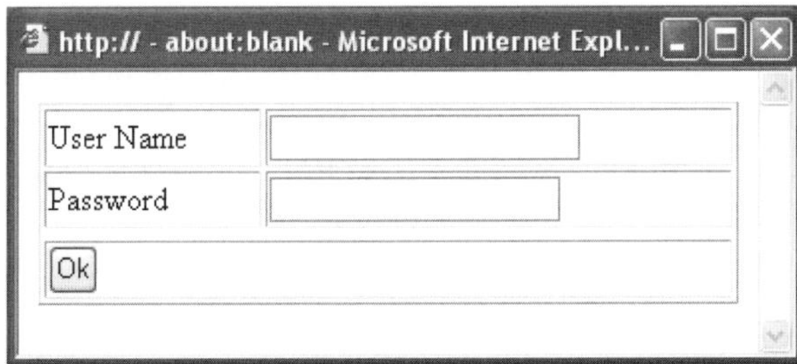

FIGURE 3.21 Internet Explorer window that uses the password text box to securely get password from the user.

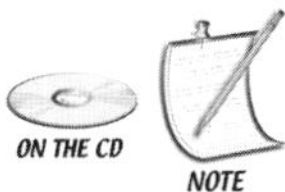

The CD-ROM includes `GetPasswordIE.vbs`. The code in `GetPasswordIE.vbs` creates a new Internet Explorer window, displays the input box, waits for the user the input the password, closes the window, and echoes the data typed by the user in the user and the password text boxes when the user clicks the `OK` button.

HTA script: HTA scripts are another method of securely getting a password from the user (Chapter 2 covered HTA scripts). Since HTA files also support HTML, you can use the password text box to securely obtain the password from the user, as shown in Figure 3.22.

The CD-ROM includes the `GetPassword.hta` script that was used to create the window shown in Figure 3.22.

FIGURE 3.22 HTA file that securely gets the password from the user.

RUNNING SCRIPTS

Similar to the other standards discussed in this chapter, it is also important to standardize how to run your scripts. Although is it not essential to decide what shell (Cscript.exe, Wscript.exe, or MSHTA) to run your scripts with, it is crucial to understand the privileges required for running a script. For example, a script that reads and displays the attributes of a file does not require administrative privilege, and therefore should be run with a user that has only read privileges to that file or the folder (it will minimize the risk of the script corrupting the file). Similarly, a script that modifies a registry value should be granted change permissions only on that value.

It can be very daunting to troubleshoot your script with lower privilege. Therefore you should run your script with administrative privileges in a test environment before running it with a user that has lower permissions. This will rule out the possibility of your script having functionality related issues when troubleshooting a problem.

However, it is impractical to get that granular (especially for scripts that will be run only once or a few times). A more practical approach would be to divide your scripts into two categories: read-only and change scripts (that is, a script that requires read-only privilege, such as a script that gets the status of a Windows service and, a script that requires more than read-only privilege such as, a script that would stop a Windows service). Read-only scripts can be run under a user that does not have administrator privilege. The change scripts on the other hand, can be run under the built-in administrator account.

Although you can run the scripts with the built-in administrator account, you should create a separate account that is administrator-equivalent and run the scripts under that account. This will help you in auditing the account. (Many entries in the log files are logged under the built-in administrator account, which makes searching information difficult. If you create a separate account for scripts, it will be easier to find.)

Using RunAs

You can either keep switching between the privileged and the non-privileged user accounts to run your scripts, or use the `RunAs` command (systems earlier than Windows 2000 do not include this command). You do the following to run scripts as a different user:

1. Open a command window.
2. Type `runas /noprofile /user:mymachine\user cmd`.

The command will prompt you for the password for the user provided to the `RunAs` command, as shown in Figure 3.23.

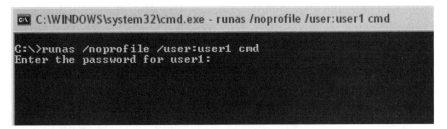

```
C:\WINDOWS\system32\cmd.exe - runas /noprofile /user:user1 cmd

C:\>runas /noprofile /user:user1 cmd
Enter the password for user1:
```

FIGURE 3.23 `RunAs` prompting you for the password.

If the authentication is successful, another command window will open (notice that the command window is now running under the context of the user you provided to the `RunAs` command), as shown in Figure 3.24. Run your scripts from this window.

```
cmd (running as WINXPCLIENT1\user1)
Microsoft Windows XP [Version 5.1.2600]
(C) Copyright 1985-2001 Microsoft Corp.

C:\WINDOWS\system32>cd\scripts

C:\Scripts>GetPassword.vbs

C:\WINDOWS\system32\cmd.exe
Microsoft Windows XP [Version 5.1.2600]
(C) Copyright 1985-2001 Microsoft Corp.

C:\Documents and Settings\ScriptAdmin>runas /noprofile /user:user1 cmd
Enter the password for user1:
Attempting to start cmd as user "WINXPCLIENT1\user1" ...

C:\Documents and Settings\ScriptAdmin>
```

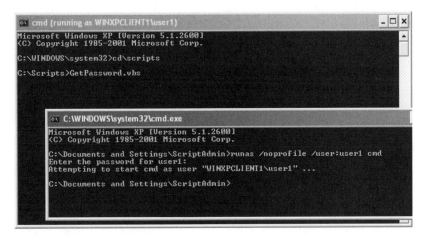

FIGURE 3.24 `RunAs` successfully opened a new command window. Running `GetPassword.vbs` will run the script under `User1` context.

Alternatively, you can also create a shortcut to your scripts and set the RunAs checkmark (under Advanced properties), as shown in Figure 3.25. After setting this, when you run your script, you will be prompted for a user and password, as shown in Figure 3.26.

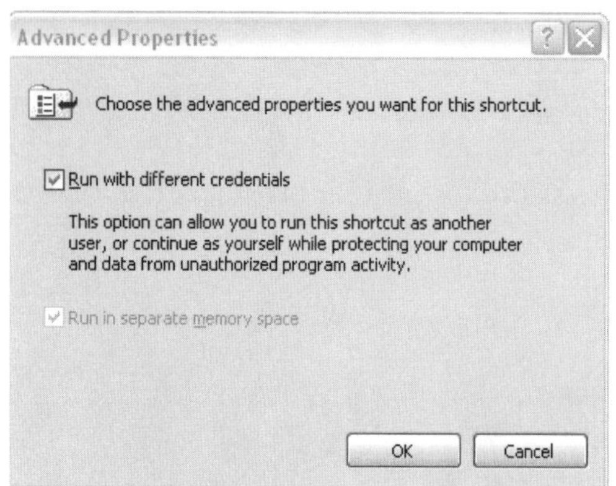

FIGURE 3.25 RunAs Advanced property of the shortcut. Displays the RunAs checkmark.

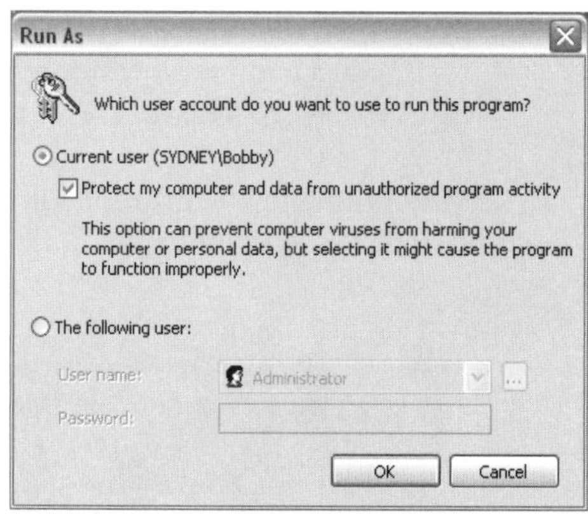

FIGURE 3.26 RunAs authentication window that appears when the RunAs Advanced property is set for the shortcut.

Choosing a Shell

It is a matter of choice how you run your scripts. For instance, you can run the script in Listing 3.14 with either Cscript.exe or Wscript.exe. Running with either of the shells will produce the same result. However, if you run your script with Cscript.exe, the result will be displayed in a command window (as seen in Figure 3.27), as compared to the result displayed in a (GUI; as seen in Figure 3.28) window if run with Wscript.exe.

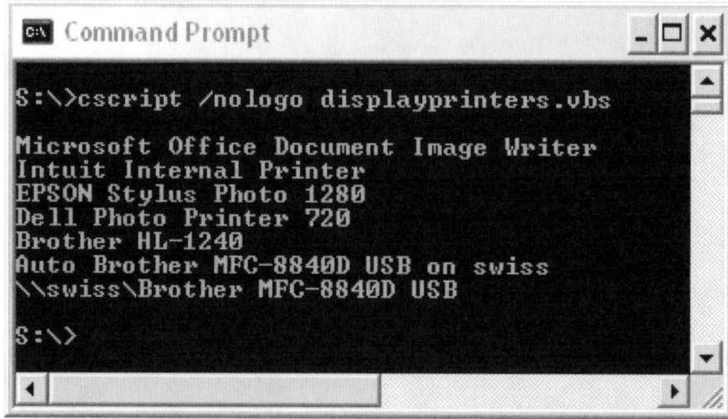

FIGURE 3.27 Script in Listing 3.14 run with Cscript.exe displays results in a command window.

FIGURE 3.28 Script in Listing 3.14 run with Wscript.exe displays results in a GUI window.

LISTING 3.14 List Installed Printers

```
set objWMI = getobject("Winmgmts:\\.\root\cimv2")
Set colPrinters = objWMI.InstancesOf("Win32_Printer")
for each item in colPrinters
    sPrinter = sPrinter & VBNewLine & item.name
next
wscript.echo sPrinter
Set colPrinters = nothing
set objWMI = nothing
```

ON THE CD

Included on the CD-ROM as `DisplayPrinters.vbs`.

NOTE

As discussed in Chapter 2, there are times when you must use a specific shell type to run a script. For example, you must use Cscript.exe if your code uses Wscript's `Wscript.StdOut` *or* `Wscript.StdIn` *methods. Similarly, you must use MSHTA (double-clicking an HTA file will automatically run with MSHTA) to run an HTA file.*

TESTING SCRIPTS

All scripts are created for a purpose. If the purpose is not met, the script fails. For example, if a script was created to check if a file exists on a remote system and it fails to connect to the remote system, the script has failed to produce the expected result. Therefore, it is important to test your scripts.

It is important to test a script for functionality and the results that it produces because:

- the script may fail when run as a user that does not have the right privilege
- the script may fail because of incompatibility with the operating system
- the script may fail if a required dependency is unavailable
- the script may fail because of a syntax, runtime error
- the script may fail because of a logical error, that is, the script will run successfully, but may not produce desired results

Testing to Identify Privilege Issues

The simplest way to test your scripts for privilege issues is to run the script as the user that is equivalent to the user that will finally run the script. For example, if you are creating a script for a normal user (user with limited rights / privileges), it is best to run the script as a user that has similar privileges as the normal user. By doing so, you will know if your script can be run by a normal user or not. Testing for privileges will allow you to identify and rectify privilege issues before the final release.

Testing to Identify Compatibility Issues

Compatibility issues may occur when a script is run on a system other than the system it was created for. For instance, a script that was created for Windows XP may fail to run on a system running Windows XP with Service Pack 2. For this purpose it is important to test your scripts and document the platforms for which the script is best suited. For example, if you create a script for Windows XP, it is best to test the script with every available service pack of Windows XP to check for compatibility.

Testing to Identify Dependency Issues

Dependency issues generally cannot be tested as they are environment-specific. However, as a best practice you can include code to check that the dependency (such as a file on a network drive) exists before attempting to open the file. Adding code to your scripts to check for dependencies will allow you to display or log a meaningful message instead of an error displayed by VBScript.

Testing to Identify Syntax and Runtime Errors

Syntax errors in the scripts can generally be tested by simply launching the scripts. Runtime errors on the other hand, may not surface until the affected code is executed, and therefore, require testing of every procedure included in the scripts.

For example, when the script in Listing 3.15 is executed, it does not immediately display any errors. However, a runtime error is displayed, when the `Check Procedure` button is clicked that executes the `DisplayMessage` procedure. Therefore, it is essential to test all features of a script to ensure that the script does not display runtime errors when a particular feature is used.

LISTING 3.15 Runtime Testing Script Example

```
<HTML>
<Script Language="vbscript">
  Sub DisplayMessage
    document.writ msg.value
End Sub
</Script>
<Body>
  <input type="text" name="msg">
  <input type="Button" Value="Check Procedure" OnClick="DisplayMessage">
 </Body>
</HTML>
```

Testing to Identify Logical Errors

As we learned in Chapter 2, logical errors are difficult to identify and troubleshoot. Scripts may generate undesired results because of the logical errors. For example, the example in Listing 3.16 displays a computer name appended with a date, where just the computer name is expected.

LISTING 3.16 Logical Error Example

```
<HTML>
<Script language="vbscript">
 Sub GetDrives
   sComputer = ComputerName.Value
   WriteLog sComputer
   msgbox sComputer
   Set objWMI = GetObject("Winmgmts://" & sComputer)
       for each item in objWMI.InstancesOf("Win32_LogicalDrive")
               sDrive = sDrive & "<br>" & item.name
       next
   Set objWMI = nothing
End Sub
Sub WriteLog(cn)
       cn = "[ " & now & " ] " & cn
       Set objFs = CreateObject("Scripting.FileSystemObject")
          Set objFile = objFs.OpenTextFile("Loginfo.log",8,true)
            objFile.WriteLine cn
               objFile.Close
          Set objFile = nothing
            Set objFs = nothing
End Sub
</Script>
<Body>
       <input type="text" name="ComputerName">
       <input type="button" value="Get Drives" OnClick="GetDrives">
</Body>
</HTML>
```

When the script in Listing 3.16 is run, it tries to connect to a computer that does not exist. It is because the computer name is prefixed with time stamp by the `WriteLog` method. This happens because by default the `Sub` procedure in VBScript treats the arguments as passed `By Reference` and not `By Value`. As a result, when the `WriteLog` method prefixes the computer name with the date and time, it actually updates the referenced `sComputer` variable, which causes the WMI connection to fail because there is no such computer on the network.

Logical problems such as this are generally difficult to identify, and therefore require thorough testing. To thoroughly test the scripts and the results that they produce, it is best to create test cases. For example, to ensure that a script can be run on all Windows platforms you may create test cases and indicate the results of the tests in a summary report as shown in Table 3.5.

TABLE 3.5 Test Case and Results Summary

Number	Test Case	Result
1.1	Run the script on a system running Windows XP	Passed
1.2	Run the script on a system running Windows 2000	Passed
1.3	Run the script on a system running Windows 2003	Failed
1.4	Run the script on a system running Windows NT 4.0	Failed
1.5	Run the script on a system running Windows 95	Failed
2.1	Test for remote machine connection	Failed
2.2	Test logging function	Passed
2.3	Test result display and layout	Failed

DEBUGGING SCRIPTS

You know by now that errors do occur; some errors are hard to find, such as logical errors, and others are easy to identify, such as syntax and run-time errors. Generally, you can identify most errors with a good test plan and thorough testing. However, if you do not have complete control of the environment in which your script will be executed, it is a best practice to include logging information that can be used for debugging scripts. Including code for logging information helps you in identifying the perpetrator(s) that may be the cause of the failure of your script.

It is best practice to at the minimum add code to trace and log error information (that is, information should be logged only when an error occurs), as the example in Listing 3.17 demonstrates.

LISTING 3.17 `LoggingError.vbs` **Script That Logs Error Information to the Application EventLog**

```
On Error Resume Next
Set objwNet = CreateObject("Wscript.Shell")
 CheckErr
  Wscript.Echo objwNet.ComputerName
       CheckErr
 Sub CheckErr
   Set objwShell = CreateObject("Wscript.Shell")
     if Err <> 0 then
            objwShell.LogEvent 1, "Ox" & hex(Err.Number) _
                                                & ", " & err.Description
     end if
  Set objwShell = nothing
End Sub
```

When the script in Listing 3.17 is run, the script does the following:

1. It continues even if an error is encountered because of the `On Error Resume Next` statement.

If the `On Error Resume Next` statement is missing in your script, the script will terminate when the error occurs. As a result the next statement to log the error information will not be executed.

2. It creates an instance of the `Wscript.Shell` object and stores it in `objwNet` variable.
3. It calls the `CheckErr` method.
4. The `CheckErr` method writes the error message to the event log if the error number is not equal to zero.
5. The script next calls the `ComputerName` method, which generates an error.

`ComputerName` method is not exposed by `Wscript.Shell` object; it is exposed by the `Wscript.Network` object. Therefore, the script in Listing 3.17 will always write the error information to the event log when the `ComputerName` method is executed. The error has been introduced in the script to demonstrate the logging feature of the script.

6. The script once again executes the `CheckErr` message that creates an event entry in the event log, as shown in Figure 3.29.

For simple scripts, adding code to capture and log error information is sufficient. However, for complicated scripts, you may want to capture more than error information to trace the script execution. For example, you may want to log information on execution of important statements in a script, along with the error information (if error

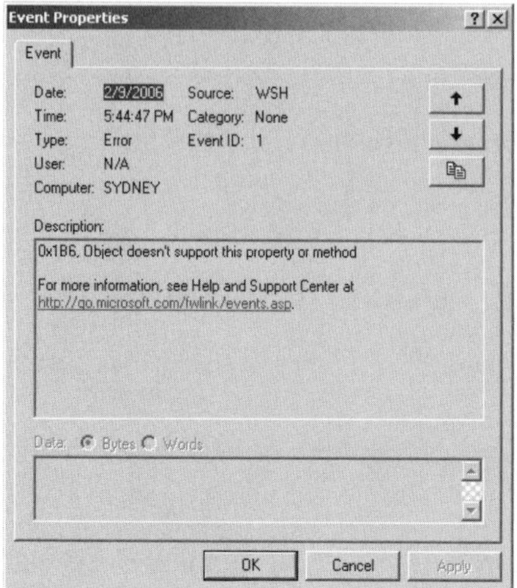

FIGURE 3.29 EventLog entry created by running the script in Listing 3.17.

occurs), to determine that the script ran as expected. Such information is generally captured to a text file rather than writing to an event log. This is because it allows you to analyze the log file at a later time and also, it does not clutter the event logs files by adding multiple entries. Therefore, if you need to trace script execution, it is a best practice to write to a log file. The following example in Listing 3.18 demonstrates how to log execution and error information to a log file.

LISTING 3.18 Trace and Log Script Execution Information Example

```
On Error Resume Next
CONST DEBUG_LOG = "Debug.Log"
  Writelog DEBUG_LOG, "Started at " & Now
   Writelog DEBUG_LOG, "Connecting to local system"
    Set objWMI = GetObject("Winmgmts:")
       CheckErr(4)
         Writelog DEBUG_LOG, "Getting Win32_ComputerSystem Class"
          Set objCs = objWMI.Get("Win32_ComputerSystem")
            CheckErr(5)
              Writelog DEBUG_LOG, "Getting properties"
              Set objCsProp = objCs.Properties_
                CheckErr(6)
                 Writelog DEBUG_LOG, "Enumerating properties"
                 For each prop in objCsProp
                   Property = prop.Name
                   propVAlue = prop.Value
                    Wscript.Echo Property & ", " & propValue
                  Writelog DEBUG_LOG, Property & " = " & PropValue
```

```
                Next
                Writelog DEBUG_LOG, "Completed"
              Writelog DEBUG_LOG, "Releasing memory"
            Set objCsProp = nothing
           Set objCs = nothing
     Set objWMI = nothing
  Writelog DEBUG_LOG, "Ended at " & Now
Sub WriteLog(ByVal LogFile, ByVal Msg)
   Set objFs = CreateObject("Scripting.FileSystemObject")
     Set objFile = objFs.OpenTextFile(LogFile,8,True)
       objFile.WriteLine Msg
       objFile.close
     Set objFile = nothing
   Set objFs = nothing
End Sub
Sub CheckErr(ByVal iLine)
       if Err.Number <> 0 then
               Writelog DEBUG_LOG, "Error at " & iLine & ", " & _
                                   Err.Number & ", " & _
                                   Err.Description & ", " & _
                                   Err.Source
               Err.Clear
       else
               Writelog DEBUG_LOG, "Completed"
       end if
End Sub
```

When the script in Listing 3.18 is executed, it writes step-by-step information about execution (that was included in the script) to the specified debug log file. The information is logged every time the script is executed. Although it is okay to log debugging information every time the script is executed, it is not the best practice.

Best practice is to provide for an option to enable or disable logging, as required. You can do so by using a combination of a variable (that can be set as `True` or `False`) and the `If…then` statement, as shown in Listing 3.19.

LISTING 3.19 Enabling / Disabling Debugging Information Example

```
On Error Resume Next
 bDebug = False
 CONST DEBUG_LOG = "Debug.Log"
  if bDebug then Writelog DEBUG_LOG, "Started at " & Now
   if bDebug then Writelog DEBUG_LOG, "Connecting to local system"
    Set objWMI = GetObject("Winmgmts:")
       if bDebug then CheckErr(4)
         if bDebug then Writelog DEBUG_LOG, _
                    "Getting Win32_ComputerSystem Class"
          Set objCs = objWMI.Get("Win32_ComputerSystem")
            if bDebug then CheckErr(5)
              if bDebug then Writelog DEBUG_LOG, "Getting properties"
              Set objCsProp = objCs.Properties_
                if bDebug then CheckErr(6)
```

```
                if bDebug then Writelog DEBUG_LOG, _
                                        "Enumerating properties"
                For each prop in objCsProp
                  Property = prop.Name
                  propVAlue = prop.Value
                   Wscript.Echo Property & ", " & propValue
                 if bDebug then Writelog DEBUG_LOG, _
                               Property & " = " & PropValue
                  Next
                  if bDebug then Writelog DEBUG_LOG, "Completed"
              if bDebug then Writelog DEBUG_LOG, "Releasing memory"
            Set objCsProp = nothing
           Set objCs = nothing
     Set objWMI = nothing
  if bDebug then Writelog DEBUG_LOG, "Ended at " & Now
Sub WriteLog(ByVal LogFile, ByVal Msg)
   Set objFs = CreateObject("Scripting.FileSystemObject")
     Set objFile = objFs.OpenTextFile(LogFile,8,True)
       objFile.WriteLine Msg
       objFile.close
     Set objFile = nothing
   Set objFs = nothing
End Sub
Sub CheckErr(ByVal iLine)
      if Err.Number <> 0 then
              Writelog DEBUG_LOG, "Error at " & iLine & ", " & _
                                     Err.Number & ", " & _
                                     Err.Description & ", " & _
                                     Err.Source
              Err.Clear
      else
              Writelog DEBUG_LOG, "Completed"
      end if
End Sub
```

When the script in Listing 3.19 is executed, the script logging statements (such as `Writelog DEBUG_LOG, "Started at " & Now`) are conditionally executed. If the value of `bDebug` flag is set to `True`, it enables logging, and the script writes the debugging information to the debug log file. On the other hand, if the `bDebug` flag is set to `False`, the script does not log any debugging information.

SUMMARY

In this chapter you learned why standardizing your scripts is essential. This chapter also described in detail how to name a script and the importance of naming it correctly. It also covered coding standards such as commenting (that is, standards for including comments in your scripts); formatting code and adding a header that provides a brief description of the script including script version, author, date the script was created, and the changes made to the script. Also in this chapter, you learned about script attributes that describe the nature of the script: that is, if the script is a read-only or a change script, will it run unattended or require user interaction, does it run against a single system or multiple systems, do you run this script only once (and never use it again) or run it repetitively, is it a low-, medium- or high-impact script. This chapter also explained how to use certificates and CAPICOM to securely include passwords in your scripts or encrypt your script that includes passwords. And as the last steps, this chapter covered how to test your scripts, and how to debug them.

This is the last chapter of Part I. In Part II, you will learn about the practical implementations of what was covered in Part I. We will delve into practical tasks that you as an administrator perform to administer your Windows environment.

Part II

Advanced Windows Administration Scripting

In This Part

- Managing IIS 6.0
- Managing Terminal Services
- Managing Windows Firewall

This part is the practical implementation of the Windows scripting technologies and scripting standards covered in Part I. This part covers automation of three new important administration tasks.

4 Managing IIS 6.0

In This Chapter

- Enumerating Web sites and Web site properties
- Enumerating virtual directories and virtual directory settings
- Creating and deleting Web sites
- Creating and deleting virtual directories

Needed for This Chapater

- Windows 2003 Server with Internet Information Server 6.0 (IIS6)
- Text editor

Before Reading This Chapter

- Read Chapter 2
- Browse through WMI IIS provider documentation at *http://msdn .microsoft.com/library/default.asp?url=/library/en-us/iissdk/html/ 852c3424-f87e-4b46-984b-815e8281bd17.asp*

This chapter introduces you to Internet Information Server (IIS6) management and configuration using scripts. It introduces you to the new IIS6 WMI provider. The IIS6 WMI provider exposes objects that you can use in your scripts to automate management of your IIS6 servers. The IIS6 WMI objects implement various classes in the namespace in WMI *MicrosoftIISv2*. Some common WMI properties and methods are inherited from the `IWbemClassObject` COM interface in WMI `IWbemClassObject` COM interface and the `SWbemObject` scripting object. These inherited methods can be used to get and set properties and create new nodes in the IIS Metabase.

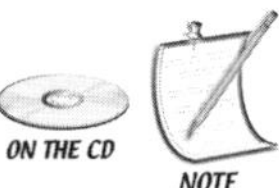

You can also use ADSI to manage IIS6 servers. However, this chapter covers only WM-based scripts. Scripts for this chapter can be found in Scripts\Chapter04 on the CD-ROM.

ENUMERATING WEB SITES AND WEB SITE PROPERTIES

The primary advantage of using scripts is that you can automate tedious tasks that are too time-consuming to perform with the GUI. For example, suppose you have multiple sites configured on a single IIS6 server and you need to list the sites and their properties. It would take a significant amount of time to carry out this task using the IIS6 manager and going through each site to get and list the properties. By contrast, you can quickly write a script that can enumerate all sites and its properties and save it to a text or an XML file format, as seen in Listing 4.1.

LISTING 4.1 List IIS Sites and Properties

```
<package>
   <job id="Enum Sites and Site Properties">
     <runtime>
         <named
             name="s"
             helpstring="Remote Server Name. Default=Localhost"
             type="string"
             required=false/>
         <named
             name="u"
             helpstring="User name for the remote computer.
Example: Domain\UserName"
             type="string"
             required=false/>
         <named
             name="p"
             helpstring="password for the remote user"
             type="string"
             required=false/>
         <named
             name="x"
             helpstring="Output XML file name. Default=EnumSitesProp.xml"
             type="string"
             required=false/>
     </runtime>
<?job debug="true"?>
<script language="vbscript">
  Option Explicit
  Dim sServer, sUser, sPassword
  Dim objXml, InitXML, OutXmlFile, RootNode
  Dim objWMI, objWebConnect, objWebServer, objSite
  Dim WebSrv, Prop
  sServer = wscript.Arguments.Named("s")
    if sServer = "" then sServer = "."
     sUser = wscript.Arguments.Named("u")
       sPassword = wscript.Arguments.Named("p")
         OutXmlFile = Wscript.Arguments.Named("x")
          if OutXmlFile = "" then OutXmlFile = "EnumSitesProp.xml"
```

```
        InitXML = "<MAIN><DATECREATED>" & now & "</DATECREATED></MAIN>"
         CONST wbemAuthenticationLevelPkt = 4, _
                         WbemAuthenticationLevelPktPrivacy = 6
     Set objXml = CreateObject("MSXML2.DomDocument")
       objXml.LoadXml InitXML
         Set RootNode = objXml.SelectSingleNode("/MAIN")
           set objWMI = CreateObject("WbemScripting.SwbemLocator")
      objWMI.Security_.AuthenticationLevel = wbemAuthenticationLevelPkt
      Set objWebConnect = objWMI.ConnectServer(sServer, _
                                                "root/MicrosoftIISv2", _
                                                    sUser, sPassword)
        set objWebServer = objWebConnect.InstancesOf("IIsWebServer")
              For each Websrv in objWebServer
                     Set objSite = WriteXMLEl(objXML, RootNode, "SITE", "")
                  WriteXmlAt objXML, objSite, "NAME",WebSrv.Name
                        for each prop in websrv.Properties_
                           for each prop in websrv.Properties_
                                 set propXml = WriteXmlEl (objXML, _
                                                 objVirDir,"PROPERTY","")
                                   WriteXmlAt objXML, propXml, "NAME", Prop.Name
                                    WriteXmlAt objXML, propXml, "VALUE",
                                                                 Prop.Value
                                 set propXml = nothing
                           Next
                       Set objSite = nothing
              Next
                 Set objWebServer = nothing
      objXml.Save OutXmlFile
   set objWebConnect = nothing
set objWMI = nothing
Function writeXmlEl(xmldoc, InCreateNode, ElName, ElValue)
   On Error Resume Next
   Dim mEl
    Set mEl = xmldoc.createNode("element", CStr(ElName), "")
       InCreateNode.appendChild (mEl)
      mEl.Text = ElValue & vbNewLine
    Set writeXmlEl = mEl
 End Function
 Function WriteXmlAt(xmldoc,InCreateNode ,AtName,AtValue)
   On Error Resume Next
    Dim mAttribute, myRootAttrib
        Set mAttrib = xmldoc.createAttribute(AtName)
          If Not IsEmpty(InCreateNode) Then
             Set myRootAttrib = InCreateNode.Attributes
          End If
        myRootAttrib.setNamedItem (mAttrib)
     InCreateNode.setAttribute AtName, AtValue
    Set WriteXmlAt = InCreateNode
 End Function
</script>
</job>
</package>
```

The Script

The script in Listing 4.1 enumerates IIS6 Web sites created on a given server. It also enumerates the properties of each Web site and saves the information to an XML file. To do this, the script performs the following steps:

1. Creates the `Named` node to accept the following arguments:
   - `s` as name (or IP address) of the IIS6 server
   - `u` as the username to connect as the specified user
   - `p` as password for the username specified in `u` argument
   - `x` as the output XML filename
2. Includes `Option Explicit` statement to enforce variable declaration.
3. Declares required variables.
4. Retrieves the argument values passed as script parameters to initialize the input and output variables. Sets the default values for the optional arguments.
5. Initializes the `InitXML` variable with the top level XML document node. Adds the `DATECREATED` node to set the value of the node with current system date and time by calling the `Now` VBScript function.
6. Initializes constants for the WMI authentication level.

NOTE

For Windows 2003 servers running Service Pack 1, it is a requirement to encrypt the connection when administering IIS6 remotely. If the connection is not encrypted, the script will fail with Access Denied Error (WBEM_E_ACCESS_DENIED, 0x80041003). Step 11 uses the constants defined in Step 6 to ensure that the connection is encrypted.

7. Creates a new MSXML DOM object.
8. Loads the initial XML data stored in the `InitXML` variable using the `LoadXml` method.
9. Retrieves the root node (`/MAIN`) using the `SelectSingleNode` method and stores it in the `RootNode` variable.
10. Creates the WMI Services object.
11. Sets the `AuthenticationLevel` of the `Security_` property to `wbemAuthenticationLevelPkt`. This ensures that the connection to the remote system is encrypted (see previous Note).
12. Connects to the WMI IIS provider using the `ConnectServer` method.
13. Retrieves the instances of the IIS Web server (`IISWebServer`).

For each instance of the server the script does the following:

- Creates a new XML node (`SITE`) in the memory for the site and stores the returned node in to `objSite` variable. The script calls the `WriteXmlEl` function to create the node. The function creates the node and returns the newly created node as an object.

NOTE

Since the XML node and attributes are created over and over again, the calls to create the nodes and attributes were put into the `WriteXmlEl` and `WriteXmlAt` functions. These functions are called in the script whenever the script needs to add a node or an attribute to a node.

- The script calls the `WriteXmlAt` to write the name of the Web site as an attribute to the `SITE` node.
- For each property of the Web site the script does the following:
  - Creates a new `PROPERTY` node
  - Adds the `NAME` attribute and sets the value to the name of the property being retrieved
  - Adds the `VALUE` attribute and sets the value to the value of the property being retrieved. For example, the `NAME` attribute may have `AppIsolated` as a value, and the `VALUE` attribute may have `2` as the retrieved value of the `AppIsolated` property of the Web site, as shown:

    ```
    <PROPERTY NAME="AppIsolated" VALUE="2" />
    ```

- The script the calls the `Save` method of the MSXML DOM object (`objXml`) to save the XML file to the disk.
- The script finally releases memory and ends.

When the script is executed, if no XML file name is passed as the command-line argument to the script, it saves the XML data (as seen in Figure 4.1) in to `EnumSites` Prop.xml file.

Input, Process, and Output Chart

As discussed earlier in Chapter 1, every script does three things: it takes an input, processes it, and outputs the results. If you follow the sample analogy, the script in Listing 4.1 can also be divided into the following:

Input: Takes the server name, username, password, and an output XML file name as optional inputs to the script.

Process: The script then connects to the remote system to retrieve the information and stores it in memory as an XML object.

Output: It saves the retrieved information to an XML file.

Figure 4.2 shows the Input, Process, and Output chart for the script in Listing 4.1.

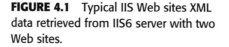

```
- <MAIN>
    <DATECREATED>11/2/2005 9:03:20
      AM</DATECREATED>
  - <SITE NAME="W3SVC/1">
      <PROPERTY NAME="AppIsolated" VALUE="2" />
      <PROPERTY NAME="AppPackageID" VALUE="" />
      <PROPERTY NAME="AppPackageName"
        VALUE="" />
      <PROPERTY NAME="AppRoot" VALUE="" />
      <PROPERTY NAME="Caption" VALUE="" />
      <PROPERTY NAME="Description" VALUE="" />
      <PROPERTY NAME="InstallDate" VALUE="" />
      <PROPERTY NAME="Name" VALUE="W3SVC/1" />
      <PROPERTY NAME="ServerState" VALUE="2" />
      <PROPERTY NAME="SSLCertHash" VALUE="" />
      <PROPERTY NAME="Status" VALUE="" />
    </SITE>
  - <SITE NAME="W3SVC/87257621">
      <PROPERTY NAME="AppIsolated" VALUE="2" />
      <PROPERTY NAME="AppPackageID" VALUE="" />
      <PROPERTY NAME="AppPackageName"
        VALUE="" />
      <PROPERTY NAME="AppRoot" VALUE="" />
      <PROPERTY NAME="Caption" VALUE="" />
      <PROPERTY NAME="Description" VALUE="" />
      <PROPERTY NAME="InstallDate" VALUE="" />
      <PROPERTY NAME="Name"
        VALUE="W3SVC/87257621" />
      <PROPERTY NAME="ServerState" VALUE="2" />
      <PROPERTY NAME="SSLCertHash" VALUE="" />
      <PROPERTY NAME="Status" VALUE="" />
    </SITE>
  </MAIN>
```


FIGURE 4.1 Typical IIS Web sites XML data retrieved from IIS6 server with two Web sites.

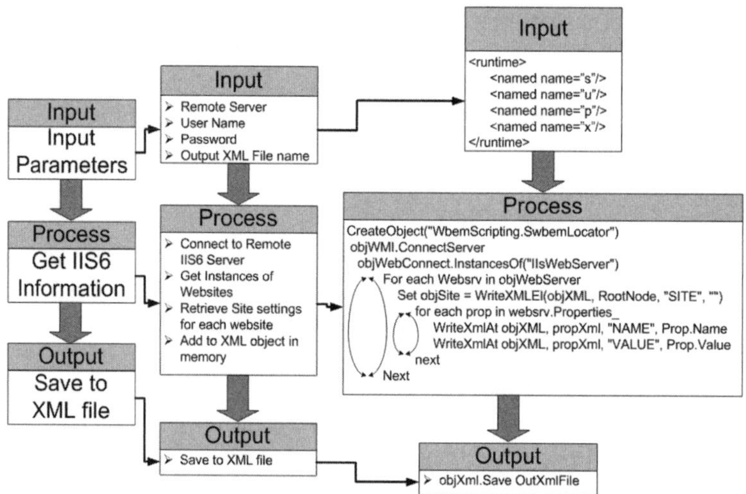

FIGURE 4.2 Input, Process, and Output chart for the script in Listing 4.1.

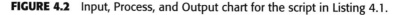

ENUMERATING VIRTUAL DIRECTORIES AND VIRTUAL DIRECTORY SETTINGS

WMI IIS provider also exposes association classes that you can use to retrieve information on virtual directories. Similar to the script in Listing 4.1, you can also create a script to enumerate the virtual directories (and the properties of the virtual directory) of a Web site, as the script in Listing 4.2 does.

LISTING 4.2 Enumerate Virtual Directories and Settings

```
<package>
<job id=" Enum Virtual Directory and Virtual Directory Properties">
<runtime>
  <named
    name="s"
    helpstring="Remote Server Name. Default=Localhost"
    type="string"
    required=false/>
  <named
    name="u"
    helpstring="User name for the remote computer. Example: Domain\UserName"
    type="string"
    required=false/>
   <named
     name="p"
     helpstring="password for the remote user"
     type="string"
     required=false/>
   <named
     name="x"
     helpstring="Output XML file name. Default=EnumSitesProp.xml"
     type="string"
     required=false/>
</runtime>
<?job debug="true"?>
<script language="vbscript">
  Option Explicit
  Dim sServer, sUser, sPassword
  Dim objXml, InitXML, OutXmlFile, RootNode
  Dim objWMI, objWebConnect, objWebServer, objSite
  Dim WebSrv, IISDirectory, objVirDir
  Dim Prop, PropXml
  sServer = wscript.Arguments.Named("s")
    if sServer = "" then sServer = "."
     sUser = wscript.Arguments.Named("u")
       sPassword = wscript.Arguments.Named("p")
         OutXmlFile = Wscript.Arguments.Named("x")
          if OutXmlFile = "" then OutXmlFile = "EnumVirtualDirProp.xml"
```

```
      InitXML = "<MAIN><DATECREATED>" & now & "</DATECREATED></MAIN>"
     CONST wbemAuthenticationLevelPkt = 4, _
WbemAuthenticationLevelPktPrivacy = 6
    Set objXml = CreateObject("MSXML2.DomDocument")
    objXml.LoadXml InitXML
    Set RootNode = objXml.SelectSingleNode("/MAIN")
    set objWMI = CreateObject("WbemScripting.SwbemLocator")
     objWMI.Security_.AuthenticationLevel = wbemAuthenticationLevelPkt
     Set objWebConnect = objWMI.ConnectServer(sServer, _
                                               "root/MicrosoftIISv2", _
                                                   sUser, sPassword)
        set objWebServer = objWebConnect.InstancesOf("IIsWebServer")
         For each Websrv in objWebServer
             Set objSite = WriteXMLEl(objXML, RootNode, "SITE", "")
            WriteXmlAt objXML, objSite, "NAME",WebSrv.Name
                 for each IISDirectory in objWebConnect.AssociatorsOf( _
                                                "IISWebVirtualDir='" & _
                                                  WebSrv.Name & "/root'", _
                                                         , "IISWebVirtualDir")
                       Set objVirDir = WriteXMLEl(objXML, _
             objSite, "VIRDIR", "")
                          WriteXMLAt objXML, objVirDir, _
                              "NAME", IISDirectory.Name
                               for each prop in IISDirectory.Properties_
                                set propXml = WriteXmlEl (objXML, _
        objVirDir,"PROPERTY","")
                                  WriteXmlAt objXML, propXml, "NAME", Prop.Name
                                   WriteXmlAt objXML, propXml, "VALUE", Prop.Value
                                set propXml = nothing
                             next
                  Set objVirDir = nothing
                  next
                 Set objSite = nothing
         Next
     objXml.Save OutXmlFile
    Set objWebServer = nothing
   set objWebConnect = nothing
  set objWMI = nothing
 Function writeXmlEl(xmldoc, InCreateNode, ElName, ElValue)
   On Error Resume Next
   Dim mEl
    Set mEl = xmldoc.createNode("element", CStr(ElName), "")
       InCreateNode.appendChild (mEl)
      mEl.Text = ElValue & vbNewLine
    Set writeXmlEl = mEl
 End Function
 Function WriteXmlAt(xmldoc,InCreateNode ,AtName,AtValue)
   On Error Resume Next
    Dim mAttribute, myRootAttrib
```

```
        Set mAttrib = xmldoc.createAttribute(AtName)
          If Not IsEmpty(InCreateNode) Then
             Set myRootAttrib = InCreateNode.Attributes
          End If
        myRootAttrib.setNamedItem (mAttrib)
     InCreateNode.setAttribute AtName, AtValue
    Set WriteXmlAt = InCreateNode
 End Function
</script>
</job>
</package>
```

The Script

When the script in Listing 4.2 is executed, it lists the virtual directories of a given Web site, retrieves the properties of each Web site, and saves the information to an XML file. To accomplish this, the script does the following:

1. Creates the `Named` node to accept the following arguments:
   - `s` as name (or IP Address) of the IIS6 server
   - `u` as the username to connect as the specified user
   - `p` as password for the username specified in `u` argument
   - `x` as the output XML filename
2. Includes `Option Explicit` statement to enforce variable declaration.
3. Declares required variables.
4. Retrieves the argument values passed as script parameters to initialize the input and output variables. Sets the default values for the optional arguments.
5. Initializes the `InitXML` variable with the top-level XML document node. Adds the `DATECREATED` node to set the value of the node with current system date and time by calling the `Now` VBScript function.
6. Initializes constants for the WMI authentication level.
7. Creates a new MSXML DOM object.
8. Loads the initial XML data stored in the `InitXML` variable using the `LoadXml` method.
9. Retrieves the root node (`/MAIN`) using the `SelectSingleNode` method and stores it in the `RootNode` variable.
10. Creates the WMI Services object.
11. Sets the `AuthenticationLevel` of the `Security_` property to `wbemAuthentication-LevelPkt`. This ensures that the connection to the remote system is encrypted (see previous Note).

12. Connects to the WMI IIS provider using the `ConnectServer` method.
13. Retrieves the instances of the IIS Web server (`IISWebServer`).

For each instance of the server does the following:

- Creates a new XML node (`SITE`) in the memory for the site and stores the returned node in the `objSite` variable. The script calls the `WriteXmlEl` function to create the node. The function creates the node and returns the newly created node as an object.
- The script calls the `WriteXmlAt` to write the name of the Web site as an attribute to the `SITE` node.
- For each associated (`AssociatorsOf`) virtual directory (`IISWebVirtualDir`) of IIS the on Web site, the script does the following:
  - Creates `VIRDIR` node.
  - Adds the name of the virtual directory to the `NAME` attribute.
- For each property of the virtual directory (`IISDirectory`):

  1. Creates a new `PROPERTY` node.
  2. Adds the `NAME` attribute and sets the value to the name of the property being retrieved.
  3. Adds the `VALUE` attribute and sets the value to the value of the property being retrieved. For example, the `NAME` attribute may have the `AppIsolated` as a value and the `VALUE` attribute may have `2` as the retrieved value of the `AppIsolated` property of the Web site as shown:

     ```
     <PROPERTY NAME="AppRoot" VALUE="/LM/W3SVC/1/ROOT" />
     ```

- The script the calls the `Save` method of the MSXML DOM object (`objXml`) to save the XML file to the disk.
- The script finally releases memory and ends.

When the script is executed, if no XML file name is passed as the command line argument to the script, it saves the XML data (as seen in Figure 4.3) to the `EnumVirtualDirProp.xml` file.

Input, Process, and Output Chart

The script in Listing 4.2 can also be divided into the following:

Input: Takes the server name, username, password, and an output XML filename as optional inputs to the script.

Process: The script then connects to the remote system to retrieve the information and stores it in memory as an XML object.

Output: It saves the retrieved information to an XML file.

C:\Bobby\Articles and Books\Scripting\Windows Scripting\SWAT\Scripts\Chapter04\EnumVirtual...

File Edit View Favorites Tools Help


```
- <MAIN>
    <DATECREATED>11/27/2005 9:59:59 PM</DATECREATED>
  - <SITE NAME="W3SVC/1">
    - <VIRDIR NAME="W3SVC/1/ROOT/CertControl">
        <PROPERTY NAME="AppIsolated" VALUE="2" />
        <PROPERTY NAME="AppPackageID" VALUE="" />
        <PROPERTY NAME="AppPackageName" VALUE="" />
        <PROPERTY NAME="AppRoot" VALUE="/LM/W3SVC/1/ROOT" />
        <PROPERTY NAME="Caption" />
        <PROPERTY NAME="Description" />
        <PROPERTY NAME="InstallDate" />
        <PROPERTY NAME="Name" VALUE="W3SVC/1/ROOT/CertControl" />
        <PROPERTY NAME="Status" />
      </VIRDIR>
    - <VIRDIR NAME="W3SVC/1/ROOT/CertEnroll">
        <PROPERTY NAME="AppIsolated" VALUE="2" />
        <PROPERTY NAME="AppPackageID" VALUE="" />
        <PROPERTY NAME="AppPackageName" VALUE="" />
        <PROPERTY NAME="AppRoot" VALUE="/LM/W3SVC/1/ROOT" />
        <PROPERTY NAME="Caption" />
        <PROPERTY NAME="Description" />
        <PROPERTY NAME="InstallDate" />
        <PROPERTY NAME="Name" VALUE="W3SVC/1/ROOT/CertEnroll" />
        <PROPERTY NAME="Status" />
      </VIRDIR>
    - <VIRDIR NAME="W3SVC/1/ROOT/CertSrv">
        <PROPERTY NAME="AppIsolated" VALUE="0" />
        <PROPERTY NAME="AppPackageID" VALUE="" />
        <PROPERTY NAME="AppPackageName" VALUE="" />
        <PROPERTY NAME="AppRoot"
          VALUE="/LM/W3svc/1/ROOT/CertSrv" />
        <PROPERTY NAME="Caption" />
        <PROPERTY NAME="Description" />
        <PROPERTY NAME="InstallDate" />
        <PROPERTY NAME="Name" VALUE="W3SVC/1/ROOT/CertSrv" />
        <PROPERTY NAME="Status" />
      </VIRDIR>
    </SITE>
    <SITE NAME="W3SVC/434112590" />
  </MAIN>
```


Done My Computer

FIGURE 4.3 Typical virtual directory settings XML data retrieved from IIS6 server with two Web sites.

Figure 4.4 shows the Input, Process, and Output chart for the script in Listing 4.2.

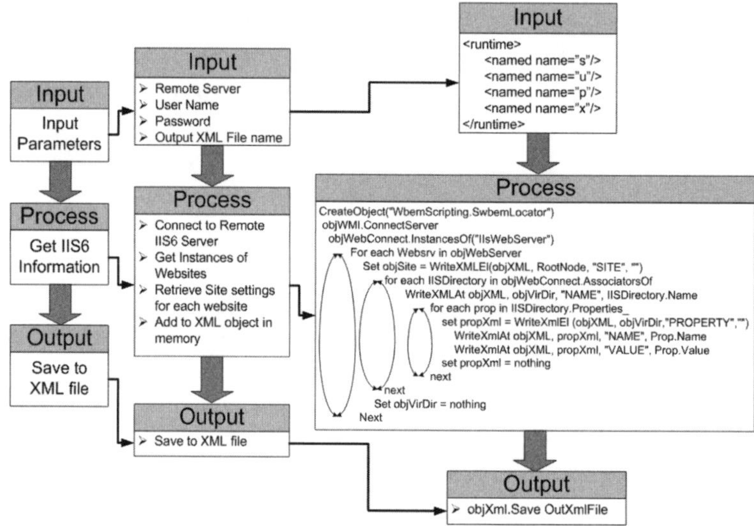

FIGURE 4.4 Input, Process, and Output chart for the script in Listing 4.2.

CREATING WEB SITES

You can easily create a new Web site using the IIS manager in Windows 2003. However, if you need to automate the Web site creation, you can write a script, such as shown in Listing 4.3.

LISTING 4.3 Create Web Site Script

```
<package>
 <job id="Enum Sites and Site Properties">
  <runtime>
        <named
            name="SiteName"
            helpstring="Name for the new website"
            type="string"
            required=true/>
        <named
            name="SitePath"
            helpstring="Directory Path for the website.
Example: c:\inetpub\wwwroot"
            type="string"
            required=true/>
        <named
            name="HostHeader"
            helpstring="Host headers for the site.
```

```
Example:10.10.10.1,80,Mysite;10.10.10.1,8080,Mysite.MyDom.Com"
             type="string"
             required=false/>
         <named
             name="s"
             helpstring="Remote Server Name. Default=Localhost"
             type="string"
             required=false/>
         <named
             name="u"
             helpstring="User name for the remote computer.
                         Example: Domain\UserName"
             type="string"
             required=false/>
         <named
             name="p"
             helpstring="password for the remote user"
             type="string"
             required=false/>
  </runtime>
 <?job debug="true"?>
 <script language="VBScript">
  Option Explicit
  Dim objWMI, objWebConnect, objWebService
  Dim sServer, sUser, sPassword
  Dim sSiteRootPath, sSiteName, inBindings
  Dim splitBindings, splitBind
  Dim sSitePath, i, Bind
  CONST wbemAuthenticationLevelPkt = 4
  CONST WbemAuthenticationLevelPktPrivacy = 6
  sSiteRootPath = wscript.Arguments.Named("SitePath")
  sSiteName = Wscript.Arguments.Named("SiteName")
  if sSiteRootPath = "" or sSiteName = "" then
        Wscript.Arguments.ShowUsage
        Wscript.Quit
  end if
  sServer = wscript.Arguments.Named("s")
    if sServer = "" then sServer = "."
     sUser = wscript.Arguments.Named("u")
       sPassword = wscript.Arguments.Named("p")
  inBindings = wscript.Arguments.Named("HostHeader")
  if inBindings = "" then inBindings = ",80,"
  set objWMI = CreateObject("WbemScripting.SWbemLocator")
  objWMI.Security_.AuthenticationLevel = wbemAuthenticationLevelPkt
   set objWebConnect = objWMI.ConnectServer(sServer, _
                                            "root/MicrosoftIISv2", _
                                                     sUser, sPassword)
  set objWebService = objWebConnect.Get("IIsWebService='W3SVC'")
  splitBindings = split(inBindings,";")
  Redim Bindings(ubound(SplitBindings))
  for i = 0 to ubound(splitbindings)
   SplitBind = split(splitbindings(i),",")
    if ubound(splitBind) = 2 then
```

```
            Set Bindings(i) = _
               objWebConnect.get("ServerBinding").SpawnInstance_()
             Bindings(i).IP = splitBind(0)
              Bindings(i).Port = splitBind(1)
                Bindings(i).Hostname = splitBind(2)
      end if
     next
     sSitePath = objWebService.CreateNewSite(sSiteName, Bindings, sSiteRootPath)
     If Err Then
           WScript.Echo "Error Creating Site: " & sSiteName & " " & _
                                   Hex(Err.Number) & ": " & Err.Description
           WScript.Quit(1)
     else
           Wscript.Echo sSiteName & " Created Successfully. " & VBNewLine &
   sSitePath
     End If
   For each bind in Bindings
           set Bind = nothing
   Next
   Set objWebService = nothing
   Set objWebConnect = nothing
   Set objWMI = nothing
   </script>
   </job>
   </package>
```

The Script

The script in Listing 4.3, when executed, creates a new Web site on a specified server. The script has two mandatory arguments (arguments that must be passed when the script is executed) and four optional arguments. You are required to pass the `SiteName` name and the `SitePath` arguments (directory path to the server) at the time the script is executed. Optionally you can pass the s (remote server name, default is localhost), u (username to connect as), p (password for the user), and the HostHeader (host headers are combination of `IPAddress`, `PortAddress`, `HeaderName`). For example, to create a new Web site on a remote MyComputer with multiple host headers and the directory path to D:\MySite folder, you can execute the command shown in Figure 4.5.

FIGURE 4.5 Create a Web site by calling `CreateWebSite.Wsf` file on a command line with parameters.

To create a new Web site, the script takes the following steps:

1. Creates the `Named` node to accept the following arguments:

   - `SiteName` as the name of the new site to be created
   - `SitePath` as directory path for the new site
   - `hostheader` as the host headers for the Web site. A host header must be in the following format:

     ```
     IP1,Port1,HostHeaderValue1
     ```

     To specify multiple host headers, separate the host headers with a semicolon (;), as in the following example:

   - `IP1,Port1,HostHeaderValue1;IP2,Port2,HostHeaderValue2`
   - `s` as name (or IP Address) of the IIS6 server
   - `u` as the username to connect as the specified user
   - `p` as password for the username specified in `u` argument

2. Includes `Option Explicit` statement to enforce variable declaration.
3. Declares required variables.
4. Parses arguments passed at the command line.
5. Creates a new WMI services object.
6. Sets the authentication level for the WMI connection to packet level encryption.
7. Connects to the `root/MicrosoftIISv2` namespace on the local or remote server.
8. Gets an instance of the IIS6 Web server service.
9. Splits the bindings passed as arguments.
10. Redims the array to match the number of host headers passed as argument.
11. For each host header set (IP, Port, HH) spawns an instance of the `ServerBindings` class.
12. Sets the IP address, Port, and HostName properties for each binding.
13. Creates a new Web site by calling the `CreateNewSite` method.
14. Echoes the error or success message.
15. Clears memory and ends.

Input, Process, and Output Chart

The script in Listing 4.3 can also be divided into the following:

> **Input:** Takes the Web site name and directory path for the Web site as required arguments and host headers, server name, username, and password as optional input arguments to the script.

Process: The script a new set of server bindings (`ServerBinding`) and creates the Web site by calling the `CreateNewSite` method.

Output: It outputs the Success or the Failure message.

Figure 4.6 shows the Input, Process, and Output chart for the script in Listing 4.3.

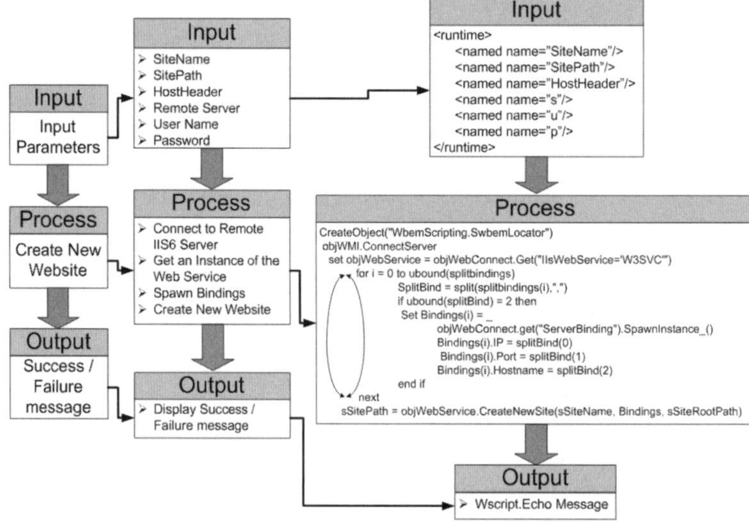

FIGURE 4.6 Input, Process, and Output chart for the script in Listing 4.3.

DELETING WEB SITES

Like Web site creation, Web site deletion can also be automated. To create the site, the script uses the `CreateNewSite` method of the `IISwebService` class. To delete a Web site, however, the script must call the `Delete` method and pass the Web site path as the argument. The script in Listing 4.4 demonstrates how to delete a Web site by calling the `Delete` method.

LISTING 4.4 Delete Web Site

```
<package>
 <job id="Enum Sites and Site Properties">
  <runtime>
     <named
       name="SiteName"
       helpstring="Website name to delete."
```

```
      type="string"
      required=true/>
    <named
      name="s"
      helpstring="Remote Server Name. Default=Localhost"
      type="string"
      required=false/>
    <named
      name="u"
      helpstring="User name for the remote computer.
                              Example: Domain\UserName"
      type="string"
      required=false/>
    <named
      name="p"
      helpstring="password for the remote user"
      type="string"
      required=false/>
 </runtime>
<?job debug="true"?>
<script language="vbscript">
 Option Explicit
 Dim sServer, sUser, sPassword
 Dim objWMI, objWebConnect, objWebServer
 Dim sSiteName, ServerRootPath, WebSrv
 sServer = wscript.Arguments.Named("s")
   if sServer = "" then sServer = "."
    sUser = wscript.Arguments.Named("u")
      sPassword = wscript.Arguments.Named("p")
        sSiteName = Wscript.Arguments.Named("SiteName")
         if sSiteName = "" then
               Wscript.Arguments.ShowUsage
               Wscript.quit(1)
         end if
   CONST wbemAuthenticationLevelPkt = 4
   CONST wbemAuthenticationLevelPktPrivacy = 6
   set objWMI = CreateObject("WbemScripting.SwbemLocator")
    objWMI.Security_.AuthenticationLevel = wbemAuthenticationLevelPkt
    Set objWebConnect = objWMI.ConnectServer(sServer, _
                                           "root/MicrosoftIISv2", _
                                               sUser, sPassword)
    Set objWebServer = objWebConnect.ExecQuery(_
                            "Select * from IISWebServerSetting " & _
                                 "where ServerComment='" & sSiteName & "'")
       For each WebSrv in objWebServer
               ServerRootPath = WebSrv.Name
       Next
       objWebConnect.delete "IISWebServer='" & ServerRootPath & "'"
       If Err Then
          WScript.Echo "Error Creating Site: " & sSiteName & " " & _
                            Hex(Err.Number) & ": " & Err.Description
          WScript.Quit(1)
       else
```

```
        Wscript.Echo sSiteName & " Deleted Successfully. "
      End If
    Set objWebServer = nothing
    Set objWebConnect = nothing
    Set objWMI = nothing
  </script>
 </job>
</package>
```

The Script

You can run the script in Listing 4.4 to delete a Web site. However, you must pass the name of the site to delete as the `SiteName` argument to the script. Optionally, you can also pass a remote server name (`s` argument), the user to authenticate as (`u` argument), and the password for the user (`p` argument) to the script as arguments. To delete a Web site, the script takes the following steps:

1. Creates the `Named` node to accept the following arguments:
   - `SiteName` as the name of the new site to be created
   - `s` as name (or IP Address) of the IIS6 server
   - `u` as the username to connect as the specified user
   - `p` as password for the use name specified in `u` argument
2. Includes `Option Explicit` statement to enforce variable declaration.
3. Declares required variables.
4. Parses arguments passed at the command line.
5. Creates a new WMI services object.
6. Sets the authentication level for the WMI connection to packet level encryption.
7. Connects to the `root/MicrosoftIISv2` namespace on the local or remote server.
8. Executes a WQL (WMI Query Language) to get the instance of the Web site.
9. The script retrieves the site's object path and stores it in the `ServerRootPath` variable.
10. The script calls the `Delete` method and passes the `IISWebServer` class with `ServerRootPath` (the `ServerRootPath` identifies the Web site to delete).
11. It displays the Success or Failure message.
12. Releases memory and ends.

Input, Process, and Output Chart

The script in Listing 4.4 can be divided into the following:

Input: Takes the Web site name as required argument and server name, user-name, and password as optional input arguments to the script.

Process: The script gets the site's root path and deletes the site.

Output: It outputs the Success or the Failure message.

Figure 4.7 shows the Input, Process, and Output chart for the script in Listing 4.4.

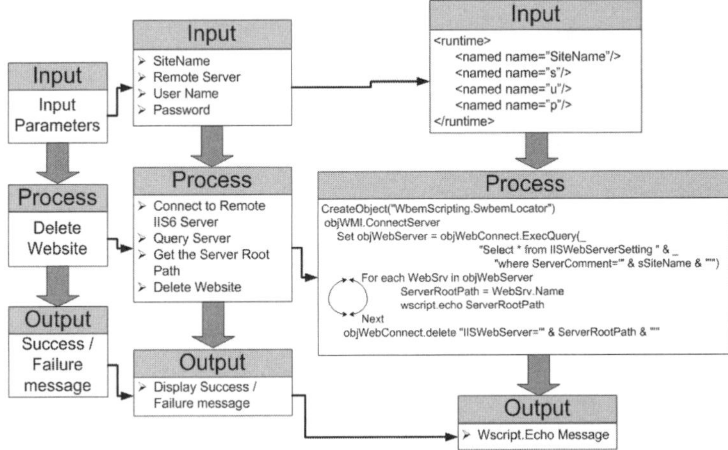

FIGURE 4.7 Input, Process, and Output chart for the script in Listing 4.4.

CREATING VIRTUAL DIRECTORIES

You can also automate the creation of a virtual directory using the IIS WMI provider. To create a virtual directory in a given Web site, after connecting to the Web site, you need to spawn an instance of the `IIsWebVirtualDirSetting` class, set its properties, and then call the `Put_` method as shown in Listing 4.5. You can chose to set all or a few of the properties of the virtual directory. The properties that you do not set inherit the settings from the parent object (site or virtual directory).

LISTING 4.5 Create Virtual Directory Script

```
<package>
 <job id=" Create Virtual Directory">
  <runtime>
     <named
       name="sitename"
       helpstring="SiteName"
       type="string"
       required=true/>
     <named
       name="s"
```

```
        helpstring="Remote Server Name. Default=Localhost"
        type="string"
        required=false/>
      <named
        name="u"
        helpstring="User name for the remote computer.
                                Example: Domain\UserName"
        type="string"
        required=false/>
      <named
        name="p"
        helpstring="password for the remote user"
        type="string"
        required=false/>
      <named
        name="x"
        helpstring="Input Xml file for the Virtual directory settings"
        type="string"
        required=True/>
   </runtime>
  <?job debug="true"?>
  <script language="vbscript">
   Option Explicit
   Dim sServer, sUser, sPassword
   Dim objWMI, objWebConnect, objWebServer
   Dim sSiteName, ServerRootPath, WebSrv
   Dim inXmlFile
   inXmlFile = Wscript.Arguments.Named("x")
    sSiteName = Wscript.Arguments.Named("SiteName")
    if inXmlFile = "" or sSiteName = "" then
         Wscript.Arguments.ShowUsage
         Wscript.quit(1)
    end if
   sServer = wscript.Arguments.Named("s")
     if sServer = "" then sServer = "."
      sUser = wscript.Arguments.Named("u")
        sPassword = wscript.Arguments.Named("p")
     CONST wbemAuthenticationLevelPkt = 4
     CONST WbemAuthenticationLevelPktPrivacy = 6
     set objWMI = CreateObject("WbemScripting.SwbemLocator")
      objWMI.Security_.AuthenticationLevel = wbemAuthenticationLevelPkt
      Set objWebConnect = objWMI.ConnectServer(sServer, _
                                              "root/MicrosoftIISv2", _
                                                  sUser, sPassword)
      Set objWebServer = objWebConnect.ExecQuery(_
                                "Select * from IISWebServerSetting " & _
                                     "where ServerComment='" & sSiteName & "'")
         For each WebSrv in objWebServer
                 ServerRootPath = WebSrv.Name
         Next
         CreateVirDir objWebConnect, ServerRootPath, inXmlFile
```

```
    Set objWebServer = nothing
    Set objWebConnect = nothing
    Set objWMI = nothing

  Function CreateVirDir(byVal objWebConnect, _
Byval ServerRootPath, byVal XmlFile)
   Dim objXml, vDirNodes, svDir, sDirPath, sNewvDir, i
   Dim objVDirSetting, objvDir
     Set ObjXml = CreateObject("MSXML2.DomDocument")
       objXml.Load XmlFile
        if objxml.parseError.errorCode <> 0 then
          Wscript.Echo "Error Validating " & XmlFile & _
                       VBNewLine & objXML.parseError.reason
          Wscript.quit
        end if
         CONST APP_POOLED = 2
           Set VDirNodes = objXml.SelectNodes("/MAIN/VDIR")
            For i = 0 to vDirNodes.Length -1
                svDir = vDirNodes(i).GetAttribute("NAME")
                sDirPath = vDirNodes(i).GetAttribute("PATH")
        if svDir = "" or sDirPath = "" then
           Wscript.Echo "Error: You must provide" & _
"a name and path for the new virtual directory"
           Wscript.quit(1)
        end if
        sNewVDir = ServerRootPath & "/Root/" & sVDir
        Set objVDirSetting = objWebConnect.Get("IIsWebVirtualDirSetting")
        Set objvDir = objVDirSetting.SpawnInstance_()
        objvDir.Name = sNewVDir
        objvDir.Path = vDirNodes(i).GetAttribute("PATH")
        objvDir.AuthFlags = _
           vDirNodes(i).SelectSingleNode("PROPERTIES/AUTHFLAGS").text
        objvDir.AccessExecute = _
         vDirNodes(i).SelectSingleNode("PROPERTIES/ACCESSEXECUTE").Text
        objvDir.AccessRead = _
         vDirNodes(i).SelectSingleNode("PROPERTIES/ACCESSREAD").Text
        objvDir.AccessWrite = _
         vDirNodes(i).SelectSingleNode("PROPERTIES/ACCESSWRITE").Text
        objvDir.AnonymousUserName = _
   vDirNodes(i).SelectSingleNode("PROPERTIES/ANONYMOUSUSERNAME").Text
        objvDir.AnonymousUserPass = _
   vDirNodes(i).SelectSingleNode("PROPERTIES/ANONYMOUSUSERPASS").Text
        objvDir.DefaultDoc = _
         vDirNodes(i).SelectSingleNode("PROPERTIES/DEFAULTDOC").Text
        objvDir.EnableDefaultDoc = _
   vDirNodes(i).SelectSingleNode("PROPERTIES/ENABLEDEFAULTDOC").Text
        objvDir.DirBrowseFlags = "&" & _
   vDirNodes(i).SelectSingleNode("PROPERTIES/DIRBROWSEFLAGS").Text
        objvDir.AccessFlags = _
   vDirNodes(i).SelectSingleNode("PROPERTIES/ACCESSFLAGS").Text
        If vDirNodes(i).SelectNodes("CREATEAPP").length then
           objvDir.AppPoolId = _
```

```
      vDirNodes(i).SelectSingleNode("CREATEAPP/APPPOOLID").Text
        End If
        objvDir.Put_()
        If Err Then
          WScript.Echo "Error Creating virtual directory: " & svDir & " " & _
                              Hex(Err.Number) & ": " & Err.Description
          WScript.Quit(1)
        else
          Wscript.Echo svDir & " Created Successfully. "
        End If
        If vDirNodes(i).SelectNodes("CREATEAPP").Length > 0 then
          Set objvDir = _
  objWebConnect.Get("IIsWebVirtualDir='" & sNewVDir & "'")
          objvDir.AppCreate2(APP_POOLED)
          Set objvDir = _
            objWebConnect.Get("IIsWebVirtualDirSetting='" & sNewVDir  & "'")
          objvDir.AppFriendlyName = _
      vDirNodes(i).SelectSingleNode("CREATEAPP/APPFRIENDLYNAME").text
          objvDir.Put_()
        End If
        Next
        set objXml = nothing
  End Function
  </script>
 </job>
</package>
```

The Script

There are a lot of properties that can be configured for a virtual directory. For example, when you create the site, you may want to change the read access, the write access, execute access, the anonymous username and password, default documents, and so on. If you need such properties to be set when the site is created, then you must somehow pass the configuration values to the script. One option is that you can pass them as arguments to the script. However, the command line will be too long and prone to errors. A better option is to add all the options in a text or an XML file that you can read the property values from and accordingly configure them as the script in Listing 4.5 does.

The script in Listing 4.5 takes an XML file (defined with properties and their values) and sets the specified properties accordingly. The XML file has the structure as shown in Figure 4.8.

As shown in Figure 4.8, the root of the document is the `<MAIN>` XML node. There can be only one root node. The `<VDIR>` under the `<MAIN>` node is the root of the virtual directory that you want to be created. For each virtual directory that you need to create, you can add a `<VDIR>` node. For example, to create two virtual directories, `Test1` and `Test2`, you can create the following XML file:

```
<MAIN>
    <VDIR NAME="Test1" PATH="C:\Test1">
            <PROPERTIES>
            ...
            </PROPERTIES>
            <CREATEAPP>
            ...
            </CREATEAPP>
    </VDIR>
    <VDIR NAME="Test2" PATH="C:\Test2">
            <PROPERTIES>
            ...
            </PROPERTIES>
            <CREATEAPP>
            ...
            </CREATEAPP>
    </VDIR>
</MAIN>
```

```
- <MAIN>
  - <VDIR NAME="TestVDIR" PATH="C:\Temp">
    - <PROPERTIES>
        <AUTHFLAGS>5</AUTHFLAGS>
        <ACCESSEXECUTE>True</ACCESSEXECUTE>
        <ACCESSREAD>True</ACCESSREAD>
        <ACCESSWRITE>True</ACCESSWRITE>
        <ANONYMOUSUSERNAME>Test</ANONYMOUSUSERNAME>
        <ANONYMOUSUSERPASS>Test</ANONYMOUSUSERPASS>
        <DEFAULTDOC>Default.asp,Default.htm</DEFAULTDOC>
        <ENABLEDEFAULTDOC>True</ENABLEDEFAULTDOC>
        <DIRBROWSEFLAGS>H4000003E</DIRBROWSEFLAGS>
        <ACCESSFLAGS>513</ACCESSFLAGS>
      </PROPERTIES>
    - <CREATEAPP>
        <APPFRIENDLYNAME>test virtual
          directory</APPFRIENDLYNAME>
        <APPPOOLID>MLIM</APPPOOLID>
      </CREATEAPP>
    </VDIR>
  </MAIN>
```

FIGURE 4.8 Input XML file sample for creating a virtual directory.

The `<PROPERTIES>` node within the `<VDIR>` node contains the nodes for the properties that you need to set for the virtual directory. The script reads each property node (such as `<ACCESSREAD>`) and sets the property (such as `AccessRead`) for the virtual directory. On the other hand, `<CREATEAPP>` node, if added to the XML file, is used by the script to set the virtual directory as an application. The properties within the `<CREATEAPP>` node (`<APPFRIENDLYNAME>` and `<APPPOOLID>`) defines the settings for the application.

All virtual directory properties are not defined in the XML file. To add other properties, you can do the following (for example, if you want to add the `AspBufferingOn` property):

1. *Add a node as property to the XML file under* `<PROPERTIES>` *node such as* `<ASPBUFFERINGON>` *(must be all uppercase). Add the value for the property (such as* `True` *or* `False`*) within the property start and end nodes (such as* `<ASPBUFFER-INGON>True</ASPBUFFERINGON>`*).*
2. *Open the script in an editor and add the property line after the objvDir.Path = statement such as follows:*

```
objvDir.AspBufferingOn =_vDirNodes(i).SelectSingleNode
("ASPBUFFERING ON").text
```

3. *Save the XML and the script file and test it.*

Besides passing the input XML file as an argument to the script, you also need to pass the name of the Web site, as an argument, where the virtual directory needs to be created. Optionally, you can also pass a remote server name, username to connect as, and the password for the specified user as arguments. When executed, the script reads the input XML file, creates a new virtual directory, and sets the properties of the newly created virtual directory. To create a new virtual directory the script does the following:

1. Creates the `Named` node to accept the following arguments:
   - `SiteName` as the name of the new site to be created
   - `s` as name (or IP Address) of the IIS6 server
   - `u` as the username to connect as the specified user
   - `p` as password for the username specified in `u` argument
2. Includes `Option Explicit` statement to enforce variable declaration.
3. Declares required variables.
4. Parses arguments passed at the command line.
5. Creates a new WMI services object.
6. Sets the Authentication level for the WMI connection to packet level encryption.
7. Connects to the root/MicrosoftIISv2 namespace on the local or remote server.
8. Executes a WQL (WMI Query Language) to get the instance of the Web site.
9. The script retrieves the site's object path and stores it in the `ServerRootPath` variable.
10. The script next calls the `CreateVirDir` function. The `CreateVirDir` does the following:
    - Creates a new instance of the MSXML DOM object.
    - Loads the XML file into memory.
    - Selects all the `VDIR` nodes. For each `VDIR` node the script does the following:
      - Spawns an instance of the `IIsWebVirtualDirSetting` class.
      - Reads the data from XML nodes and sets the properties.

- Calls the `Put_` method that creates the virtual directory and sets the virtual directory properties.
- The script displays the success or failure message
- The script then checks to see if the `CREATEAPP` node exists.
- It creates an application for the virtual directory and sets the friendly name for the application if the `CREATEAPP` node exists.
- The script releases the `objXml` object and exits the function.

11. The script clears the memory and exits.

Input, Process, and Output Chart

The script in Listing 4.5 can be divided into the following:

> **Input:** Takes the Web site name and the input XML file as required arguments. It also takes server name, username, and password as optional input arguments.
>
> **Process:** The script gets the site's root path, creates a new virtual directory, sets the newly created virtual directory settings and ends.
>
> **Output:** It outputs the Success or the Failure message.

Figure 4.9 shows the Input, Process, and Output chart for the script in Listing 4.5.

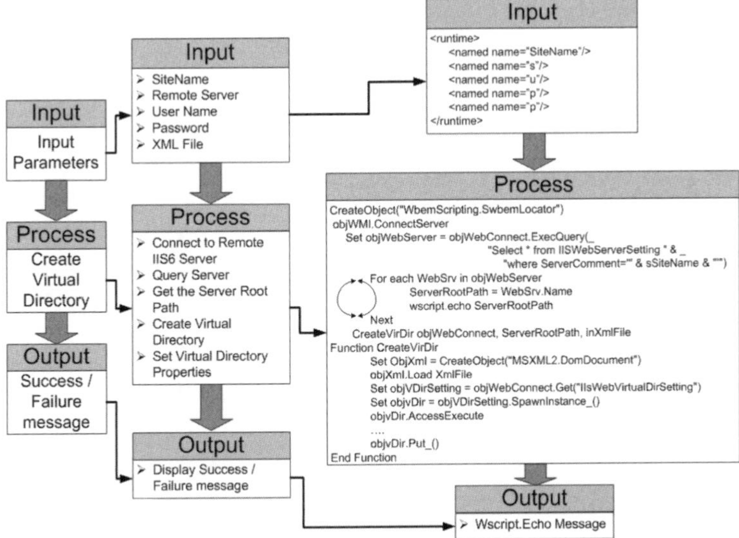

FIGURE 4.9 Input, Process, and Output chart for the script in Listing 4.5.

DELETING VIRTUAL DIRECTORIES

Deleting virtual directories is similar to deleting Web sites. To delete a virtual directory, you must call the `Delete` method and pass `IISWebVitrualDir` with the virtual directory name that you need to delete. For example, to delete a virtual directory called `Test` in the default Web site, you would to the following:

```
objWebConnect.Delete "IISWebVirtualDir='/W3SVC/1/Root/Test'"
```

The script in Listing 4.6 shows the complete script that can be used to delete a virtual directory from a specified Web site.

LISTING 4.6 Delete Virtual Directory Script

```
<package>
 <job id=" Delete Virtual Directory">
  <runtime>
     <named
       name="SiteName"
       helpstring="Website name to delete."
       type="string"
       required=true/>
     <named
       name="vDir"
       helpstring="virtual directory path from the root.
Example: /Test/SubTest"
       type="string"
       required=true/>
     <named
       name="s"
       helpstring="Remote Server Name. Default=Localhost"
       type="string"
       required=false/>
     <named
       name="u"
       helpstring="User name for the remote computer.
                                Example: Domain\UserName"
       type="string"
       required=false/>
     <named
       name="p"
       helpstring="password for the remote user"
       type="string"
       required=false/>
  </runtime>
 <?job debug="true"?>
 <script language="vbscript">
  Option Explicit
  Dim sServer, sUser, sPassword
  Dim objWMI, objWebConnect, objWebServer
  Dim sSiteName, ServerRootPath, WebSrv
```

```
Dim VirtualDirectoryPath, VirtualRootPath
sServer = wscript.Arguments.Named("s")
  if sServer = "" then sServer = "."
   sUser = wscript.Arguments.Named("u")
     sPassword = wscript.Arguments.Named("p")
       sSiteName = Wscript.Arguments.Named("SiteName")
        VirtualDirectoryPath = Wscript.Arguments.Named("vDir")
        if sSiteName = "" or VirtualDirectoryPath = "" then
              Wscript.Arguments.ShowUsage
              Wscript.quit(1)
        end if
  CONST wbemAuthenticationLevelPkt = 4
  CONST WbemAuthenticationLevelPktPrivacy = 6
  On Error Resume Next
  set objWMI = CreateObject("WbemScripting.SwbemLocator")
   objWMI.Security_.AuthenticationLevel = wbemAuthenticationLevelPkt
   Set objWebConnect = objWMI.ConnectServer(sServer, _
                                     "root/MicrosoftIISv2", _
                                         sUser, sPassword)
   Set objWebServer = objWebConnect.ExecQuery(_
                       "Select * from IISWebServerSetting " & _
                            "where ServerComment='" & sSiteName & "'")
     For each WebSrv in objWebServer
             ServerRootPath = WebSrv.Name
     Next
     if left(VirtualDirectoryPath,1) <> "/" then
             VirtualDirectoryPath = "/" & VirtualDirectoryPath
     end if
       VirtualRootPath = ServerRootPath & "/root" & VirtualDirectoryPath
          objWebConnect.delete "IISWebVirtualDir='" & VirtualRootPath & "'"
           If Err Then
             WScript.Echo "Error Creating Site: " & sSiteName & " " & _
                             Hex(Err.Number) & ": " & Err.Description
             WScript.Quit(1)
           else
             Wscript.Echo sSiteName & " Deleted Successfully. "
           End If
   Set objWebServer = nothing
   Set objWebConnect = nothing
   Set objWMI = nothing
</script>
</job>
</package>
```

The Script

To delete a Web site, the script takes the following steps:

1. Creates the `Named` node to accept the following arguments:
   - `SiteName` as the name of the new site to be created
   - s as name (or IP Address) of the IIS6 server

- `u` as the username to connect as the specified user
- `p` as password for the username specified in `u` argument

2. Includes `Option Explicit` statement to enforce variable declaration.
3. Declares required variables.
4. Parses arguments passed at the command line.
5. Creates a new WMI services object.
6. Sets the authentication level for the WMI connection to packet level encryption.
7. Connects to the `root/MicrosoftIISv2` namespace on the local or remote server.
8. Executes a WQL (WMI Query Language) to get the instance of the Web site.
9. The script retrieves the site's object path and stores it in the `ServerRootPath` variable.
10. It then creates the root path of the virtual directory that needs to be deleted and stores the value in the `VirtualRootPath` variable.

You must pass the complete path to the virtual directory. For example, to delete a `Test` virtual directory that is a sub virtual directory of `TestVDIR` virtual directory, you must pass `/TestVDIR/Test` as the `vDir` argument to the script. To delete a virtual directory that is in the root of the Web site, you can simply pass the name of the virtual directory. For example, to delete the `TestVDIR` virtual directory, simply pass `/vDir:TestVDIR` as an argument to the script.

11. The script calls the `Delete` method and passes the `IISWebVirtualDir` class passes the `VirtualRootPath` variable.
12. The script echoes the Success or Failure message and ends.

Input, Process, and Output Chart

The script in Listing 4.6 can be divided into the following:

Input: Takes the Web site name and the path to the virtual directory as required arguments. It also takes server name, username, and password as optional input arguments.

Process: The script gets the site's root path, deletes the specified virtual directory, and ends.

Output: It outputs the Success or the Failure message.

Figure 4.10 shows the Input, Process, and Output chart for the script in Listing 4.6.

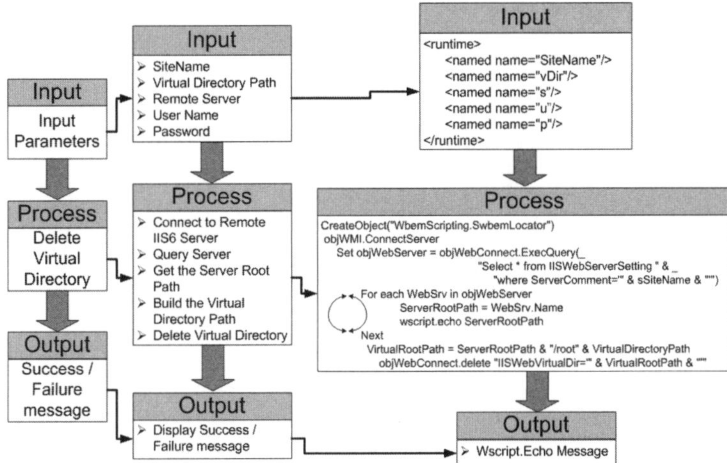

FIGURE 4.10 Input, Process, and Output chart for the script in Listing 4.6.

SUMMARY

This chapter covered IIS6 automation and management. In this chapter you learned how to create a Web site, delete a Web site, create virtual directories, and delete a virtual directory with scripts. This chapter also discussed the input, process, and output relationships of each script. This chapter was based on the WMI IIS provider that is included with Windows 2003 servers only. This chapter gave you a starting point for the IIS6 automation and management using scripts. A complete reference of the IIS6 provider (the classes, properties, and methods provided by the IIS6 provider) is available at the MSDN site *http://msdn.microsoft.com/library/default.asp?url=/library/en-us/iissdk/html/852c3424-f87e-4b46-984b-815e8281bd17.asp.*

The next chapter covers the Terminal Services automation. You will learn how to use scripts to manage Windows Terminal Services using the Terminal Services WMI provider.

5 Managing Terminal Services

In This Chapter

- Listing and configuring Terminal Services
- Listing and configuring Terminal properties
- Listing and configuring Terminal permissions

Needed for This Chapter

- Windows 2003 Server
- Text editor

Before Reading This chapter

- Read Chapter 2
- Browse through WMI TS provider documentation at *http://msdn.microsoft.com/library/default.asp?url=/library/en-us/termserv/termserv/terminal_services_wmi_provider_reference.asp*

This chapter introduces you to Terminal Services (TS) server management and configuration using scripts. It introduces you to the new Terminal Services WMI provider. The TS WMI provider exposes objects that you can use in your scripts to automate management of your Windows 2003 terminal servers. The TS WMI objects implement various classes in the `CIMV2` namespace in WMI.

Scripts for this chapter can be found in Scripts\Chapter05 on the CD-ROM.

LISTING AND CONFIGURING TERMINAL SERVICES

Before WMI, you had to write applications using programming languages such as Visual Basic or C++ to manage Terminal Services. It was because no scripting interface was available and the applications had to call the Terminal Service APIs directly. These APIs can now be accessed through the WMI.

A Terminal Service WMI provider has been added in Windows 2003. The TS WMI provider exposes WMI classes (that expose properties and methods) that can be used in scripts to automate Terminal Services (WMI provider is available and included only in Windows 2003) management. For example, you can use the script in Listing 5.1 to list the Terminal Server settings.

LISTING 5.1 Listing Terminal Server Settings

```
<package>
 <job id=" List Terminal Server Settings">
  <runtime>
     <named
       name="s"
       helpstring="Remote Server Name. Default=Localhost"
       type="string"
       required=false/>
     <named
       name="u"
       helpstring="User name for the remote computer.
                               Example: Domain\UserName"
       type="string"
       required=false/>
     <named
       name="p"
       helpstring="password for the remote user"
       type="string"
       required=false/>
     <named
       name="l"
       helpstring="Output log file name. Default=ListTsSettings.txt"
       type="string"
       required=false/>
  </runtime>
 <?job debug="true"?>
 <script language="vbscript">
  Option Explicit
  Dim sServer, sUser, sPassword, sLogFile
  Dim objWMI, objTsConnect, objTsSettings
  Dim objSwat
  Dim item, prop
  sServer = wscript.Arguments.Named("s")
    if sServer = "" then sServer = "."
     sUser = wscript.Arguments.Named("u")
       sPassword = wscript.Arguments.Named("p")
```

```
        sLogFile = wscript.Arguments.Named("l")
       if sLogFile = "" then sLogFile = "ListTsSettings.txt"
         CONST wbemAuthenticationLevelPkt = 4
           CONST WbemAuthenticationLevelPktPrivacy = 6
   Set objSwat = CreateObject("Swat.1.00")
    set objWMI = CreateObject("WbemScripting.SwbemLocator")
     objWMI.Security_.AuthenticationLevel = wbemAuthenticationLevelPkt
       Set objTsConnect = objWMI.ConnectServer(sServer, _
                                                     "root/CIMv2", _
                                                     sUser, sPassword)
        set objTsSettings = _
                   objTsConnect.InstancesOf("Win32_terminalServiceSetting")
         for each item in objTsSettings
           for each prop in item.Properties_
              objSwat.WriteLog sLogFile, _
                          objSwat.SplitOnCap(prop.name) & _
                                               " = " & prop.value
           next
     next
    set objTsSettings = nothing
   set objWMI = nothing
 set objSwat = nothing
</script>
</job>
</package>
```

The Script

The script in Listing 5.1 lists all the properties of Terminal Services and saves the information into a text file. To do this the script performs the following steps:

1. Creates the `Named` node to accept the following arguments:
   - `s` as name (or IP Address) of the TS server
   - `u` as the username to connect as the specified user
   - `p` as password for the username specified in `u` argument
   - `l` as output log filename
2. Includes `Option Explicit` statement to enforce variable declaration.
3. Declares required variables.
4. Retrieves the argument values passed as script parameters to initializes the input and output variables. Sets the default values for the optional arguments.
5. Initializes constants for the WMI authentication level.
6. Creates an instance of the custom `Swat.1.00` object.
7. Creates the WMI Services object.
8. Sets the `AuthenticationLevel` of the `Security_` property to `wbemAuthentication-LevelPkt`. This ensures that the connection to the remote system is encrypted.
9. Gets instances of the `Win32_TerminalServerSetting` class.

10. For each instance of the Terminal Server Settings does the following:
    - Gets the properties name and value collection.
    - For each property in the properties collection:
        - Calls the `WriteLog` method of the `Swat.1.00` object to write the `Name` and the `Value` to the specified test file.
        - Before the `WriteLog` method is called, the script calls the `SplitOnCap` method exposed by the `Swat.1.00` object. The `SplitOnCap` function correctly formats the `Name` property for display by splitting the value passed to the function on the basis of the uppercase characters. For example, it formats `ServerName` value to Server Name.
11. Finally, the script releases memory and ends.

The script, when executed, creates a text file with the specified name (if the output filename is not passed to the script, the script creates ListTsSettings.txt) and writes the properties and values to the text file similar to the following:

```
Active Desktop = 1
Allow TSConnections = 1
Caption =
Delete Temp Folders = 1
Description =
Direct Connect License Servers =
Disable Forcible Logoff = 0
Fallback Print Driver Type = 0
Home Directory =
Licensing Description = This policy provides two concurrent connections.
Licensing Name = Remote Desktop for Administration
Licensing Type = 1
Logons = 0
Profile Path =
Server Name = W2K3IISCERT
Setting ID =
Single Session = 0
Terminal Server Mode = 0
Time Zone Redirection = 0
User Permission = 0
Use Temp Folders = 1
```

The value of the properties can also be formatted to make it more meaningful. For example, you can format `1` returned by the `ActiveDesktop` property as `Active Desktop = Active Desktop is allowed in each user session`. This will make it more meaningful to the reader rather than displaying `1`. To do this, you can add a function and use a select statement such as the following:

```
Function FormatActiveDesktop(v)
   Select Case v
    Case 1 : sValue = _
                 "Active Desktop is allowed in each user session."
    Case else : sValue = _
                 "Active Desktop is not allowed in each user session."
   End Select
  FormatActiveDesktop = sValue
End Function
```

You will have to write a function for each value that you want to format and use an `if then...else` statement to ensure that the right function is called for the right property. For example, the following `if then...else` statement will ensure that the `ActiveDesktop` format function is called for the `ActiveDesktop` property:

```
If prop.Name = "ActiveDesktop" then sValue = FormatActiveDesktop
(prop.Value)
```

Alternatively, you can also use a select statement to call the right formatting function for the property as follows:

```
for each prop in item.Properties_
Select Case prop.Name
    Case "ActiveDesktop" : sValue = FormatActiveDesktop(prop.Value)
    Case "AllowTSConnections" : sValue = FormatATSCon(prop.Value)
    ...
End Select
             objSwat.WriteLog sLogFile, _
                          objSwat.SplitOnCap(prop.name) & _
                                            " = " & sValue
next
```

ADD AND REMOVE DIRECT CONNECT LICENSE SERVER

Direct license server is used by the Terminal Services to get a license for the client when the Terminal Services is running in the application mode. You set or delete the direct license server name by calling the `AddDirectConnectLicenseServer` and `DeleteDirect-LicenseServer` methods of the `Win32_TerminalServiceSetting` class. Listing 5.2 shows how to add or delete a server using a script.

LISTING 5.2 Adding Removing Direct Connect License Server Script

```
<package>
 <job id=" Set Direct Connect License Server">
  <runtime>
     <named
       name="s"
```

```
        helpstring="Remote Server Name. Default=Localhost"
        type="string"
        required=false/>
      <named
        name="u"
        helpstring="User name for the remote computer.
                              Example: Domain\UserName"
        type="string"
        required=false/>
      <named
        name="p"
        helpstring="password for the remote user"
        type="string"
        required=false/>
      <named
        name="LServer"
        helpstring="License Server Name."
        type="boolean"
        required=true/>
      <named
        name="AddRemove"
        helpstring="Add or Remove a License Server. Default=+"
        type="boolean"
        required=false/>
   </runtime>
  <?job debug="true"?>
  <script language="vbscript">
   Option Explicit
   Dim sServer, sUser, sPassword, sLogFile
   Dim objWMI, objTsConnect, objTsSettings
   Dim objSwat
   Dim item, prop
   sServer = wscript.Arguments.Named("s")
     if sServer = "" then sServer = "."
      sUser = wscript.Arguments.Named("u")
        sPassword = wscript.Arguments.Named("p")
         sLicenseServerName = wscript.Arguments.Named("LServer")
           if LServer = "" then
                 Wscript.Arguments.ShowUsage
                 Wscript.Quit(1)
           end if
            bAddRemove = wscript.Arguments.Named("AddRemove")
             if bAddRemove = "" then bAddRemove = True
              CONST wbemAuthenticationLevelPkt = 4
               CONST WbemAuthenticationLevelPktPrivacy = 6
       On Error Resume Next
       set objWMI = CreateObject("WbemScripting.SwbemLocator")
        objWMI.Security_.AuthenticationLevel = wbemAuthenticationLevelPkt
          Set objTsConnect = objWMI.ConnectServer(sServer, _
                                          "root/CIMv2", _
                                              sUser, sPassword)
            set objTsSettings = _
                                  objTsConnect.InstancesOf( _
```

```
"Win32_terminalServiceSetting")
            for each item in objTsSettings
                if bAddRemove then
                        item.AddDirectConnectLicenseServer sLicenseServerName
                        if Err then
                          Wscript.Echo "Error adding License Server " & _
                                        Err.Number & ", " & Err.Description
                        else
                          Wscript.Echo "License Server added successfully"
                        end if
                else
                        item.DeleteDirectConnectLicenseServer sLicenseServerName
                        if Err then
                          Wscript.Echo "Error deleting License Server " & _
                                        Err.Number & ", " & Err.Description
                        else
                          Wscript.Echo "License Server deleted successfully"
                        end if
                end if
       next
      set objTsSettings = nothing
     set objWMI = nothing
  set objSwat = nothing
 </script>
 </job>
</package>
```

The Script

The script takes the `LServer` name argument as the required argument and the remote server name, connect as user, password for the user and `AddRemove` as optional arguments. The `AddRemove` argument takes the `Boolean` value. A + sign sets the value to true and – sign sets the value to false. The script when executed takes the following steps to add or remove the Direct Connect License server:

1. Creates the `Named` node to accept the following arguments:
   - `s` as name (or IP Address) of the TS server
   - `u` as the username to connect as the specified user
   - `p` as password for the username specified in `u` argument
   - `LServer` as the Direct Connect License server name
   - `AddRemove` as the action for the script (+ adds the server and – removes the server)
2. Includes `Option Explicit` statement to enforce variable declaration.
3. Declares required variables.
4. Retrieves the argument values passed as script parameters to initialize the input and output variables. Sets the default values for the optional arguments.

5. Initializes constants for the WMI authentication level.
6. Creates the WMI Services object.
7. Sets the `AuthenticationLevel` of the `Security_` property to `wbemAuthentication-LevelPkt`. This ensures that the connection to the remote system is encrypted.
8. Connects to the WMI TS provider using the `ConnectServer` method.
9. Retrieves the instances of the `Win32_TerminalServiceSetting` class.
10. For each instance of the TS setting does the following:
    - If the `AddRemove` is set to `True`
        - Calls the `AddDirectConnectLicense` method to add the server.
        - Displays Success or Failure message.
    - If the `AddRemove` is set to `False`
        - Calls the `DeleteDirectConnectLicense` method to delete the server.
        - Displays Success or Failure message.
11. The script releases memory and ends.

CHANGING TERMINAL SERVER LICENSE TYPE

A default installation of Windows 2003 sets the TS to Remote Desktop (RDP) for Administration (commonly known as Admin mode). The Admin License allows 2 RDP connections to the TS server. However, TS running in application mode supports the following modes:

Per Device/Per Seat: Valid for application servers only.

Per User: Valid for applications servers only.

You can change these modes using scripts by calling the `ChangeMode` method of the `Win32_TerminalServiceSetting` class as shown in Listing 5.3.

LISTING 5.3 Changing Terminal Server License Mode

```
<package>
 <job id="Change TS License Mode">
  <runtime>
     <named
       name="s"
       helpstring="Remote Server Name. Default=Localhost"
       type="string"
       required=false/>
     <named
       name="u"
       helpstring="User name for the remote computer.
                                   Example: Domain\UserName"
```

```
        type="string"
        required=false/>
      <named
        name="p"
        helpstring="password for the remote user"
        type="string"
        required=false/>
      <named
        name="Mode"
        helpstring="TS License Mode.
                 0 = Personal Terminal Server
                 1 = Remote Desktop for Administration
                 2 = Per Device / Per Seat
                 3 = Internet Connector
                 4 = Per User"
        type="Simple"
        required=true/>
 </runtime>
<?job debug="true"?>
<script language="vbscript">
 Option Explicit
 Dim sServer, sUser, sPassword, iMode
 Dim objWMI, objTsConnect, objTsSettings
 Dim item
 sServer = wscript.Arguments.Named("s")
   if sServer = "" then sServer = "."
    sUser = wscript.Arguments.Named("u")
      sPassword = wscript.Arguments.Named("p")
       iMode = wscript.Arguments.Named("Mode")
     On Error Resume Next
         if iMode = "" then
               Wscript.Arguments.ShowUsage
               Wscript.Quit(1)
         else
               iMode = cInt(iMode)
         end if
            CONST wbemAuthenticationLevelPkt = 4
             CONST WbemAuthenticationLevelPktPrivacy = 6
     set objWMI = CreateObject("WbemScripting.SwbemLocator")
      objWMI.Security_.AuthenticationLevel = wbemAuthenticationLevelPkt
        Set objTsConnect = objWMI.ConnectServer(sServer, _
                                                     "root/CIMv2", _
                                                        sUser, sPassword)
          set objTsSettings = _
               objTsConnect.InstancesOf("Win32_terminalServiceSetting")
             for each item in objTsSettings
                 item.ChangeMode iMode
                 if Err then
                   Wscript.Echo "Error changing License mode " & _
                               Hex(Err.Number) & ", " & Err.Description
                 else
                   Wscript.Echo "License mode changed successfully"
```

```
                end if
            next
        set objTsSettings = nothing
      set objWMI = nothing
</script>
 </job>
</package>
```

The Script

The script in Listing 5.3 can be used to change the licensing mode of the Terminal Services.

NOTE

Change mode script does not change the Terminal Server mode from Remote Desktop to Application Server. It changes the Licensing type of the Terminal Server based on the Terminal Server mode. Therefore, if you try to set the license type to 2 (Per Device) on a server that is running in Remote Desktop mode, you will receive an `Invalid` *operation error. However, if the script is run on the server running in Application Server mode, the script will successfully set the mode to Per Device.*

When executed, the script takes the following steps to change the Terminal Server mode:

1. Creates the `Named` node to accept the following arguments:
   - `s` as name (or IP Address) of the TS server
   - `u` as the username to connect as the specified user
   - `p` as password for the username specified in `u` argument
   - `Mode` as the License mode
2. Includes `Option Explicit` statement to enforce variable declaration.
3. Declares required variables.
4. Retrieves the argument values passed as script parameters to initialize the input and output variables.
5. Sets the default values for the optional arguments.
6. Checks to ensure that the `Mode` argument was passed.
7. Converts the `Mode` argument value to integer type.
8. Initializes constants for the WMI authentication level.
9. Creates the WMI Services object.
10. Sets the `AuthenticationLevel` of the `Security_` property to `wbemAuthentication-LevelPkt`. This ensures that the connection to the remote system is encrypted.
11. Connects to the WMI TS provider using the `ConnectServer` method.
12. Retrieves the instances of the `Win32_TerminalServiceSetting` class.
13. For each instance of the TS setting does the following:

- Attempts to change the type of licensing for the Terminal Server.
- Displays Success or Failure message.

14. Releases memory and ends.

ENABLE AND DISABLE TERMINAL SERVICES CONNECTIONS

Using scripts you can set the Terminal Services to accept or deny new Terminal Server connections. Listing 5.4 shows the script that can be used to enable or disable TS connections.

LISTING 5.4 Enable / Disable Terminal Services Connections Script

```
<package>
 <job id="Enable Disable TS Connections">
  <runtime>
     <named
       name="s"
       helpstring="Remote Server Name. Default=Localhost"
       type="string"
       required=false/>
     <named
       name="u"
       helpstring="User name for the remote computer.
                                Example: Domain\UserName"
       type="string"
       required=false/>
     <named
       name="p"
       helpstring="password for the remote user"
       type="string"
       required=false/>
     <named
       name="EnableDisable"
       helpstring="Enable or Disable TS connections. Default=+"
       type="Boolean"
       required=true/>
  </runtime>
 <?job debug="true"?>
 <script language="vbscript">
  Option Explicit
  Dim sServer, sUser, sPassword, bEnableDisable
  Dim objWMI, objTsConnect, objTsSettings
  Dim item
  sServer = wscript.Arguments.Named("s")
    if sServer = "" then sServer = "."
     sUser = wscript.Arguments.Named("u")
       sPassword = wscript.Arguments.Named("p")
        bEnableDisable = wscript.Arguments.Named("EnableDisable")
```

```
        if bEnableDisable = "" then bEnableDisable = True
            CONST wbemAuthenticationLevelPkt = 4
             CONST WbemAuthenticationLevelPktPrivacy = 6
    On Error Resume Next
    set objWMI = CreateObject("WbemScripting.SwbemLocator")
     objWMI.Security_.AuthenticationLevel = wbemAuthenticationLevelPkt
       Set objTsConnect = objWMI.ConnectServer(sServer, _
                                            "root/CIMv2", _
                                                sUser, sPassword)
         set objTsSettings = _
              objTsConnect.InstancesOf("Win32_terminalServiceSetting")
          for each item in objTsSettings
            if bEnableDisable then
              item.SetAllowTsConnections(1)
              if Err then
                Wscript.Echo "Error enabling connections " & _
                              Hex(Err.Number) & ", " & Err.Description
              else
                Wscript.Echo "Terminal Server will accept new connections"
              end if
            else
              item.SetAllowTsConnections 0
              if Err then
                Wscript.Echo "Error disable connections " & _
                              Hex(Err.Number) & ", " & Err.Description
              else
                Wscript.Echo "Terminal Server will not accept new
                    connections"
              end if
            end if
          next
    set objTsSettings = nothing
   set objWMI = nothing
</script>
</job>
</package>
```

The Script

The script in Listing 5.4 can be used to enable or disable the Terminal Services connections. Disabling the connections will not allow new connections to be made to the Terminal Services, and enabling the connections will allow new connections.

When executed, the script takes the following steps to enable or disable the Terminal Services connections:

1. Creates the `Named` node to accept the following arguments:

   - s as name (or IP Address) of the TS server
   - `u` as the username to connect as the specified user

- `p` as password for the username specified in `u` argument
- `EnableDisable` as boolean value that will be used to enable or disable the connections.

2. Includes `Option Explicit` statement to enforce variable declaration.
3. Declares required variables.
4. Retrieves the argument values passed as script parameters to initialize the input and output variables. Sets the default values for the optional arguments.
5. Sets the default value of the `bEnableDisable` variable.
6. Initializes constants for the WMI authentication level.
7. Creates the WMI Services object.
8. Sets the `AuthenticationLevel` of the `Security_` property to `wbemAuthenticationLevelPkt`. This ensures that the connection to the remote system is encrypted.
9. Connects to the WMI TS provider using the `ConnectServer` method.
10. Retrieves the instances of the `Win32_TerminalServiceSetting` class.
11. For each instance of the TS setting does the following:

- If the `bEnableDisable` variable is set to `True`
  - Sets the TS to allow connections.
  - Displays Success or Failure message.
- If the `bEnableDisable` variable is set to `False`
  - Sets the TS to deny new connections.
  - Displays Success or Failure message.

12. Releases memory and ends.

LISTING AND CONFIGURING TERMINAL PROPERTIES

Terminal properties (such as Environment, Session, etc.) can be set using the Terminal Service configuration utility included with Windows 2003. WMI TS provider also exposes classes that allow you to remotely configure the configuration settings that you can set using the Terminal Service configuration utility.

General Settings

General settings that you can set on the General page of the Terminal Services configuration utility (as shown in Figure 5.1) can be retrieved and set using a script.

Listing 5.5 demonstrates how to set and retrieve General Settings properties using the `Win32_GeneralSetting` class exposed by the TS WMI provider.

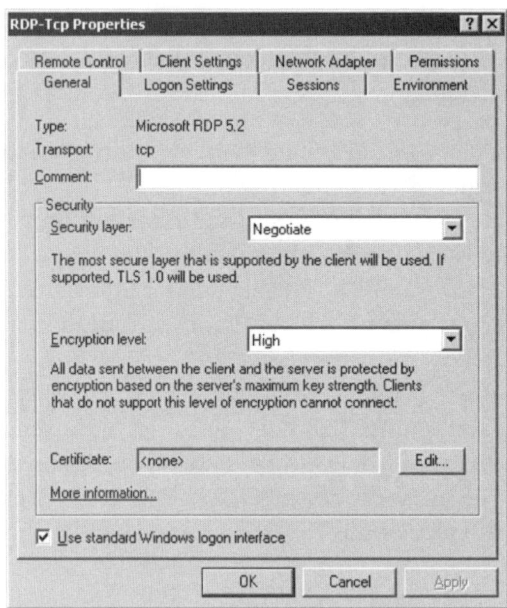

Figure 5.1 General settings tab of the TS configuration utility that lists and sets the properties of the RDP-tcp terminal.

LISTING 5.5 `GeneralSettings.wsf` Script Retrieves and Sets General Terminal Settings

```
<package>
 <job id="Get and Set General Settings">
  <runtime>
     <named
       name="s"
       helpstring="Remote Server Name. Default=Localhost"
       type="string"
       required=false/>
     <named
       name="u"
       helpstring="User name for the remote computer.
                               Example: Domain\UserName"
       type="string"
       required=false/>
     <named
       name="p"
       helpstring="password for the remote user"
       type="string"
       required=false/>
     <named
       name="x"
```

```
      helpstring="Input Xml file"
      type="string"
      required=false/>
 </runtime>
<?job debug="true"?>
<script language="vbscript" src="helperfunctions.vbs">
 Option Explicit
 Dim sServer, sUser, sPassword, sXmlFile
 Dim objWMI, objTsConnect
 Dim objXml,objXmlChild, objRoot
 sServer = wscript.Arguments.Named("s")
   if sServer = "" then sServer = "."
    sUser = wscript.Arguments.Named("u")
      sPassword = wscript.Arguments.Named("p")
       sXmlFile = wscript.Arguments.Named("x")
            CONST wbemAuthenticationLevelPkt = 4
             CONST WbemAuthenticationLevelPktPrivacy = 6
     set objWMI = CreateObject("WbemScripting.SwbemLocator")
      objWMI.Security_.AuthenticationLevel = _
                                wbemAuthenticationLevelPkt
        Set objTsConnect = objWMI.ConnectServer(sServer, _
                                       "root/CIMv2", _
                                           sUser, sPassword)
       if sXmlFile = "" then
               GetGeneral
       else
          Set objXml = CreateObject("MSXML2.DomDocument")
             objXml.Async = false
                objXml.Load sXmlFile
                  Set objRoot = objXml.SelectSingleNode("/MAIN")
                    set objXmlChild = objRoot.SelectNodes("GENERAL")
                if objXmlChild.Length > 0 then
                        SetGeneral
                End if
             set objRoot = nothing
           set objXmlChild = nothing
          Set objXml = nothing
       end if
     Set objTsConnect = nothing
    set objWMI = nothing
 Sub SetGeneral
       Dim WindowsAuthentication,EncryptionLevel, SecurityLayer
       Dim objXmlGen, ChildNode, objGenSettings, item
       set objxmlGen = objRoot.SelectSingleNode("GENERAL")
       if objXmlGen.HasChildNodes then
          for each ChildNode in objXmlGen.ChildNodes
               Select Case ChildNode.NodeName
                       Case "WINDOWSAUTHENTICATION"
                               WindowsAuthentication = ChildNode.Text
                               Select Case UCase(WindowsAuthentication)
                                  Case "STANDARD"
                                       WindowsAuthentication = 1
                                  Case "NONSTANDARD"
```

```
                                        WindowsAuthentication = 0
                                   Case else
                                        WindowsAuthentication = 1
                                End Select
                        Case "ENCRYPTIONLEVEL"
                                EncryptionLevel = ChildNode.Text
                                Select Case Ucase(EncryptionLevel)
                                   Case "LOW" : EncryptionLevel = 1
                                   Case "CLIENT" : EncryptionLevel = 2
                                   Case "HIGH" : EncryptionLevel = 3
                                   Case "FIPS" : EncryptionLevel = 4
                                   Case else : EncryptionLevel = 1
                                End Select
                        Case "SECURITYLAYER"
                                SecurityLayer = ChildNode.Text
                                Select Case Ucase(SecurityLayer)
                                   Case "RDP" : SecurityLayer = 0
                                   Case "NEGOTIATE" : SecurityLayer = 1
                                   Case "SSL" : SecurityLayer = 2
                                   Case else : SecurityLayer = 0
                                End Select
                End Select
            next
           Set objXmlGen = nothing
          Set objGenSettings = _
                        objTsConnect.InstancesOf("Win32_TSGeneralSetting")
          For each item in objGenSettings
                if WindowsAuthentication <> "" then _
                        item.WindowsAuthentication = WindowsAuthentication
                        item.Put_
                if EncryptionLevel <> "" then _
                        item.SetEncryptionLevel EncryptionLevel
                if SecurityLayer <> 0 then _
                        item.SetSecurityLayer SecurityLayer
          Next
          Set objGenSettings = nothing
        end if
End Sub
Sub GetGeneral
     Dim objGenSettings
     Dim item, DispValue
        Set objGenSettings = objTsConnect.InstancesOf("Win32_TSGeneralSetting")
         For each item in objGenSettings
                DispValue = "Caption = " & item.Caption
                DispValue = DispValue & VBNewLine & _
                                "Comment = " & item.Comment
                DispValue = DispValue & VBNewLine & _
                                "Description = " & item.Description
                DispValue = DispValue & VBNewLine & _
                                "Min Encryption Level =" & _
                                        FormatEncryptLevel( _
                                                item.MinEncryptionLevel)
                DispValue = DispValue & VBNewLine & _
```

```
                                "Security Layer = " & _
                                       FormatSecurityLayer( _
                                               item.SecurityLayer)
                DispValue = DispValue & VBNewLine & _
                                "Setting ID = " & item.SettingID
                DispValue = DispValue & VBNewLine & _
                                "SSL Certificate SHA1 Hash = " & _
                                        item.SSLCertificateSHA1Hash
                DispValue = DispValue & VBNewLine & _
                                "Terminal Name = " & item.TerminalName
                DispValue = DispValue & VBNewLine & _
                                "Transport = " & item.Transport
                DispValue = DispValue & VBNewLine & _
                                "Windows Authentication = " & _
                                    FormatWindowsAuth( _
                                            item.WindowsAuthentication)
        Next
        Wscript.Echo DispValue
        Set objGenSettings = nothing
End Sub
</script>
 </job>
</package>
```

The Script

The script in Listing 5.5 may seen complicated, however, it is a simple script that either displays the General settings or sets the General settings from the XML file passed as parameter to the script.

The script has two sub procedures: `SetGeneral` and `GetGeneral`. The `SetGeneral` sub procedure is called when an XML file is passed as an argument to the script, and `GetGeneral` is called when the XML file is not passed to the script.

The `SetGeneral` sub procedure reads the XML file to retrieve the values and changes the settings accordingly. It sets the following three configuration settings that you can find on the General tab in TS configuration utility:

Windows Authentication: Changes the `WindowsAuthentication` property.

Minimum Encryption Level: Changes the `MinEncryptionLevel` property.

Security Layer: Changes the `SecurityLayer property`.

It reads the property settings from the XML file that has the following schema:

```
<MAIN>
    <GENERAL>
    <WINDOWSAUTHENTICATION>Standard</WINDOWSAUTHENTICATION>
            <ENCRYPTIONLEVEL>High</ENCRYPTIONLEVEL>
            <SECURITYLAYER>Negotiate</SECURITYLAYER>
    </GENERAL>
</MAIN>
```

The XML file has `<MAIN>` as the root node. The `<GENERAL>` node is the root node for the General properties. `<WINDOWSAUTHENTICATION>`, `<ENCRYPTIONLEVEL>`, and `<SECURITYLAYER>` nodes hold the values for the General properties. When the script is executed, it reads the text from these nodes to set the values of the properties. The property nodes can have the values as defined in Table 5.1.

TABLE 5.1 General Properties XML File Nodes and Values

Node	Setable Values	
WINDOWSAUTHENTICATION	**Value**	**Description**
	Standard	Defaults to the standard Windows authentication process
	NonStandard	Does not default to the standard Windows authentication process
ENCRYPTIONLEVEL	**Value**	**Description**
	Low	Low level of encryption
	Client	Client compatible level of encryption
	High	High level of encryption
	Fips	FIPS compliant encryption
SECURITYLAYER	**Value**	**Description**
	Rdp	Native Rdp encryption
	Negotiate	The most secure layer used by the client will be used
	Ssl	SSL (TLS 1.0) will be used for server authentication and for encrypting all data transferred between the server and the client

The values in Table 5.1 must be used to define the settings in the XML file. For example, if you want to change the `SecurityLayer` property to `Negotiate` from `RDP`, you should set the `<SECURITYLAYER>` node as follows:

```
<SECURITYLAYER>Negotiate</SECURITYLAYER>
```

When the script is executed with the XML file as an argument as shown in Listing 5.6, it will change the `SecurityLayer` to `Negotiate`.

LISTING 5.6 Executing `GeneralSettings.wsf` to Change the General Properties

```
GeneralSettings /x:GeneralSettings.xml
```

When the script is run without the `/x:` parameter (that is, the XML file is not passed as an argument), the script queries the Terminal and displays the current General settings as shown in Figure 5.2.

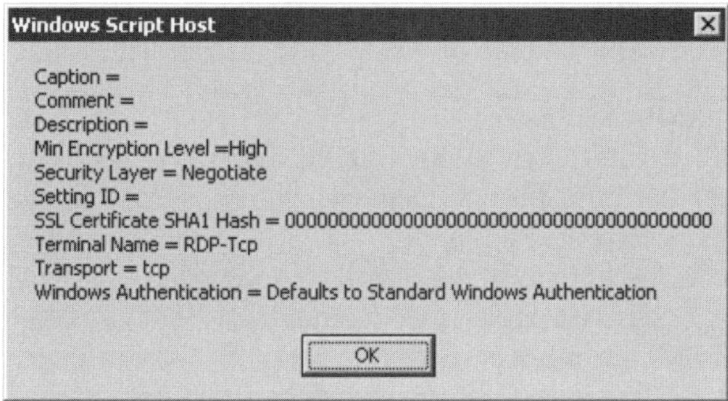

FIGURE 5.2 General settings displayed by the script when the /x: argument is not passed.

NOTE

The `GeneralSettings.wsf` file includes the `HerlperFunctions.vbs` script using the `src` attribute of the `<script>` tag. The `HelperFunctions.vbs` script has functions that format the output returned to make it more meaningful. For example, the `SecurityLayer` property returns an integer value of `0`, `1`, or `2` that the `FormatSecurityLayer` function converts to a text value for display. The script also includes the `Select` statements to convert the text value defined in the XML file (such as `Rdp`) to a numeric value (such as `0`) that the `SetSecurityLayer` method expects. It is easier to remember text and numeric values that may signify something.

The `GeneralSettings.wsf` script (shown in Listing 5.5) when executed takes the following steps to set or retrieve the properties:

1. Creates the `Named` node to accept the following arguments:
   - `s` as name (or IP Address) of the TS server
   - `u` as the username to connect as the specified user
   - `p` as password for the username specified in `u` argument
   - `x` as XML filename
2. Includes `Option Explicit` statement to enforce variable declaration.
3. Declares required variables.
4. Retrieves the argument values passed as script parameters to initializes the input and output variables. Sets the default values for the optional arguments.

5. Initializes constants for the WMI authentication level.
6. Creates the WMI Services object.
7. Sets the `AuthenticationLevel` of the `Security_` property to `wbemAuthenticationLevelPkt`. This ensures that the connection to the remote system is encrypted.
8. Connects to the WMI TS provider using the `ConnectServer` method.
9. Checks to see if an XML file was passed as argument:

- If XML file is passed
  - Creates a new MSXML DOM object
  - Loads the file into memory
  - Selects the Root node
  - Checks to see if the `<GENERAL>` node exists in the XML data in memory
  - Calls `SetGeneral` sub procedure
- If XML file is not passed
  - Calls `GetGeneral` sub procedure

10. If the `SetGeneral` sub procedure is called

- Declares variables
- Selects the `<GENERAL>` node
- Checks to verify that the child nodes exist in the `<GENERAL>` node
- For each child node: selects case based on the node name
  - If case is `WINDOWSAUTHENTICATION`
    - Gets the text of the child node
    - Selects case for authentication to set the value for `WindowAuthentication` property
  - If case is `ENCRYPTIONLEVEL`
    - Gets the text of the child node
    - Selects case for encryption level to set the value for `EncryptionLevel` property
  - If case is `SECURITYLAYER`
    - Gets the text of the child node
    - Selects case for Security layer to set the value for `SecurityLayer` property
- Gets instances of `Win32_TSGeneralSetting` class
- For each instance of the class
  - Sets the `WindowsAuthentication` property in cache
  - Calls the `Put_` method to save the property
  - Calls the `SetEncryptionLevel` method to set the encryption level
  - Calls the `SetSecurityLayer` method to set the security layer

11. If the `GetGeneral` procedure is called
    - Declares variables
    - Gets instances of `Win32_TSGeneralSetting` class
    - For each setting in class
        - Retrieves individual property values
        - Calls the formatting functions as needed (from included `HelperFunctions.vbs` script)
12. Displays the retrieved values
13. Releases memory and ends

Logon Settings

Like the General settings, the settings on the Logon tab can be set using the `Win32_LogonSetting` class. The script in Listing 5.7 can be used to set the Logon properties.

LISTING 5.7 Script for Getting and Setting Logon Properties

```
<package>
 <job id="Get and Set Logon Settings">
  <runtime>
     <named
       name="s"
       helpstring="Remote Server Name. Default=Localhost"
       type="string"
       required=false/>
     <named
       name="u"
       helpstring="User name for the remote computer.
                                Example: Domain\UserName"
       type="string"
       required=false/>
     <named
       name="p"
       helpstring="password for the remote user"
       type="string"
       required=false/>
     <named
       name="x"
       helpstring="Input Xml file"
       type="string"
       required=false/>
  </runtime>
 <?job debug="true"?>
 <script language="vbscript" src="helperfunctions.vbs">
  Option Explicit
  Dim sServer, sUser, sPassword, sXmlFile
  Dim objWMI, objTsConnect
```

```
Dim objXml,objXmlChild, objRoot
sServer = wscript.Arguments.Named("s")
  if sServer = "" then sServer = "."
   sUser = wscript.Arguments.Named("u")
     sPassword = wscript.Arguments.Named("p")
      sXmlFile = wscript.Arguments.Named("x")
           CONST wbemAuthenticationLevelPkt = 4
            CONST WbemAuthenticationLevelPktPrivacy = 6
    set objWMI = CreateObject("WbemScripting.SwbemLocator")
     objWMI.Security_.AuthenticationLevel = _
                                wbemAuthenticationLevelPkt
       Set objTsConnect = objWMI.ConnectServer(sServer, _
                                       "root/CIMv2", _
                                           sUser, sPassword)
      if sXmlFile = "" then
              GetLogon
      else
         Set objXml = CreateObject("MSXML2.DomDocument")
            objXml.Async = false
               objXml.Load sXmlFile
                 Set objRoot = objXml.SelectSingleNode("/MAIN")
                   set objXmlChild = objRoot.SelectNodes("LOGON")
               if objXmlChild.Length > 0 then
                      SetLogon
               End if
            set objRoot = nothing
          set objXmlChild = nothing
         Set objXml = nothing
      end if
    Set objTsConnect = nothing
   set objWMI = nothing
Sub SetLogon
      Dim ClientLogonInfoPolicy,PromptForPassword
      Dim sUser, sDomain, sPassword
      Dim objXmlLog, ChildNode, objLogSettings, item
      set objxmlLog = objRoot.SelectSingleNode("LOGON")
      if objXmlLog.HasChildNodes then
         for each ChildNode in objXmlLog.ChildNodes
              Select Case ChildNode.NodeName
                      Case "CLIENTLOGONINFOPOLICY"
                              ClientLogonInfoPolicy = ChildNode.Text
                              Select Case UCase(ClientLogonInfoPolicy)
                                 Case "PERUSER"
                                      ClientLogonInfoPolicy = 1
                                 Case "SERVEROVERRIDE"
                                      ClientLogonInfoPolicy = 0
                                 Case else
                                      ClientLogonInfoPolicy = 1
                              End Select
                      Case "PROMPTFORPASSWORD"
                              PromptForPassword = ChildNode.Text
                              Select Case Ucase(PromptForPassword)
                                 Case "PROMPT" : PromptForPassword = 1
```

```
                                Case "NOPROMPT" : PromptForPassword = 0
                                Case else : PromptForPassword = 1
                            End Select
                    Case "EXPLICITLOGON"
                            if ChildNode.HasChildNodes then
                              sUser = ChildNode.SelectSingleNode("USER").Text
                              sDomain = ChildNode.SelectSingleNode("DOMAIN")
                              .Text
                              sPassword = _
                                ChildNode.SelectSingleNode("PASSWORD").Text
                            end if
            End Select
        next
        Set objXmlLog = nothing
       Set objLogSettings = objTsConnect.InstancesOf("Win32_TSLogonSetting")
       For each item in objLogSettings
             if ClientLogonInfoPolicy <> "" then _
                     item.ClientLogonInfoPolicy = ClientLogonInfoPolicy
             if PromptForPassword <> "" then _
                     item.SetPromptForPassword PromptForPassword
             item.Put_
             if item.ClientLogonInfoPolicy = 0 and sUser <> "" then _
                     item.ExplicitLogon sUser, sDomain, sPassword
       Next
       Set objLogSettings = nothing
     end if
End Sub
Sub GetLogon
     Dim objLogonSettings
     Dim item, prop, DispValue
     Dim sPropName, sPropValue
        Set objLogonSettings = objTsConnect.InstancesOf("Win32_TSLogonSetting")
         For each item in objLogonSettings
               For each prop in item.Properties_
                       sPropName = prop.Name
                       Select Case lcase(sPropName)
                         Case "promptforpassword"
                               sPropValue = FormatPromptForPass(prop.value)
                         Case "clientlogoninfopolicy"
                               sPropValue = Formatclipol(prop.value)
                         Case else
                               sPropValue = prop.Value
                       End Select
                       DispValue = DispValue & VBNewLine & _
                                   sPropName & " = " & sPropValue
               Next
        Next
        Wscript.Echo DispValue
        Set objLogonSettings = nothing
End Sub
</script>
 </job>
</package>
```

The Script

Similar to the `GeneralSettings.wsf` file, the `LogonSettings.wsf` script shown in Listing 5.7 has two sub procedures: `SetLogon` and `GetLogon`. The `Setlogon` sub procedure is called when an XML file is passed as an argument to the script and the `GetLogon` is called when the XML file is not passed to the script.

The `SetLogon` sub procedure reads the XML file to retrieve the values and changes the settings accordingly. It sets the following three configuration settings that you can find on the Logon tab in TS configuration utility:

Client Logon Info Policy: Changes the `ClientLogonInfoPolicy` property.

Prompt For Password: Changes the `PromptForPassword` property.

Explicit Logon User Settings: Changes the `UserID`, `Domain` and `Password` properties. This can be set only if the `ClientLogonInfoPolicy` property is set to `ServerOverride` (that is, the property is set to `0`).

It reads the property settings from the XML file that has the following schema:

```
<MAIN>
    <LOGON>
            <CLIENTLOGONINFOPOLICY></CLIENTLOGONINFOPOLICY>
            <EXPLICITLOGON>
                    <USER></USER>
                    <DOMAIN></DOMAIN>
                    <PASSWORD></PASSWORD>
            </EXPLICITLOGON>
            <PROMPTFORPASSWORD></PROMPTFORPASSWORD>
    </LOGON>
</MAIN>
```

The XML file has `<MAIN>` as the root node. The `<LOGON>` node is the root node for the Logon properties. `<CLIENTLOGONINFOPOLICY>`, `<EXPLICITLOGON>` and `<PROMPTFORPASSWORD>` nodes hold the values for the Logon properties. The `<USER>`, `<DOMAIN>` and `<PASSWORD>` nodes can be used to specify the username, domain, and password respectively. When the script is executed, it reads the text from these nodes to set the values of the properties. The property nodes can have the values as defined in Table 5.2.

The values in Table 5.2 must be used to define the settings in the XML file. For example, if you want to change the `PromptForPassword` property to `Prompt`, you should set the `<PROMPTFORPASSWORD>` node as follows:

```
<PROMPTFORPASSWORD>Prompt</PROMPTFORPASSWORD>
```

TABLE 5.2 Logon Properties XML File Nodes and Values

Node	Setable Values	
CLIENTLOGONINFOPOLICY	**Value**	**Description**
	PerUser	Individual user connection settings are in effect
	ServerOverride	Individual user connection settings are overridden by the server
EXPLICITLOGON	**Node**	**Value**
	USER	User's nameUsername
	DOMAIN	Domain of the user. Leave it blank for local user
	<PASSWORD>	Password for the user
PROMPTFORPASSWORD	**Value**	**Description**
	Prompt	The user is prompted for a password
	NoPrompt	The user is not prompted for a password

When the script is executed with the XML file as an argument, as shown in Listing 5.8, it will change the `PromptForPassword` to `Prompt`.

LISTING 5.8 Executing `LogonSettings.wsf` to Change the Logon Properties

```
LogonSettings /x:LogonSettings.xml
```

When the script is run without the `/x:` parameter (that is, the XML file is not passed as an argument), the script queries the Terminal and displays the current Logon settings as shown in Figure 5.3.

NOTE

Similar to `GeneralSettings.wsf` script, the `LogonSettings.wsf` file also has functions that format the output returned to make it more meaningful. The `SecurityLayer` property returns an integer value of `0`, `1`, or `2` that the `FormatSecurityLayer` function converts to a text value for display. The script also includes the `Select` statements to convert the text value defined in the XML file (such as `Rdp`) to a numeric value (such as `0`) that the `SetSecurityLayer` method expects. It is easier to remember text and numeric values that may signify something.

When executed, the `LogonSettings.wsf` script (shown in Listing 5.7) takes the following steps to set or retrieve the properties:

FIGURE 5.3 Logon settings displayed by the script when the `/x:` argument is not passed.

1. Creates the `Named` node to accept the following arguments:
   - `s` as name (or IP Address) of the TS server
   - `u` as the username to connect as the specified user
   - `p` as password for the username specified in `u` argument
   - `x` as XML filename
2. Includes `Option Explicit` statement to enforce variable declaration.
3. Declares required variables.
4. Retrieves the argument values passed as script parameters to initialize the input and output variables. Sets the default values for the optional arguments.
5. Initializes constants for the WMI authentication level.
6. Creates the WMI Services object.
7. Sets the `AuthenticationLevel` of the `Security_` property to `wbemAuthentication-LevelPkt`. This ensures that the connection to the remote system is encrypted.
8. Connects to the WMI TS provider using the `ConnectServer` method.
9. Checks to see if an XML file was passed as argument:
   - If XML file is passed
   - Creates a new MSXML DOM object
   - Loads the file into memory
   - Selects the root node
   - Checks to see if the `<LOGON>` node exists in the XML data in memory
   - Calls `SetLogon` sub procedure

11. If XML file is not passed

    - Calls `GetLogon` sub procedure

12. If the `SetLogon` sub procedure is called

    - Declares variables
    - Selects the `<LOGON>` node
    - Checks to verify that the child nodes exist in the `<LOGON>` node
    - For each child node: selects case based on the node name
        - If case is `CLIENTLOGONINFOPOLICY`
            - Gets the text of the child node
            - Select case for client logon info policy to set the value for `ClientLogonInfoPolicy` property
        - If case is `PROMPTFORPASSWORD`
            - Gets the text of the child node.
            - Select case for prompt for password to set the value for `PROMPTFORPASSWORD` property
        - If case is `EXPLICITLOGON`
            - If the `EXPLICITLOGON` has child nodes gets the text `USER`, `DOMAIN`, and `PASSWORD` nodes

13. Gets instances of `Win32_TSLogonSetting` class.
14. For each instance of the class

    - Sets the `ClientLogonInfoPolicy` property in cache
    - Sets the `PromptForPassword` property in cache
    - Calls the `Put_` method to save the property
    - If the `ClientLogonInfoPolicy` is set to `ServerOverrides`, sets the `User`, `Domain`, and `Password` by calling the `ExplicitLogon` method

15. If the `GetLogon` procedure is called

    - Declares variables
    - Gets instances of `Win32_TSLogonSetting` class
    - For each setting in class
        - Retrieves individual property names and their values
        - Calls the formatting functions as needed (from included `HelperFunctions.vbs` script)

16. Displays the retrieved values.
17. Releases memory and ends.

Session Settings

The Session settings properties can be set using the `Win32_SessionSetting` class. The `Win32_SessionSetting` class exposes several properties and two methods that you can use to retrieve and set the session properties. The script in Listing 5.9 uses these properties and methods to list the current settings and modify them based on the properties specified in the XML file.

LISTING 5.9 Script for Getting and Setting Session Properties

```
<package>
 <job id="Get and Set Session Settings">
  <runtime>
     <named
       name="s"
       helpstring="Remote Server Name. Default=Localhost"
       type="string"
       required=false/>
     <named
       name="u"
       helpstring="User name for the remote computer.
                               Example: Domain\UserName"
       type="string"
       required=false/>
     <named
       name="p"
       helpstring="password for the remote user"
       type="string"
       required=false/>
     <named
       name="x"
       helpstring="Input Xml file"
       type="string"
       required=false/>
  </runtime>
 <?job debug="true"?>
 <script language="vbscript" src="helperfunctions.vbs">
  Option Explicit
  Dim sServer, sUser, sPassword, sXmlFile
  Dim objWMI, objTsConnect, objSwat
  Dim objXml,objXmlChild, objRoot
  sServer = wscript.Arguments.Named("s")
    if sServer = "" then sServer = "."
     sUser = wscript.Arguments.Named("u")
       sPassword = wscript.Arguments.Named("p")
        sXmlFile = wscript.Arguments.Named("x")
             CONST wbemAuthenticationLevelPkt = 4
              CONST WbemAuthenticationLevelPktPrivacy = 6
      Set objSwat = CreateObject("Swat.1.00")
```

```
set objWMI = CreateObject("WbemScripting.SwbemLocator")
 objWMI.Security_.AuthenticationLevel = wbemAuthenticationLevelPkt
   Set objTsConnect = objWMI.ConnectServer(sServer, _
                                                   "root/CIMv2", _
                                             sUser, sPassword)
  if sXmlFile = "" then
          GetSession
  else
     Set objXml = CreateObject("MSXML2.DomDocument")
        objXml.Async = false
           objXml.Load sXmlFile
             Set objRoot = objXml.SelectSingleNode("/MAIN")
               set objXmlChild = objRoot.SelectNodes("SESSION")
           if objXmlChild.Length > 0 then
                  SetSession
           End if
        set objRoot = nothing
      set objXmlChild = nothing
     Set objXml = nothing
  end if
Set objTsConnect = nothing
set objWMI = nothing
set objSwat = nothing
Sub SetSession
   Dim BrokenConnectionAction,BrokenConnectionPolicy
   Dim ReconnectionPolicy, TimeLimitPolicy
   Dim ActiveSessionLimit, DisconnectSessionLimit, IdleSessionLimit
   Dim objXmlSes, ChildNode, objSesSettings, item
   set objxmlSes = objRoot.SelectSingleNode("SESSION")
   if objXmlSes.HasChildNodes then
      for each ChildNode in objXmlSes.ChildNodes
           Select Case ChildNode.NodeName
                   Case "BROKENCONNECTIONACTION"
                       BrokenConnectionAction = ChildNode.Text
                       Select Case Ucase(BrokenConnectionAction)
                   Case "DISCONNECT" : BrokenConnectionAction = 0
                   Case "TERMINATE" : BrokenConnectionAction = 1
                          Case else : BrokenConnectionAction = 0
                       End Select
                   Case "BROKENCONNECTIONPOLICY"
                       BrokenConnectionPolicy = ChildNode.Text
                       Select Case Ucase(BrokenConnectionPolicy)
                          Case "USER" : BrokenConnectionPolicy = 1
                          Case "SERVER" : BrokenConnectionPolicy = 0
                          Case else : BrokenConnectionPolicy = 1
                       End Select
                   Case "RECONNECTIONPOLICY"
                       ReconnectionPolicy = ChildNode.Text
                       Select Case Ucase(ReconnectionPolicy)
                          Case "ANY" : ReconnectionPolicy = 0
                          Case "PREVIOUS" : ReconnectionPolicy = 1
                          Case else : ReconnectionPolicy = 1
                       End Select
```

```
                    Case "TIMELIMITPOLICY"
                            TimeLimitPolicy = ChildNode.Text
                            Select Case Ucase(TimeLimitPolicy)
                               Case "USER" : TimeLimitPolicy = 1
                               Case "SERVER" : TimeLimitPolicy = 0
                               Case else : TimeLimitPolicy = 1
                            End Select
                    Case "TIMELIMIT"
                            if ChildNode.HasChildNodes then
                              ActiveSessionLimit = _
                                    ChildNode.SelectSingleNode( _
                                       "ACTIVESESSIONLIMIT").Text
                              DisconnectSessionLimit = _
                                    ChildNode.SelectSingleNode( _
                                       "DISCONNECTSESSIONLIMIT").Text
                            IdleSessionLimit = _
                                    ChildNode.SelectSingleNode( _
                                       "IDLESESSIONLIMIT").Text
                            end if
            End Select
        next
       Set objXmlSes = nothing
      Set objSesSettings = _
                    objTsConnect.InstancesOf("Win32_TSSessionSetting")
      For each item in objSesSettings
            if BrokenConnectionPolicy <> "" then _
                    item.BrokenConnectionPolicy = BrokenConnectionPolicy
            if TimeLimitPolicy <> "" then _
                    item.TimeLimitPolicy = TimeLimitPolicy
            item.Put_
            if item.BrokenConnectionPolicy = 0 then
              if BrokenConnectionAction <> "" then _
                    item.BrokenConnection BrokenConnectionAction
            end if
            if item.TimeLimitPolicy = 0 then
              if ActiveSessionLimit <> "" then _
                    item.TimeLimit "ActiveSessionLimit", _
                        Conv2Milisec(ActiveSessionLimit)
                if DisconnectSessionLimit <> "" then _
                    item.TimeLimit "DisconnectSessionLimit", _
                        Conv2Milisec(DisconnectSessionLimit)
              if IdleSessionLimit <> "" then _
                   item.TimeLimit "IdleSessionLimit", _
                                    Conv2Milisec(IdleSessionLimit)
          end if
      Next
      Set objSesSettings = nothing
    end if
End Sub
Sub GetSession
 Dim objSessionSettings
 Dim item, prop, DispValue
```

```
     Dim sPropName, sPropValue
Set objSessionSettings = _
objTsConnect.InstancesOf("Win32_TSSessionSetting")
        For each item in objSessionSettings
              For each prop in item.Properties_
                     sPropName = prop.Name
                     Select Case lcase(sPropName)
                       Case "brokenconnectionaction"
                             sPropValue = FormatBConAct(prop.value)
                       Case "brokenconnectionpolicy"
                             sPropValue = FormatBConPol(prop.value)
                       Case "reconnectionpolicy"
                             sPropValue = FormatReconPol(prop.value)
                       Case "timelimitpolicy"
                             sPropValue = FormatTimeLimitpol(prop.value)
                       Case else
                             sPropValue = prop.Value
                     End Select
                     DispValue = DispValue & VBNewLine & _
                        objSwat.SplitOnCap(sPropName) & " = " & sPropValue
              Next
       Next
       Wscript.Echo DispValue
       Set objSessionSettings = nothing
    End Sub
 </script>
 </job>
</package>
```

The Script

The `SessionSettings.wsf` script shown in Listing 5.9 also has two sub procedures: `GetSession` and `SetSession`. Therefore, the `SessionSettings.wsf` script also performs two functions; it retrieves and displays the values of the Session properties and sets the values of the Session properties as specified in the XML file passed as an argument to the script.

The `SetSession` sub procedure reads the XML file to retrieve the values and changes the settings accordingly. It sets the following three configuration settings that you can find on the Logon tab in TS configuration utility:

Broken Connection Policy: Changes the `BrokenConnectionPolicy` property.

Broken Connection Action: Changes the `BrokenConnectionAction` property.

Reconnection Policy: Changes the `ReconnectionPolicy` property.

Time Limit: Changes the `SessionLimitType` property and its value. It sets the time limit for `ActiveSessionLimit`, `DisconnectedSessionLimit`, and `IdleSessionLimit` properties.

It reads the property settings from the XML file that has the following schema:

```
<MAIN>
    <SESSION>
    <BROKENCONNECTIONACTION></BROKENCONNECTIONACTION>
    <BROKENCONNECTIONPOLICY></BROKENCONNECTIONPOLICY>
    <RECONNECTIONPOLICY></RECONNECTIONPOLICY>
    <TIMELIMITPOLICY></TIMELIMITPOLICY>
    <TIMELIMIT>
       <ACTIVESESSIONLIMIT></ACTIVESESSIONLIMIT>
       <DISCONNECTSESSIONLIMIT></DISCONNECTSESSIONLIMIT>
       <IDLESESSIONLIMIT></IDLESESSIONLIMIT>
    </TIMELIMIT>
    </SESSION>
</MAIN>
```

The XML file has `<MAIN>` as the root node. The `<SESSION>` node is the root node for the Session properties. `<BROKENCONNECTIONACTION>`, `<BROKENCONNECTIONPOLICY>`, `<RECONNECTIONPOLICY>`, `<TIMELIMITPOLICY>`, and `<TIMELIMIT>` nodes hold the values for the Session properties. The `<ACTIVESESSIONLIMIT>`, `<DISCONNECTSESSIONLIMIT>`, and `<IDLESESSIONLIMIT>` nodes can be used to specify the session limit-type property values. When the script is executed, it reads the text from these nodes to set the values of the properties. The property nodes can have the values as defined in Table 5.3.

TABLE 5.3 Session Properties XML File Nodes and Values

Node	Setable Values	
BROKENCONNECTIONACTION	**Value**	**Description**
	Disconnect	The user is disconnected from the session
	Terminate	The session is permanently deleted from the server
BROKENACTIONPOLICY	**Node**	**Value**
	User	The user's disconnection policy settings are in effect
	Server	The user's disconnection policy settings are overridden by the server
RECONNECTIONPOLICY	**Value**	**Description**
	Any	Any client will be used to reconnect
	Previous	Previous client connection used in connection will be used to reconnect
TIMELIMITPOLICY	**Value**	**Description**
	User	The user's time limit policy settings are in effect
	Server	The user's time limit policy settings are overridden by the server →

NODE	SETABLE VALUES	
TIMELIMIT	**Node**	**Value**
	ACTIVESESSIONLIMIT	Number of minutes. For example: 10
	DISCONNECTSESSIONLIMIT	Number of minutes. For example: 10
	IDLESESSIONLIMIT	Number of minutes. For example: 10

The values in Table 5.3 must be used to define the settings in the XML file. For example, if you want to change the `ReconnectionPolicy` property to `Any`, you should set the `<ReconnectionPolicy>` node as follows:

```
<RECONNECTIONPOLICY>Any</RECONNECTINPOLICY>
```

When the script is executed with the XML file as an argument, as shown in Listing 5.10, it will change the `ReconnectionPolicy` to `Any`.

LISTING 5.10 Executing `SessionSettings.wsf` to Change the Session Properties

```
SessionSettings /x:SessionSettings.xml
```

When the script is run without the `/x:` parameter (that is, the XML file is not passed as an argument), the script queries the Terminal and displays the current Session settings, as shown in Figure 5.4.

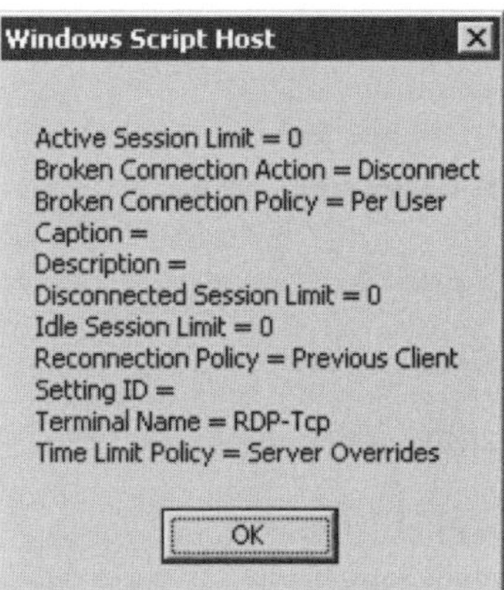

FIGURE 5.4 Session settings displayed by the script when the `/x:` argument is not passed.

The `SessionSettings.wsf` file also includes the `HelperFunctions.vbs` script that contains functions that format the output returned to make it more meaningful. Additionally it also contains the `Con2MiliSec` function that converts the minutes for the Time Limit properties to milliseconds expected by the `TimeLimit` method.

To accomplish the two tasks, the script takes the following steps:

1. Creates the `Named` node to accept the following arguments:
   - `s` as name (or IP Address) of the TS server
   - `u` as the username to connect as the specified user
   - `p` as password for the username specified in `u` argument
   - `x` as XML filename
2. Includes `Option Explicit` statement to enforce variable declaration.
3. Declares required variables.
4. Retrieves the argument values passed as script parameters to initialize the input and output variables. Sets the default values for the optional arguments.
5. Initializes constants for the WMI authentication level.
6. Creates the WMI Services object.
7. Sets the `AuthenticationLevel` of the `Security_` property to `wbemAuthenticationLevelPkt`. This ensures that the connection to the remote system is encrypted.
8. Connects to the WMI TS provider using the `ConnectServer` method.
9. Checks to see if an XML file was passed as argument.
10. If XML file is passed
    - Creates a new MSXML DOM object
    - Loads the file into memory
    - Selects the root node
    - Checks to see if the `<SESSION>` node exists in the XML data in memory
    - Calls `SetSession` sub procedure
11. If XML file is not passed
    - Calls `GetSession` sub procedure
12. If the `SetSession` sub procedure is called
    - Declares variables
    - Selects the `<SESSION>` node
    - Checks to verify that the child nodes exist in the `<SESSION>` node
    - For each child node: selects case based on the node name
      - If case is `BROKENCONNECTIONACTION`

    - Gets the text of the child node
    - Selects case for broken connection action to set the value for `BrokenConnectionAction` property
  - If case is `BROKENCONNECTIONPOLICY`
    - Gets the text of the child node
    - Selects case for broken connection policy to set the value for `BrokenConnectionPolicy` property
  - If case is `RECONNECTIONPOLICY`
    - Gets the text of the child node
    - Selects case for reconnection connection policy to set the value for `ReconnectionPolicy` property
  - If case is `TIMELIMITPOLICY`
    - Gets the text of the child node
    - Selects case for time limit policy to set the value for `TimeLimit-Policy` property
  - If case is `TIMELIMIT`
    - Checks to see if the `<TIMELIMIT>` node has child nodes
    - Gets text for `<ACTIVESESSIONLIMIT>`, `<DISCONNECTSESSIONLIMIT>`, and `<IDLESESSIONLIMIT>` nodes

13. Gets instances of `Win32_TSSessionSetting` class.
14. For each instance of the class

    - Sets the `BrokenConnectionPolicy` property in cache
    - Sets the `TimeLimitPolicy` property in cache
    - Calls the `Put_` method to save the properties
    - If the `BrokenConnectionPolicy` is set to `Server`
      - Sets the `BrokenConnectionAction` property
    - If the `TimeLimitPolicy` property is set to `Server`
      - Sets the `ActiveSessionLimit`, `DisconnectSessionLimit`, and `IdleSes-sionLimit` properties (converts the values from minutes to milliseconds by calling the `Conv2MiliSec` function before setting the values with the `TimeLimit` method)

15. If the `GetSession` procedure is called

    - Declares variables
    - Gets instances of `Win32_TSSessionSetting` class
    - For each setting in class
      - Retrieves individual property names and their values
      - Calls the formatting functions as needed (from included `Helper-Functions.vbs` script)

16. Displays the retrieved values.
17. Releases memory and ends.

Environment Settings

Environment settings can be changed using the `Win32_EnvironmentSetting` class. This class provides eight properties and two methods. Only the `InitialProgramPolicy` property is Read/Write (that is, the value of this property can be read and changed). All other properties are read-only (that is, you can only retrieve the value). The script in Listing 5.11 uses these properties and methods to display the current settings and configure the properties.

LISTING 5.11 Script for Getting and Setting Environment Properties

```
<package>
 <job id="Get and Set Environment Settings">
  <runtime>
     <named
       name="s"
       helpstring="Remote Server Name. Default=Localhost"
       type="string"
       required=false/>
     <named
       name="u"
       helpstring="User name for the remote computer.
                              Example: Domain\UserName"
       type="string"
       required=false/>
     <named
       name="p"
       helpstring="password for the remote user"
       type="string"
       required=false/>
     <named
       name="x"
       helpstring="Input Xml file"
       type="string"
       required=false/>
  </runtime>
 <?job debug="true"?>
 <script language="vbscript" src="helperfunctions.vbs">
  Option Explicit
  Dim sServer, sUser, sPassword, sXmlFile
  Dim objWMI, objTsConnect, objSwat
  Dim objXml,objXmlChild, objRoot
  sServer = wscript.Arguments.Named("s")
    if sServer = "" then sServer = "."
     sUser = wscript.Arguments.Named("u")
       sPassword = wscript.Arguments.Named("p")
        sXmlFile = wscript.Arguments.Named("x")
             CONST wbemAuthenticationLevelPkt = 4
              CONST WbemAuthenticationLevelPktPrivacy = 6
```

```
    Set objSwat = CreateObject("Swat.1.00")
    set objWMI = CreateObject("WbemScripting.SwbemLocator")
     objWMI.Security_.AuthenticationLevel = wbemAuthenticationLevelPkt
       Set objTsConnect = objWMI.ConnectServer(sServer, _
                                               "root/CIMv2", _
                                                   sUser, sPassword)
      if sXmlFile = "" then
              GetEnvironment
      else
         Set objXml = CreateObject("MSXML2.DomDocument")
            objXml.Async = false
               objXml.Load sXmlFile
                 Set objRoot = objXml.SelectSingleNode("/MAIN")
                   set objXmlChild = objRoot.SelectNodes("ENVIRONMENT")
               if objXmlChild.Length > 0 then
                      SetEnvironment
               End if
            set objRoot = nothing
          set objXmlChild = nothing
         Set objXml = nothing
      end if
    Set objTsConnect = nothing
   set objWMI = nothing
  set objSwat = nothing
  Sub SetEnvironment
      Dim ClientWallPaper,InitialProgramPolicy
      Dim StartIn, InitialProgramPath
      Dim objXmlEnv, ChildNode, objEnvSettings, item
      set objxmlEnv = objRoot.SelectSingleNode("ENVIRONMENT")
      if objXmlEnv.HasChildNodes then
         for each ChildNode in objXmlEnv.ChildNodes
              Select Case ChildNode.NodeName
                      Case "CLIENTWALLPAPER"
                              ClientWallPaper = ChildNode.Text
                              Select Case Ucase(ClientWallPaper)
                                 Case "HIDE" : ClientWallPaper = 0
                                 Case "DISPLAY" : ClientWallPaper = 1
                                 Case else : ClientWallPaper = 0
                              End Select
                      Case "INITIALPROGRAMPOLICY"
                              InitialProgramPolicy = ChildNode.Text
                              Select Case Ucase(InitialProgramPolicy)
                                 Case "USER" : InitialProgramPolicy = 1
                                 Case "SERVER" : InitialProgramPolicy = 0
                                 Case "DESKTOP" : InitialProgramPolicy = 2
                                 Case else : InitialProgramPolicy = 1
                              End Select
                      Case "INITIALPROGRAM"
                              if ChildNode.HasChildNodes then
                                InitialProgramPath = _
                                      ChildNode.SelectSingleNode( _
                                          "INITIALPROGRAMPATH").Text
```

```
                                StartIn = _
                              ChildNode.SelectSingleNode("STARTIN").Text
                              end if
                End Select
            next
           Set objXmlEnv = nothing
          Set objEnvSettings = _
                        objTsConnect.InstancesOf("Win32_TSEnvironmentSetting")
          For each item in objEnvSettings
                if ClientWallPaper <> "" then _
                        item.ClientWallPaper = ClientWallPaper
                if InitialProgramPolicy <> "" then _
                        item.InitialProgramPolicy = InitialProgramPolicy
                item.Put_
                if item.InitialProgramPolicy = 0 then
                  if InitialProgramPath <> "" and StartIn <> "" then _
                        item.InitialProgram InitialProgramPath, StartIn
                end if
          Next
          Set objEnvSettings = nothing
        end if
    End Sub
    Sub GetEnvironment
     Dim objEnvironmentSettings
     Dim item, prop, DispValue
     Dim sPropName, sPropValue
        Set objEnvironmentSettings = _
                        objTsConnect.InstancesOf("Win32_TSEnvironmentSetting")
         For each item in objEnvironmentSettings
                For each prop in item.Properties_
                        sPropName = prop.Name
                        Select Case lcase(sPropName)
                          Case "clientwallpaper"
                                sPropValue = FormatClientWallPaper(prop.value)
                          Case "initialprogrampolicy"
                                sPropValue = FormatIProgPol(prop.value)
                          Case else
                                sPropValue = prop.Value
                        End Select
                        DispValue = DispValue & VBNewLine & _
                            objSwat.SplitOnCap(sPropName) & " = " & sPropValue
                Next
        Next
        Wscript.Echo DispValue
        Set objEnvironmentSettings = nothing
    End Sub
 </script>
 </job>
</package>
```

The Script

The `EnvironmentSettings.wsf` script shown in Listing 5.11 also has two sub procedures: `GetEnvironment` and `SetEnvironment`. Therefore, the `EnvironmentSettings.wsf` script also performs two functions; it retrieves and displays the values of the Environment properties and sets the values of the Environment properties as specified in the XML file passed as an argument to the script.

The `SetEnvironment` sub procedure reads the XML file to retrieve the values and changes the settings accordingly. It sets the following three configuration settings that you can find on the Environment tab in TS configuration utility:

Client Wallpaper: Changes the ClientWallpaper property.

Initial Program Policy: Changes the InitialProgramPolicy property.

The `InitialProgramPolicy` can have three settings `0`, `1`, and `2`. The Terminal Services documentation at http://msdn.microsoft.com *only states `0` and `1`. The script in Listing 5.11 can, however, set all three values.*

Initial Program: Changes the startup program properties, such as the username and the working directory for the initial program.

The documentation on Terminal Services at http://msdn.microsoft.com *incorrectly states that the `InitialProgram` method also changes the `Name` of the path. However, `Name` is not an argument that you can pass to the `InitialProgram` method; you can only pass program path and working directory as the arguments of the `InitialProgram`.*

It reads the property settings from the XML file that has the following schema:

```
<MAIN>
 <ENVIRONMENT>
   <CLIENTWALLPAPER>Display</CLIENTWALLPAPER>
   <INITIALPROGRAMPOLICY></INITIALPROGRAMPOLICY>
   <INITIALPROGRAM>
      <INITIALPROGRAMPATH></INITIALPROGRAMPATH>
      <STARTIN></STARTIN>
   </INITIALPROGRAM>
 </ENVIRONMENT>
</MAIN>
```

The XML file has `<MAIN>` as the root node. The `<ENVIRONMENT>` node is the root node for the Environment properties. `<CLIENTWALLPAPER>`, `<INITIALPROGRAMPOLICY>`, and `<INITIALPROGRAM>` nodes hold the values for the Environment properties. The `<INITIALPROGRAMPATH>` and `<STARTIN>` nodes can be used to specify the startup program and the working directory property values. When the script is executed, it reads the text from these nodes to set the values of the properties. The property nodes can have the values as defined in Table 5.4.

TABLE 5.4 Environment Properties XML File Nodes and Values

Node	Setable Values	
CLIENTWALLPAPER	**Value**	**Description**
	Hide	The wallpaper image is not displayed on the client
	Display	The wallpaper image is displayed on the client
INITIALPROGRAMPOLICY	**Value**	**Description**
	User	Run the initial program specified in the user profile
	Server	Run initial program specified at the server
	Desktop	Do not allow running initial program. Always show the desktop
INITIALPROGRAM	**Node**	**Value**
	INITIALPROGRAMPATH	The startup program (including path). For example: Notepad.exe
	STARTIN	C:\Temp

The values in Table 5.4 must be used to define the settings in the XML file. For example, if you want to change the `ClientWallPaper` property to `Display`, you should set the `<CLIENTWALLPAPER>` node as follows:

```
<CLIENTWALLPAPER>Display</CLIENTWALLPAPER>
```

When the script is executed with the XML file as an argument, as shown in Listing 5.12, it will change the `ClientWallPaper` to `Display`.

LISTING 5.12 Executing `EnvironmentSettings.wsf` to Change the Environment Properties

```
EnvironmentSettings /x:EnvironmentSettings.xml
```

When the script is run without the `/x:` parameter (that is, the XML file is not passed as an argument), the script queries the Terminal and displays the current Environment settings, as shown in Figure 5.5.

NOTE

The `EnvironmentSettings.wsf` file also includes the `HelperFunctions.vbs` script that contains functions that format the output returned to make it more meaningful.

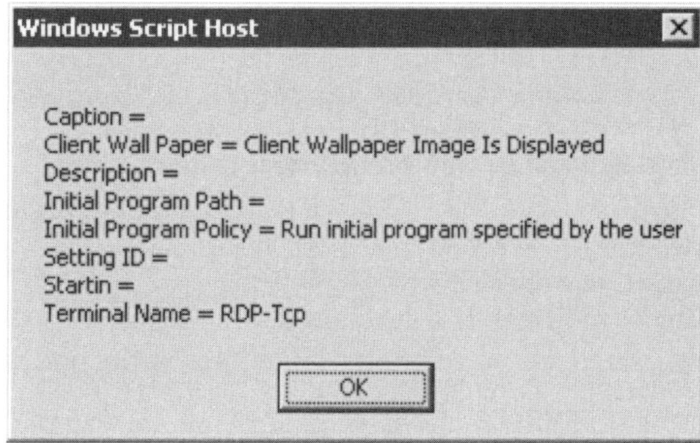

FIGURE 5.5 Environment settings displayed by the script when the `/x:` argument is not passed.

To accomplish the two tasks, the script in Listing 5.11 takes the following steps:

1. Creates the `Named` node to accept the following arguments:
   - `s` as name (or IP Address) of the TS server
   - `u` as the username to connect as the specified user
   - `p` as password for the username specified in `u` argument
   - `x` as XML filename
2. Includes `Option Explicit` statement to enforce variable declaration.
3. Declares required variables.
4. Retrieves the argument values passed as script parameters to initializes the input and output variables. Sets the default values for the optional arguments.
5. Initializes constants for the WMI authentication level.
6. Creates the WMI Services object.
7. Sets the `AuthenticationLevel` of the `Security_` property to `wbemAuthenticationLevelPkt`. This ensures that the connection to the remote system is encrypted.
8. Connects to the WMI TS provider using the `ConnectServer` method.
9. Checks to see if an XML file was passed as argument.
10. If XML file is passed
    - Creates a new MSXML DOM object
    - Loads the file into memory
    - Selects the root node
    - Checks to see if the `<ENVIRONMENT>` node exists in the XML data in memory
    - Calls `SetEnvironment` sub procedure

11. If XML file is not passed
    - Calls `GetEnvironment` sub procedure
12. If the `SetEnvironment` sub procedure is called
    - Declares variables
    - Selects the `<ENVIRONMENT>` node
    - Checks to verify that the child nodes exist in the `<ENVIRONMENT>` node
    - For each child node: selects case based on the node name
        - If case is `CLIENTWALLPAPER`
            - Gets the text of the child node
            - Select case for client wallpaper to set the value for `ClientWallPaper` property
        - If case is `INITIALPROGRAMPOLICY`
            - Gets the text of the child node
            - Select case for initial startup program policy to set the value for `InitialProgramPolicy` property
        - If case is `INITIALPROGRAM`
            - Checks to see if the `<INITIALPROGRAM>` node has child nodes
            - Gets text for `<INITIALPROGRAMPATH>` and `<STARTIN>` nodes
13. Gets instances of `Win32_TSEnvironmentSetting` class.
14. For each instance of the class
    - Sets the `ClientWallPaper` property in cache
    - Sets the `InitialProgramPolicy` property in cache
    - Calls the `Put_` method to save the properties
    - If the `InitialProgramPolicy` is set to `Server`
    - Calls the `InitialProgram` method to set the `InitialProgramPath` and `StartIn` properties
15. If the `GetEnvironment` procedure is called
    - Declares variables
    - Gets instances of `Win32_TSEnvironmentSetting` class
    - For each setting in class:
        - Retrieves individual property names and their values
        - Calls the formatting functions as needed (from included `HelperFunctions.vbs` script)
16. Displays the retrieved values.
17. Releases memory and ends.

Remote Control Settings

The `Win32_RemoteControlSetting` class provides the properties and methods that can be used to configure the Remote Control options of the Terminal. You can set the Remote Control policy and the level of control for a session, which specifies whether the session will be viewed only by the remote user, or viewed and remote controlled through a mouse or a keyboard. The following four settings for remote controlling the sessions can be set:

Disable: The Remote Control is disabled.

Enable Input Notify: The user of the Remote Control has full control over the user's session. The Remote Control user needs to be permitted by the user to take control of the session.

Enable Input No Notify: The user of the Remote Control has full control over the user's session. The Remote Control user does not require the user's permission to take control of the session.

Enable No Input Notify: The Remote Control user can only view the user's session. Remote Control user needs to be permitted by the user to view the session.

Enable No Input No Notify: The Remote Control user can only view the user's session. Remote Control user does not need permission from the user to view the remote control session.

The script in Listing 5.13 illustrates how to display and set these configuration settings by calling the `RemoteControl` method and the `RemoteControlPolicy` property exposed by the `Win32_RemoteControlSetting` class.

LISTING 5.13 Script for Getting and Setting Remote Control Properties

```
<package>
 <job id="Get and Set Remote Control Settings">
  <runtime>
     <named
       name="s"
       helpstring="Remote Server Name. Default=Localhost"
       type="string"
       required=false/>
     <named
       name="u"
       helpstring="User name for the remote computer.
                               Example: Domain\UserName"
       type="string"
       required=false/>
```

```
    <named
      name="p"
      helpstring="password for the remote user"
      type="string"
      required=false/>
    <named
      name="x"
      helpstring="Input Xml file"
      type="string"
      required=false/>
 </runtime>
<?job debug="true"?>
<script language="vbscript" src="helperfunctions.vbs">
 Option Explicit
 Dim sServer, sUser, sPassword, sXmlFile
 Dim objWMI, objTsConnect, objSwat
 Dim objXml,objXmlChild, objRoot
 sServer = wscript.Arguments.Named("s")
   if sServer = "" then sServer = "."
    sUser = wscript.Arguments.Named("u")
      sPassword = wscript.Arguments.Named("p")
       sXmlFile = wscript.Arguments.Named("x")
            CONST wbemAuthenticationLevelPkt = 4
             CONST WbemAuthenticationLevelPktPrivacy = 6
     Set objSwat = CreateObject("Swat.1.00")
     set objWMI = CreateObject("WbemScripting.SwbemLocator")
      objWMI.Security_.AuthenticationLevel = wbemAuthenticationLevelPkt
        Set objTsConnect = objWMI.ConnectServer(sServer, _
                                                "root/CIMv2", _
                                                    sUser, sPassword)
       if sXmlFile = "" then
               GetRemoteControl
       else
          Set objXml = CreateObject("MSXML2.DomDocument")
             objXml.Async = false
                objXml.Load sXmlFile
                  Set objRoot = objXml.SelectSingleNode("/MAIN")
                    set objXmlChild = objRoot.SelectNodes("REMOTECONTROL")
                if objXmlChild.Length > 0 then
                       SetRemoteControl
                End if
             set objRoot = nothing
           set objXmlChild = nothing
          Set objXml = nothing
       end if
     Set objTsConnect = nothing
    set objWMI = nothing
   set objSwat = nothing
   Sub SetRemoteControl
       Dim LevelOfControl,RemoteControlPolicy
       Dim objXmlRc, ChildNode, objRcSettings, item
       set objxmlRc = objRoot.SelectSingleNode("REMOTECONTROL")
```

```
      if objXmlRc.HasChildNodes then
         for each ChildNode in objXmlRc.ChildNodes
              Select Case ChildNode.NodeName
                      Case "LEVELOFCONTROL"
                            LevelOfControl = ChildNode.Text
                            Select Case Ucase(LevelOfControl)
                              Case "DISABLE" : LevelOfControl = 0
                              Case "ENABLEINPUTNOTIFY" : LevelOfControl = 1
                              Case "ENABLEINPUTNONOTIFY" : LevelOfControl = 2
                              Case "ENABLENOINPUTNOTIFY" : LevelOfControl = 3
                              Case "ENABLENOINPUTNONOTIFY" : LevelOfControl = 4
                              Case else : LevelOfControl = 0
                              End Select
                      Case "REMOTECONTROLPOLICY"
                            RemoteControlPolicy = ChildNode.Text
                            Select Case Ucase(RemoteControlPolicy)
                              Case "USER" : RemoteControlPolicy = 1
                              Case "SERVER" : RemoteControlPolicy = 0
                              Case else : RemoteControlPolicy = 3
                              End Select
              End Select
          next
         Set objXmlRc = nothing
        Set objRcSettings = _
              objTsConnect.InstancesOf("Win32_TSRemoteControlSetting")
        For each item in objRcSettings
              if lcase(item.terminalname) <> "console" then
              if RemoteControlPolicy <> "" then _
                      item.RemoteControlPolicy = RemoteControlPolicy
                  item.Put_
                  if item.RemoteControlPolicy = 0 and _
                    LevelOfControl <> "" then _
                                    item.RemoteControl LevelOfControl
              end if
        Next
        Set objRcSettings = nothing
      end if
  End Sub
 Sub GetRemoteControl
   Dim objRemoteControlSettings
   Dim item, prop, DispValue
   Dim sPropName, sPropValue
      Set objRemoteControlSettings = _
              objTsConnect.InstancesOf("Win32_TSRemoteControlSetting")
       For each item in objRemoteControlSettings
             if lcase(item.terminalname) <> "console" then
              For each prop in item.Properties_
                      sPropName = prop.Name
                      Select Case lcase(sPropName)
                        Case "levelofcontrol"
                              sPropValue = prop.value
                        Case "remotecontrolpolicy"
                              sPropValue = FormatRCPol(prop.value)
```

```
                    Case else
                          sPropValue = prop.Value
                  End Select
                  DispValue = DispValue & VBNewLine & _
                     objSwat.SplitOnCap(sPropName) & " = " & sPropValue
          Next
          DispValue = DispValue
          End if
      Next
      Wscript.Echo DispValue
      Set objRemoteControlSettings = nothing
  End Sub
</script>
</job>
</package>
```

The Script

The `RemoteControlSettings.wsf` script shown in Listing 5.13 has two sub procedures: `GetRemoteControl` and `SetRemoteControl`. Therefore, the `RemoteControlSettings.wsf` script also performs two functions; it retrieves and displays the values of the Remote Control properties and sets the values of the Remote Control properties as specified in the XML file passed as an argument to the script.

The `SetRemoteControl` sub procedure reads the XML file to retrieve the values and changes the settings accordingly. It sets the following two configuration settings that you can find on the Remote Control tab in TS configuration utility:

Remote Control Policy: Changes the `RemoteControlPolicy` property.

Level Of Control: Changes the `LevelOfControl` property. This property can only be set if the `RemoteControlPolicy` property is set to `Server` (that is, the user's Remote Control settings are overridden by the server).

It reads the property settings from the XML file that has the following schema:

```
<MAIN>
   <REMOTECONTROL>
       <REMOTECONTROLPOLICY></REMOTECONTROLPOLICY>
       <LEVELOFCONTROL></LEVELOFCONTROL>
   </REMOTECONTROL>
</MAIN>
```

The XML file has `<MAIN>` as the root node. The `<REMOTECONTROL>` node is the root node for the Remote Control properties. `<REMOTECONTROLPOLICY>` and `<LEVELOFCONTROL>` nodes hold the values for the Remote Control properties. When the script is executed, it reads the text from these nodes to set the values of the properties. The property nodes can have the values as defined in Table 5.5.

TABLE 5.5 Remote Control Properties XML File Nodes and Values

Node	Setable Values	
REMOTECONTROLPOLICY	**Value**	**Description**
	User	The user's Remote Control policies are in effect.
	Server	The user's Remote Control policies are overridden by the server.
LEVELOFCONTROL	**Value**	**Description**
	Disable	The user has no control over the session
	EnableInputNotify	The user of the Remote Control has full control over the user's session. The Remote Control user needs to be permitted by the user to take control of the session.
	EnableInputNoNotify	The user of the Remote Control has full control over the user's session. The Remote Control user does not require the user's permission to take control of the session.
	EnableNoInputNotify	The Remote Control user can only view the user's session. Remote Control user does not need permission from the user to view the remote control session.
	EnableNoInputNoNotify	The Remote Control user can only view the user's session. Remote Control user does not need permission from the user to view the remote control session.

The values in Table 5.5 must be used to define the settings in the XML file. For example, if you want to change the `LevelOfControl` property to `Disable`, you should set the `<LEVELOFCONTROL>` node as follows:

```
<LEVELOFCONTROL>Disable</LEVELOFCONTROL>
```

When the script is executed with the XML file as an argument, as shown in Listing 5.14, it will change the `LevelOfControl` to `Disable`.

LISTING 5.14 Executing `RemoteControlSettings.wsf` to Change the Remote Control Properties

```
RemoteControlSettings /x:RemoteControlSettings.xml
```

When the script is run without the `/x:` parameter (that is, the XML file is not passed as an argument), the script queries the Terminal and displays the current Remote Control settings, as shown in Figure 5.6.

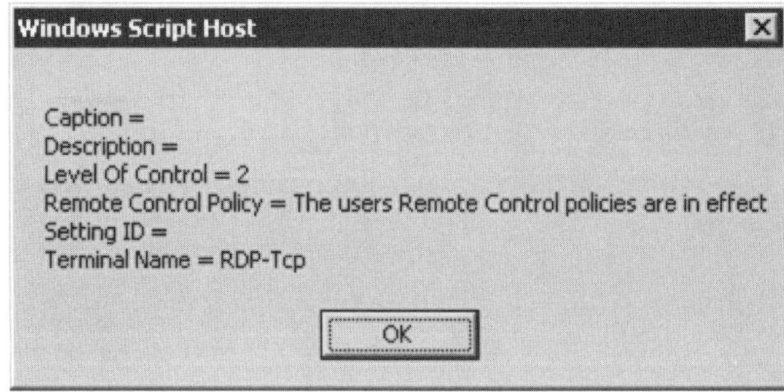

FIGURE 5.6 Remote Control settings displayed by the script when the `/x:` argument is not passed.

The `RemoteControlSettings.wsf` file also includes the `HelperFunctions.vbs` script that contains functions that format the output returned to make it more meaningful.

The script in Listing 5.13 takes the following steps to accomplish the two tasks:

1. Creates the `Named` node to accept the following arguments:
   - `s` as name (or IP Address) of the TS server
   - `u` as the username to connect as the specified user
   - `p` as password for the username specified in `u` argument
   - `x` as XML filename
2. Includes `Option Explicit` statement to enforce variable declaration.
3. Declares required variables.
4. Retrieves the argument values passed as script parameters to initialize the input and output variables. Sets the default values for the optional arguments.
5. Initializes constants for the WMI authentication level.
6. Creates the WMI Services object.

7. Sets the `AuthenticationLevel` of the `Security_` property to `wbemAuthenticationLevelPkt`. This ensures that the connection to the remote system is encrypted.
8. Connects to the WMI TS provider using the `ConnectServer` method.
9. Checks to see if an XML file was passed as argument.
10. If XML file is passed
    - Creates a new MSXML DOM object
    - Loads the file into memory
    - Selects the root node
    - Checks to see if the `<REMOTECONTROL>` node exists in the XML data in memory
    - Calls `SetRemoteControl` sub procedure
11. If XML file is not passed
    - Calls `GetRemoteControl` sub procedure
12. If the `SetRemoteControl` sub procedure is called
    - Declares variables
    - Selects the `<REMOTECONTROL>` node
    - Checks to verify that the child nodes exist in the `<REMOTECONTROL>` node
    - For each child node: selects case based on the node name
        - If case is `LEVELOFCONTROL`
            - Gets the text of the child node
            - Selects case for client wallpaper to set the value for `LevelOfControl` property
        - If case is `REMOTECONTROLPOLICY`
            - Gets the text of the child node
            - Selects case for initial startup program policy to set the value for `RemoteControlPolicy` property
13. Gets instances of `Win32_TSRemoteControlSetting` class
14. For each instance of the class
    - Sets the `RemoteControlPolicy` property in cache
    - Calls the `Put_` method to save the properties
    - If the `RemoteControlPolicy` is set to `Server`
    - Sets the `LevelOfControl` property by calling the `LevelOfControl` method
15. If the `GetRemoteControl` procedure is called
    - Declares variables
    - Gets instances of `Win32_TSRemoteControlSetting` class

- For each setting in class
  - Retrieves individual property names and their values
  - Calls the formatting functions as needed (from included `Helper-Functions.vbs` script)

16. Displays the retrieved values.
17. Releases memory and ends.

Client Settings

Client Settings define the configuration settings, such as connection setting, the color depth setting, drive mapping, printer mapping, COM and LPT port mappings for the client. These settings can be configured either from the Client Settings tab of the TS configuration utility or using a script, such as shown in Listing 5.15.

LISTING 5.15 Script for Getting and Setting Client Properties

```
<package>
 <job id="Get and Set Session Settings">
  <runtime>
     <named
       name="s"
       helpstring="Remote Server Name. Default=Localhost"
       type="string"
       required=false/>
     <named
       name="u"
       helpstring="User name for the remote computer.
                            Example: Domain\UserName"
       type="string"
       required=false/>
     <named
       name="p"
       helpstring="password for the remote user"
       type="string"
       required=false/>
     <named
       name="x"
       helpstring="Input Xml file"
       type="string"
       required=false/>
  </runtime>
 <?job debug="true"?>
 <script language="vbscript" src="helperfunctions.vbs">
  Option Explicit
  Dim sServer, sUser, sPassword, sXmlFile
  Dim objWMI, objTsConnect, objSwat
  Dim objXml,objXmlChild, objRoot
  sServer = wscript.Arguments.Named("s")
    if sServer = "" then sServer = "."
```

```
    sUser = wscript.Arguments.Named("u")
      sPassword = wscript.Arguments.Named("p")
       sXmlFile = wscript.Arguments.Named("x")
            CONST wbemAuthenticationLevelPkt = 4
             CONST WbemAuthenticationLevelPktPrivacy = 6
     Set objSwat = CreateObject("Swat.1.00")
     set objWMI = CreateObject("WbemScripting.SwbemLocator")
      objWMI.Security_.AuthenticationLevel = wbemAuthenticationLevelPkt
        Set objTsConnect = objWMI.ConnectServer(sServer, _
                                            "root/CIMv2", _
                                                  sUser, sPassword)
  if sXmlFile = "" then
               GetClient
       else
          Set objXml = CreateObject("MSXML2.DomDocument")
             objXml.Async = false
                objXml.Load sXmlFile
                  Set objRoot = objXml.SelectSingleNode("/MAIN")
                    set objXmlChild = objRoot.SelectNodes("CLIENT")
                if objXmlChild.Length > 0 then
                       SetClient
                End if
             set objRoot = nothing
           set objXmlChild = nothing
          Set objXml = nothing
       end if
     Set objTsConnect = nothing
    set objWMI = nothing
   set objSwat = nothing
Sub SetClient
        Dim ConnectClientDrivesAtLogon, ConnectPrinterAtLogon
Dim DefaultToClientPrinter
        Dim LPTPortMapping, COMPortMapping, AudioMapping
        Dim ClipboardMapping, DriveMapping, WindowsPrinterMapping
        Dim ColorDepth, ColorDepthPolicy
        Dim ConnectionPolicy
        Dim objXmlCli, ChildNode, objCliSettings, item
        set objxmlCli = objRoot.SelectSingleNode("CLIENT")
        if objXmlCli.HasChildNodes then
           for each ChildNode in objXmlCli.ChildNodes
                Select Case ChildNode.NodeName
                        Case "CONNECTIONSETTINGS"
                           if ChildNode.HasChildNodes then
                             ConnectClientDrivesAtLogon = _
                               ChildNode.SelectSingleNode( _
                                    "CONNECTDRIVESATLOGON").Text
                             Select Case Ucase(ConnectClientDrivesAtLogon)
                              Case "NOAUTOMAP" : ConnectClientDrivesAtLogon = 0
                              Case "AUTOMAP" : ConnectClientDrivesAtLogon = 1
                              Case else : ConnectClientDrivesAtLogon = 0
                                End Select
                             ConnectPrinterAtLogon = _
                                ChildNode.SelectSingleNode( _
```

```
                "CONNECTPRINTERATLOGON").Text
          Select Case Ucase(ConnectPrinterAtLogon)
               Case "NOAUTOMAP" : ConnectPrinterAtLogon = 0
               Case "AUTOMAP" : ConnectPrinterAtLogon = 1
               Case else : ConnectPrinterAtLogon = 0
            End Select
         DefaultToClientPrinter = _
             ChildNode.SelectSingleNode( _
                "DEFAULTTOCLIENTPRINTER").Text
          Select Case Ucase(DefaultToClientPrinter)
               Case "NOAUTOMAP" : DefaultToClientPrinter = 0
               Case "AUTOMAP" : DefaultToClientPrinter = 1
               Case else : DefaultToClientPrinter = 0
            End Select
      end if
   Case "CLIENTPROPERTY"
         LPTPortMapping = _
          ChildNode.SelectSingleNode("LPTPORTMAPPING").Text
         Select Case Ucase(LPTPortMapping )
               Case "DISABLE" : LPTPortMapping  = 0
               Case "ENABLE" : LPTPortMapping  = 1
               Case else : LPTPortMapping  = 0
            End Select

         COMPortMapping = _
          ChildNode.SelectSingleNode("COMPORTMAPPING").Text
         Select Case Ucase(COMPortMapping)
               Case "DISABLE" : COMPortMapping  = 0
               Case "ENABLE" : COMPortMapping  = 1
               Case else : COMPortMapping  = 0
            End Select
         AudioMapping = _
           ChildNode.SelectSingleNode("AUDIOMAPPING").Text
         Select Case Ucase(AudioMapping)
               Case "DISABLE" : AudioMapping  = 0
               Case "ENABLE" : AudioMapping  = 1
               Case else : AudioMapping  = 0
            End Select
         ClipboardMapping = _
        ChildNode.SelectSingleNode("CLIPBOARDMAPPING").Text
         Select Case Ucase(ClipboardMapping)
               Case "DISABLE" : ClipboardMapping  = 0
               Case "ENABLE" : ClipboardMapping  = 1
               Case else : ClipboardMapping  = 0
            End Select
         DriveMapping = _
           ChildNode.SelectSingleNode("DRIVEMAPPING").Text
         Select Case Ucase(DriveMapping)
               Case "DISABLE" : DriveMapping  = 0
               Case "ENABLE" : DriveMapping  = 1
               Case else : DriveMapping  = 0
            End Select
```

```
                        WindowsPrinterMapping = _
                           ChildNode.SelectSingleNode( _
                              "WINDOWSPRINTERMAPPING").Text
                        Select Case Ucase(WindowsPrinterMapping)
                              Case "DISABLE" : WindowsPrinterMapping  = 0
                              Case "ENABLE" : WindowsPrinterMapping  = 1
                              Case else : WindowsPrinterMapping  = 0
                           End Select
                   Case "COLORDEPTH"
                           ColorDepth = ChildNode.Text
                           Select Case Ucase(ColorDepth)
                              Case "8BIT" : ColorDepth = 1
                              Case "15BIT" : ColorDepth = 2
                              Case "16BIT" : ColorDepth = 3
                              Case "24BIT" : ColorDepth = 4
                              Case else : ColorDepth = 3
                           End Select
                   Case "COLORDEPTHPOLICY"
                           ColorDepthPolicy = ChildNode.Text
                           Select Case Ucase(ColorDepthPolicy)
                              Case "SERVER" : ColorDepthPolicy = 0
                              Case "USER" : ColorDepthPolicy = 1
                              Case else : ColorDepthPolicy = 1
                           End Select
                   Case "CONNECTIONPOLICY"
                           ConnectionPolicy = ChildNode.Text
                           Select Case Ucase(ConnectionPolicy)
                              Case "SERVER" : ConnectionPolicy = 0
                              Case "USER" : ConnectionPolicy = 1
                              Case else : ConnectionPolicy = 1
                           End Select
           End Select
       next
      Set objXmlCli = nothing
     Set objCliSettings = _
            objTsConnect.InstancesOf("Win32_TSClientSetting")
     For each item in objCliSettings
           if ConnectionPolicy <> "" then
                   item.ConnectionPolicy = _
                                   ConnectionPolicy
                   item.Put_
           end if
           if item.ConnectionPolicy = 0 then
             if ConnectClientDrivesAtLogon <> "" and _
                   ConnectPrinterAtLogon <> "" and _
                   DefaultToClientPrinter <> "" then _
                      item.ConnectionSettings _
                              ConnectClientDrivesAtLogon, _
                                   ConnectPrinterAtLogon, _
                                        DefaultToClientPrinter
           end if
           if LPTPortMapping <> "" then _
                   item.SetClientProperty _
```

```
                                "LPTPortMapping", LPTPortMapping
                if COMPortMapping <> "" then _
                        item.SetClientProperty _
                                "COMPortMapping", COMPortMapping
                if AudioMapping <> "" then _
                        item.SetClientProperty _
                                "AudioMapping", AudioMapping
                if ClipboardMapping <> "" then _
                        item.SetClientProperty _
                                "ClipboardMapping", ClipboardMapping
                if DriveMapping <> "" then _
                        item.SetClientProperty _
                                "DriveMapping", DriveMapping
                if WindowsPrinterMapping <> "" then _
                        item.SetClientProperty _
                                "WindowsPrinterMapping", _
                                                WindowsPrinterMapping
                if ColorDepthPolicy <> "" then _
                        item.SetColorDepthPolicy ColorDepthPolicy
                if ColorDepth <> "" and _
                                item.ColorDepthPolicy = 1 then _
                                        item.SetColorDepth ColorDepth
          Next
          Set objCliSettings = nothing
        end if
End Sub
Sub GetClient
     Dim objClientSettings
     Dim item, prop, DispValue
     Dim sPropName, sPropValue
        Set objClientSettings = _
                        objTsConnect.InstancesOf("Win32_TSClientSetting")
         For each item in objClientSettings
                For each prop in item.Properties_
                        sPropName = prop.Name
                        Select Case lcase(sPropName)
                          Case "audiomapping"
                                sPropValue = FormatAudioMap(prop.value)
                          Case "clipboardmapping"
                                sPropValue = FormatClipMap(prop.value)
                          Case "colordepth"
                                sPropValue = FormatColorDepth(prop.value)
                          Case "colordepthpolicy"
                                sPropValue = FormatCDepthPol(prop.value)
                          Case "comportmapping"
                                sPropValue = FormatComPortMap(prop.value)
                          Case "connectclientdrivesatlogon"
                                sPropValue = FormatConDrive(prop.value)
                          Case "connectionpolicy"
                                sPropValue = FormatConPol(prop.value)
                          Case "connectprinteratlogon"
                                sPropValue = FormatConPrinter(prop.value)
                          Case "defaulttoclientprinter"
```

```
                        sPropValue = FormatDefClientPrinter(prop.value)
                  Case "drivemapping"
                        sPropValue = FormatDriveMap(prop.value)
                  Case "lptportmapping"
                        sPropValue = FormatLptMap(prop.value)
                  Case "windowsprintermapping"
                        sPropValue = FormatWindowsPrintMap(prop.value)
                  Case else
                        sPropValue = prop.Value
                End Select
                DispValue = DispValue & VBNewLine & _
                        objSwat.SplitOnCap(sPropName) & _
                           " = " & sPropValue
        Next
    Next
    Wscript.Echo DispValue
    Set objClientSettings = nothing
End Sub
</script>
</job>
</package>
```

The Script

The script in Listing 5.15 when executed without passing the `/X:` argument will display the Client settings for the Terminal. Whereas, if the XML file (containing the Client Settings configuration) is passed as the /x: argument, the script will read the XML file and perform the configuration changes specified in the XML file.

Like other scripts, if the XML file is passed to the script as an argument, the script will call the `SetClient` sub procedure to change the configuration settings. It will call the `GetClient` sub procedure if the XML file is not passed as the argument.

The `SetClient` sub procedure reads the XML file to retrieve the values and change the specified settings. It sets the following configuration settings that you can find on the Client Settings tab in TS configuration utility:

Connection Settings: Changes the `ConnectClientDrivesAtLogon`, `ConnectPrinterAtLogon`, `DefaultToClientPrinter` properties by calling the `ConnectionSettings` method of the `Win32_TSClientSetting` class. These properties can be set only if the `ConnectionPolicy` property is set to `Server` (that is, the server overrides the user's settings).

Client Property Settings: Changes the `LPTPortMapping`, `COMPortMapping`, `Audio-Mapping`, `ClipboardMapping`, `DriveMapping`, or `WindowsPrinterMapping` properties. `SetClientProperty` method is called to disable or enable each property.

Color Depth: Changes the `ColorDepth` property of the class. This property can be set only if the `ColorDepthPolicy` property is set to `Server` (that is, the server overrides the user's settings).

It reads the property settings from the XML file that has the following schema:

```
<MAIN>
   <CLIENT>
     <CONNECTIONPOLICY></CONNECTIONPOLICY>
     <CONNECTIONSETTINGS>
         <CONNECTDRIVESATLOGON></CONNECTDRIVESATLOGON>
         <CONNECTPRINTERATLOGON></CONNECTPRINTERATLOGON>
       <DEFAULTTOCLIENTPRINTER></DEFAULTTOCLIENTPRINTER>
     </CONNECTIONSETTINGS>
     <CLIENTPROPERTY>
       <LPTPORTMAPPING></LPTPORTMAPPING>
       <COMPORTMAPPING></COMPORTMAPPING>
       <AUDIOMAPPING></AUDIOMAPPING>
       <CLIPBOARDMAPPING></CLIPBOARDMAPPING>
       <DRIVEMAPPING></DRIVEMAPPING>
       <WINDOWSPRINTERMAPPING></WINDOWSPRINTERMAPPING>
     </CLIENTPROPERTY>
     <COLORDEPTH></COLORDEPTH>
     <COLORDEPTHPOLICY></COLORDEPTHPOLICY>
   </CLIENT>
</MAIN>
```

The XML file has `<MAIN>` as the root node. The `<CLIENT>` node is the root node for the Client Settings. `<CONNECTIONPOLICY>`, `<CONNECTIONSETTINGS>`, `<CLIENTPROPERTY>`, `<COLORDEPTH>` and `<COLORDEPTHPOLICY>` nodes hold the values for the Client Settings. The `<LPTPORTMAPPING>`, `<COMPORTMAPPING>`, `<AUDIOMAPPING>`, `<CLIPBOARDMAPPING>`, `<DRIVEMAPPING>`, and `<WINDOWSPRINTERMAPPING>` nodes hold the values for the Client Property settings. Whereas `<CONNECTDRIVESATLOGON>`, `<CONNECTPRINTERATLOGON>`, and `<DEFAULTTOCLIENTPRINTER>` hold the values for the Connection Settings property. When the script is executed, it reads the text from these nodes to set the values of the properties. The property nodes can have the values as defined in Table 5.6.

TABLE 5.6 Client Settings XML File Nodes and Values

Node	Setable Values	
CONNECTIONPOLICY	**Value**	**Description**
	User	The user's Connection Settings policies are in effect.
	Server	The user's Connection Settings policies are overridden by the server.
CONNECTIONSETTINGS	**Node**	**Value**
	CONNECTDRIVESATLOGON	Automap or NoAutomap
	CONNECTPRINTERATLOGON	Automap or NoAutomap
	DEFAULTTOCLIENTPRINTER	Automap or NoAutomap →

Node	Setable Values	
CLIENTPROPERTY	**Node**	**Value**
	LPTPORTMAPPING	Enable or Disable
	COMPORTMAPPING	Enable or Disable
	AUDIOMAPPING	Enable or Disable
	CLIPBOARDMAPPING	Enable or Disable
	DRIVEMAPPING	Enable or Disable
	WINDOWSPRINTERMAPPING	Enable or Disable
COLORDEPTH	**Value**	**Description**
	8bit	8 bit
	15bit	15 bit
	16bit	16 bit
	24bit	24 bit
COLORDEPTHPOLICY	**Value**	**Description**
	User	The user's Color Depth policy is in effect.
	Server	The user's Color Depth policy is overridden by the server.

The values in Table 5.6 must be used to define the settings in the XML file. For example, if you want to change the `ColorDepth` property to `24bit`, you should set the `<COLORDEPTH>` node as follows:

```
<COLORDEPTH>24bit</COLORDEPTH>
```

When the script is executed with the XML file as an argument, as shown in Listing 5.16, it will change the `ColorDepth` to `Disable`.

LISTING 5.16 Executing `ClientSettings.wsf` to Change the Client Settings Properties

```
ClientSettings /x:ClientSettings.xml
```

When the script is run without the `/x:` parameter (that is, the XML file is not passed as an argument), the script queries the Terminal and displays the current Client settings as shown in Figure 5.7.

NOTE

The `ClientSettings.wsf` file also includes the `HelperFunctions.vbs` script that contains functions that format the output returned to make it more meaningful.

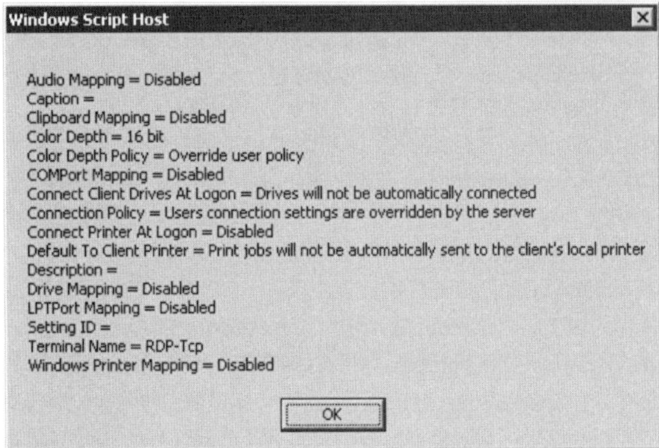

FIGURE 5.7 Client Settings displayed by the script when the `/x:` argument is not passed.

The script in Listing 5.15 takes the following steps to accomplish the two tasks:

1. Creates the `Named` node to accept the following arguments:
   - `s` as name (or IP Address) of the TS server
   - `u` as the username to connect as the specified user
   - `p` as password for the username specified in `u` argument
   - `x` as XML filename
2. Includes `Option Explicit` statement to enforce variable declaration.
3. Declares required variables.
4. Retrieves the argument values passed as script parameters to initialize the input and output variables. Sets the default values for the optional arguments.
5. Initializes constants for the WMI authentication level.
6. Creates the WMI Services object.
7. Sets the `AuthenticationLevel` of the `Security_` property to `wbemAuthenticationLevelPkt`. This ensures that the connection to the remote system is encrypted.
8. Connects to the WMI TS provider using the `ConnectServer` method.
9. Checks to see if an XML file was passed as argument.
10. If XML file is passed
    - Creates a new MSXML DOM object
    - Loads the file into memory
    - Selects the root node
    - Checks to see if the `<CLIENT>` node exists in the XML data in memory
    - Calls `SetClient` sub procedure

11. If XML file is not passed

    - Calls `GetClient` sub procedure

12. If the `SetClient` sub procedure is called

    - Declares variables
    - Selects the `<CLIENT>` node
    - Checks to verify that the child nodes exist in the `<CLIENT>` node
    - For each child node: selects case based on the node name
        - If case is `LEVELOFCONTROL`
            - Gets the text of the child node
            - Selecst case for client wallpaper to set the value for `LevelOfControl` property
        - If case is `REMOTECONTROLPOLICY`
            - Gets the text of the child node
            - Select case for initial startup program policy to set the value for `RemoteControlPolicy` property

13. Gets instances of `Win32_TSRemoteControlSetting` class.
14. For each instance of the class

    - Sets the `RemoteControlPolicy` property in cache
    - Calls the `Put_` method to save the properties
    - If the `RemoteControlPolicy` is set to `Server`
    - Sets the `LevelOfControl` property by calling the `LevelOfControl` method

15. If the `GetRemoteControl` procedure is called

    - Declares variables
    - Gets instances of `Win32_TSClientSetting` class
    - For each setting in class
        - Retrieves individual property names and their values
        - Calls the formatting functions as needed (from included `Helper-Functions.vbs` script)

16. Displays the retrieved values.
17. Releases memory and ends.

Network Adapter Settings

TS Service allows you to select a specific adapter or all adapters that have the RDP protocol installed. Selection can be made from the Network Adapter tab in the TS configuration utility. Alternatively, the Network Adapter settings can also be changed using a script.

However, before changing the configuration, if you want to list the network adapters installed on the system that can be configured for TS, you can create a script, such as shown in Listing 5.17.

LISTING 5.17 Listing TS Configurable Network Adapters

```
<package>
<job id=" List TS ready adapters">
 <runtime>
    <named
      name="s"
      helpstring="Remote Server Name. Default=Localhost"
      type="string"
      required=false/>
    <named
      name="u"
      helpstring="User name for the remote computer.
                            Example: Domain\UserName"
      type="string"
      required=false/>
    <named
      name="p"
      helpstring="password for the remote user"
      type="string"
      required=false/>
 </runtime>
<?job debug="true"?>
<script language="vbscript">
 Option Explicit
 Dim sServer, sUser, sPassword
 Dim objWMI, objTsConnect
 Dim objSwat, objTsNetworkAdapters
 Dim item, prop
 Dim objIe, objDoc
 sServer = wscript.Arguments.Named("s")
   if sServer = "" then sServer = "."
    sUser = wscript.Arguments.Named("u")
      sPassword = wscript.Arguments.Named("p")
     Set objIe = CreateObject("InternetExplorer.Application")
       objIe.Navigate "about:blank"
         objIe.ToolBar = 0
           objIe.StatusBar = 0
           objIe.Height = 200
         objIe.Left = 0
       objIe.Top = 0
       Do While (objIe.Busy)
               Wscript.Sleep 200
       Loop
         objIe.Visible = 1
           set objDoc = objIe.document
            set objSwat = CreateObject("SWAT.1.00")
```

```
                CONST wbemAuthenticationLevelPkt = 4
                 CONST WbemAuthenticationLevelPktPrivacy = 6
                   set objWMI = CreateObject( _
                                   "WbemScripting.SwbemLocator")
                    objWMI.Security_.AuthenticationLevel = _
                                   wbemAuthenticationLevelPkt
                     Set objTsConnect = objWMI.ConnectServer( _
                                              sServer, _
                                                "root/CIMv2", _
                                                   sUser, sPassword)
             set objTsNetworkAdapters = _
                          objTsConnect.InstancesOf( _
                                  "Win32_TSNetworkAdapterListSetting")
              for each item in objTsNetworkAdapters
                  for each prop in item.properties_
                     objDoc.write _
                       "<b>" & objSwat.SplitOnCap(prop.name) & "</b>"_
                                             & " = " & prop.Value & "<br>"
                  next
                  objDoc.Write "<hr><br>"
              next
          Set objIe = nothing
         Set objDoc = nothing
        set objTsNetworkAdapters = nothing
       set objTsConnect = nothing
      set objWMI = nothing
     set objSwat = nothing
   </script>
   </job>
  </package>
```

The Script

The script in Listing 5.17 queries the properties of the `Win32_TSNetworkAdapterListSetting` class to list the TS-ready network adapters. To accomplish this task, the script takes the following steps:

1. Creates the `Named` node to accept the following arguments:
   - `s` as name (or IP Address) of the TS server
   - `u` as the username to connect as the specified user
   - `p` as password for the username specified in `u` argument
2. Includes `Option Explicit` statement to enforce variable declaration.
3. Declares required variables.
4. Retrieves the argument values passed as script parameters to initialize the input.
5. Creates a new `InternetExplorer.Application` (IEA) object and stores it in the `objIe` variable.

NOTE

All this while, you have seen that the examples in this chapter have been using `Wscript.Echo` *to display the results. This script, however, uses the* `InternetExplorer.Application` *object (covered in Chapter 2) to display the enumerated results in an IE window. This is another method of displaying results. You can also write the results to a text file or an XML file instead, by using the* `Scripting.FileSystemObject` *or the MSXML DOM object. Alternatively, you can also create an MSHTA script that can also display results in an IE window.*

6. Navigates to a blank page.
7. Sets the properties (such as `StatusBar, Height, Left, Top`) of the IEA object.
8. Loops for the IEA object to completely load the IE window.
9. Makes the IE window visible to the user (see Figure 5.8).

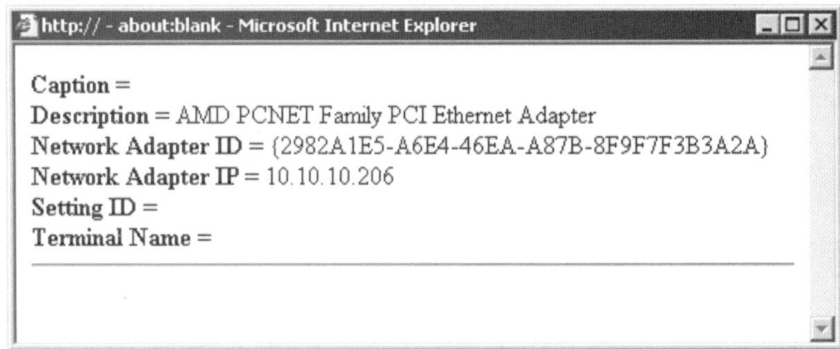

FIGURE 5.8 Network Adapter Settings displayed in an IE window.

10. Creates the `Swat.1.00` object and stores it in `objSwat` variable.
11. Initializes constants for the WMI authentication level.
12. Creates the WMI Services object.
13. Sets the `AuthenticationLevel` of the `Security_` property to `wbemAuthenticationLevelPkt`. This ensures that the connection to the remote system is encrypted.
14. Connects to the WMI TS provider using the `ConnectServer` method.
15. Gets instances of `Win32_TSNetworkAdapterListSetting` class.
16. For each instance in class, and for each property of the instance, writes individual property name and its value to the IE document.
17. Releases memory and ends.

Similar to the script in Listing 5.17 that lists the network adapter settings, the script in Listing 5.18 also displays the properties of the network adapter of the Terminal. Like the script in Listing 5.17, the script in Listing 5.18 also takes the same steps (as listed for

5.17 above) to accomplish the task. However, instead of calling the `Win32_TSNetworkAdapterListSetting` class, lists the properties of the `Win32_TSNetworkAdapterSetting` class.

LISTING 5.18 Enumerating Network Adapter Setting

```
<package>
 <job id="List Network Adapter Settings">
  <runtime>
     <named
       name="s"
       helpstring="Remote Server Name. Default=Localhost"
       type="string"
       required=false/>
     <named
       name="u"
       helpstring="User name for the remote computer.
                               Example: Domain\UserName"
       type="string"
       required=false/>
     <named
       name="p"
       helpstring="password for the remote user"
       type="string"
       required=false/>
  </runtime>
 <?job debug="true"?>
 <script language="vbscript">
  Option Explicit
  Dim sServer, sUser, sPassword
  Dim objWMI, objTsConnect
  Dim objSwat, objTsNetworkAdapters
  Dim item, prop
  Dim objIe, objDoc
  sServer = wscript.Arguments.Named("s")
    if sServer = "" then sServer = "."
     sUser = wscript.Arguments.Named("u")
       sPassword = wscript.Arguments.Named("p")
      Set objIe = CreateObject("InternetExplorer.Application")
        objIe.Navigate "about:blank"
          objIe.ToolBar = 0
            objIe.StatusBar = 0
            objIe.Height = 200
          objIe.Left = 0
        objIe.Top = 0
        Do While (objIe.Busy)
                Wscript.Sleep 200
        Loop
          objIe.Visible = 1
            set objDoc = objIe.document
```

```
            set objSwat = CreateObject("SWAT.1.00")
             CONST wbemAuthenticationLevelPkt = 4
              CONST WbemAuthenticationLevelPktPrivacy = 6
                set objWMI = CreateObject( _
                               "WbemScripting.SwbemLocator")
                 objWMI.Security_.AuthenticationLevel = _
                               wbemAuthenticationLevelPkt
                  Set objTsConnect = objWMI.ConnectServer( _
                                          sServer, _
                                            "root/CIMv2", _
                                               sUser, sPassword)
          set objTsNetworkAdapters = _
                       objTsConnect.InstancesOf( _
                               "Win32_TSNetworkAdapterSetting")
           for each item in objTsNetworkAdapters
               for each prop in item.properties_
                  objDoc.write _
                    "<b>" & objSwat.SplitOnCap(prop.name) & "</b>"_
                                     & " = " & prop.Value & "<br>"
               next
               objDoc.Write "<hr><br>"
           next
       Set objIe = nothing
      Set objDoc = nothing
     set objTsNetworkAdapters = nothing
    set objTsConnect = nothing
   set objWMI = nothing
  set objSwat = nothing
 </script>
 </job>
</package>
```

The scripts in Listing 5.17 and Listing 5.18 are same. Therefore both the scripts take the same steps to enumerate the settings. Except the script in Listing 5.17 calls `Win32_TSNetworkAdapterListSetting`*, and the script in Listing 5.18 calls the* `Win32_TSNetworkAdapterSetting`*. Therefore, to learn about the steps that the script in Listing 5.18 takes, see "The Script" section immediately following the script in Listing 5.17.*

The `Win32_TSNetworkAdapterSetting` class provides the properties and methods to manage the network adapter settings for the Terminal. The class exposes two (`SelectAllNetworkAdapters` and `SelectNetworkAdapterIP`) methods that you can call to either set the network adapter to select all network adapters or select a specific adapter based on the IP Address of a specific network adapter. The script shown in Listing 5.19 calls these methods to change the network adapter settings.

LISTING 5.19 Set Network Adapter Setting

```
<package>
 <job id="Get and Set Session Settings">
  <runtime>
     <named
       name="s"
       helpstring="Remote Server Name. Default=Localhost"
       type="string"
       required=false/>
     <named
       name="u"
       helpstring="User name for the remote computer.
                              Example: Domain\UserName"
       type="string"
       required=false/>
     <named
       name="p"
       helpstring="password for the remote user"
       type="string"
       required=false/>
     <named
       name="ip"
       helpstring="Network Adapter type. Example:
                       /ip:All
                       /ip:192.168.1.1"
       type="string"
       required=true/>
  </runtime>
 <?job debug="true"?>
 <script language="vbscript" src="helperfunctions.vbs">
  Option Explicit
  Dim sServer, sUser, sPassword, sIP
  Dim objWMI, objTsConnect, objNASettings
  Dim item
  sServer = wscript.Arguments.Named("s")
    if sServer = "" then sServer = "."
     sUser = wscript.Arguments.Named("u")
       sPassword = wscript.Arguments.Named("p")
        sIP = wscript.Arguments.Named("ip")
          if sIP = "" then
                Wscript.Arguments.ShowUsage
                Wscript.Quit(1)
          end if
             CONST wbemAuthenticationLevelPkt = 4
              CONST WbemAuthenticationLevelPktPrivacy = 6
       set objWMI = CreateObject("WbemScripting.SwbemLocator")
       objWMI.Security_.AuthenticationLevel = _
                                 wbemAuthenticationLevelPkt
         Set objTsConnect = objWMI.ConnectServer(sServer, _
                                            "root/CIMv2", _
                                          sUser, sPassword)
        Set objNASettings = _
```

```
                objTsConnect.InstancesOf( _
                        "Win32_TSNetworkAdapterSetting")
        For each item in objNASettings
            if lcase(item.TerminalName) <> "console" then
                if lcase(sIP) = "all" then
                        item.SelectAllNetworkAdapters
                else
                        itemp.SelectNetworkAdapterIP sIP
                end if
            end if
        Next
        Set objNASettings = nothing
      Set objTsConnect = nothing
     set objWMI = nothing
    set objSwat = nothing
 </script>
 </job>
</package>
```

The Script

The script in Listing 5.19 can be used to either enable all network adapters or a single adapter based on the provided IP Address. To set an adapter by IP Address, you must pass the IP Address as an argument. For example to set the network adapter to a network adapter with 192.168.1.1 IP Address, you can do the following:

1. Open a command prompt window (or the Start > Run window).
2. On the TS server type:

```
cscript /nologo SetNetworkAdapterSetting.wsf /c:192.168.1.1
```

3. Execute the command by pressing the `Enter` key.

The script will do the following to change the network adapter setting:

1. Creates the `Named` node to accept the following arguments:

   - `s` as name (or IP Address) of the TS server
   - `u` as the username to connect as the specified user
   - `p` as password for the username specified in `u` argument
   - `c` as the IP address argument (it can take a specific IP address or the key word `All`)

2. Includes `Option Explicit` statement to enforce variable declaration.
3. Declares required variables.
4. Retrieves the argument values passed as script parameters to initializes the input.

5. Initializes constants for the WMI authentication level.
6. Creates the WMI Services object.
7. Sets the `AuthenticationLevel` of the `Security_` property to `wbemAuthenticationLevelPkt`. This ensures that the connection to the remote system is encrypted.
8. Connects to the WMI TS provider using the `ConnectServer` method.
9. Gets instances of `Win32_TSNetworkAdapterSetting` class.
10. For each instance in class
    - Checks to ensure that the Terminal is not a console
    - Checks to see if the `All` keyword was passed (`LCase` function is used to convert the case to lowercase characters before comparison. This makes the argument case insensitive)
    - If the `All` keyword is passed as an argument
        - Calls the `SelectAllNetworkAdapters` method
    - If the `All` key word is not passed as an argument
        - Calls the `SelectNetworkAdapterIP` and passes the value (of `/c` argument) as an argument to the method
11. Releases memory and ends.

The Network Adapter tab also allows you to set the number of connections to unlimited or limit the number of connections to a specified number. However, the `Win32_NetworkAdapterSetting` does not provide a method to configure this setting.

You can, however, change the setting directly in the registry. To remotely change the registry, you can use the WMI Registry provider. The registry provider provides the `StdRegProv` class that exposes methods for managing the Windows registry. `StdRegProv` resides in the `Default` WMI namespace. You can use the `Get` method of the WMI services object to get an instance of the `StdRegProv` class.

The `MaxInstanceCount` value in the registry can be changed to change the connection count. It can be either set to a specified number or to `4294967295`. Setting it to `4294967295` sets the Terminal to accept an unlimited number of connections. The script in Listing 5.20 demonstrates how to set change registry to limit the number of connections.

The maximum number of connections can only be set if the TS is running in application mode. Changing the `MaxInstanceCount` value in the registry when TS is running in Administration mode or in RDP mode, will not enable more than two allowed sessions.

LISTING 5.20 Set Registry to Limit Maximum Connections for a Terminal

```
<package>
<job id="Get and Set Session Settings">
 <runtime>
```

```
    <named
      name="s"
      helpstring="Remote Server Name. Default=Localhost"
      type="string"
      required=false/>
    <named
      name="u"
      helpstring="User name for the remote computer.
                              Example: Domain\UserName"
      type="string"
      required=false/>
    <named
      name="p"
      helpstring="password for the remote user"
      type="string"
      required=false/>
    <named
      name="c"
      helpstring="Number of Connections"
      type="string"
      required=true/>
 </runtime>
<?job debug="true"?>
<script language="vbscript" src="helperfunctions.vbs">
 Option Explicit
 Dim sServer, sUser, sPassword, iMaxConnections
 Dim objWMI, objConnect, objReg
 Dim sKeyPath, sValueName
 sServer = wscript.Arguments.Named("s")
   if sServer = "" then sServer = "."
    sUser = wscript.Arguments.Named("u")
      sPassword = wscript.Arguments.Named("p")
       iMaxConnections = wscript.Arguments.Named("c")
         if iMaxConnections = "" then
               Wscript.Arguments.ShowUsage
               Wscript.Quit(1)
         end if
          CONST HKEY_LOCAL_MACHINE = &H80000002
          sKeyPath = "SYSTEM\CurrentControlSet\Control\" & _
                         "Terminal Server\WinStations\RDP-Tcp"
           sValueName = "MaxInstanceCount"
            CONST wbemAuthenticationLevelPkt = 4
             CONST WbemAuthenticationLevelPktPrivacy = 6
              set objWMI = CreateObject( _
                               "WbemScripting.SwbemLocator")
               objWMI.Security_.AuthenticationLevel = _
                               wbemAuthenticationLevelPkt
             Set objConnect = objWMI.ConnectServer(sServer, _
                                              "root/Default", _
                                              sUser, sPassword)
           Set objReg = _
                objConnect.Get("StdRegProv")
         objReg.SetDWORDValue HKEY_LOCAL_MACHINE, _
```

```
                                          sKeyPath, _
                                         sValueName, _
                                         iMaxConnections
        Set objReg = nothing
      Set objConnect = nothing
     set objWMI = nothing
 </script>
 </job>
</package>
```

The Script

When the script in Listing 5.20 is executed, it takes the following steps to change the number of connections in the registry:

1. Creates the `Named` node to accept the following arguments:
   - `s` as name (or IP Address) of the TS server
   - `u` as the username to connect as the specified user
   - `p` as password for the username specified in `u` argument
   - `c` as the maximum number of connections
2. Includes `Option Explicit` statement to enforce variable declaration.
3. Declares required variables.
4. Retrieves the argument values passed as script parameters to initialize the input.
5. Initializes the constant for the root of the `HKey_Local_Machine` hive.
6. Initializes the key path and the value (`MaxInstanceCount`).
7. Initializes constants for the WMI authentication level.
8. Creates the WMI Services object.
9. Sets the `AuthenticationLevel` of the `Security_` property to `wbemAuthenticationLevelPkt`. This ensures that the connection to the remote system is encrypted.
10. Connects to the WMI registry provider in `Root\Default` namespace.
11. Gets an instance of the `StdRegProv` class.
12. Calls the `SetDwordValue` method to set the `MaxInstanceCount` value passed as the parameter.
13. Releases memory and ends.

Permission Settings

By default all administrators and the members of the `Remote Desktop Users` group are granted permissions to connect to Terminal Services. You can view the current permissions and revoke or grant permissions to other groups and users from the TS configuration utility's Permissions tab. As an alternative, you can also create a script to automate these tasks.

Listing Permissions

You can view the permissions granted to the users and groups on the Permissions tab of the TS configuration utility. The same permissions can be listed by querying the `Win32_TSAccount` class. The class exposes properties that return the currently set permissions. The script in Listing 5.21 shows how to retrieve the values of the properties and list the current permissions of the Terminal.

LISTING 5.21 Listing Terminal Permissions

```
<package>
<job id="Get and Set Session Settings">
 <runtime>
    <named
      name="s"
      helpstring="Remote Server Name. Default=Localhost"
      type="string"
      required=false/>
    <named
      name="u"
      helpstring="User name for the remote computer.
                              Example: Domain\UserName"
      type="string"
      required=false/>
    <named
      name="p"
      helpstring="password for the remote user"
      type="string"
      required=false/>
 </runtime>
 <?job debug="true"?>
 <script language="vbscript" src="helperfunctions.vbs">
 Option Explicit
  Dim sServer, sUser, sPassword
  Dim objWMI, objTsConnect
  Dim objPermissionsSettings
  Dim item, prop, DispValue
  Dim sPropName, sPropValue
  Dim objSwat
  CONST wbemAuthenticationLevelPkt = 4
  CONST WbemAuthenticationLevelPktPrivacy = 6
   sServer = wscript.Arguments.Named("s")
    if sServer = "" then sServer = "."
     sUser = wscript.Arguments.Named("u")
      sPassword = wscript.Arguments.Named("p")
       Set objSwat = CreateObject("SWAT.1.00")
        set objWMI = CreateObject("WbemScripting.SwbemLocator")
         objWMI.Security_.AuthenticationLevel = _
                                wbemAuthenticationLevelPkt
         Set objTsConnect = objWMI.ConnectServer(sServer, _
                                        "root/CIMv2", _
                                        sUser, sPassword)
```

```
        Set objPermissionsSettings = _
                objTsConnect.InstancesOf("Win32_TSAccount")
         For each item in objPermissionsSettings
             if lcase(item.terminalname) <> "console" then
                For each prop in item.Properties_
                   sPropName = prop.Name
                   sPropValue = perm(prop.value)
                   DispValue = DispValue & VBNewLine & _
                   sPropName & " = " & spropvalue
                Next
             end if
           DispValue = Dispvalue & VbNewLine
         Next
       Wscript.Echo DispValue
      Set objPermissionsSettings = nothing
    Set objWMI = nothing
   Set objSwat = nothing
  </script>
 </job>
</package>
```

The Script

The script in Listing 5.21 can be used to list the current Terminal permissions. The script does the following to retrieve the permissions information:

1. Creates the `Named` node to accept the following arguments:
   - `s` as name (or IP Address) of the TS server
   - `u` as the username to connect as the specified user
   - `p` as password for the username specified in `u` argument
2. Includes `Option Explicit` statement to enforce variable declaration.
3. Declares required variables.
4. Retrieves the argument values passed as script parameters to initialize the input.
5. Creates the `Swat.1.00` object and stores it in `objSwat` variable.
6. Initializes constants for the WMI authentication level.
7. Creates the WMI Services object.
8. Sets the `AuthenticationLevel` of the `Security_` property to `wbemAuthentication-LevelPkt`. This ensures that the connection to the remote system is encrypted.
9. Connects to the WMI TS provider using the `ConnectServer` method.
10. Gets instances of `Win32_TSAccount` class.
11. For each instance in class
    - Checks to ensure that the Terminal is not a console
    - For each property of the class

- Gets the property name; formats it using the `SplitOnCap` method of `SWAT.1.00` common component
- Gets the value of the property. The script formats the value using the perm function defined in the helperfunctions.vbs script file. The perm function, at first, compares the value, passed as the argument to the function, with 983999 to identify if the user or the group has been granted Full Control. It then uses logical AND VBScript operator to identify individual permissions. It returns the cumulative permissions identified by the function.
- Adds the formatted property and value to the `DispValue` variable
- Adds an additional line as separator between permissions by adding `VBNewLine` character to the `DispValue` variable

12. Displays the accumulated permissions.
13. Releases memory and ends.

Deleting Permissions

The `Win32_Account` class also exposes the `Delete` method that can be used to delete an account from the Terminal Permissions. The method can be called to delete a user or a group account. The script in Listing 5.22 queries a specified server to retrieve and delete a specified account passed as an argument to the script.

LISTING 5.22 Delete Account from Terminal Permissions

```
<package>
<job id="Delete Account from Terminal Permissions">
 <runtime>
    <named
      name="s"
      helpstring="Remote Server Name. Default=Localhost"
      type="string"
      required=false/>
    <named
      name="u"
      helpstring="User name for the remote computer.
                            Example: Domain\UserName"
      type="string"
      required=false/>
    <named
      name="p"
      helpstring="password for the remote user"
      type="string"
      required=false/>
    <named
      name="TSAccount"
      helpstring="Terminal Server
account to delete. Example: MyDomain\MyUser"
```

```
        type="Boolean"
        required=true/>
   </runtime>
  <?job debug="true"?>
  <script language="vbscript">
   Option Explicit
   Dim sServer, sUser, sPassword, sTsAccount
   Dim objWMI, objTsConnect, objTsAccount
   Dim item, result
    sServer = wscript.Arguments.Named("s")
     if sServer = "" then sServer = "."
      sUser = wscript.Arguments.Named("u")
        sPassword = wscript.Arguments.Named("p")
         sTsAccount = wscript.Arguments.Named("tsaccount")
           if sTsAccount = "" then
                 Wscript.Arguments.ShowUsage
                 Wscript.Quit(1)
           end if
           CONST wbemAuthenticationLevelPkt = 4
           CONST WbemAuthenticationLevelPktPrivacy = 6
            On Error Resume Next
             set objWMI = CreateObject("WbemScripting.SwbemLocator")
               objWMI.Security_.AuthenticationLevel = _
                                          wbemAuthenticationLevelPkt
                 Set objTsConnect = objWMI.ConnectServer(sServer, _
                                                      "root/CIMv2", _
                                                     sUser, sPassword)
         Set objTsAccount = objTsConnect.ExecQuery( _
                         "Select * from Win32_TSAccount " & _
                                 "where accountname='" & _
                                 replace(sTsAccount,"\","\\") & "'")
          For each item in objTsAccount
             if lcase(item.terminalname) <> "console" then
                 item.delete
             end if
         Next
            Set objTsAccount = nothing
         Set objTsConnect = nothing
        Set objWMI = nothing
     </script>
    </job>
   </package>
```

The Script

When executing the script, the `AccountName` argument must be passed to the script. If the script is executed without the required parameter, it will display the script usage by calling the `Wscript.Arguments.Usage` statement. The `AccountName` argument is the account name that you want to revoke the permissions for. The argument must be passed in `Domain\User` format. For example, to delete `User1` account of `Domain1`, you can run the following command:

```
DeletePermissions /AccountName:Domain1\User1
```

To delete a local account, i.e., an account on the local system, you can use `ComputerName\AccountName`. To delete a builtin account such as the `Administrator` account, you must specify `builtin\Administrator` (built-in is a keyword that identifies that the account was created by the OS). You can run the `ListPermissions.wsf` script to view the existing permissions.

The script in Listing 5.22 takes the following steps to delete a specified account from the Terminal Permissions:

1. Creates the `Named` node to accept the following arguments:
   - `s` as name (or IP Address) of the TS server
   - `u` as the username to connect as the specified user
   - `p` as password for the username specified in `u` argument
   - `tsaccount` as the account name to delete
2. Includes `Option Explicit` statement to enforce variable declaration.
3. Declares required variables.
4. Retrieves the argument values passed as script parameters to initialize the input.
5. Checks to see if the `TsAccount` name argument was passed to the script. Displays the script syntax and quits.
6. Initializes constants for the WMI authentication level.
7. Creates the WMI Services object.
8. Sets the `AuthenticationLevel` of the `Security_` property to `wbemAuthenticationLevelPkt`. This ensures that the connection to the remote system is encrypted.
9. Connects to the WMI TS provider using the `ConnectServer` method.
10. Calls the `ExecQuery` method to retrieve the account object that matches the account name passed as the `TsAccount` argument.

Since the `\` is a reversed character, it must be escaped using an additional `\` character. The `Replace` command replaces the `\` with `\\` to include the escape character.

11. For each item in the collection (only one item is returned because of filtering in the select statement using the where clause)
    - Checks to see if the Terminal is not a console
    - Calls the `Delete` method to delete the account
12. Releases memory and exits.

Modifying Permissions

In addition to the `Delete` method, the `Win32_TSAccount` class also exposes the `ModifyPermissions` and `ModifyAuditPermissions` methods. The `ModifyPermissions` method can be used to associate a more granular permission set with the specified account. The `ModifyAuditPermissions` method can be called to set the audit permissions (`Success` or `Failure`) for a specified account. As the names of the methods state, both the `ModifyPermissions` and the `ModifyAuditPermissions` can be used to modify existing permissions (to add permissions for a new account, you must use the `AddAccount` method covered next in this chapter). Both the `ModifyPermissions` and `ModifyAuditPermissions` can set the permissions listed in Table 5.7.

TABLE 5.7 Permission Mask for `ModifyPermissions` and `ModifyAuditPermissions` Class

Permission	Value	Description
WINSTATION_QUERY	0	Permission to query information about a session
WINSTATION_SET	1	Permission to modify connection parameters
WINSTATION_LOGOFF	2	Permission to log off a user from a session
WINSTATION_VIRTUAL	3	Permission to use virtual channels
WINSTATION_SHADOW	4	Permission to shadow another user's session
WINSTATION_LOGON	5	Permission to log on to a session on the server
WINSTATION_MSG	7	Permission to send a message to another user's session
WINSTATION_CONNECT	8	Permission to connect to another session
WINSTATION_DISCONNECT	9	Permission to disconnect a session

NOTE

`WINSTATION_RESET` (value = 6) is not listed in the table because it is not supported in Windows 2003.

The permissions listed in Table 5.7 are the permissions that you can set for a specified account using a script, such as shown in Listing 5.23.

LISTING 5.23 Modify Permissions and Audit Permissions of a Terminal

```
<package>
<job id="Modify Terminal Permissions and Audit Permissions">
  <runtime>
     <named
       name="s"
       helpstring="Remote Server Name. Default=Localhost"
       type="string"
       required=false/>
     <named
```

```
        name="u"
        helpstring="User name for the remote computer.
                               Example: Domain\UserName"
        type="string"
        required=false/>
      <named
        name="p"
        helpstring="password for the remote user"
        type="string"
        required=false/>
      <named
        name="x"
        helpstring="Input Xml file"
        type="string"
        required=false/>
  </runtime>
 <?job debug="true"?>
 <script language="vbscript" src="helperfunctions.vbs">
  Option Explicit
  Dim sServer, sUser, sPassword, sXmlFile
  Dim objWMI, objTsConnect
  Dim objXml,Child, objXmlChild, objRoot
  CONST wbemAuthenticationLevelPkt = 4
  CONST WbemAuthenticationLevelPktPrivacy = 6
  sServer = wscript.Arguments.Named("s")
    if sServer = "" then sServer = "."
     sUser = wscript.Arguments.Named("u")
       sPassword = wscript.Arguments.Named("p")
        sXmlFile = wscript.Arguments.Named("x")
         if sXmlFile = "" then
                Wscript.Arguments.showusage
                Wscript.quit(1)
         end if
         set objWMI = CreateObject("WbemScripting.SwbemLocator")
           objWMI.Security_.AuthenticationLevel = _
                                   wbemAuthenticationLevelPkt
         Set objTsConnect = _
                      objWMI.ConnectServer(sServer, _
                                   "root/CIMv2", _
                                       sUser, sPassword)
           Set objXml = CreateObject("MSXML2.DomDocument")
              objXml.Async = false
                 objXml.Load sXmlFile
                   Set objRoot = objXml.SelectSingleNode("/MAIN")
                    for each child in objRoot.ChildNodes
                       Select Case child.nodename
                          Case "AUDIT"
                              SetPerms 0
                          Case "MODIFY"
                              SetPerms 1
                       End select
                   next
              set objRoot = nothing
```

```
        set objXmlChild = nothing
       Set objXml = nothing
  Set objTsConnect = nothing
 set objWMI = nothing
Sub SetPerms(v)
    Dim objPerms, objDict
    Dim sText, sNodeName
    Dim AccountName, ChildNode
    Dim item, Key
    Set objDict = CreateObject("Scripting.Dictionary")
    AccountName = child.GetAttribute("NAME")
    if AccountName = "" or isNull(AccountName) then exit Sub
    AccountName = trim(Replace(AccountName,"\","\\"))
    if Child.HasChildNodes then
       for each ChildNode in Child.ChildNodes
            sText = ChildNode.Text
            sNodeName = ChildNode.NodeName
            Select case sNodeName
               Case "QUERY" : sNodeName = 0
               Case "SET" : sNodeName = 1
               Case "LOGOFF" : sNodeName = 2
               Case "VIRTUAL" : sNodeName = 3
               Case "SHADOW" : sNodeName = 4
               Case "LOGON" : sNodeName = 5
               Case "MSG" : sNodeName = 7
               Case "CONNECT" : sNodeName = 8
               Case "DISCONNECT" : sNodeName = 9
            End Select
            if ChildNode.Text <> "" then
               Select Case Ucase(sText)
                 Case "DENY" : sText = 0
                 Case "ALLOW" : sText = 1
                 Case else : sText = 0
               End Select
              objDict.Add sNodeName, sText
            End if
        next
      Set objPerms = objTsConnect.ExecQuery( _
                   "Select * from Win32_TSAccount " & _
                           "where accountname='" & _
                             AccountName & "'")
      For each item in objPerms
        if lcase(item.terminalname) <> "console" then
            for each key in objDict.Keys
              Select Case v
               Case 0
                 item.ModifyAuditPermissions key, _
                                   objDict.Item(Key)
               Case 1
                 item.ModifyPermissions key, _
                                   objDict.Item(Key)
              End Select
            next
```

```
          end if
        Next
        Set objPerms = nothing
        Set objDict = nothing
      end if
    End Sub
 </script>
 </job>
</package>
```

The Script

The script in Listing 5.23 can be used to modify the permissions and the audit permissions of an existing account. It reads the permissions settings from the XML file passed as an argument to the script. The XML file has the following format:

```
<MAIN>
    <AUDIT NAME="">
            <QUERY></QUERY>
            <SET></SET>
            <VIRTUAL></VIRTUAL>
            <SHADOW></SHADOW>
            <LOGON></LOGON>
            <LOGOFF></LOGOFF>
            <MSG></MSG>
            <CONNECT></CONNECT>
            <DISCONNECT></DISCONNECT>
    </AUDIT>
    <MODIFY NAME="">
            <QUERY></QUERY>
            <SET></SET>
            <VIRTUAL></VIRTUAL>
            <SHADOW></SHADOW>
            <LOGON></LOGON>
            <LOGOFF></LOGOFF>
            <MSG></MSG>
            <CONNECT></CONNECT>
            <DISCONNECT></DISCONNECT>
    </MODIFY>
</MAIN>
```

The XML file has `<MAIN>` as the root node. The `<AUDIT>` and `<MODIFY>` nodes are the root nodes for the permissions and audit permissions settings. The `NAME` attribute of the nodes is used to specify the account name permissions which have to be modified. The `<QUERY>`, `<SET>`, `<VIRTUAL>`, `<SHADOW>`, `<LOGON>`, `<LOGOFF>`, `<MSG>`, `<CONNECT>`, and `<DISCONNECT>` nodes hold the *Allow* values of the *PermissionMask*. The *Allow* value can only have `Allow` or `Deny`. For example, if you want to grant the `QUERY` (`WINSTATION_QUERY`) permission to `Builtin\Administrators` group, you should set the `<QUERY>` node of `<MODIFY>` node as follows:

```
<MODIFY NAME="BUILTIN\Administrators">
<QUERY>allow</QUERY>
</MODIFY>
```

Similarly, if you want to enable auditing for the `Builtin\Administrators` group, you should set the `<QUERY>` node of `<AUDIT>` node as follows:

```
<AUDIT NAME="BUILTIN\Administrators">
<QUERY>allow</QUERY>
</AUDIT>
```

When the script is executed, it takes the following steps to modify the permissions and (or) the audit permissions of the Terminal:

1. Creates the `Named` node to accept the following arguments:
   - `s` as name (or IP Address) of the TS server
   - `u` as the username to connect as the specified user
   - `p` as password for the username specified in `u` argument
   - `x` as the input XML filename
2. Includes `Option Explicit` statement to enforce variable declaration.
3. Declares required variables and constants.
4. Retrieves the argument values passed as script parameters to initialize the input.
5. Checks to see if the XML filename was passed to the script. If the XML filename is not passed, the script displays the script syntax and quits.
6. Creates the WMI Services object.
7. Sets the `AuthenticationLevel` of the `Security_` property to `wbemAuthenticationLevelPkt`. This ensures that the connection to the remote system is encrypted.
8. Connects to the WMI TS provider using the `ConnectServer` method.
9. Creates MSXML `DOMDocument` object.
10. Loads the XML file into memory.
11. Selects the root node.
12. For each child node of the root node
    - If node name is `AUDIT`
      - Calls the `SetPerms` sub procedure and passes `0` (zero) as an argument
    - If the node name is `MODIFY`
      - Calls the `SetPerms` sub procedure and passes `1` (one) as an argument

13. `SetPerms` method when called:

    - Declares variables
    - Creates a dictionary object (the dictionary object is used to temporarily store the `PermissionMask` and its `Allow` value. The combination of the `PermissionMask` and the `Allow` (`1` = allowed, `0` = denied) is used to set the permissions and the audit permissions
    - Calls the `GetAttribute` method to read the account name for which the permission is to be set. It stores the retrieved value in the `AccountName` variable
    - Checks to see if the `AccountName` was passed. Exits the `SetPerms` sub procedure if the `AccountName` value is not passed or is `NULL`

14. Escapes the `\` character using the `Replace` method.
15. Verifies if the current node (`AUDIT` or `MODIFY`) has child nodes.
16. For each child node of the current node

    - Reads the text of the node
    - Reads the node name
    - Converts the `String` into corresponding `Integer` value (this is needed because the `ModifyPermissions` and `ModifyAuditPermissions` methods expect `PermissionMask` parameter to be `Integer` type). The type is converted as per the values shown in Table 5.7. For example, `QUERY` (`WINSTATION_QUERY`) `PermissionMask` is converted to `0` and `SET` (`WINSTATION_SET`) is converted to `1` and so on.
    - Converts the `Allow` permission `String` to `Integer` value (`DENY` = `0` and `ALLOW` = `1`)
    - Finally adds the `PermissionMask` and `Allow` integer values as the `Key`, `Value` combination to the dictionary object
    - Calls the `ExecQuery` method to retrieve the account object that matches the account name stored in the `AccountName` variable. Stores the returned collection as object in `objPerms` variable.
    - For each item in the collection
        - Checks to see if the terminal name is not Console
    - For each key in the dictionary
        - Calls `ModifyAuditPermissions` method if `0` is passed as an argument to the `SetPerms` sub procedure
        - Calls `ModifyPermissions` method if `1` is passed as an argument to the `SetPerms` sub procedure

17. Releases memory and exits `SetPerms` sub procedure.
18. Releases memory by setting object variables to nothing and ends.

Adding Permissions

Using the Terminal Services WMI provider you can also add accounts to the Terminal permission set. The `AddAccount` method of the `Win32_TSPermissionSetting` class can be used to grant permissions to the new accounts. The `AddAccount` method takes two arguments: `AccountName` and `PermissionPreSet`. The `AccountName` argument is the account that you want to add to the Terminal (for example, `MyDomain\User1`). The `PermissionPreSet` is the set of permissions to associate with the specified account. The `PermissionPreSet` can have any of the following three values shown in Table 5.8.

TABLE 5.8 Values of `PermissionPreSet` Argument

Value	Permission	Description
0	WINSTATION_GUEST_ACCESS	The account has Logon permission
1	WINSTATION_USER_ACCESS	The account has: Logon, Query, Message and Connect permissions
2	WINSTATION_ALL_ACCESS	The account has full permissions

The script in Listing 5.24 illustrates how to add or restore default permissions.

LISTING 5.24 Add a Specified Account to Terminal and Grant Permissions

```
<package>
 <job id="Add Permissions">
  <runtime>
     <named
       name="s"
       helpstring="Remote Server Name. Default=Localhost"
       type="string"
       required=false/>
     <named
       name="u"
       helpstring="User name for the remote computer.
                             Example: Domain\UserName"
       type="string"
       required=false/>
     <named
       name="p"
       helpstring="password for the remote user"
       type="string"
       required=false/>
     <named
       name="AccountName"
       helpstring="Terminal Server account to delete.
Example: MyDomain\MyUser"
       type="String"
```

```
      required=false/>
    <named
      name="Perm"
      helpstring="Account permissions to associate.
                  Options:Guest, User, Full
                  Default:User"
      type="String"
      required=false/>
 </runtime>
<?job debug="true"?>
<script language="vbscript">
 Option Explicit
 Dim sServer, sUser, sPassword
 Dim sAccountName, sPerm, bRestore
 Dim objWMI, objTsConnect, objTsAccount
 Dim item, iPermission
  sServer = wscript.Arguments.Named("s")
   if sServer = "" then sServer = "."
    sUser = wscript.Arguments.Named("u")
      sPassword = wscript.Arguments.Named("p")
       sAccountName = wscript.Arguments.Named("accountname")
        sPerm = wscript.Arguments.Named("perm")
         if sAccountName = "" then
               Wscript.Arguments.ShowUsage
               Wscript.Quit(1)
         end if
          Select Case ucase(sPerm)
            Case "GUEST"
               iPermission = 0
            Case "USER"
               iPermission = 1
            Case "FULL"
               iPermission = 2
            Case else
               iPermission = 1
          End Select
         CONST wbemAuthenticationLevelPkt = 4
         CONST WbemAuthenticationLevelPktPrivacy = 6
          On Error Resume Next
           set objWMI = CreateObject("WbemScripting.SwbemLocator")
             objWMI.Security_.AuthenticationLevel = _
                                   wbemAuthenticationLevelPkt
               Set objTsConnect = objWMI.ConnectServer(sServer, _
                                                 "root/CIMv2", _
                                                sUser, sPassword)
               Set objTsAccount = objTsConnect.ExecQuery( _
                    "Select * from Win32_TSPermissionsSetting")
        For each item in objTsAccount
               if lcase(item.TerminalName) <> "console" then
                 item.AddAccount sAccountName, iPermission
               end if
       Next
          Set objTsAccount = nothing
```

```
      Set objTsConnect = nothing
     Set objWMI = nothing
  </script>
 </job>
</package>
```

The Script

The script in Listing 5.24 adds a specified account (user or group) to the Terminal and associates specified permissions to the account. It takes the following steps to complete the task:

1. Creates the `Named` node to accept the following arguments:
   - `s` as name (or IP Address) of the TS server
   - `u` as the username to connect as the specified user
   - `p` as password for the username specified in `u` argument
   - `accountname` as the account name to add
   - `perm` as the permission set to add (`Guest`, `User`, and `Full`)
2. Includes `OptionExplicit` statement to enforce variable declaration.
3. Declares required variables.
4. Retrieves the argument values passed as script parameters to initialize the input.
5. Checks to see if the `AccountName` name argument was passed to the script. If the `AccountName` value is not passed then the script displays the script syntax and quits.
6. Initializes constants for the WMI authentication level.
7. Converts the permission set from string to integer value.
8. Declares authentication level constants.
9. Creates the WMI Services object.
10. Sets the `AuthenticationLevel` of the `Security_` property to `wbemAuthentication-LevelPkt`. This ensures that the connection to the remote system is encrypted.
11. Connects to the WMI TS provider using the `ConnectServer` method.
12. Queries the `Win32_TSPermissionSetting` class using the `ExecQuery` method.
13. For each item in collection
    - Checks to see if the Terminal is not a console
    - Calls the `AddAccount` method to add the specified account and associate the specified permission set
14. Releases memory and exits.

Restoring Default Permissions

The TS configuration utility can be used to restore the TS permissions to default permissions. The same can be accomplished by calling the `RestoreDefaults` method of the `Win32_TSPermissionSetting` class in a script, such as shown in Listing 5.25.

LISTING 5.25 Restore Default Permissions

```
<package>
<job id="Restore Default Permissions">
 <runtime>
    <named
      name="s"
      helpstring="Remote Server Name. Default=Localhost"
      type="string"
      required=false/>
    <named
      name="u"
      helpstring="User name for the remote computer.
                             Example: Domain\UserName"
      type="string"
      required=false/>
    <named
      name="p"
      helpstring="password for the remote user"
      type="string"
      required=false/>
 </runtime>
<?job debug="true"?>
<script language="vbscript">
 Option Explicit
 Dim sServer, sUser, sPassword
 Dim objWMI, objTsConnect, objTsAccount
 Dim item, Choice
  sServer = wscript.Arguments.Named("s")
   if sServer = "" then sServer = "."
    sUser = wscript.Arguments.Named("u")
      sPassword = wscript.Arguments.Named("p")
         CONST wbemAuthenticationLevelPkt = 4
         CONST WbemAuthenticationLevelPktPrivacy = 6
          On Error Resume Next
           set objWMI = CreateObject("WbemScripting.SwbemLocator")
             objWMI.Security_.AuthenticationLevel = _
                                  wbemAuthenticationLevelPkt
               Set objTsConnect = objWMI.ConnectServer(sServer, _
                                              "root/CIMv2", _
                                             sUser, sPassword)
               Set objTsAccount = objTsConnect.ExecQuery( _
                    "Select * from Win32_TSPermissionsSetting")
        For each item in objTsAccount
          if lcase(item.TerminalName) <> "console" then
            Choice = msgbox("Are you sure you want to " & _
                       "restore default permissions for " _
```

```
                                    & item.TerminalName, _
                                     VBCritical+VBYesNo, _
                                                "Confirm")
                    if Choice = VBYes then
                         item.RestoreDefaults
                    end if
                  end if
          Next
             Set objTsAccount = nothing
          Set objTsConnect = nothing
         Set objWMI = nothing
    </script>
  </job>
</package>
```

The Script

The script in Listing 5.25 when called will restore the settings of all the terminals besides the console terminal. To accomplish the task, the script takes the following steps:

1. Creates the `Named` node to accept the following arguments:
   - `s` as name (or IP Address) of the TS server
   - `u` as the username to connect as the specified user
   - `p` as password for the username specified in `u` argument
2. Includes `Option Explicit` statement to enforce variable declaration.
3. Declares required variables.
4. Retrieves the argument values passed as script parameters to initialize the input.
5. Initializes constants for the WMI authentication level.
6. Declares authentication level constants.
7. Creates the WMI Services object.
8. Sets the `AuthenticationLevel` of the `Security_` property to `wbemAuthenticationLevelPkt`. This ensures that the connection to the remote system is encrypted.
9. Connects to the WMI TS provider using the `ConnectServer` method.
10. Queries the `Win32_TSPermissionSetting` class using the `ExecQuery` method.
11. For each item in collection
    - Checks to see if the Terminal is not a console
    - Calls `Msgbox` function that prompts the user to confirm if the permissions for the Terminal should be restored
    - Calls the `RestoreDefaults` method if the user answers `Yes` to the confirm question
12. Releases memory and ends.

SUMMARY

This chapter covered Terminal Services automation and management. In this chapter you learned how to List Terminal Services configuration settings, how to change or add a TS connections license server, how to enable and disable Terminal connections and how to configure Terminal Properties that can be set using the TS configuration utility. You learned how to automate configuration of General Settings, Logon Settings, Session Settings, Environment Settings, Remote Control Settings, Client Settings, Network Adapter Settings, and Permission Settings. You also learned how to use XML files as an input settings file and how to read the nodes and attributes defined in the XML file. You also learned how to use the IE object to display information in an IE window.

This chapter covered the TS WMI provider which exposes various classes for Terminal Services automation. A complete reference of the Terminal Services WMI provider (the classes, properties, and methods of the TS WMI provider) is available at the MSDN site *http://msdn.microsoft.com/library/default.asp?url=/library/en-us/termserv/termserv/terminal_services_wmi_provider_reference.asp.*

In the next, and the final chapter, you will learn how to manage Windows Firewall that was included in Windows XP Service Pack 2.0 and Windows 2003 Service Pack 1.

6 Managing Windows Firewall

In This Chapter

- Enable and disable Windows Firewall
- Managing exceptions
- Enable and disable services
- Enabling and disabling ports
- Configuring ICMP settings

Needed for This Chapter

- Windows 2003 Server Service Pack 1
- Windows XP Service Pack 2
- Text editor

Before Reading This Chapter

- Read Chapter 2

In Windows 2003 Service Pack 1 and Windows XP Service Pack 2 Microsoft includes the Windows Firewall. If enabled, Windows Firewall can help protect your system by monitoring and restricting information that travels between computers and networks or the Internet. It does this by blocking unauthorized access to your system.

Windows Firewall can be managed either by using the GUI utility that is installed as a `Control Panel` applet, the `NetSH` command-line utility, Group Policies or through customized scripts. In this chapter you will learn about writing customized scripts for managing Windows Firewall.

Scripts for this chapter can be found in Scripts\Chapter06 on the CD-ROM.

ENABLING AND DISABLING FIREWALL

When you install Service Pack 1 on Windows 2003 or Service Pack 2 on Windows XP operating system, by default it installs the Windows Firewall (WFW). WFW allows you to block unauthorized applications and services from accessing the network or the Internet. It also allows you to define what and who is authorized to access your system from the network or the Internet.

Upon installation, WFW is enabled by default on Windows XP and disabled on Windows 2003. You can enable or disable WFW through the configuration utility included in the Control Panel. Alternatively, you can also write a script to enable and disable the firewall as shown in Listing 6.1.

LISTING 6.1 Enable and Disable Firewall

```
<package>
 <job>
  <runtime>
     <named
       name="enable"
       helpstring="Enable or Disable Firewall"
       type="boolean"
       required=true/>
   </runtime>
   <script Language="vbscript">
    Option Explicit
     Dim objFWmgr, objCurProfile, bEnabled
      bEnabled = wscript.Arguments.named("enable")
        if bEnabled = "" then
          Wscript.Arguments.ShowUsage
          Wscript.Quit(1)
        end if
       Set objFWmgr = CreateObject("HNetCfg.FWmgr")
        Set objCurProfile = objFWmgr.LocalPolicy.CurrentProfile
         if bEnabled and objCurProfile.FirewallEnabled then
            Wscript.Echo "Firewall already enabled"
         elseif Not bEnabled and objCurProfile.FirewallEnabled then
             objCurProfile.FirewallEnabled = false
             if Err <> 0 then
                Wscript.Echo Err.Number & ", " & Err.Description
             else
                Wscript.Echo "Firewall Disabled Successfully"
             end if
         elseif bEnabled and Not objCurProfile.FirewallEnabled then
             objCurProfile.FirewallEnabled = true
             if Err <> 0 then
                Wscript.Echo Err.Number & ", " & Err.Description
             else
                Wscript.Echo "Firewall Enabled Successfully"
             end if
         end if
```

```
      Set objCurProfile = nothing
     Set objFWmgr = nothing
  </script>
 </job>
</package>
```

The Script

The script in Listing 6.1 can be executed to enable or disable the WFW on the local computer. The script takes `enable+-` (+ = true, - = false) `Boolean` argument. The script enables the WFW if + (true) is passed as an argument and disables the WFW if – (false) is passed as an argument. The script displays the script syntax if the `/enable` argument is missing. To enable or disable the WFW, the script takes the following steps:

1. Creates the `Named` node to accept the following arguments:
   - enable as `Boolean` argument (+ will enable the WFW and – will disable the WFW)
2. Includes `Option Explicit` statement to enforce variable declaration.
3. Declares required variables.
4. Retrieves the argument values passed as script parameter.
5. Checks to ensure that the `enable` argument was passed. Displays the script usage and ends if the `enable` argument is not passed.
6. Creates the `HNetCfg.Fwmgr` WFW management object.
7. Retrieves the current WFW profile by retrieving the `LocalPolicy.CurrentProfile` property. Stores the retrieved object in `objCurProfile` variable.
8. If + is passed as the `enable` argument and the WFW is enabled, the script displays the `Firewall is already enabled` message.
9. If – is passed as the enable argument and the WFW is enabled, the script disables the WFW by setting the `FirewallEnabled` property to `False` and displays the `Firewall Enabled Successfully` message.
10. If + is passed and the firewall is currently disabled, the script enables the WFW by setting the `FirewallEnabled` property to `True` and displays the `Firewall Enabled Successfully` message.
11. If none of the conditions match, that is, if the WFW is currently disabled and – is passed as the argument, the script displays `Firewall is already disabled` message.
12. Releases memory and ends.

CONFIGURING EXCEPTION SERVICES

Remote Desktop, File and Print Sharing, and UPnP Framework services are added to the exception list of the WFW (as built-in services) when Service Pack 2 is installed on Windows XP and when Service Pack 1 is installed on Windows 2003.

By default WFW also adds and enables the Remote Assistance application to the exception list in Windows XP. That is, only the Remote Assistance application is allowed to communicate on the network or the Internet. All other applications and services, such as Remote Desktop service, File and Print Sharing service are blocked by default. These services can be enabled or disabled and configured from the Control Panel and also through a script such as shown in Listing 6.2.

LISTING 6.2 Enabling and Disabling and Configuring Built-in Services

```
<package>
 <job>
  <runtime>
     <named
       name="Service"
       helpstring="Service Name to enable or disable. Example: RDP"
       type="string"
       required=true/>
     <named
       name="enable"
       helpstring="Enable or Disable Service"
       type="boolean"
       required=true/>
     <named
       name="addresses"
       helpstring="Remote Addresses for the service (comma separated).
Default:*"
       type="boolean"
       required=false/>
     <named
       name="scope"
       helpstring="Scope of the Service. Options: All / Local. Default:All"
       type="string"
       required=false/>
   </runtime>
   <script Language="vbscript">
    Option Explicit
     Dim objFWmgr, objCurProfile, objService
     Dim sService, sScope, sRemoteAddresses, bEnabled
     Const FILE_AND_PRINT = 0
     Const UPNP = 1
     Const REMOTE_DESKTOP = 2
     Const SCOPE_ALL = 0
     Const SCOPE_LOCAL_SUBNET = 1
      bEnabled = wscript.Arguments.named("enable")
      sService = Wscript.Arguments.named("service")
```

```
            if bEnabled = "" or sService = "" then
              Wscript.Arguments.ShowUsage
              Wscript.Quit(1)
            end if
             sScope = Wscript.Arguments.named("scope")
              if sScope = "" then sScope = SCOPE_ALL
              sRemoteAddresses = wscript.Arguments.named("addresses")
               if sRemoteAddresses = "" then sRemoteAddresses = "*"
                Select Case ucase(sService)
                   Case "RDP"
                           sService = REMOTE_DESKTOP
                   Case "FP"
                           sService = FILE_AND_PRINT
                   Case "UPNP"
                           sService = UPNP
                 End Select
          Set objFWmgr = CreateObject("HNetCfg.FWmgr")
           Set objCurProfile = objFWmgr.LocalPolicy.CurrentProfile
              Set objService = objCurProfile.Services.Item(sService)
                   if bEnabled and objService.Enabled then
                     Wscript.Echo objService.Name & " is already enabled"
                   elseif bEnabled and Not objService.Enabled then
                     objService.Enabled = true
                      if Err <> 0 then
                       Wscript.Echo Err.Number & ", " & Err.Description
                      else
                       Wscript.Echo objService.Name & " enabled successfully"
                      end if
                   elseif Not bEnabled and objService.Enabled then
                     objService.Enabled = false
                      if Err <> 0 then
                       Wscript.Echo Err.Number & ", " & Err.Description
                      else
                       Wscript.Echo objService.Name & " disabled successfully"
                      end if
                   else
                       Wscript.Echo objService.Name & " is already disabled"
                   end if
                   objService.Scope = SScope
                   objService.RemoteAddresses = sRemoteAddresses
            Set objService = nothing
          Set objCurProfile = nothing
         Set objFWmgr = nothing
      </script>
    </job>
  </package>
```

The Script

The script in Listing 6.2 can enable or disable File and Print Sharing, Remote Desktop, and UPnP Framework services. It can also set the network scope by setting the `Scope` property and remote addresses by setting the `RemoteAddresses` property. To accomplish these tasks the script takes the following steps:

1. Creates the `Named` node to accept the following arguments:
   - `Service` as Service name to enable or disable (`RDP` = Remote Desktop, `FP` = File and Print Sharing, `UPNP` = UPnP Framework)
   - `enable` as `Boolean` argument (`+` will enable the WFW and – will disable the WFW)
   - `addresses` as remote addresses for the service (comma separated. `Default=*`)
   - `scope` as the scope of the service (`All` or `Local Subnet` only, `Default=All`)
2. Includes `Option Explicit` statement to enforce variable declaration.
3. Declares required variables and constants.
4. Retrieves the argument values passed as script parameter.
5. Checks to ensure that the `enable` and the `service` arguments were passed. Displays the script usage and ends if either of the arguments is not passed.
6. Sets defaults for the `Scope` and `RemoteAddresses` values.
7. Identifies the service type.
8. Creates the `HNetCfg.Fwmgr` WFW management object.
9. Retrieves the current WFW profile by retrieving the `LocalPolicy.CurrentProfile` property. Stores the retrieved object in `objCurProfile` variable.
10. Gets the specified service by calling the `Item` method.
11. If `+` is passed as the `enable` argument and the specified service is enabled, the script displays the `[Service Name] is already enabled` message.
12. If `+` is passed as the `enable` argument and the specified service is not enabled, the script enables the specified service by setting the `Enabled` property to `True` and displays the `[Service Name] Enabled Successfully` message.
13. If `-` is passed and the specified service is currently enabled, the script disables the service by setting the `Enabled` property to `False` and displays the `[Service Name] Disabled Successfully` message.
14. If none of the conditions match, that is, if the specified service is currently disabled and – is passed as the argument, the script displays `[Service Name] is already disabled` message.

NOTE

`[Service Name]` is substituted by the actual name of the service, such as File and Printer Sharing.

15. Changes the scope of the service.
16. Changes the Remote Addresses of the service.
17. Releases memory and ends.

CONFIGURING SERVICE PORT

Some services, such as the File and Print Sharing service allow communication on multiple built-in ports, such as 137, 138. These ports can be individually enabled or disabled through a script such as shown in Listing 6.3.

LISTING 6.3 Enabling and Disabling Service Ports and Changing Port Scope

```
<package>
 <job>
  <runtime>
     <named
       name="Service"
       helpstring="Service Name to enable or disable. Example: RDP"
       type="string"
       required=true/>
     <named
       name="enable"
       helpstring="Enable or Disable Service"
       type="boolean"
       required=false/>
     <named
       name="port"
       helpstring="Port of the service to enable or disable"
       type="string"
       required=true/>
     <named
       name="protocol"
       helpstring="Protocol of the Port. Options:UDP | TCP"
       type="string"
       required=true/>
     <named
       name="Addresses"
       helpstring="Remote addresses for Custom scope"
       type="string"
       required=false/>
     <named
       name="scope"
       helpstring="Scope of the Port of the specified service.
                   Options=Any|Local|Specific IPs"
       type="string"
       required=false/>
   </runtime>
   <script Language="vbscript">
    Option Explicit
     Dim objFWmgr, objCurProfile, objService, objPort
     Dim sService, sPort, bEnabled
     Dim sRemoteAddresses, sScope, sProtocol, port
     Const FILE_AND_PRINT = 0
     Const UPNP = 1
     Const REMOTE_DESKTOP = 2
     Const SCOPE_ANY = 0
```

```
Const SCOPE_LOCAL_SUBNET = 1
Const SCOPE_CUSTOM = 2
 bEnabled = wscript.Arguments.named("enable")
  sService = Wscript.Arguments.named("service")
   sPort = wscript.Arguments.named("port")
    sScope = Wscript.Arguments.named("scope")
     sProtocol = wscript.Arguments.named("protocol")
      sRemoteAddresses = wscript.Arguments.named("addresses")
      if sService = "" or sPort = "" or sProtocol = "" then
          Wscript.Arguments.ShowUsage
         Wscript.Quit(1)
      end if
       Select Case ucase(sProtocol)
           Case "UDP"
                   sProtocol = 17
           Case "TCP"
                   sProtocol = 6
        End Select
        Select Case UCase(sScope)
           Case "ANY"
                   sScope = SCOPE_ANY
           Case "LOCAL"
                   sScope = SCOPE_LOCAL_SUBNET
           Case "CUSTOM"
                   sScope = SCOPE_CUSTOM
                   if sRemoteAddresses = "" then
                     Wscript.Echo "Remote Addresses " & _
                                    "must be specified" & _
                                    " for Custom scope"
                     Wscript.Arguments.ShowUsage
                     Wscript.Quit(1)
                   end if
         End Select
         Select Case ucase(sService)
           Case "RDP"
                   sService = REMOTE_DESKTOP
           Case "FP"
                   sService = FILE_AND_PRINT
           Case "UPNP"
                   sService = UPNP
          End Select
  Set objFWmgr = CreateObject("HNetCfg.FWmgr")
    Set objCurProfile = objFWmgr.LocalPolicy.CurrentProfile
     Set objService = objCurProfile.Services.Item(sService)
       Set objPort = objService.GloballyOpenPorts
         for each port in objPort
          if port.port = cint(sPort) and _
                     port.Protocol = cint(sProtocol) then
           if bEnabled <> "" then
              EnableDisablePort
           end if
           if sScope = SCOPE_CUSTOM then
               port.RemoteAddresses = sRemoteAddresses
```

```
                else
                  if port.Scope <> sScope and sScope <> "" then
                    port.Scope = sScope
                    Wscript.echo "Scope changed successfully"
                  end if
                end if
              end if
            next
        Set objPort = nothing
      Set objService = nothing
    Set objCurProfile = nothing
  Set objFWmgr = nothing
  Sub EnableDisablePort
     if bEnabled and port.enabled then
       Wscript.Echo  Port.Name & " is already enabled"
     elseif bEnabled and Not Port.Enabled then
       Port.Enabled = true
       if Err <> 0 then
        Wscript.Echo Err.Number & ", " & Err.Description
       else
        Wscript.Echo  Port.Name & " enabled successfully"
       end if
     elseif Not bEnabled and Port.Enabled then
       Port.Enabled = false
       if Err <> 0 then
        Wscript.Echo Err.Number & ", " & Err.Description
       else
        Wscript.Echo  Port.Name & " disabled successfully"
       end if
     else
        Wscript.Echo  Port.Name & " is already disabled"
     end if
  End Sub
</script>
</job>
</package>
```

The Script

The script in Listing 6.3 can enable and disable the ports of a specified service. For example, the following command will disable 137 (UDP) port of the File and Print Sharing service:

```
ServicePorts /service:fp /port:137 /protocol:udp /enable
```

The script in Listing 6.3 can also change the port scope of a specified service. For example, the following command will change the scope of the port to custom scope with `10.10.10.0` network as the remote address:

```
ServicePorts /service:fp /port:137 /protocol:udp /scope:custom
/addresses:10.10.10.0
```

To enable and disable ports of a specified service and change the scope of the port of a specified service, the script in Listing 6.3 takes the following steps:

1. Creates the `Named` node to accept the following arguments:
   - `Service` as Service name to enable or disable (`RDP` = Remote Desktop, `FP` = File and Print Sharing, `UPNP` = UPnP Framework)
   - enable as `Boolean` argument (+ will enable the WFW and – will disable the WFW)
   - `port` as the port number of the specified service
   - `protocol` as the protocol (TCP or UDP) assigned to the port
   - `addresses` as remote addresses for the service (comma separated); required for `Custom` scope only.
   - `scope` as the scope of the service (`Any` or `Local` or `Custom`)
2. Includes `Option Explicit` statement to enforce variable declaration.
3. Declares required variables and constants.
4. Retrieves the argument values passed as script parameter.
5. Checks to see if the `service`, `port`, and `protocol` arguments were passed to the script; displays script usage and ends if either of the arguments is not passed.
6. Converts `protocol` argument from string to integer type.
7. Converts the `scope` argument from string to integer type.
8. Converts `service` argument from string to integer type.
9. Creates the `HNetCfg.Fwmgr` WFW management object.
10. Retrieves the current WFW profile by retrieving the `LocalPolicy.CurrentProfile` property. Stores the retrieved object in `objCurProfile` variable.
11. Gets the specified service item and stores it as object in `objService` variable.
12. Gets the `Globally Open Ports` of the specified service and stores it as object in `objPort` variable.
13. For each port in ports collection (`objPort`).
    - Checks to see if the port and protocol match with the passed arguments
    - Checks to see if the `enable` argument was passed
    - If the `enable` was passed, calls `EnableDisablePort` sub procedure
    - The `EnableDisablePort` sub procedure does the following:
      - If `enable` argument is `True` and the port is currently enabled
        - Display message that the port is already enabled
      - Else if the `enable` argument is `True` and the port is disabled
        - Enable the port
        - Display `[Port Name] enabled successfully`

    - Else if the `enable` argument is `False` and the port is enabled
        - Disable the port
        - Display `[Port Name] disabled successfully`
    - If no conditions match, that is, the service is disabled and the `enable` argument is `False`
        - Display `[Port Name] is already disabled` message
    - Exit sub procedure
- Check if `scope` argument is custom
    - If custom
        - Call `RemoteAddresses` method to set the custom addresses
    - If the port scope is not the same as the `scope` argument and the `scope` argument is not empty
        - Change the scope by setting the `Scope` property
        - Display `Scope change successfully` message

14. Releases memory and ends.

LISTING EXCEPTION SERVICES AND SERVICES CONFIGURATION

Current configuration settings for Remote Desktop, File and Print Sharing, and UPnP Framework services can also be listed using a script such as shown in Listing 6.4.

Unlike the other scripts in this chapter, this script is an HTML Application (HTA) script that displays the information in an HTML window. HTAs allow you to create a script that can be formatted for a better display using the HTML tags. In this script, the `<TABLE>` tag is used to create a table with a header for the services and their settings. The same script can be written in WSF or VBS file format if you need to display the properties in a command window. You can also convert the script to use the IE object (see Listing 5.17, Chapter 5) to display the results in an HTML window. See Chapter 2 to learn more about Microsoft HTML Applications .

LISTING 6.4 Listing Exception Services and Services Configuration

```
<HTML>
<HEAD>
    <TITLE>List Services and Settings</TITLE>
</HEAD>
<BODY>
    <TABLE BORDER=0 CELLSPACING=1 CELLPADDING=1 BGCOLOR=#EEEEEE WIDTH=100% >
    <TR>
        <TH><FONT SIZE=2>NAME</FONT></TH>
        <TH><FONT SIZE=2>ENABLED</FONT></TH>
```

```
            <TH><FONT SIZE=2>CUSTOMIZED</FONT></TH>
            <TH><FONT SIZE=2>OPEN PORTS</FONT></TH>
            <TH><FONT SIZE=2>IP VERSION</FONT></TH>
            <TH><FONT SIZE=2>REMOTE ADDRESSES</FONT></TH>
            <TH><FONT SIZE=2>SCOPE</FONT></TH>
            <TH><FONT SIZE=2>TYPE</FONT></TH>
        </TR>
<Script language="vbscript">
 Dim objFWmgr, objCurProfile
   Set objFWmgr = CreateObject("HNetCfg.FWmgr")
    Set objCurProfile = objFWmgr.LocalPolicy.CurrentProfile
          for each service in objCurProfile.Services
            sName = UCase(Service.Name)
            bEnabled = Service.Enabled
            for each Port in Service.GloballyOpenPorts
                sGloballyOpenPorts = sGloballyOpenPorts _
                                   & "," & Port.Port
            next
                sGloballyOpenPorts = right(sGloballyOpenPorts,_
                                          Len(sGloballyOpenPorts) -1)
                sIPVersion = GetIpVersion(Service.IpVersion)
                sRemoteAddresses = Service.RemoteAddresses
                sScope = GetServiceScope(Service.Scope)
                sType = GetServiceType(Service.Type)
                    Document.Write  "<TR BGCOLOR=#ffffff>" & _
                                "<TD><font size=2>" & _
                                        sName & "</font></TD>" & _
                                "<TD><font size=2>" & _
                                        bEnabled & "</font></TD>" & _
                                "<TD><font size=2>" & _
                                        bCustomized & "</font></TD>" & _
                                "<TD><font size=2>" & _
                                        sGloballyOpenPorts & _
                                                "<font></TD>" & _
                                "<TD><font size=2>" & _
                                        sIpVersion & "</font></TD>" & _
                                "<TD><font size=2>" & _
                                        sRemoteAddresses & "</font></TD>" & _
                                "<TD><font size=2>" & _
                                        sScope & "</font></TD>" & _
                                "<TD><font size=2>" & _
                                        sType & "</font></TD></TR>"
     next
   Set objCurProfile = nothing
  Set objFWmgr = nothing
  Function GetServiceScope(s)
    Select Case s
        Case 0
            GetServiceScope = "All"
        Case 1
            GetServiceScope = "Local Subnet"
        Case 2
            GetServiceScope = "Custom"
```

```
            Case 3
                GetServiceScope = "MAX"
            Case else
                GetServiceScope = s
        End Select
    End Function
    Function GetServiceType(t)
        Select Case t
            Case 0
                GetServiceType = "File and Print Sharing"
            Case 1
                GetServiceType = "UPnP Framework"
            Case 2
                GetServiceType = "Remote Desktop"
            Case 3
                GetServiceType = "None"
            Case 4
                GetServiceType = "MAX"
            Case else
                GetServiceType = t
      End Select
    End Function
    Function GetIpVersion(v)
      Select Case v
            Case 0
                    GetIpVersion = "IPv4"
            Case 1
                    GetIpVersion = "IPv6"
            Case 2
                    GetIpVersion = "ANY"
            Case 3
                    GetIpVersion = "MAX"
            Case else
                    GetIpVersion = v
      End Select
    End Function
</script>
</TABLE>
</BODY>
</HTML>
```

The Script

The script in Listing 6.4 enumerates the services, retrieves the services configuration, and displays it in an HTML window. To do this, the script takes the following steps:

1. Declares the <HTML> top level tag.
2. Defines the title of the html page.
3. Starts a new HTML table (<TABLE> tag).
4. Writes the headers for the columns.

5. Starts the `<script>` tag for writing VBScript code.
6. Declares variables.
7. Creates an `HNetCfg.FWmgr` WFW management object and stores it in the `objFWmgr` variable.
8. Retrieves the current WFW profile by retrieving the `LocalPolicy.CurrentProfile` property. Stores the retrieved object in `objCurProfile` variable.
9. For each service in services of the current profile
   - Retrieves `Name` property and converts the name to upper case.
   - Retrieves the `Enabled` property.
   - Retrieves the collection of open ports.
     - For each port in the collection, the script retrieves and appends the `Port` property to `sGlopballyOpenPorts` variable. It separates the port numbers by a comma
   - Cleans the port list by removing the prefixed comma. Calls the `Right` VBScript method to remove the first character (prefixed comma) and stores the result back into `sGlopballyOpenPorts`.
   - Retrieves the `IPVersion` property of the service. Formats it to string by calling the `GetIpVersion` custom function.
   - Retrieves the `Scope` property of the service. Formats it to string by calling the `GetServiceScope` custom function.
   - Retrieves the `Type` property of the service. Formats it to string by calling the `GetServiceType` custom function.
   - Writes the formatted table information about the service to the document.
10. Releases memory.
11. Closes the `<script>` tag.
12. Closes the `<TABLE>`, `<BODY>`, and `<HTML>` tags and ends.

LISTING AUTHORIZED APPLICATIONS

Similar to enumerating the list of services, you can also enumerate the list of authorized applications by retrieving the collection of authorized applications from the `AuthorizedApplications` property of the `HNetCfg.FWmgr` WFW manager. The HTA script in Listing 6.5 retrieves and displays the authorized application information in an HTML format similar to the script in Listing 6.4.

LISTING 6.5 Enumerating and Displaying Authorized Applications

```
<HTML>
<HEAD>
    <TITLE>List Authorized Applications and Settings</TITLE>
```

```
</HEAD>
<BODY>
    <TABLE BORDER=0 CELLSPACING=1 CELLPADDING=1 BGCOLOR=#EEEEEE WIDTH=100% >
    <TR>
        <TH><FONT SIZE=2>NAME</FONT></TH>
        <TH><FONT SIZE=2>ENABLED</FONT></TH>
        <TH><FONT SIZE=2>IMAGE FILE NAME</FONT></TH>
        <TH><FONT SIZE=2>IP VERSION</FONT></TH>
        <TH><FONT SIZE=2>REMOTE ADDRESSES</FONT></TH>
        <TH><FONT SIZE=2>SCOPE</FONT></TH>
    </TR>
<Script language="vbscript">
 Dim objFWmgr, objCurProfile
   Set objFWmgr = CreateObject("HNetCfg.FWmgr")
    Set objCurProfile = objFWmgr.LocalPolicy.CurrentProfile
          for each App in objCurProfile.AuthorizedApplications
            sName = UCase(App.Name)
             bEnabled = App.Enabled
              sImageFileName = App.ProcessImageFileName
               sIPVersion = GetIpVersion(App.IpVersion)
                sRemoteAddresses = App.RemoteAddresses
                  sScope = GetAppScope(App.Scope)
                    Document.Write  "<TR BGCOLOR=#ffffff>" & _
                                "<TD><font size=2>" & _
                                        sName & "</font></TD>" & _
                                "<TD><font size=2>" & _
                                        bEnabled & "</font></TD>" & _
                                "<TD><font size=2>" & _
                                        sImageFileName & "</font></TD>" & _
                                "<TD><font size=2>" & _
                                        sIpVersion & "</font></TD>" & _
                                "<TD><font size=2>" & _
                                        sRemoteAddresses & "</font></TD>" & _
                                "<TD><font size=2>" & _
                                        sScope & "</font></TD></TR>"
                next
   Set objCurProfile = nothing
  Set objFWmgr = nothing
  Function GetAppScope(s)
    Select Case s
        Case 0
            GetAppScope = "All"
        Case 1
            GetAppScope = "Local Subnet"
        Case 2
            GetAppScope = "Custom"
        Case 3
            GetAppScope = "MAX"
        Case else
            GetAppScope = s
    End Select
 End Function
 Function GetIpVersion(v)
```

```
    Select Case v
         Case 0
                 GetIpVersion = "IPv4"
         Case 1
                 GetIpVersion = "IPv6"
         Case 2
                 GetIpVersion = "ANY"
         Case 3
                 GetIpVersion = "MAX"
         Case else
                 GetIpVersion = v
    End Select
  End Function
</script>
</TABLE>
</BODY>
</HTML>
```

The Script

The script in Listing 6.5 enumerates the services, retrieves the services configuration, and displays it in an HTML window. To do this, the script takes the following steps:

1. Declares the `<HTML>` top level tag.
2. Defines the title of the html page.
3. Starts a new HTML table (`<TABLE>` tag).
4. Writes the headers for the columns.
5. Starts the `<script>` tag for writing VBScript code.
6. Declares variables.
7. Creates an `HNetCfg.FWmgr` WFW management object and stores it in the `objFWmgr` variable.
8. Retrieves the current WFW profile by retrieving the `LocalPolicy.CurrentProfile` property. Stores the retrieved object in the `objCurProfile` variable.
9. For each application in authorized applications of the current profile

   - Retrieves `Name` property and converts the name to uppercase.
   - Retrieves the `Enabled` property of the application.
   - Retrieves Process Image File Name (path to the program file and its name. For example: `C:\WINDOWS\system32\sessmgr.exe` for `Remote Assistance` program) of the application.
   - Retrieves the `IPVersion` property of the application. Formats it to string by calling the `GetIpVersion` custom function.
   - Retrieves the `RemoteAddresses` property of the application.
   - Retrieves the `Scope` property of the application. Formats it to string by calling the `GetAppScope` custom function.
   - Writes the formatted table information about the application to the document.

10. Releases memory.
11. Closes the <script> tag.
12. Closes the <TABLE>, <BODY>, and <HTML> tags and ends.

ADDING AND REMOVING APPLICATION FROM EXCEPTION LIST

Besides using the WFW manager object (`HNetCfg.FWmgr`) to view the applications and services, you can also add and remove applications from the WFW exception list as the script in Listing 6.6 demonstrates. The script in Listing 6.6 can be used both for removing and adding new applications to the WFW exceptions list. The information about the application to add or remove can be passed as arguments to the script on the command line.

LISTING 6.6 Adding and Removing Application from Exception List

```
<package>
<job>
 <runtime>
    <named
      name="Action"
      helpstring="Add or Remove action. Options:A|R"
      type="string"
      required=false/>
    <named
      name="IFName"
      helpstring="Image file name. for
example:C:\WINDOWS\system32\sessmgr.exe"
      type="string"
      required=true/>
    <named
      name="AppName"
      helpstring="Application name. Example:Remote Assistance"
      type="string"
      required=true/>
    <named
      name="enable"
      helpstring="Enable or disable the application."
      type="boolean"
      required=false/>
    <named
      name="IPVersion"
      helpstring="IP Version. Options:IPV6|IPV4|ANY"
      type="string"
      required=false/>
    <named
      name="Addresses"
```

```
     helpstring="Remote Addresses (comma delimited list)."
     type="string"
     required=false/>
   <named
     name="Scope"
     helpstring="Scope of the application. Options:Any|Local|Custom"
     type="string"
     required=false/>
 </runtime>
 <script Language="vbscript">
  Option Explicit
  Dim sAction, sImageFileName, sAppName, bEnabled
  Dim sIPVersion, sRemoteAddresses, sScrope, sXmlFile
  Dim objFWmgr, objAuthApp
   sAction = wscript.Arguments.named("action")
      if sAction = "" then
        Wscript.Arguments.ShowUsage
        Wscript.Quit(1)
      else
        if UCase(sAction) = "A" then
              bAction = true
        else
              bAction = false
        end if
      end if
      sAppName = Wscript.Arguments.named("appname")
       sImageFileName = Wscript.Arguments.named("ifname")
        sIPVersion = Wscript.Arguments.named("ipversion")
         sAddresses = Wscript.Arguments.named("addresses")
          sScope = Wscript.Arguments.named("scope")
   Set objFWmgr = CreateObject("HNetCfg.FWmgr")
    Set objCurProfile = objFWmgr.LocalPolicy.CurrentProfile
      if bAction then
          if sImageFileName = "" or sAppName = "" then
              Wscript.Echo "You must provide " & _
                           "the Application name " & _
                           "and the Image file name " & _
                           "in the A action mode"
              Wscript.arguments.ShowUsage
              Wscript.quit(1)
           else
              if sScope <> "" then
                Select Case UCase(sScope)
                  Case "ANY"
                   sScope = SCOPE_ANY
                  Case "LOCAL"
                   sScope = SCOPE_LOCAL_SUBNET
                  Case "CUSTOM"
                   sScope = SCOPE_CUSTOM
                    if sRemoteAddresses = "" then
                      Wscript.Echo "Remote Addresses " & _
                                   "must be specified" & _
                                     " for Custom scope"
```

```
                    Wscript.Arguments.ShowUsage
                    Wscript.Quit(1)
                   end if
                End Select
             end if
         end if
      Set objAuthApp = CreateObject("HNetCfg.FWAuthorizedApplication")
      objAuthApp.Name = sAppName
      objAuthApp.ProcessImageFileName = sImageFileName
      if sIPVersion <> "" then
            Select Case UCase(sIPVersion)
               Case "IPV4"
                    sIPVersion = 0
               Case "IPV6"
                    sIPVersion = 1
               Case "ANY"
                    sIPVersion = 2
               Case "MAX"
                    sIPVersion = 3
            End Select
            objAuthApp.sIPVersion = sIPVersion
      end if
      if sScope <> "" then
            if sScope = SCOPE_CUSTOM then
               objAuthApp.RemoteAddresses = sRemoteAddresses
            else
               objAuthApp.Scope = sScope
            end if
      end if
      if bEnabled <> "" then
        if not bEnabled then objAuthApp.Enabled = false
      end if
        objCurProfile.AuthorizedApplications.Add objAuthApp
          if Err <> 0 then
            Wscript.Echo Err.NUmber & ", " & Err.Description
          else
            Wscript.Echo sAppName & " added successfully."
          end if
    else
         if sAppName = "" then
            Wscript.Echo "You must provide " & _
                         "the Application name " & _
                         "in the R action mode"
            Wscript.Quit(1)
          end if
      for each App in objCurProfile.AuthorizedApplications
       if UCase(App.Name) = UCase(sAppName) then
            objCurProfile.AuthorizedApplications.Remove _
App.ProcessImageFileName
            if Err <> 0 then
              Wscript.Echo Err.Number & ", " & Err.Description
            else
              bFound = true
```

```
            end if
        end if
       next
       if bFound then
         Wscript.Echo sAppName & " removed from the exception list."
       end if
     end if
     Set objAuthApp = nothing
   Set objFWmgr = nothing
  </script>
 </job>
</package>
```

The Script

The script in Listing 6.6 can perform an `A` (add) or `R` (remove) action. When run in `A` action mode, the script can be used to add applications to the WFW exceptions list. For example, to add the Microsoft Anti Spyware application to the exception list, so that it can connect to the internet to get updates, you can run the following command:

```
AddRemoveExceptions.wsf /action:A /appname:"Microsoft Anti Spyware"
/ifname:"C:\Program Files\Microsoft AntiSpyware\GIANTAntiSpywareMain.exe"
```

The script expects at the minimum `Action`, `AppName`, and `IFName` (`Process Image File Name`) arguments when run in `A` mode. The other arguments—`IPVersion`, `Enable`, `Addresses`, and `Scope`—are optional arguments that when omitted, as in the above example, inherit the default settings. For example, when the `Enable` argument is empty, the application is enabled by default when added to the exception list.

When run in `R` action mode, the script runs to remove an application from the WFW exception list. In `R` mode the script expects only the `Action` and the `AppName` arguments. For example, to remove the Microsoft Anti Sypware application from the exception list, you can run the following command:

```
AddRemoveExceptions.wsf /action:R /appname:"Microsoft Anti Spyware"
```

The `AppName` argument is not case sensitive, that is, to remove Microsoft AntiSpyware application, you can pass `Microsoft anti spyware` as the `AppName` argument. The script will convert the `AppName` to all uppercase characters before comparison.

To Add and Remove the applications from the exception list, the script does the following:

1. Creates the `Named` nodes to accept the following arguments:
   - `Action` as Add or Remove action to perform
   - `IFName` as the Image File Name (for example, `%windir%\system32\notepad.exe`)

- `AppName` as the application name for the Image File Name
- `Enable` as `Boolean` argument (+ will enable the WFW and – will disable the WFW)
- `IPVersion` as IP Version setting for the application (Options: `Any|IPV4|IPV6`)
- `addresses` as remote addresses for the application (comma separated)
- `scope` as the scope of the application (`Any` or `Local` or `Custom`)

2. Includes `Option Explicit` statement to enforce variable declaration.
3. Declares required variables and constants.
4. Retrieve the `Action` argument.
5. Check to see if the `Action` argument was passed. If passed set the `bAction` mode variable (`True` for Add and `False` for remove) else display message and end the script.
6. Retrieves the argument values passed as script parameter.
7. Creates an `HNetCfg.FWmgr` WFW management object and stores it in the `objFWmgr` variable.
8. Retrieves the current WFW profile by retrieving the `LocalPolicy.CurrentProfile` property. Stores the retrieved object in `objCurProfile` variable.
9. If `bAction` is set to `True`.

- Check to see that the `IFName` and `AppName` arguments were passed. Display message and end the script if either of the arguments was not passed.
- If the arguments were passed
  - Initialize the `Scope` setting if the `Scope` argument was passed.
  - If the `Scope` is custom, check to see that the `Addresses` argument was passed. Display message and end if not passed.
- Create `HNetCfg.FWAuthorizedApplication` application object (used for setting the properties of the new application being added) and store the object in `objAuthApp` variable.
- Pass `sAppName` (`AppName` argument) to the `Name` property.
- Pass `sImageFileName` (`IFName` argument) to the `ProcessImageFileName` property.
- Check to see if the `IPVersion` argument was passed.
  - Convert the `IPVersion` string value to integer value that is acceptable to the `IPVersion` property of the application.
  - Pass the `sIPVersion` (`IPVersion` argument) to the `IPVersion` property.
- Check to see if the `Scope` argument was passed.
  - Check to see if the `Scope` argument is `Custom` type.
    - If `Custom`
    - Pass the `sRemoteAddresses` (`Addresses` argument) to the `RemoteAddresses` property.

    - If not `Custom`
    - Pass `sScope` (`Scope` argument) to the `Scope` property.
- Pass the `bEnabled` (`Enable` argument) to the `Enabled` property if the `Enable` argument was passed.
- Call the `Add` method of the `AuthorizedApplications` of the current profile. Pass the `FWAuthorizedApplication` object (`objAuthApp`) to the method.
- If there was an error adding the application, display the error message else display a success message.

10. If `bAction` is `False`

- Loop through all authorized applications.
- If the Authorized Application name matches the `AppName` argument
    - Call the `Remove` method of the `AuthorizedApplications` of the current profile to remove the application from the exception list. Pass the Image File Name to the remove method.
    - If there is an error removing the application, display the error message else set the `bFound` variable to True.
- Display the Success message if `bFound` variable is True.

11. Release memory and end.

NOTE

The `UCase` function is used to convert both the Application name returned by the `App.Name` property and the `AppName` argument. As a result, the `AppName` argument is not case sensitive.

TURNING OFF EXCEPTIONS

Most times you would want to allow exceptions in WFW. However, if for any reason you decide not to allow exceptions in WFW (for example, when you are connected to an unsecured network), WFW allows you to turn off the exceptions. When the exceptions are turned off, the authorized applications on the exception list are ignored and treated as not authorized applications and services.

It is simple to turn off the exception list using the WFW control panel utility; you can check mark the `Don't Allow Exceptions` check box on the General page. The same can also be accomplished through a script such as shown in Listing 6.7.

LISTING 6.7 Allowing and Disallowing Exceptions

```
if Wscript.Arguments.Count <> 1 then
    Wscript.Echo "AllowExceptions.vbs Allow|Deny"
else
    Select Case Ucase(Wscript.Arguments(0))
      Case "ALLOW"
          bAllowed = False
          sAllowed = "Enabled"
      Case "DENY"
          bAllowed = True
          sAllowed = "Disabled"
    End Select
    Set objFWmgr = CreateObject("HNetCfg.FWmgr")
      Set objCurProfile = objFWmgr.LocalPolicy.CurrentProfile
        objCurProfile.ExceptionsNotAllowed = bAllowed
         if Err <> 0 then
           Wscript.Echo Err.Number & ", " & Err.Description
else
           Wscript.Echo "Exceptions list is " & sAllowed
         end if
  Set objCurProfile = nothing
 Set objFWmgr = nothing
end if
```

The Script

The script in Listing 6.7 can be used to enable or disable the exceptions list. The script takes `Allow` or `Deny` as an unnamed argument. For example, to deny the exception list (that is, the exception list should be ignored) you can type the following at the command line:

```
AllowExceptions.vbs deny
```

To allow the exceptions (that is, the exception list should not be ignored), you can type the following at the command line:

```
AllowExceptions.vbs allow
```

NOTE

The `Allow` and `Deny` arguments are not case sensitive.

To accomplish these tasks, the script takes the following steps:

1. Checks to see that the `Allow` or `Deny` (only one) argument is passed to the script.
2. If argument is not passed
   - Display the script usage and end

3. If the argument is passed
   - Set the `bAllowed` variable to `True` or `False` based on the argument passed
   - Also set the `sAllowed` display message variable
4. Creates an `HNetCfg.FWmgr` WFW management object and stores it in the `objFWmgr` variable.
5. Retrieves the current WFW profile by retrieving the `LocalPolicy.CurrentProfile` property. Stores the retrieved object in the `objCurProfile` variable.
6. Sets the `ExceptionsNotAllowed` property by passing the `bAllowed` (`True` or `False`) variable.
7. If there errors then display the error else display the success message (append the `sAllowed` (`Enabled` or `Disabled`) variable to the end of the message).
8. Release memory and end.

ENABLING AND DISABLING NOTIFICATIONS

By default the user is notified when a program is blocked by WFW. You can enable or disable the notification from the control panel utility or using a script as shown in Listing 6.8.

LISTING 6.8 Disable and Enable Notification

```
if Wscript.Arguments.Count <> 1 then
  Wscript.Echo "AllowNotification.vbs Allow|Deny"
else
    Select Case Ucase(Wscript.Arguments(0))
      Case "ENABLE"
        bAllowed = False
        sAllowed = "Enabled"
      Case "DISABLE"
        bAllowed = True
        sAllowed = "Disabled"
 End Select
 Set objFWmgr = CreateObject("HNetCfg.FWmgr")
 Set objCurProfile = objFWmgr.LocalPolicy.CurrentProfile
   objCurProfile.NotificationsDisabled = bAllowed
 if Err <> 0 then
  Wscript.Echo Err.Number & ", " & Err.Description
 else
  Wscript.Echo "Notifications are " & sAllowed
 end if
 Set objCurProfile = nothing
     Set objFWmgr = nothing
end if
```

The Script

Similar to the script in Listing 6.7, the script in Listing 6.8 enables and disables WFW notifications. The script in Listing 6.8 also takes only one argument: `Enable` or `Disable`.

To disable the notifications, you can run the following command:

```
AllowNotifications.vbs Deny
```

And to allow notifications, you can run the following command:

```
AllowNotifications.vbs Allow
```

To enable and disable the notifications, the script takes the following steps:

1. Checks to see that the `Enable` or `Disable` (only one) argument is passed to the script.
2. If argument is not passed
   - Display the script usage and end
3. If the argument is passed
   - Set the `bAllowed` variable to `True` or `False` based on the argument passed
   - Also set the `sAllowed` display message variable
4. Creates an `HNetCfg.FWmgr` WFW management object and stores it in the `objFWmgr` variable.
5. Retrieves the current WFW profile by retrieving the `LocalPolicy.CurrentProfile` property. Stores the retrieved object in the `objCurProfile` variable.
6. Set the `NotificationsDisabled` property by passing the `bAllowed` (`True` or `False`) variable. A `True` value sets the `NotificationsDisabled` to `Yes` (that is, do not display notifications) and a `False` value sets `NotificationsDisabled` to `No` (that is display notifications).
7. If there errors then display the error else display the success message (append the `sAllowed` (`Enabled` or `Disabled`) variable to the end of the message).
8. Release memory and end.

CONFIGURING ICMP SETTINGS

ICMP settings allow you to control the behavior of the ICMP packets. ICMP packets are generally used for troubleshooting IP communications issues. For example, you can use the Ping utility to check if a host with a specific IP address is available on the network before attempting to connect to the remote host. However, ICMP is vulnerable to DOS (denial of service) attacks and therefore you may want to control how your system responds to the incoming ICMP requests. WFW can be configured to control ICMP packets through the control panel utility and through a script, such as shown in Listing 6.9.

LISTING 6.9 Displaying and Configuring ICMP Settings

```
<package>
<job>
 <runtime>
    <named
      name="AllowInboundEchoRequest"
      helpstring="Allow Inbound Echo Request"
      type="boolean"
      required=false/>
    <named
      name="AllowInboundMaskRequest"
      helpstring="Allow Inbound Mask Request"
      type="boolean"
      required=false/>
    <named
      name="AllowInboundRouterRequest"
      helpstring="Allow Inbound Router Request"
      type="boolean"
      required=false/>
    <named
      name="AllowInboundTimestampRequest"
      helpstring="Allow Inbound Timestamp Request"
      type="boolean"
      required=false/>
    <named
      name="AllowOutboundDestinationUnreachable"
      helpstring="Allow Outbound Destination Unreachable"
      type="boolean"
      required=false/>
    <named
      name="AllowOutboundPacketTooBig"
      helpstring="Allow Outbound Packet Too Big"
      type="boolean"
      required=false/>
    <named
      name="AllowOutboundParameterProblem"
      helpstring="Allow Outbound Parameter Problem"
      type="boolean"
      required=false/>
    <named
      name="AllowOutboundSourceQuench"
      helpstring="Allow Outbound Source Quench"
      type="boolean"
      required=false/>
    <named
      name="AllowOutboundTimeExceeded"
      helpstring="Allow Outbound Time Exceeded"
      type="boolean"
```

```
      required=false/>
    <named
      name="AllowRedirect"
      helpstring="Allow Redirect"
      type="boolean"
      required=false/>
    <named
      name="All"
      helpstring="All ICMP Settings"
      type="boolean"
      required=false/>
    <unnamed
      name = "help"
      helpstring="Show Script usage"
      required=false/>
  </runtime>
  <script Language="vbscript">
   set Args = Wscript.Arguments.unnamed
   if Args.Count > 0 then
       if LCase(Args(0)) = "help" or Args(0) = "?" then
        Wscript.Arguments.ShowUsage
        Wscript.Quit
       end if
   end if
   Set objFWmgr = CreateObject("HNetCfg.FWmgr")
     Set objCurProfile = objFWmgr.LocalPolicy.CurrentProfile
       set objICMP = objCurProfile.ICMPSettings
        if Wscript.Arguments.Count = 0 then
         Wscript.echo "Allow Inbound Echo Request: " & _
                        objICMP.AllowInboundEchoRequest
         Wscript.echo "Allow Inbound Mask Request: " & _
                        objICMP.AllowInboundMaskRequest
         Wscript.echo "Allow Inbound Router Request: " & _
                            objICMP.AllowInboundRouterRequest
         Wscript.echo "Allow Inbound Timestamp Request: " & _
                          objICMP.AllowInboundTimestampRequest
         Wscript.echo "Allow Outbound Destination Unreachable: " & _
                          objICMP.AllowOutboundDestinationUnreachable
         Wscript.echo "Allow Outbound Packet Too Big: " & _
                               objICMP.AllowOutboundPacketTooBig
         Wscript.echo "Allow Outbound Parameter Problem: " & _
                               objICMP.AllowOutboundParameterProblem
         Wscript.echo "Allow Outbound Source Quench: " & _
                               objICMP.AllowOutboundSourceQuench
         Wscript.echo "Allow Outbound Time Exceeded: " & _
                               objICMP.AllowOutboundTimeExceeded
         Wscript.echo "Allow Redirect: " & _
                                objICMP.AllowRedirect
        else
         bAll = wscript.Arguments.named("all")
         if bAll then
               bAllowInboundEchoRequest = true
               bAllowInboundMaskRequest = true
```

```
                bAllowInboundRouterRequest = true
                bAllowInboundTimestampRequest = true
                bAllowOutboundDestinationUnreachable = true
                bAllowOutboundPacketTooBig = true
                bAllowOutboundParameterProblem = true
                bAllowOutboundSourceQuench = true
                bAllowOutboundTimeExceeded = true
                bAllowRedirect = true
           else
                bAllowInboundEchoRequest= _
                 Wscript.Arguments.named("AllowInboundEchoRequest")
                bAllowInboundMaskRequest = _
                 Wscript.Arguments.named("AllowInboundMaskRequest")
                bAllowInboundRouterRequest = _
                 Wscript.Arguments.named("AllowInboundRouterRequest")
                bAllowInboundTimestampRequest = _
                 Wscript.Arguments.named("AllowInboundTimestampRequest")
                bAllowOutboundDestinationUnreachable = _
                 Wscript.Arguments.named("AllowOutboundDestinationUnreachable")
                bAllowOutboundPacketTooBig = _
                 Wscript.Arguments.named("AllowOutboundPacketTooBig")
                bAllowOutboundParameterProblem = _
                 Wscript.Arguments.named("AllowOutboundParameterProblem")
                bAllowOutboundSourceQuench = _
                 Wscript.Arguments.named("AllowOutboundSourceQuench")
                bAllowOutboundTimeExceeded = _
                 Wscript.Arguments.named("AllowOutboundTimeExceeded")
                bAllowRedirect = _
                 Wscript.Arguments.named("AllowRedirect")
          end if
          objICMP.AllowInboundEchoRequest = bAllowInboundEchoRequest
          objICMP.AllowInboundMaskRequest = bAllowInboundMaskRequest
          objICMP.AllowInboundRouterRequest = bAllowInboundRouterRequest
          objICMP.AllowInboundTimestampRequest = bAllowInboundTimestampRequest
          objICMP.AllowOutboundDestinationUnreachable = _
                                        bAllowOutboundDestinationUnreachable
          objICMP.AllowOutboundPacketTooBig = bAllowOutboundPacketTooBig
          objICMP.AllowOutboundParameterProblem = _
                                              bAllowOutboundParameterProblem
          objICMP.AllowOutboundSourceQuench = bAllowOutboundSourceQuench
          objICMP.AllowOutboundTimeExceeded = bAllowOutboundTimeExceeded
          objICMP.AllowRedirect = bAllowRedirect
        end if
        Set objICMP = nothing
      Set objCurProfile = nothing
     Set objFWmgr = nothing
    </script>
   </job>
</package>
```

The Script

The script in Listing 6.9 can be used to view the current ICMP settings and change all or individual ICMP settings. To display the current ICMP settings you must run the script without the command-line arguments. To display help for the script (the script usage) you can do the following:

```
Icmpsettings.wsf help
```

The help argument is an unnamed argument. Unnamed arguments are not prefixed with / (forward slash).

To enable all ICMP settings, you can do the following:

```
Icmpsettings.wsf /all+
```

And to disable all ICMP settings, you can run the following command:

```
Icmpsettings.wsf /all-
```

Individual settings can be changed by passing the individual setting as the command-line argument with + or – (`True` or `False`) as the argument value. For example, to enable `AllowRedirect` and `AllowOutboundSourceQuench` ICMP properties, you would execute the following command:

```
Icmpsettings /AllowRedirect+ /AllowOutboundSourceQuench+
```

Similarly to disable an individual property, such as `AllowRedirect` property, you would execute the following command:

```
Icmpsettings /AllowRedirect-
```

To display and enable or disable the ICMP settings the script does the following:

1. Creates the `Named` nodes to accept the following arguments:
   - `AllowInboundEchoRequest` as Allow Inbound Echo Request setting
   - `AllowInboundMaskRequest` as Allow Inbound Mask Request setting
   - `AllowInboundRouterRequest` as Allow Inbound Router Request setting
   - `AllowInboundTimestampRequest` as Allow Inbound Timestamp Request setting
   - `AllowOutboundDestinationUnreachable` as Allow Outbound Destination Unreachable setting
   - `AllowOutboundPacketTooBig` as Allow Outbound Packet Too Big setting
   - `AllowOutboundParameterProblem` as Allow Outbound Parameter Problem setting

- `AllowOutboundSourceQuench` as Allow Outbound Source Quench setting
- `AllowOutboundTimeExceeded` as Allow Outbound Time Exceeded setting
- `AllowRedirect` as Allow Redirect setting
- `All` as special argument that the script uses to set all the ICMP settings

2. Creates the `UnNamed` arguments.
3. `Help` argument used to display script usage.
4. Retrieves the `UnNamed` arguments.
5. Checks to see if there are any `UnNamed` arguments.

- If `Help` unnamed argument is passed
- Displays the script usage and end

6. Creates an `HNetCfg.FWmgr` WFW management object and stores it in the `objFWmgr` variable.
7. Retrieves the current WFW profile by retrieving the `LocalPolicy.CurrentProfile` property. Stores the retrieved object in the `objCurProfile` variable.
8. Retrieves the `ICMPSettings` property. Stores the retrieved object in the `objICMP` variable.
9. Checks to see if any arguments are passed.

- If no arguments are passed: display each ICMP Setting
- If arguments are passed
  - `All` argument is passed: set all variables for the ICMP settings to `True`
  - Retrieve each arguments to set individual variables for the ICMP settings
  - Pass each variable to the property (for example: `bAllowRedirect` is passed to the `AllowRedirect` property)

10. Release memory and end

SUMMARY

This chapter covers automation of the Windows Firewall that is installed on Windows XP when Service Pack 2 is installed, and Windows 2003 when Service Pack 1 is installed. In this chapter you learned how to enable and disable the firewall, how to configure Exception Services and Applications, how to disable or enable exceptions, how to add or remove applications from the exceptions list, how to enable or disable notifications and finally how to configure ICMP settings.

This is the last chapter of the book. Additional information, such as references and additional links and information about tools and scripts included in this book, is covered in the Appendix.

Appendix

In This Appendix

- Script Store utility
- Installing Script Store
- Script Store how to(s)
- About the CD-ROM
- Helpful resources
- Creating Common Component

This appendix covers tools, lists references, and describes the contents of the CD-ROM.

SCRIPT STORE UTILITY

The Script Store utility can be used to store scripts in a centralized location. It converts the VBS files to text files before storing them in the centralized location. The Script Store utility is great for storing scripts that may cause damage to the environment if they are accidentally run. By converting the scripts to text, the utility eliminates the possibility of accidentally running the scripts.

PREREQUISITES

MSXML 4.0: The Script Store utility is based uses the MSXML DOM object. Therefore, you must install MSXML 4.0 before using this utility. MSXML 4.0 is a free download that you can download from the Microsoft Web site. (The link for download is available in the "Helpful Resources" section.)

CAPICOM: CAPICOM is the Microsoft's encryption automation object that the Script Store utility uses to encrypt the scripts that it stores as text files. The data encrypted with CAPICOM can only be decrypted using CAPICOM. You must download and install CAPICOM on your system before you can use Script Store.

NOTE

CAPICOM uses a password that you specify to encrypt the files. There is no way you can decrypt the scripts without the password that was used to encrypt the scripts. Therefore, you should backup your original scripts and store them safely, if you plan to delete the original scripts after importing them to Script Store. (Script Store does not delete the original scripts; it only copies the original script.)

CAPICOM is a free automation object that you can download from the Microsoft's Web site. (The link for download is available in the "Helpful Resources" section.) After downloading CAPICOM, you must extract the CAPICOM DLL from the zip file and register it using the following command

```
Regsvr32 "CAPICOM 2.1.0.1\x86\capicom.dll"
```

INSTALLING SCRIPT STORE

ON THE CD

To install the Script Store utility, from the Programs folder on the CD-ROM do the following:

1. Double-click Setup.exe
2. Click OK to continue
3. Click the `Install` button (located on the left side of the dialog box shown in Figure A.1)
4. Click the `Continue` button to continue (select a program group)
5. Click OK to finish the installation

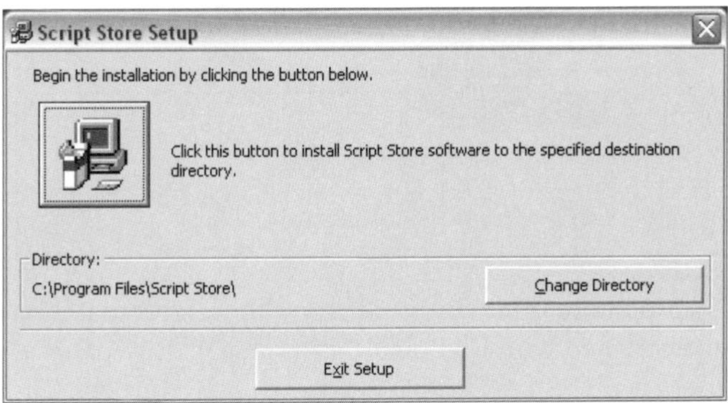

FIGURE A.1 Install dialog box.

HOW TO SET-UP SCRIPT STORE PATH

1. From the Program > Script Store menu (or from the program group where you chose to install the application), launch ScriptStore.exe
2. When you launch the application for the first time, it prompts you to set the Script Store path. All scripts will be stored in this location until you change the location using the "Storage Path" option under the settings menu. Figure A.2 shows the dialog box that appears at set-up.

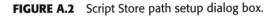

FIGURE A.2 Script Store path setup dialog box.

HOW TO CHANGE SCRIPT STORE PATH

1. Click Settings > Storage Path from the menu as shown in Figure A.3
2. Type the path (or select the path from by clicking the ... button) in the Set Storage Path dialog box (see Figure A.2 earlier) and click OK

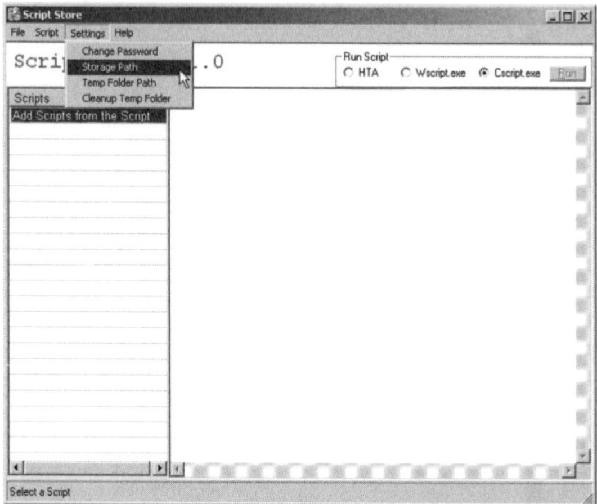

FIGURE A.3 Storage Path menu item.

Changing the Script Store path does not move the existing scripts to the new location. The scripts located at the old location (location prior to the change) are, however, still available; they are neither moved to the new location or deleted, therefore you still have access to the existing scripts. After the change, any new scripts added to the Script Store will be saved to the new location.

WHAT TEMP FOLDER IS AND HOW TO SET IT

Script Store uses this space to temporarily store and execute the scripts. You can designate any location as long as you have read, write, and delete access to the folder. When you launch the application for the first time, the program prompts you to set this location. You can change the location at any time from the "Temp Folder Path" menu under the Settings menu.

HOW TO ADD A SCRIPT TO THE STORE

1. Click on Script > Add menu item to open the "Select a Script to Add" dialog box.
2. In this box, you can either type the script location or click on the `Select` button to browse for a script that you wish to add.
3. Click the `Add` button when done.

NOTE

Browsing for and selecting a script will add the script name to the Script Display Name text box. If you want, you can change this to a more meaningful name. You do not have to include the file extension.

HOW TO REMOVE A SCRIPT FROM THE STORE

1. Select the script you want to remove
2. Click on Script > Remove menu item
3. A confirmation box will appear that will allow you to either remove the entry from the store or remove the entry and delete the script from the store as shown in Figure A.4
4. Click OK to remove the script

FIGURE A.4 Remove Script confirmation dialog box.

NOTE

Deleting the script is not reversible. You can, however, manually create an entry in SSList.xml to recover the script if you choose to only remove the entry.

HOW TO EDIT AND RUN A SCRIPT

1. Selecting a script in the left window loads the script into the right text window.
2. This enables the `Run` command (`Run` button and the Script > Run menu item).
3. Click the Shell that you want the script to run with
4. Click the `Run` button or click Script > Run menu item to run the script with the selected shell
5. Confirm that you want to run the script
6. Confirm that you are authorized to run the script

You can edit the script in the right text window before running the script. The `Run` *command runs the temporary script file for execution from this window. You cannot save the changes that you make to the script at this time. If you need to change the content, do the following:*

a) edit the text in the right window
b) select and copy the contents of the script to the clipboard
c) paste and save the contents to a file (outside of Script Store)
d) remove and delete the script file
e) add the new script file using the Script > Add menu.

HOW TO DELETE SCRIPTS IN THE TEMP FOLDER

1. Click Settings > Cleanup Temp Folder menu
2. Click Yes on the confirmation window

HOW TO CHANGE LOCATION OF THE XML FILES (OR USE XML FILES FROM ANOTHER SCRIPT STORE)

1. Create an ss.ini file in the same folder where ScriptStore.exe is located.
2. Add the following entry:

```
l=<path to the xml files>
```

   For example, if the files are located in K:\scripts. create the ss.ini file as follows:

```
l=D:\Scripts
```

3. Save the INI file and launch ScriptStore.exe

ABOUT THE CD-ROM

The CD-ROM included with this book contains complete scripts for each chapter and additional scripts in Scripts.msi.

Additional scripts include:

- `Addva.vbs`: Sample script that demonstrates addition of two variables.
- `AvailableDiskspace.js` / `AvailableDiskSpace.vbs`: Scripts that display the available disk space on the C drive.

- `Echo.js`: Jscript script showing how to echo information.
- `First.vbs`: Echoes date, time, and a message.
- `ListProperties.vbs`: WMI script that writes the properties of a specified class of `CIMV2` namespace.
- `ListPropertiesAndValues.wsf`: WMI script that writes the properties of a spefied class of `CIMV2` namespace. The script is created as a WSF file as compared to the ListProperties.vbs script
- `OperatingSystem.vbs`: Writes specified properties to a text file.
- `SWAT_1.wsc`: The common component with several functions that can be called in scripts.
- `SWAT_1.hta`: The sample file that demonstrates how to add and use `SWAT_1.wsc` component in your scripts.
- `Programs Folder`: Includes Script Store application installation files
- Figures, Tables, and Listings folder: Includes text files that list the figure, tables, and listings of each chapter

HELPFUL RESOURCES

Reference	Link
CAPICOM	*http://www.microsoft.com/downloads/details.aspx?FamilyID=860ee43a-a843-462f-abb5-ff88ea5896f6&DisplayLang=en*
MSXML 4.0 SP2	*http://www.microsoft.com/downloads/details.aspx?FamilyID=3144b72b-b4f2-46da-b4b6-c5d7485f2b42&DisplayLang=en*
Terminal Services WMI Provider Reference	*http://msdn.microsoft.com/library/default.asp?url=/library/en-us/termserv/termserv/terminal_services_wmi_provider_reference.asp*
WMI Reference	*http://msdn.microsoft.com/library/default.asp?url=/library/en-us/wmisdk/wmi/wmi_reference.asp*
MSDN Scripting	*http://msdn.microsoft.com/library/default.asp?url=/library/en-us/dnanchor/html/scriptinga.asp*
MSDN Home	*http://msdn.microsoft.com*
Microsoft Technet Script Center	*http://www.microsoft.com/technet/scriptcenter/default.mspx*
Windows Firewall API Reference	*http://msdn.microsoft.com/library/default.asp?url=/library/en-us/ics/ics/inetfwmgr.asp*
IIS Programmatic Administration Reference	*http://msdn.microsoft.com/library/default.asp?url=/library/en-us/iissdk/html/c0d7e907-89b1-4752-940f-2cfe7276928e.asp*
Troubleshooting Windows Firewall Settings	*http://support.microsoft.com/default.aspx?kbid=875357*

Reference	Link
Comparison of the IIS Administration Features	*http://msdn.microsoft.com/library/default.asp?url=/library/en-us/iissdk/html/df6d787b-95a1-4ae3-b746-94f35caeeab3.asp*
Microsoft Windows *2000 Scripting Guide*	*http://www.microsoft.com/technet/scriptcenter/guide/default.mspx*
World Wide Web Consortium	*http://www.w3.org*
Free Online Learning School	*http://www.w3schools.com*

CREATING COMMON SCRIPT COMPONENTS

As discussed in Chapter 2, you can create a COM component with Windows Script Components and register it as a DLL using Regsvr32.exe. These COM components work like a common library of functions that can be included in your scripts. The functions exposed by the components can be used over and over again in your scripts.

In this section, we will create a `SWAT.1.00` component and add the `GetComputerName` and `SplitOnCap` sample functions that will be used by the scripts in Part II. The common functions will be exposed to the scripts by creating an instance of the `SWAT.1.00` component.

To create a new `SWAT.1.00` component, do the following:

1. Launch Windows Script Component Wizard (if you have not already downloaded and installed the Windows Script Component Wizard, now is the time to do it; you can download the Windows Script Component Wizard installation package from `msdn.microsoft.com/scripting`).
2. Type the text in Step 1 of the wizard as shown in Figure A.5. Click the `Next` button when completed.
3. Click the `Next` button 4 times (selects defaults).
4. Click the `Finish` button.
5. Click the `Ok` button to close the wizard. (The wizard will create the `SWAT.1.00.WSC` file in the folder that you specified in Step 1.)
6. Click the `Ok` button to close the wizard.
7. Navigate to the folder where the `SWAT.1.00.WSC` file exists, right-click the file and select `Register` from the menu. Click OK to close the registration successful window.

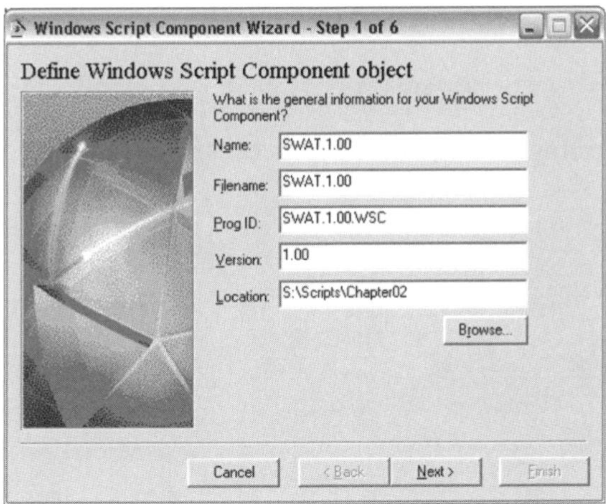

FIGURE A.5 Windows Script Component Wizard Step 1 of SWAT.1.00.

You now have the structure of the component ready. You can add other functions and properties to the component as required. To add a function to the script component, for example to add the GetComputerName function, do the following:

1. Double-click SWAT.1.00.WSC file
2. Type the following within <public> and </public> nodes

```
<method name="GetComputerName" />
```

3. Type the following within the <![CDATA[and]]> nodes

```
Function GetComputerName
   Set objwNet = CreateObject("Wscript.Network")
     GetComputerName = UCase(objwNet.ComputerName)
   Set objwNet = nothing
End Function
```

4. Save the WSC file

Now that the GetComputerName function has been added to the SWAT.1.00 component, you can use it in your scripts as follows:

1. Create a SWAT.1.00 component using the CreateObject method. For example, the following will create the component and store it in the objSwat variable:

```
Set objSwat = CreateObject("SWAT.1.00")
```

2. Call the `GetComputerName` method as follows:

```
objSwat.GetComputerName
```

Figure A.6 shows the relationship between the calling script and the `SWAT.1.00` component.

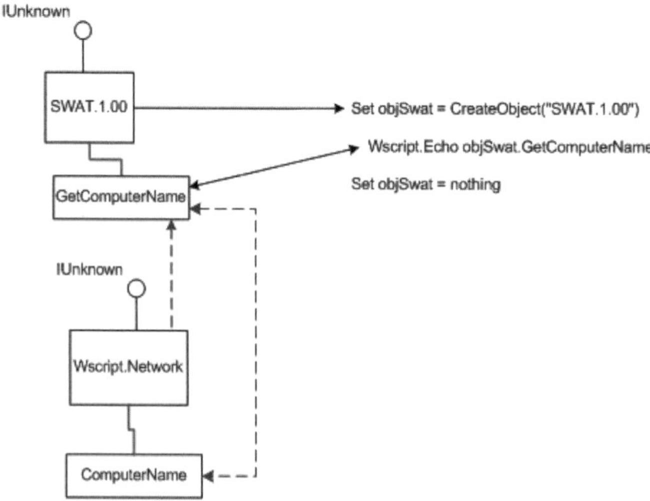

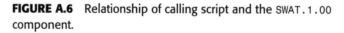

FIGURE A.6 Relationship of calling script and the `SWAT.1.00` component.

Index

S